NEW TRADE STRATEGY FOR THE WORLD ECONOMY

by Harry Johnson

Economic Nationalism in Old and New States
(*Editor*)

Economic Policies Towards Less Developed Countries

Essays in Monetary Economics

International Trade and Economic Growth:
Studies in Pure Theory

Money, Trade and Economic Growth:
Survey Lectures in Economic Theory

etc.

New Trade Strategy for the World Economy

EDITED BY
HARRY G. JOHNSON

London
GEORGE ALLEN AND UNWIN LTD
RUSKIN HOUSE . MUSEUM STREET

FIRST PUBLISHED IN 1969

SECOND IMPRESSION 1970

© *Atlantic Trade Study 1969*

ISBN 0 04 330143 6 *cased*
0 04 330169 x *paper*

PRINTED IN GREAT BRITAIN
in 10 on 12 point Baskerville
by Compton Printing Ltd.
London and Aylesbury

THE ATLANTIC TRADE STUDY PROGRAMME

The Atlantic Trade Study, registered as an educational trust, was formed in December, 1966, by a private group in London to sponsor a programme of policy research on the implications for Britain of participating in a broadly based free trade association as possibly the next phase in the liberalisation of international trade.

It is under the chairmanship of Sir Michael Wright, formerly Permanent Head of the British Delegation to the Geneva Disarmament Conference, while the Director of Studies is Professor Harry G. Johnson, of the London School of Economics and Political Science and the University of Chicago. The programme is now being administered by the recently established Trade Policy Research Centre, the Director of which is Mr. Hugh Corbet, previously of *The Times*. Set out below is the committee responsible for the programme:

As a basis on which to proceed with research, the proposed free trade association was defined as initially embracing the United States, Canada, Britain and other member countries of the European Free Trade Association; open to the European Communities and to Japan, Australia and New Zealand, as well as other industrially advanced nations; and affording less developed countries greater access to their markets.

Several proposals along these lines had already been receiving serious attention at academic, business and official levels in North America. The ATS was in fact a British response to a new trade strategy proposed in May, 1966, by the Canadian-American Committee, a non-official group sponsored by the Private Planning Association of Canada and the National Planning Association in the United States.

With the expiry on June 30, 1967, of President Johnson's authority under the Trade Expansion Act of 1962 to negotiate trade agreements with other countries, and the completion of the so-called Kennedy Round of multilateral tariff negotiations, made possible by the Act and conducted under the auspices of the General Agreement on Tariffs and Trade, the United States Administration and Congress was expected to embark upon a thorough reappraisal of trade policies and practices with a view to formulating a fresh negotiating authority. The proposal for a multilateral free trade association initiated by North Atlantic countries has been one of the policy options to have subsequently come under consideration.

Meanwhile, the British Government had made a second application for United Kingdom membership of the European Communities. But whether Britain gained admission or not, the concept of a potentially world-wide free trade association was deemed, in either eventuality, as likely to prove of large significance. For in the event of membership being negotiated it was considered that the United Kingdom would then require an informed policy for the development of closer commercial and political relations between Western Europe and North America. If on the other hand the European Communities rejected Britain again, even if only temporarily, it would be important to have examined beforehand whether there exists a viable alternative.

PREFACE

With the exception of the introductory part, the studies in this volume, dealing with the proposal for a multilateral free trade association initiated by North Atlantic countries, were substantially written during 1967 and the first half of 1968 and have since been brought up to date with subsequent developments. But the personnel of governments change. All the same, until policy is revised, the past statements of official spokesmen remain authoritative and that is how they have been treated here.

The study by Maxwell Stamp and Harry Cowie was first published as a pamphlet in November, 1967, under the title "The Free Trade Area Option"; that of Gerard and Victoria Curzon in February, 1968, as "After the Kennedy Round"; Lionel Gelber's, in July, 1968, as "World Politics and Free Trade"; and the study by David Robertson first appeared in July, 1968, under its title here, "Scope for New Trade Strategy".

While the Atlantic Trade Study programme has provided the opportunity, the views expressed in the papers are the responsibility of the various authors.

HARRY G. JOHNSON

London,
Autumn, 1968

CONTENTS

Part I

TIME FOR CHANGE IN TRADE STRATEGY

by

HARRY G. JOHNSON

Professor of Economics, London School of Economics and Political Science and the University of Chicago; formerly Professor of Economic Theory, University of Manchester; author of "The World Economy at the Crossroads" (1965), "Economic Policies Toward Less Developed Economies" (1967) and "Essays in Monetary Economics" (1967).

Part II

OPTIONS AFTER THE KENNEDY ROUND

by

GERARD CURZON

Professor of International Economics, Graduate Institute of International Studies, University of Geneva; author of "Multilateral Commercial Diplomacy" (1965),

and

VICTORIA CURZON

Research Fellow, Graduate Institute of International Studies, University of Geneva; co-author of "The European Free Trade Association and the Crisis of European Integration "(1968).

Part III

WORLD POLITICS AND TRADE STRATEGY

by

LIONEL GELBER

*Historian; author of "The Rise of Anglo-American Friendship"
(1938 and 1966), "America in Britain's Place" (1961) and
"The Alliance of Necessity" (1967); formerly Special Assistant
to the Prime Minister of Canada.*

Part IV

BRITAIN AND THE FREE TRADE AREA OPTION

by

MAXWELL STAMP

*Managing Director, Maxwell Stamp Associates, economic
consultants; formerly Adviser to the Bank of England and a one-
time executive director of the International Monetary Fund,*

and

HARRY COWIE

*Director, Maxwell Stamp Associates; formerly Research Director
of the Liberal Party.*

Part V

SCOPE FOR NEW TRADE STRATEGY

by

DAVID ROBERTSON

Lecturer in Economics, University of Reading; co-author of "The European Free Trade Association and the Crisis of European Integration" (1968).

Part I

TIME FOR CHANGE IN TRADE STRATEGY

by

Harry G. Johnson

1 PROPOSAL FOR A MULTILATERAL FREE TRADE ASSOCIATION

In the spring of 1966 an influential body of American and Canadian business, labour and university leaders proposed "A New Trade Strategy for Canada and the United States". It was in similar vein to proposals earlier mooted by Senator Jacob Javits, of New York, and others published shortly afterwards by Senator Paul Douglas, as he then was, of Illinois.[1] The idea struck a chord in Britain and ever since it has been gradually gathering momentum.

What is broadly being proposed is the establishment of a free trade association in industrial products among a group of countries centred on the Atlantic, together with some subsidiary proposals for action in related areas of trade policy. The nucleus of what would thus initially be a North Atlantic free trade area (NAFTA) would be the United States, Canada and Britain and other members of the European Free Trade Association (EFTA). But the plan would be an "open-ended" arrangement which other industrial nations—Japan, Australia, New Zealand and the countries of the European Communities, if they so desired—could also join provided they were prepared to confrom to the relatively simple rules that such a scheme would entail.

Because of this open-ended feature, the term "North Atlantic free trade area" is something of a misnomer, since the prospective members do not constitute a geographical region, as do the members of the Common Market; rather the participants in the New Trade Strategy would constitute an association of geographically separated states. Moreover, not all would be located in the vicinity of the North Atlantic; membership could well extend around the world, from Europe to the Antipodes. While posing a problem of semantics, the NAFTA label has possibly caught on precisely because, in the Great Debate over Britain's place in the world, it is relevant to the difference between the Atlanticist and Europeanist schools of

[1]See "A New Trade Strategy for Canada and the United States" (Canadian-American Committee, Washington, D.C., and Montreal, May, 1966); Jacob Javits, "The Second Battle of Britain", *Congressional Record*, US Congress, Washington, D.C., August 12, 1965, Vol. 111, No. 148, pp. 19421-25; and Paul Douglas, "America in the Market Place" (Holt Rinehart and Winston, New York, 1966).

3

opinion. The term is in any case convenient and has become sufficiently established in common usage to warrant employing it as briefly descriptive of the concept of a multilateral free trade association of like-minded nations.

Retention of Sovereignty

A free trade association is an arrangement under which members eliminate tariffs on their imports of goods from one another while retaining their existing tariffs on imports from non-members. It is to be distinguished from a customs union, under which members take the additional step of unifying their original national tariffs into a common tariff against imports from the outside world. It is to be distinguished still more from a common market, in which members commit themselves additionally to freedom of internal movements of labour and capital as well as goods and, also, to the harmonisation and co-ordination of national problems in such areas as monopolies control, social insurance, the structure of taxation and agricultural policy.

This distinction with respect to economic scope and commitment has an important political corollary. Whereas customs unions and common markets have usually been designed either to underpin an existing, or to lay the foundations for an ultimate, political federation or union, this being the political objective justifying the effort and strain of negotiating compromises among the member states, a free trade area is on the other hand a purely economic arrangement without ulterior political objectives. Instead, the appeal of a free trade association consists in the attainment of the economic benefits of free trade and competition over an enlarged market area consistently with the retention of the maximum feasible political sovereignty.

Understanding of this difference of political objectives and implications is especially important in any assessment of the NAFTA proposals, because it is tempting for anyone who has followed the discussion about the pros and cons of British entry into the EEC to assume, quite wrongly, that NAFTA would entail the same type of political relationship with other members of the association and hence to be distracted by irrelevant questions about whether Britain as a member could hope to exercise political leadership with the same leverage as she might hope to do in the new Europe. The argument for British participation in a broadly based

4

free trade association is not that it would provide Britain with an enlarged base for potential political power, but that it would strengthen the economic base of the political power Britain now possesses, much of which she would have to jettison to win admission to the EEC.[2]

With this as a starting point, the NAFTA proposal must be evaluated in two contexts: (a) the international interest in the liberalisation of trade among nations and (b) the national interests —both economic and political—in international trade of the prospective members.

Momentum of Trade Liberalisation

With respect to the international interest in trade liberalisation, the open-ended free trade area approach constitutes a strategy for continuing the momentum of the movement towards free trade expressed in the successive rounds of multilateral negotiation of non-discriminatory tariff reduction within the machinery of the General Agreement on Tariffs and Trade (GATT) which culminated in the successful completion of the Kennedy Round in 1967. For various reasons it is improbable that further liberalisation can proceed on the traditional GATT lines. NAFTA offers an alternative technique by which those countries which are interested in continuing the process of trade liberalisation can do so without being held back by the reluctance to negotiate of those that are fearful or cautious about further liberalisation. The free trade area approach, in contrast to some other possibilities, is sanctioned by the principles of GATT. While a free trade association confined to industrial products might be held to fall short of the virtually complete freeing of internal trade required by those principles, ample precedent exists in GATT's reception of the formation of the EEC and of EFTA for expecting that a NAFTA arrangement would nevertheless be accepted as complying with the spirit of the GATT rules.

For other reasons, however, the treaty providing for the establishment of a multilateral free trade association would have to make additional provision, beyond the elimination of internal tariffs on industrial products within a defined period of time, for the liberalisation of trade or of trading conditions. For one thing, the gradual lowering of tariffs has enhanced the significance of distortions of international competition resulting from the presence of non-tariff

[2]On this subject see Lionel Gelber's study, Part III below.

5

barriers to trade in industrial products. These barriers would probably have to be brought in some fashion within the scope of NAFTA, probably under the rubric of harmonisation of other policies. On another aspect, the agricultural exporting interests of Canada and the USA and the still more important agricultural exporting interests of Australia and New Zealand, as prospective members, would require some sort of agreement or understanding on how trade in agricultural products should be regulated—presumably via some sort of co-ordination of national agricultural support and export marketing policies. Apart from these predominantly internal trade policy problems, the growing demands of the developing countries for increased export opportunities would in all probability have to be accommodated by special arrangements facilitating entry of their exports to the markets of NAFTA countries. The growing interest on both sides in the expansion of East-West trade would probably dictate the desirability of special provisions with respect to such trade.

Varying National Interests

National interests in the formation of NAFTA naturally differ according to the country under consideration. The Canadian interest, for example, would be predominantly economic. The large body of economic research that has been undertaken in recent years into the causes of the historically invariant differential in living standards between Canada and the USA and the implications for Canada of the Canadian and American tariff structures confirms the hypothesis that the comparative inefficiency of Canadian industry is to be attributed in large part to the short production runs, the excessive diversification and the oligopolistic market structure entailed in producing for a small national market. This research confirms the view, too, that the solution lies in the specialisation and concentration of industrial effort that only free access to a really large external market could make economically feasible and profitable. Reciprocal free trade with the USA alone would probably suffice to serve Canada's economic ends. But for historical and political as well as current cosmopolitan reasons, a bilateral regional arrangement would suit Canada's international interests far less well than a broader, and especially a more outward-looking, free trade arrangement spanning the Atlantic (and possibly including the Pacific as well).

6

The American interest would necessarily be predominantly political in the broad sense; that is, an expression of the responsibility the USA has assumed (and must assume) as leader of the Western industrial nations. The continental near self-sufficiency of the USA makes the material economic gains that might ensue from free trade a peripheral—though not necessarily negligible—element in American policy calculations. For thirty-odd years, America has taken the lead in working for a more liberal international trading system, through the negotiation of reciprocal tariff reductions on a multilateral non-discriminatory basis. During the period since World War II, the USA has also promoted the economic integration of Western Europe, for a variety of economic and politico-strategic reasons. And it has been under increasing pressure in recent years to use its international leadership to facilitate the export interests of the developing countries.

The conclusion of the Kennedy Round obliges the USA to devise a new international trade strategy for the post-Kennedy Round era. The evolution of relations between the USA and Russia towards a co-operative world peace-keeping role, and the circumstances of the failure of Britain's second application to join the EEC, require a re-thinking of the Grand Design which envisaged European economic integration as a means of building a powerful but loyal political and military ally in Europe against the threat of Communist aggression. The failure of the second United Nations Conference on Trade and Development, held in Delhi in March, 1968, to produce any concrete new proposals to meet the needs of the developing countries leaves the problems of the latter still outstanding. The launching of a multilateral free trade association could be the means of continuing the momentum towards world trade liberalisation, countering the inward-looking tendencies of the EEC as it stands at present (with Britain waiting forlornly on the doorstep) and achieving changes in the trade policies of the advanced industrial nations effectively favourable to the developing countries.

Embracing Global Trading Interests

For Britain, the national interest in such a NAFTA initiative would be both economic and political. Economically, NAFTA offers that access to a really large, rich and competitive market, permitting the full exploitation of British technological accomplishments, which has been the strongest—if not the only—economic argument

7

for attempting to gain membership in the EEC. It does so without the expensive commitment to the EEC's common agricultural policy and the necessity of discriminating against trade with the other members of the Commonwealth. While some fear that British industry would be unable to hold its own in open competition with American industry, there is the counter-consideration that, as in the case of the establishment of Imperial Preference in the 1930s, membership of the EEC would provide a protected market in the short run at the expense of weakening the competitiveness of the British economy in the long run.

In any case, NAFTA is not strictly speaking an alternative to membership in the Common Market. If British admission to the EEC is to be delayed indefinitely, it may well be judged that the Common Market has ceased to be a relevant alternative and that NAFTA offers the only remaining chance of achieving the desired benefits for Britain of free competition in a large and technologically advanced international market. If, on the other hand, political circumstances were to change unexpectedly and Britain were to be rushed into membership, the new Europe would have to assume the responsibility, commensurate with its enhanced world status, of formulating a commercial policy for its trading relations with the outside world. Britain's farflung trading interests would indicate the desirability of a more liberal international trading system, the best route towards which might be a free trade arrangement in industrial products among the enlarged Europe, North America and the advanced industrial nations of the Pacific.

Politically, Britain has one foot in Europe and one in the outside world of the English-speaking people. She has still to carve out for herself an appropriate place in the post-imperial, non-Eurocentric world politics of the latter twentieth century. In seeking to join the EEC, she has been attempting to found a new world role on her European geographical location and potential capacity for leadership of the European nations. Her overseas political connections, reinforced by closer trading ties and by the renewed economic strength that free competition and access to large markets could bring, might well provide both a firmer and a more congenial foundation for a world role appropriate to Britain's experience of and potentialities for leadership.

At the present time, British policy is suspended in the limbo of rejection by the Common Market accompanied by a faint hope of eventual admission. There are those, both in Britain and in the official circles in Washington, still wedded to the Grand Design of a European Union in junior partnership with the American Union. They counsel unending patience and warn against any action or even discussion that might be construed as "anti-European". Such advice comes uncomfortably close to that of the doctor who is prepared to see the patient die so long as the operation is a success. To follow it would be to preserve the present stasis in Britain's relations with the Six, without improving Britain's chances of gaining admission or her claim to membership. To explore the NAFTA proposals seriously would give warning that Britain is not prepared to wait for ever on Europe's doorstep and that she is not compelled by lack of alternatives to do so.

The formation of a broad free trade association might indeed be the most effective intermediate step towards obtaining the kind of economic and political relationships with Europe that Britain would like to have. For successful adaptation to the competitive conditions of NAFTA would relieve European fears of having to carry the burden of a sick British economy and a vulnerable international role of sterling, while the attractions of reciprocal free trade with the whole NAFTA group would obviously be far greater to European eyes than those of access to the UK market alone.

2 PUBLIC DISCUSSION OF
POLICY ISSUES

The broad considerations behind the proposal for a multilateral free trade association are analysed in the succeeding papers in this book. Published earlier as pamphlets, they form part of a series of research papers commissioned by the Atlantic Trade Study (ATS), a registered educational trust. The ATS was formed at the end of 1966, following the publication of "A New Trade Strategy for Canada and the United States", referred to at the outset. Its instigators were a group of people of diverse origins and interests who were united in the belief that the trade policy options open to Britain, and to the advanced Western nations in general, required urgent and serious scientific study in Britain.

Members of the group felt, in particular, that the NAFTA proposal was interesting and promising enough to deserve careful and comprehensive investigation whether—as some hoped—Britain succeeded in gaining admission to the EEC or—as others feared and expected, correctly as it transpired—France once more slammed the door in Britain's face. In either event, it was felt that for the world economy the formation of a broadly based free trade association, within the rules of GATT, could be the next logical step in trade strategy.

The tradition of private sponsorship of independent scientific study of national policy problems is well established in North America, and especially in the USA, where such bodies as the Brookings Institution and the Council on Foreign Relations produce a steady stream of publications oriented towards the rational evaluation of current policy issues and alternative solutions to them. A similar tradition is by no means as firmly established in Britain at the present time. Important policy decisions have frequently been taken in the UK by government in the virtually complete absence of independent outside studies of the alternatives among which choice has been made. This has not always been the case. Indeed, in an earlier period, independent studies sponsored by the Fabian Society and by Political and Economic Planning not only influenced the formation of policy, but were the envy of informed opinion in other countries for the high standard of quality they set and maintained.

Omniscience of British Press

The decline in the influence of independent studies of policy alternatives on actual policy-making, and therefore on the incentives to sponsor and to undertake such studies, in the quarter century that has elapsed since World War II, has had a variety of causes, some with deep-seated roots in Britain's deteriorating position in the world economy and the bitter legacies of the mass unemployment of the inter-war period. One obvious contributory factor has been the attitude of the British press. It has done disservice to the cause of rational discussion of and decision on Britain's policy problems in two major ways. First, the press has been excessively prone to assess news values and present the news according to its judgment of what is currently politically acceptable or unacceptable. In so doing it has not hesitated to interpret the news according to its own views as to the desirable direction of policy. The penalty for a highly centralised system of communication media is the propagation of the establishment line by an ostensibly independent press and broadcasting system. Second, the press has typically assumed an omniscience on complex questions of economic fact with respect to which scientific research results are either non-existent, controversial, or contradictory to the press's own assertions. The price of spurious omniscience is unnecessary ignorance and dangerous self-deception. To paraphrase Frank Knight, it isn't what people don't know that gets them into trouble, it's what they think they know that isn't so.

The negative contribution of the press to public enlightenment on policy issues in Britain is well illustrated by two examples, both drawn from *The Economist*, of London. The first of a series of articles promoting a renewed British application to join the Common Market in February, 1966, was summarised in part as follows: "In Britain pretty well everyone who matters now knows that Europe is the only solution of Britain's problems. So why not have another try?"[3] Note the assumption of indisputable veracity in the use of the word "knows". Subsequent articles stressed the Six's need for British membership: "General de Gaulle's *realpolitik* has so

[3]"Go for Europe", *The Economist*, London, February 5, 1966, p. 487, the quotation being taken from a summary, p. 471.

destroyed the old trust between them that they need Britain in there with them to restore their balance and mutual confidence."[4] They also belittled the cost to Britain of accepting the EEC's common agricultural policy. An article on "The Economics of Entry" declared:

"It really is not a major obstacle that a switch to the Common Market's agricultural policy might raise Britain's cost of living by between $2\frac{1}{2}$ and $3\frac{1}{2}$ per cent over a number of years; many other, much lesser, policies of successive governments have managed to change the cost of living by far more than that. Nor, in the context of this historic venture, is it really a matter of quite overwhelming importance that the Common Market's agricultural policy might eventually swell Britain's import bill by between £175 and £200m per annum; that is equal to something under 3 per cent of Britain's total exports of goods and services in any one year, and of course entry into the market would affect our exports by considerably more."[5]

Apart from the fact that between £175 and £200m per annum is somewhat below some later and more authoritative estimates, it is illegitimate to compare an increase in the cost of living that results from a deliberate decision to pay out more resources for imports with increases that have generally been the counterpart of rising domestic incomes involving no national loss of real resources. And it is misleading to ignore the fact that additional exports cost additional resources to produce and that to the extent that those resources are absorbed in paying higher prices for existing imports instead of buying more imports they are lost to the British economy.

As a second example, *The Economist* of March 30, 1968, contained an article on the NAFTA proposals entitled "North Atlantic Non-Alternative", subtitled "A north Atlantic free trade area is a pipedream today—and, unless much more convincing arguments are found for it, should remain so". The text of the article begins by (1) dismissing the Stamp-Cowie estimates of NAFTA'S effects on Britain's trade as dependent on "some startlingly optimistic assumptions about the response of demand to price changes" (the assumptions were deliberately chosen to be conservative), (2) attempts to brand NAFTA supporters as anti-European, (3) asserts that the strongest single objection to NAFTA is that it would cut off Britain

[4]"The Road into Europe", *The Economist*, April 2, 1966, p. 17.
[5]"The Economics of Entry", *The Economist*, November 19, 1966, p. 77.

from the EEC for the foreseeable future (as if the French had not already wielded that particular knife), (4) declares that the USA would not accept it because it would divide the Western world into two economic and therefore political blocks and (5) ends up by conjuring up the bogey of American domination of the British economy if NAFTA were nevertheless established. The reader of these studies is invited to judge for himself how far, if at all, the available evidence justifies these sweeping *a priori* generalisations.

Stereotyping of Issues

In using the news relevant to policy issues to generate heat rather than to spread light, however, the press is essentially responding to the contemporary mood of policy discussion in the UK, a mood which emphasises the stereotyping of issues in terms calculated to generate or justify positive or negative emotional responses. This mood is exemplified by three "gut-reactions" commonly encountered by attempts to evoke rational discussion of the NAFTA proposals with otherwise intelligent and responsible British people.

The first such gut-reaction is that discussion of NAFTA is a waste of time, because it is obvious that the USA would not be interested. The parallel question, it may be noted, was raised in connection with Britain's application to join the Common Market, if at all, only as a prelude to explaining how Britain would out-manoeuvre France by appealing to the other Five. Giving it priority over the question of whether NAFTA might be sufficiently in Britain's interests to justify attempting to interest the USA reflects the Micawberish approach that has bedevilled British foreign policy since the war, as well as an undue implicit reliance on American leadership. More important, it is not at all obvious that the USA would not be interested, particularly if a response were sought to a British initiative. The USA has proved itself in the past responsive to interests and initiatives on the European side of the Atlantic, notably in the invention of the Marshall Plan and the passage of the Trade Expansion Act of 1962. There has always been a body of opinion in the USA favouring Anglo-American co-operation. The USA is currently in the process, moreover, of re-thinking its foreign trade strategy in the light of the successful conclusion of the Kennedy Round. Now, if ever, is the time for Britain to seek to define as clearly as possible her interests in the future structure of the world trading system.

The second gut-reaction is that a NAFTA would be fatal to Britain, because the result would be that the big American corporations would take over British industry. This argument, it should be noted, is totally inconsistent with the first: if US industry is lusting to take over British industry, the US Administration cannot be utterly opposed to giving it the opportunity. Apart from that, the argument demonstrates complete ignorance of the economics and politics of foreign corporate take-overs, which to begin with are transactions between willing buyers and willing sellers, generally aimed at increasing productive efficiency (a goal not as yet regarded as contrary to the British public interest); which tend to be promoted by tariff protection rather than by free trade; and which are already subject to control by the British Government. To determine both the likely effects of NAFTA on US direct investment in the UK, and the economic and political consequences of such effects, is a complex problem for empirical economic research, not one to be settled by conjuring up bogey men.

The third gut-reaction is to assert that the proposals are "completely impractical". This is the kind of conversation-stopping fatuity used by people who have not thought about something to bully others out of thinking about it. If a particular proposal is in the common interest of a group of nations, it is usually possible for intelligent and reasonable men to produce an operational solution to the practical problems of implementation.

Intelligent policy-making cannot be based on emotional reactions to political stereotypes. If Britain is to serve her own interests well, and to remain an influential power in the evolving world environment of the latter twentieth century, she must give careful and sustained thought to her international trading interests and to how these might best be implemented by choice among the alternative trade strategies open to her. The broad objective of the ATS programme is to contribute to this process by a thorough exploration of the NAFTA idea.

In this context, the ATS takes some pride in the fact that, in spite of a wide-spread popular belief that the NAFTA proposals were a complete political non-starter, it has been possible to persuade so many distinguished experts and scholars to undertake independent studies of the possibilities and the problems of the concept. It is also proud of the fact, in view of the propensity of commentators both outside and inside Britain to disparage British efficiency, initiative, and organising ability, that it has been able to commence publication of the studies it has commissioned within less than a year of the first tentative discussions among those responsible for getting them under way and that most of the study programme will have been published within two years of that starting point, in ample time to be of use and topical relevance to those concerned about the future of Britain's commercial policy.

Research Requirements

It is easy to get excited about the economic and political possibilities of new international trading arrangements—and equally easy to become frightened by the conceivably possible adverse consequences. Discussion of policy issues in a factual vacuum can proceed only by assertion and counter-assertion, with victory going quite fortuitously to the cleverest word-spinners and image-builders. Intelligent resolution of policy issues and adoption of strategies conducive to securing the national interest requires thorough expert exploration of the problems suggested by general debate as possibly important, with a view to assessing their magnitude and indicating ways of resolving them.

The programme of ATS research projects has been designed to explore the problems and potentialities of participation in a multilateral free trade association initiated by Atlantic countries from the point of view of the UK. The Canadian (and to a lesser extent the American) national interest in a NAFTA initiative have been investigated in depth in a comprehensive series of research studies sponsored by the Private Planning Association, while the American national interest is being studied by a group based at the Centre for International Studies, New York University, and by various branches of the US governmental system concerned with the formulation of future American trade policy. It should also be mentioned that relevant studies of the interests of the Pacific countries—which include the USA and Canada—in free trade arrangements are being produced by a programme of research into proposals for a Pacific free trade area (PAFTA) sponsored by the Japan Economic Research Center in Tokyo.

The specific topics of the ATS programme have been selected partly on the basis of logical analysis of the probable problem areas entailed in the NAFTA proposals, based on past experience of and theory about similar trading arrangements, and partly on the basis

15

of extensive discussions with public figures and academic and governmental experts about the problems they foresee as most likely to arouse concern in Britain. While some of these topics are of equal interest to all possible participants in NAFTA, and others of primary concern to people in the UK, all the studies have been written with the British interest in mind.

The NAFTA proposal raises, to begin with, the problem of how such an arrangement would fit in with the GATT, the international institution which governs world trading relationships, and with the general trend towards trade liberalisation that has characterised the period since World War II; also of how it compares with alternative strategies for continuing the movement towards freer world trade. Then there are the problems of the scope and structure of the proposed free trade association, the principles to be embodied in the treaty and the countries that might wish to participate; of the relations of the association to the developing countries and to the problem of East-West trade, which involve both economic and political questions; and of the special difficulties that might be encountered on admitting Japan as a member, as might be required by the trading interests of Australia and New Zealand and the general interests of the USA in the Pacific region. There are also problems with respect to other possible aspects of international economic co-operation in NAFTA besides the freeing of trade in industrial products: what NAFTA could do to liberalise trade in agricultural products, a special concern of Australia and New Zealand but also an interest of Canada and the USA; what sort and degree of co-operation might be required or desirable in the international monetary sphere; and how much harmonisation of economic policies other than tariff policies might be required, and how such harmonisation could best be effected.

From the point of view of Britain's interests in the NAFTA strategy, there are the economic questions of how NAFTA would affect Britain's overall balance of payments, international trade position and prospects for economic growth, and what its impact would be on major British industries. Then there are the political questions of how participation in NAFTA would affect Britain's position and status in world politics in general and in the Indo-Pacific theatre in particular. On the economic plane, there is the specific problem concerning which the NAFTA proposals have generated the most heated, but at the same time the most purely speculative and uninformed, opposition, namely the probable effects of NAFTA on investment by the large American corporations in Britain and the economic and political implications of such effects for Britain's national interests.

Dramatic Counter to Protectionism

All of the problems just listed call for careful research and the marshalling of all available knowledge. The ATS has set the research in train and will be endeavouring to promote research on new problems as they arise in public debate so far as resources permit. The four major studies in this volume are concerned with the more general aspects of the various proposals for a broadly based free trade association and the British national interest in them.

Professor Gerard Curzon and Mrs. Victoria Curzon, who are authorities on the history and operation respectively of the GATT and EFTA, analyse and compare the alternative strategies for the pursuit of liberalisation of world trade that are available after the Kennedy Round—a second Kennedy Round, the conditional most-favoured-nation approach, the free trade area approach typified by NAFTA and the sector-by-sector approach favoured by the GATT itself. They provide a dispassionate statement on the advantages and disadvantages of each and are concerned to encourage Britain to think beyond her immediate preoccupation with the Six to her responsibilities to the world as a whole. In the pamphlet version of their paper they seemed to lean slightly towards the last of the above policy options. But when it came to up-dating the paper for publication in this volume, the husband and wife team have shifted the emphasis towards the free trade area approach, this being preferred as probably the most dramatic and effective way of countering the mood of protectionism on both sides of the Atlantic that has deepened since the paper was first written.

Mr. Gelber, who has devoted much of his career to studying the Anglo-American relationship, analyses the political case for British participation in a loose trading arrangement. While it has been customary for proponents of British membership of the EEC to argue that the political gains from membership would be so great as to override any petty concern about adverse economic consequences, Mr. Gelber shows that the political case for membership is fraught with contradictions and argues that a NAFTA initiative would make much more sense for Britain, and for the USA, in the emerging politico-strategic realities of contemporary international relations.

The probable economic consequences for Britain of participation in NAFTA are analysed by Mr. Maxwell Stamp and Mr. Harry Cowie, of Maxwell Stamp Associates, a London firm of economic consultants. Their study, the first such study to make full allowance for the tariff reductions of the Kennedy Round, shows that participation in NAFTA would have beneficial effects on the volume of British trade and the British balance of payments, provided that British export prices were kept competitive—a proviso about which there is much less doubt, now that the pound has been devalued, than there was when their study was prepared. The study also produces preliminary evidence that fears of British inability to compete with the Americans in technologically advanced industries, and of a "take-over" of British industry by American corporations, are probably grossly exaggerated.

Finally, Mr. David Robertson, formerly an economist with the EFTA Secretariat, examines in detail the principles that should be embodied in the NAFTA treaty and the probability of the various countries concerned being motivated to join: for this latter purpose he conducted extensive field enquiries among the EFTA countries. He reaches the important conclusions that, though there are strong forces of inertia to overcome, a British proposal to initiate discussion of the formation of NAFTA would probably win the support of Canada, the USA and the EFTA countries.

Part II

OPTIONS AFTER THE
KENNEDY ROUND

by

Gerard and Victoria Curzon

1 FROM RICARDO TO KENNEDY

Our purpose is to discuss the future. As the gift of prophecy is not given to ordinary mortals (not even to economists) we can do no more than to take our bearings from the past in order to take a hazardous peek at tomorrow. The reader will forgive us if we return briefly to the nineteenth century.

In economic theory free trade has a respectable ancestry and it may appear paradoxical that commercial practice has often been out of step with it. But there was once a time when theory and practice coincided.

The theory grew out of the observation of the effects of the industrial revolution. Increased productivity and specialisation of the manufacturing industry led to the desire and ability to exchange one's own goods for those of another in order to enjoy a wider variety of consumer pleasures. In the middle of the nineteenth century Marx said of the manufacturing class that ". . . during its rule of scarce one hundred years [it] has created more massive and more colossal productive forces than have all preceding generations together. Subjection of nature's forces to man, machinery, application of chemistry to industry and agriculture, steam navigation, railways, electric telegraphs, clearing of whole continents for cultivation, canalisation of rivers, whole populations conjured out of the ground—what earlier century had even a presentiment that such productive forces slumbered in the lap of social labour?"[1]

More than half a century earlier Adam Smith had been puzzled by this same phenomenon of economic development and found that one of its major ingredients was the "division of labour"—or specialisation.

One can hardly quarrel with what nearly two centuries later has become such a truism that it is difficult to imagine that it can be attributed to a particular man. Adam Smith drew the conclusion that if specialisation was the basis of high productivity and consequent wealth, the limits of our wealth would be determined by the limits of specialisation. But he also saw that the extent of specialisation was limited by the size of the market within which the fruits of increased

[1]Karl Marx, "Communist Manifesto" (London, 1848).

productivity could be exchanged. This remains as true today as it was then and is behind much of the *rationale* in favour not only of free trade but also, nowadays, of regional economic integration. What can be added today is that since technology itself appears to have few bounds, the limits of specialisation are to be found in the finite nature of our planet alone. Indeed the limits to our potential wealth are determined only by the limits of the world itself and man's manifest capacity for irrational behaviour.

Adam Smith's line of reasoning was taken up by David Ricardo who formulated the theory of comparative advantage in international trade. He explained the observed phenomenon that inefficient as well as efficient producers found gains in trade and were, in their inefficiency, better off with trade than without it. A century of analysis and examination followed which seemed to confirm the findings of the classical economists. Their advocacy of free trade was tempered by only two exceptions—the "infant industry" argument and the terms of trade argument.[2]

Then came the Great Depression and understandably one became far more preoccupied with the problem of unemployment than with the gains from trade. If unemployment could be cured by sacrificing the gains from trade, then so be it. The conflict between the full employment policy theories and the freer trading theories was to preoccupy economists in the inter-war and immediate post-war periods. But as the spectre of unemployment receded, the gains from trade once more became attractive, even to debtor countries with balance of payments difficulties.

The old arguments of infant industry protection and terms of trade effects, and some new ones such as employment generation in countries with disguised unemployment, are now issues only between countries with substantially different incomes and economic structures; that is, the rich and poor countries of the world. This is not the place to discuss the merits of protection for the purposes of economic development—the "economic arguments", the "non-economic arguments" and the "non-arguments", as Professor Harry G. Johnson, of the London School of Economics, so nicely puts

[2]The first argument related to the non-existent or inefficient industry that, with the help of protection from imports, was deemed to become efficient with the passage of time. The second argument related to the exceptional case where a country had an effect on world prices through variations in its demand for foreign goods. In such cases it could be demonstrated that a country gained from imposing a tariff because it was the foreigner who paid for it.

it.[3] It is sufficient to retain that protectionism *versus* free trade is no longer an issue among developed countries: the problem is no longer *should we have free trade* but *how do we get there?*

Modern trade theory, in the meantime, rejects all arguments for protection save one or two at the most—the "optimum tariff" argument and some other "second best" arguments such as protection for infant industries or the case for customs unions and free trade areas.

Barring the inevitable exceptions that prove the rule, economic theory has now reached the conclusion that, taking as the standard of economic welfare the satisfaction of needs of individuals as consumers, freer trade is preferable to more restricted trade between countries with similar economic structures and at similar stages of development.

In economics, however, theory is almost always notoriously out of line with practice. Smith and Ricardo lived in a world that abounded in restrictions to trade, though the rising manufacturing classes (to use Marxist terminology) were haunted by the belief that their ever-increasing output would need ever larger markets.[4]

Cobden-Chevalier Treaty

By 1846 the contemporary theory got into step with policy when Britain, the most important trading nation of the time, repealed the Corn Laws and accepted the doctrine of free trade as its official policy. Even before this Prussia, in 1818, had adopted a low tariff policy as being preferable to a high one and, as the nucleus of a large customs union, had created favourable preconditions for free trade to spread throughout Europe. The event that sparked off general free trade was the Cobden-Chevalier commercial treaty between France and England signed in 1860. Though Napoleon III at the time agreed to the treaty largely for political reasons, it nevertheless opened Europe's richest market—France—to Europe's most competitive producer—Britain. Other European countries found such discrimination unacceptable and before long a system of

[3]Harry G. Johnson, "Tariffs and Economic Development", *The Journal of Development Studies*, October, 1964.
[4]Sceptical or unaware of the concept of effective demand, they mistook populations and inhabitants for exploitable markets, thus giving nineteenth century imperialism its impetus and misleading Marxists in their analysis of the inevitable self-destruction of the "capitalist" nations as they engaged in a suicidal battle for markets.

commercial treaties was negotiated by all European countries except Russia and, outside Europe, the USA. Every treaty contained the most-favoured-nation clause, whereby each partner in a bilateral agreement promised to grant the other treatment in no way inferior to that granted to the "most favoured nation". In this way negotiations were multilateralised and discrimination among countries entering the system was precluded. The level of protection in Europe was thus rapidly reduced and a free trading zone was, to all intents and purposes, established.

European Agricultural Protectionism

When did we lose our primitive innocence? Free trade in Europe survived largely intact until the outbreak of World War I, though exceptions had begun to creep in from 1880 onwards. These exceptions took the form of occasional tariffs that we should nowadays call modest and quantitative restrictions on imports were practically unknown. The first major difficulty that the most-favoured-nation (MFN) treaty system encountered was the inflow of agricultural products from the New World. At the start of the nineteenth century Malthusian fear of over-population and consequent famine had caused Europe's peasantry to be encouraged, by means more foul than fair, to cultivate the new lands overseas. But by the end of the century they had been so successful in their endeavours as to completely reverse the problem. They were now threatening the very existence of the European peasant with their cheap and plentiful grain products. The problem of the survival of the European peasant persists to this day to cloud the issue of commercial policy. North America's comparative advantage in the production of foodstuffs, especially grain products, has made of it the world's largest food exporting area and Europe's relative wealth has caused the Old World to become the world's largest food importing area. Conflict arises because all European countries, for non-economic reasons, desire to maintain at least a part of their peasantry. This problem engendered protectionist policies in 1880, led to the introduction of quantitative restrictions as a new commercial policy tool in the 1930's and returned to plague the Kennedy Round in the 1960's.

Circumstances change, but the problem has so far remained the same. And it is fascinating to see that this is also true for individual countries. Never has the proverb *plus ça change plus c'est la même chose* been truer than in the field of commercial policy.

24

The first massive attack on the European free trade system came from France, the most agriculturally inclined of all industrial countries in Western Europe. French agriculture needed protection in the face of American imports in order to survive. Of course there had always been the protectionist industrial lobbies (particularly since the Franco-Prussian War of 1871 when heavy taxes had been introduced to pay German war reparations). But the man who first attacked the *système des traités* and whose name was to become synonymous with protectionism in France was Jules Méline, an Inspector of Customs, who introduced the first really protectionist tariff in France in 1892. His argument for protection was based on the needs of the French peasant and it was agricultural products that reaped the full benefits of his policy.

Méline's reaction to the cheap grain imports from the newly settled continents was not the only course open to the countries of Europe. Denmark and Holland, for instance, instead of keeping the cheap grains out ceased their own inefficient production and used imports as a basis for efficient dairy farming. Unequal levels of agricultural productivity in Europe were the inevitable result of differing attitudes to cheap imports of grain from the New World and free trade among European countries did not long survive it. Europe became divided between those countries which had chosen a protectionist attitude to cheap grain imports and which adopted a high level of tariffs as a result and those which had chosen the road of adaption to changed circumstances. These countries became the low-tariff countries of Europe and formed the majority of the group that in the post-war years was to become known as the "low-tariff club".

If anyone remains mystified as to why a high level of agricultural protection should lead to a high level of industrial protection, he has but to consider protectionists' arguments that are still being pressed today, as they were many years ago. These claim that high domestic food prices warrant a high degree of protection because of the high level of wages they entail. In countries that practise low food prices and protect their farmers through direct subsidies the protectionist argument is based on the high level of taxation industry must suffer in order to pay the farming subsidy. It is always assumed that conditions are worse at home than they are abroad and that protection from the foreign competitor is essential.

One of the best empirical examples of the self-defeating nature of excessive protection and the merits of relative free trade is furnished by the experience of European agriculture. The Dutch and Danish farmer, who was forced to adapt to evolving circumstances at the end of the last century, is today wealthier and more efficient than his French or German counterpart.

The second massive move towards protectionism also took place in France, where quantitative restrictions were imposed to protect the peasant population from an indigestible bumper crop of Australian wheat that flooded European markets in 1930 and thoroughly upset the balance of European food prices. And in the post-war years, when the tide of protectionism generally speaking receded, it was once more concern for the French peasant that gave rise to the most sophisticated protectionist device that the world has yet witnessed—the EEC's common agricultural policy. If we are correct in assuming that a high level of agricultural protection creates forces in favour of a high level of industrial protection, the implication of the common agricultural policy for freer world trade is not encouraging.

Freer Trade Efforts

The economic (not to speak of the social and political) disruptions of the inter-war period were an excellent breeding ground for nationalist and protectionist policies, and the pre-1914 MFN treaty system was not re-established, in spite of many high-powered attempts to do so. This is not the place to give an exhaustive account of the inter-war attempts to free trade. It is enough to recall that they were numerous and that from the Covenant of the League of Nations, through the interminable inter-war economic conferences, to the outbreak of war in 1939, the desire to return to a more reasonable form of trade policy was apparent. But no one knew how to cut through the maze of restrictions and the Great Depression only made matters worse.

World War II ushered in a new age for more things than just commercial policy. It is of relevance to our story that it for instance made the USA a world power with world interests.

In August, 1941, Roosevelt and Churchill met secretly in mid-Atlantic to determine joint war aims. France, Germany and Italy, the other "strong economic powers" to whom the League had appealed in vain during the 1920s and the 1930s to adopt freer trading policies, were now out of it and the foundations laid for post-war economic co-operation were a strictly bilateral affair. Even so, Churchill was surprised to be asked by Roosevelt to subscribe to a precise (though limited) commitment: to "strive to promote mutually advantageous economic relations between them through the elimination of any discrimination in either the USA or in the UK against the importation of any product originating in the other country; and they will endeavour to further the enjoyment by all peoples of access on equal terms to the markets and to the raw materials which are needed for their economic prosperity." Churchill threw out "without discrimination" and added "with due respect for existing obligations" to safeguard Imperial Preference.

This reaction was to be typical for much that followed when for some years to come American initiatives for freer trade were watered down by British reservations and, towards the end of the war, by those of many of the allies. Professor Richard Gardner, of Columbia University, who has made an exhaustive study of the stillborn International Trade Organisation (ITO) (it was to have been the incarnation of the economic war aims of the Atlantic Charter), puts its failure to materialise down to the lack of provision for the special needs of the under-developed countries and for adequate transitional arrangements.[5] Professor Gardner adds that the two major sponsors of the ITO each sought to implement their favourite economic doctrines. For the USA the elimination of preferences, quotas and discrimination was all important; for Britain, freedom to pursue domestic full-employment policies and to maintain the Commonwealth preference system was considered essential.

After the end of the war, the whole issue of how to achieve freer trade became multilateral once again, and the two signatories of the Atlantic Charter were soon to be outpaced in this by the countries of continental Western Europe.

The first post-war attack on tariffs occurred in 1947, within the framework of the temporary and incomplete General Agreement on Tariffs and Trade (GATT) and under the auspices of renewed US trade legislation which authorised the Administration to grant tariff cuts of up to 50 per cent on a basis of reciprocity. The negotiations were an undoubted success. Impressive tariff cuts were negotiated, on paper at least. What in fact happened was that the USA gave real concessions in return for sham ones because the

[5]Richard N. Gardner, "Sterling-Dollar Diplomacy: Anglo-American Collaboration in the Reconstruction of Multilateral Trade" (Clarendon Press, Oxford, 1956).

majority of European countries maintained quantitative restrictions on dollar imports for balance of payments reasons. But it must not be thought that this was an exercise of no consequence. In 1948 the USA sponsored the creation of the Organisation for European Economic Co-operation (OEEC), and the attack on intra-European quotas began. A decade later the Europeans were no longer able to justify dollar import restrictions on balance of payments grounds and the sham tariff cuts of 1947 came into their own.

The item-by-item type of tariff negotiation, however, proved to be subject to diminishing returns. It had been very successful in reducing inflated tariff positions, but was powerless to bring about tariff cuts that really hurt—the very nature of item-by-item negotiation being to pursue the path of least resistance, since it allows each negotiator to select himself those items on which he is prepared to give concessions, leaving the real strongholds of protection untouched.

Most continental European countries were quick to realise this. Successive renewals of the US Reciprocal Trade Agreements Act gave the Administration power to negotiate on the basis of tariff cuts of only 5 per cent a year for three years at a time, and even this power was limited by all sorts of "peril point" procedures, national security considerations and the like. Since the USA, the original proponent of multilateral freeing of trade, had little to offer in negotiation, it received correspondingly little in exchange, and already in 1951 a number of continental European countries began pressing for a new negotiating procedure to replace the item-by-item technique.

Another reason for the need to find a new approach to tariff reduction lay in the weak negotiating position of the countries with relatively low tariffs. In the first tariff rounds the low tariff countries had been able to offer a binding of their low tariffs against a possible increase in exchange for a reduction in their partners' high tariffs. But in successive rounds high tariff countries were not prepared to make further reductions in return for a rebinding of low rates, which was all the low tariff countries were prepared to offer in order to retain some kind of bargaining power for the future.

In March, 1951, eleven governments,[6] among whom the UK was conspicuous for its absence, submitted a memorandum on the

[6]Austria, Belgium, Denmark, France, Italy, Luxembourg, the Netherlands, Norway, Sweden, the USA and West Germany.

"Problem of the Disparity of European Tariffs" to be discussed by the contracting parties (signatory countries) of GATT. Before discussions could mature, the French delegate, M. Pflimlin, surprised his colleagues by submitting a specific proposal for a linear reduction of tariffs by 30 per cent over a period of three years on a multilateral basis.

The GATT Plan

A working party was established to study these initiatives and after two years produced a synthesis which became known as the GATT Plan for Tariff Reduction.[7] If the GATT Plan had ever been applied it would have gone a long way to meeting the difficulties of the low tariff countries while at the same time making tariff cuts in sensitive areas. Each government participating in the plan would have undertaken to reduce the average unweighted incidence of its customs tariff by 10 per cent in three successive years. Within certain limits governments would have been free to choose the items for reduction, but so as to make sure that no country could concentrate all its reductions in a single area, ten broad sectors of traded goods were defined to which the 30 per cent reduction was to apply. Reduction by 30 per cent was the general rule, but countries with comparatively low tariff rates would not be required to make the full cut if their average duty incidence for a given sector stood below an agreed "ceiling". Furthermore, if their average duty incidence for a given sector stood at or below an agreed "floor", no reduction would be required of them. In short, the GATT Plan was a proposal for linear tariff reductions which anticipated the problem of exception lists and attempted to find a solution to the disparity problem in advance of any actual negotiation. Though it never came to anything, it does at least show that one does not necessarily have to go as far as to form a free trade area or a customs union in order to agree on tariff reductions according to a fixed timetable.

In addition to the specific provision for tariff reductions according to the plan, the working party also proposed that certain prescribed tariff levels for individual categories of goods should be decided upon. Imports were divided into four broad sectors—agricultural products,

[7]"A New Proposal for the Reduction of Customs Tariffs" (General Agreement on Tariffs and Trade, Geneva, January, 1954).

industrial raw materials, industrial semi-manufactures and finished manufactured products. An attempt was made to divide agricultural products into raw materials, semi-manufactures and manufactured goods, but was abandoned owing to the fact that many agricultural products were found to be raw materials and finished products at the same time. It was also found that tariff rates on agricultural goods did not seem to be dictated by the stage of processing reached, as was (and is) the case of most industrial tariff rates.

The working party proposed ceiling rates in each of the four sectors with the intention of eliminating tariff "peaks". The suggested ceilings were computed on the unweighted average of reporting countries' tariffs and as a result were roughly twice the ceilings that would have been attained if a weighted average had been taken. It is of interest to see what this attempt at tariff harmonisation would have produced. There would have been no tariff on industrial raw materials exceeding 5 per cent; none on industrial semi-manufactures exceeding 15 per cent; none on industrial manufactured products exceeding 30 per cent; and none on agricultural products exceeding 27 per cent.

In those days of innocence it was thought that agricultural products could be treated like any other traded article. Indeed, the working party never considered agriculture to be a special case and their plan was to have applied to it fully.

The GATT Plan for Tariff Reduction contained two further points of interest. First it was made clear again and again that the sponsoring governments considered that the initial 30 per cent reduction would be followed by further cuts, leading to substantially free trade the world over. Secondly, it made specific provisions for the problems of the less developed countries, by permitting them to retain tariffs for the protection of infant industries while allowing them access to industrial markets in accordance with the provisions of the plan. The permitted infant industry tariffs, however, were to be subject to inspection and supervision on the part of the contracting parties and countries were to be permitted to retain them only as long as they could be justified (that is, only so long as these countries had not become exporters of the products concerned).

The reason for the failure of the GATT Plan to materialise was the reluctance and/or inability of the two major trading countries to subscribe to it—the USA because it did not have Congressional permission (and did not attempt to obtain it) and the UK because it preferred to develop its Commonwealth markets and objected to "the excessive complexity of the scheme".[8]

During the years that the discussion took place various spokesmen for the continental European countries pointed out that the failure of the British and the Americans to participate in the scheme would force a number of European countries to negotiate freer trade among themselves. To this both laggards replied that they would insist on MFN treatment.

Two Strands of History Meet

At this point of the story two strands of European history meet. This is not the place to describe the trials and tribulations of the European integration movement. It is enough to record that after the brave hopes of the early post-war era, a number of frustrations had accumulated. The latest of these was the rejection of the treaty creating a European army—the European Defence Community— by the French National Assembly in August, 1954. The political and military approaches to European integration having failed, its proponents seized upon the economic one as being the only remaining avenue of possible progress open to them. They found the ground well prepared. The story of the EEC is often told in too simple terms. It did not spring fully armed from the head of M. Jean Monnet at Messina in 1955 and it was not only the result of the common political will of the six countries concerned. It is frequently forgotten that it has its own very respectable economic antecedents born of the inability of GATT to deal with the European tariff problem. When the more credulous students of European history point to the rapidity with which the Treaty of Rome was drawn up as proof of the staunch political will of the six countries they forget that they had for years presented a common economic front within GATT. But because the EEC was as much a political animal as it was an economic one, the Six failed to take with them in their enterprise Austria and the Scandinavian countries which had also been among their *compagnons de guerre*.

The British and American attitude to the European tariff problem having forced the major continental European countries to proceed to complete trade integration as the only legal means open to them under GATT rules, the USA and UK found themselves

[8]*GATT Press Release* 140, Geneva, October 15, 1953.

31

faced with the prospect of discrimination in important export markets. Britain reacted with unwonted rapidity. She changed almost overnight from being one of the principal detractors of tariff reductions to being the prime mover in a scheme for European free trade. History is written by the victors, not the vanquished, and the "Maudling negotiations" within the OEEC, as the attempt to form a European-wide free trade area came to be known, are too often thought to have been hopelessly unrealistic from the start. In fact they came so close to success that one must give credit to them as a realistic policy, even if they came to naught. In November, 1958, General de Gaulle's first *Non* shook the five other members of the new-born Community to the core and brought the efforts of Mr. Reginald Maudling, Britain's negotiator, to an abrupt end. From the ashes rose the European Free Trade Association (EFTA), no phoenix but a stop-gap solution for those countries remaining outside the EEC and wishing to find at least a partial solution to the discrimination problem they were presented with.

Trade Expansion Act of 1962

The American reaction to this double discrimination in important export markets did not take so revolutionary a form as to propose regional free trade too. Using the only administrative means at its disposal, the USA set about obtaining a reduction in the proposed common outer tariff of the EEC by conventional means. The Dillon Round of multilateral negotiations within the GATT framework was the result of this initiative. Though to European observers it was quite clear from the start that this would prove to be totally inadequate for the purpose, the occasion was taken to help the US Administration to obtain more negotiating freedom from Congress. The chosen bait was a linear cut of 20 per cent in the Community's common external tariff which was to become fully operative if and when Congress gave the US Administration power to reciprocate. But this was not all. In order to make the whole packet more attractive to Congress, the Europeans were made to promise that in any successor to the Dillon Round agricultural goods would be included in the negotiations. Armed with this impressive array of inducements to persuade Congress to grant the US Government negotiating leeway, the Dillon Round negotiators returned home in the summer of 1961. In the meantime they had stopped over in Brussels to negotiate a stand-still agreement with the EEC whereby both parties promised not to change their tariffs during the interval.[9]

The outgoing Eisenhower Administration left a number of plans for changing the old Reciprocal Trade Agreements Act to meet the result of the Dillon Round in the In-trays of the new Kennedy Administration. The new life that President John Kennedy infused into American policy did not leave commercial policy untouched. Instead of unimaginatively meeting the EEC half way by reciprocating the proposed 20 per cent tariff cut, President Kennedy seized the occasion to promote the economic aspect of his Grand Design for Atlantic partnership. The Trade Expansion Act of 1962 was the result, and it of course went further along the road to free trade than the Community had bargained for. Instead of proposing 20, it proposed a 50 per cent linear tariff cut and it furthermore proposed the complete elimination of duties on those products in which the USA and the EEC accounted for more than 80 per cent of free-world exports. Since it was at the time assumed that the UK and other EFTA members would shortly join the EEC, the so-called "dominant supplier authority" was tantamount to initiating a discussion on North Atlantic free trade on a sector-by-sector basis. In the event the failure of the EEC to enlarge its circle of membership reduced the number of product categories to which the "dominant supplier" authority applied from some 26 to 2—aircraft and margarine—and nothing came of this imaginative appeal to free trade among industrialised countries.

Depending on how the future may evolve, the hopes of the Kennedy-inspired Trade Expansion Act may stand out as a landmark in the history of commercial policy. It was planned and designed almost exactly one hundred years after the Cobden-Chevalier treaty of 1860 initiated free trade for the latter half of the nineteenth century. If we have dwelt on the historical perspective, it is because we have wished to show that the wheel is in the process of turning full circle and that if nothing develops to prevent its progress we may expect substantially free trade to characterise the latter half of the twentieth century as it did the nineteenth. But just as free trade in the nineteenth century was first arrested by economic disruption and then destroyed by political disaster, so the present trend in the direction of free trade may, of course, be reversed.

[9]For those who today remember the "chicken war", the violence of the American reaction to the EEC's attempt to stem the flow of frozen fowl across the Atlantic is explained by the fact that the USA took the stand-still agreement seriously.

2   WHAT THE KENNEDY ROUND TAUGHT

"The industrialised countries participating in the Kennedy Round made duty reductions on 70 per cent of their dutiable imports, excluding cereals, meat and dairy products. Moreover, two thirds of these cuts were of 50 per cent or more. Around another fifth were between 25 and 50 per cent. Of the total dutiable imports on which no tariff cuts have been negotiated (31 per cent of the total), one third are subject to duties of 5 per cent *ad valorem* or less. All this can be stated in another way. Of the imports by the participating industrialised countries (other than cereals, meat and dairy products) 66 per cent are either duty-free or are to be subject to cuts of 50 per cent or more; on another 15 per cent there are to be cuts of less than 50 per cent and 19 per cent remain unaffected. As for cereals, meat and dairy products, the aim was the negotiation of general arrangements. In the case of cereals, agreement relating to prices and food aid has been reached. Some bilateral agreements have been concluded on meat. Very little has been obtained in the negotiations on dairy products. On scores of other agricultural products, significant duty reductions were made . . .

"In addition to these tariff cuts, agreements were also reached on chemical products and on anti-dumping policies which will contribute in an important way to the reduction of non-tariff barriers to trade."[10]

Tariff Disparities

This is not the place to enter the labyrinth of the Kennedy Round negotiations, to trace the crises or even to analyse the successes. But the Kennedy Round, in the give and take of negotiations, has laid bare the real obstacles to freer trade and unmasked the bogies. The main difficulties encountered on the way appear to have been the problem of tariff disparities, non-tariff barriers to trade and trade in agricultural products.

The problem of tariff disparities arose in the Kennedy Round over the fact that some countries (particularly the USA) had some very

[10]Eric Wyndham White, "GATT Trade Negotiations", *GATT Press Release* 993, Statement to GATT Trade Negotiations Committee, Geneva, June 30, 1967.

high tariffs indeed—60 or 80 per cent and more *ad valorem*—while other important trading partners (notably the Community) considered that they had comparatively low tariffs. The Community felt that a 50 per cent reduction on either side would leave the protective effect of the high tariffs substantially untouched while reducing that of the lower tariffs considerably. In other words, to cut an 80 per cent tariff to 40 was not thought to be sufficient "payment" for reducing a 30 per cent tariff to 15. This led to involved discussions as to whether equal linear cuts were justified when disparities of this type arose. The GATT Plan ten years earlier had foreseen that this problem might arise when it became a question of negotiating on a linear and not item-by-item basis and had made some provision for low tariffs to be reduced by less than high ones. But before one can agree on such a procedure, one has to define tariff disparity and this proved to be impossible. Discussions were nominally confined to the USA, the UK and the EEC, but when they centered on products that involved third countries as well, the problem became more complex than ever. If, for instance, two countries (say the USA and the EEC) agree on the existence of a tariff disparity where a particular commodity is concerned and a third country (say Switzerland) is found to be a principal supplier, then Switzerland would be the main victim of an agreement between the other two to reduce a tariff by less than 50 per cent because of a "disparity". The problem was ultimately settled when the Community agreed to the "European clause" which took the rights of smaller European countries into account.

It was found in the discussion on tariff disparities that the direction of trade flows had to be taken into account and this of course widened the scope of the problem to such an extent that negotiations might have continued happily for years. But in all the discussions that actually took place on how to define a disparity, and in all the proposed mathematical definitions, no attempt was made to account for the different levels of productivity in the various countries. As a result it was impossible to determine whether in fact a tariff of 40 per cent was more or less protective than one of 20 per cent. Towards the end of the Kennedy Round the problem faded away and was not heard of again.

It is still a moot point whether the Community raised the disparity issue at the outset of the Kennedy Round as a red herring, without any serious intention of pursuing it, or whether the fact that many of the notorious disparities were to be found in the chemical sector meant that the problem was solved pragmatically in the separate agreement on chemicals that forms a supplement to the Kennedy Round protocol to the General Agreement.

Whichever it may be, the experience of the Kennedy Round suggests that the problem of disparities has been exaggerated and with luck (and good will) it will not recur in future trade negotiations. In the first place it has proved to be impossible to arrive at an objective definition of disparity and in the second place the further one proceeds along the road to freer trade, the less flagrant the disparities become. The Kennedy Round has done its work in reducing a great number of tariff positions by 50 per cent. Whatever form the next steps towards freer trade may take, they should start from lower positions than those faced by the Kennedy Round, so what turned out to be a bogey then would, hopefully, not be raised again. Incidentally, should the next steps take the form of an agreement to achieve free trade, whether on a discriminatory basis or not, the disparity issue would of course be only of temporary significance and would disappear once all tariffs reached zero position.

Non-tariff Barriers

At an early stage of the Kennedy Round negotiations it was agreed that non-tariff barriers to trade would have to be included in the negotiations. It was felt that the expected benefits from substantial tariff reductions which were anticipated should not be frustrated by the existence of non-tariff barriers in one or the other country. The experience of 1947, when no attempt was made to deal with quotas, thus making tariff cuts ineffective, was not to be repeated.

As always in these matters, there was no objection to the proposal so long as it was kept in these vague terms. But discussions on details brought the contracting parties down to earth. An invitation to all contracting parties to bring details of all non-tariff barriers they encountered in their trade relations led to a consolidated list of eighteen protectionist devices[11] which, if all applied by a single

[11]Non-tariff barriers identified by GATT contracting parties: escape clauses, anti-dumping practices, customs valuations, government procurement policies, state-trading, border tax adjustment, dumping and restrictive import policies on coal, bilateral quotas, residual quantitative restrictions, mixing regulations, variable levies, administrative and technical regulations, administrative guidance, subsidiaries' trading policies, import collateral, subsidies, internal fiscal charges and the US system of wine gallon assessment on imported bottled spirits.

country, would indeed render the value of any tariff concessions doubtful, if not meaningless.

Happily, most of the devices to which objection could be taken were identified as this or that country's practice and then only in this or that particular field of economic activity. As so frequently in GATT discussions the attempt to identify the problem cut it down to size.

No single country complained of encountering all the non-tariff barriers listed and no one country was found to be using all of them simultaneously. It therefore became a matter of distinguishing between general issues which could be dealt with by drawing up new rules or codes of conduct and specific issues which required bilateral or multilateral negotiations on particular measures affecting specific products and which did not warrant anything so far reaching as a whole new code of conduct.

Anti-Dumping Code

Among the multilateral issues loomed largely the anti-dumping legislations of many countries which were mandatory and which were therefore little affected by GATT's scanty article 6 on anti-dumping action. There seemed to be evidence that such legislation, frequently far broader in its definition of what dumping consisted of than what economists would normally accept as being justified, had been used to vary tariffs in response to foreign price changes. The new anti-dumping code of the GATT, negotiated as part of the Kennedy Round, tries to bring some order into the divergent and often too permissive national practices, by attempting to establish an internationally accepted administration of national anti-dumping legislation.

American Selling Price Procedure

Valuation for customs purposes was another issue on which there was basic agreement, as laid down in the GATT article 7 some twenty years earlier. Though some of the less-developed countries were known to sin in this respect, the most serious case concerned the American selling price (ASP) procedure of valuation for customs purposes which was obtained by the US chemical industry in 1922 as a protectionist device to keep out foreign benzenoid chemicals. This matter, too, received the attention of the Kennedy Round negotiators and the inclusion of chemicals in the negotiations, as opposed to their being put on the exception list, was of sufficient importance to the USA for them to negotiate a separate protocol on chemicals which the Trade Expansion Act had not authorised and which now needs the separate endorsement of Congress. It is interesting to see that the only equivalent non-tariff barriers the USA could find in Europe for the purpose of achieving at least nominal reciprocity were discriminatory road taxes in West Germany, France and Italy which penalised high powered, hence American, cars; Swiss restrictions on the use of corn syrup for fruit preserves; and the UK fiscal charge on tobacco where the Commonwealth preference margin was reduced by 25 per cent.

It is worth mentioning for the record that the European countries at one point drew up a chemical agreement of their own and were considering the possibility of applying it among themselves on a conditional MFN basis should the USA not play ball. If Congress fails to abolish ASP this agreement could presumably be revived.

State-Trading Practices

State-trading measures received less widespread attention and were confined to the special issue of Polish accession to the GATT. The full implications of once again a separate protocol for the accession of Poland will only be seen with time. Two important new elements have been introduced by the Kennedy Round into the world trading system. The first is that a planned increase of imports in socialist countries is to be considered equivalent to a tariff concession on the part of a market economy country. The second is that in the absence of comparable price systems in the market economies and in collectivist countries, matters such as anti-dumping and market disruption measures have been provided for in an additional protocol, thus laying down the first code of conduct between state trading and market economy countries. This may turn out to be a revolutionary break-through and it seems only a matter of time before Hungary, Rumania and Bulgaria (whose observers attended the first GATT ministerial meeting after the Kennedy Round) will join the GATT under conditions not requiring tariff negotiations. Quite apart from the positive political implications, the knowledge which will be acquired in dealing with these wholly state-trading countries in the years to come will no doubt help to solve problems of partial state-trading as practised by many of the less-developed and some of the market economy countries.

The Kennedy Round confined itself to these three major issues because the confrontation of countries and problems soon showed that the non-tariff barrier issue was an unknown quantity. Many of the remaining items on the list clearly were of the two-country, one-product type of problem: the US system of wine gallon assessment on imported bottled spirit bothered Britain, restrictive import policies on coal were a Community problem, residual quantitative restrictions were mainly part of the problems of trade with the less-developed countries[12] and so forth. Even the frequently cited government procurement problem faded out in the course of the negotiations. It is not clear whether this was due to the overwhelmingly military aspect of the question, leaving economic considerations to some marginal cases which then became bilateral problems between such countries as the USA and UK over power station contracts, or because governments preferred to retain the freedom to sin by permitting others to do so in their turn.

Some think that the border tax issue and the problem of harmonising different national tax and social welfare structures will dominate the non-tariff barrier discussions in the near future. The Kennedy Round did not give a clear pointer in this issue, probably for lack of time. The working group on non-tariff barriers set up some six sub-groups to investigate the other problems that had been brought to the attention of the signatory countries. But interest in them was so small that they never met.

Ministers meeting in Geneva in November, 1967, the first such gathering after the Kennedy Round, admitted being in the dark over the extent of the non-tariff barrier problem. They decided that "an inventory on non-tariff and para-tariff barriers affecting international trade will be drawn up (by the end of April, 1968)". In addition, they set up a special committee on trade in industrial products "to explore the opportunities for making progress toward further liberalisation of trade", instructing it to report on the non-tariff barrier problem. And they instructed the Council of the General Agreement to initiate appropriate machinery to deal with the problems identified in the inventory. If the opinion of a high

[12]The Kennedy Round yielded no official results in this field, but some quotas are said to have been removed bilaterally as part of the bargaining process, often behind the backs of other contracting parties. Thus it is said that Japan dismantled restrictions on a discriminatory basis in favour of the USA, but that this did not lead to complaints because quota restrictions are relatively unimportant factors in the trade relations among developed countries in the industrial sector.

official in GATT is anything to go by ("The more I hear and read about non-tariff barriers the less I understand them") no one really yet knows whether the issue is large or small, whether it must be attacked globally or on a country-by-country or sector-by-sector basis.

Nonetheless, the overwhelming impression at the end of the Kennedy Round is that the remaining government controlled non-tariff barriers are not sufficient to frustrate the expected benefits of the negotiated tariff reductions. But similarly strong is the impression that business itself has set up non-tariff barriers to trade much more effective than those imposed by governments and that any further progress in this field will need the effective participation of private interests.

Agriculture in World Trade

Ever since the scales turned and the nineteenth century vision of famine in a Europe of population explosion gave way to surpluses from overseas which threatened the very existence of European peasants, less favoured by nature and capital in raising their productivity, agriculture has been a spanner in the freer trade works.

The International Trade Charter, and with it the GATT, made no distinction in trading rules for agricultural and industrial goods. No universalist trade charter would have been accepted by the agricultural exporting countries if trade in agricultural products had been left out. But similarly the support policies, import regulations and other measures to protect agriculture in industrialised countries for the most diverse reasons makes it unreasonable to expect the same trading rules to apply to agricultural as to industrial products. The world's trading nations have been living with this problem for many years now, but not very happily. Since the re-examination of the world trading system began as a consequence of the creation of the EEC in 1957, at least the problem is being talked about. In 1958 a GATT group of experts under the chairmanship of Professor Gottfried Haberler, in a report entitled "Trends in World Trade", suggested that the problem of trade in agricultural goods should be dealt with. A committee was set up to review the agricultural policies of member governments and to examine the effect of agricultural protection on international trade. This helped to develop a better understanding of countries' agricultural problems and prepared the inclusion of agriculture in the Kennedy Round.

It also led to sectoral investigations into the meat, cereal and dairy product categories.

The EEC's common agricultural policy as it has now developed promises an intensification of protectionist policies in Europe with an extreme anti-trade bias which does not augur well for future trade negotiations. The Kennedy Round was the first serious post-war effort to include agriculture in the bargaining process, and discussions centered on the three main product groups already defined in former years—meat, dairy products and cereals. Only limited success was achieved, and that only with respect to trade in wheat, where a common fund for food aid to poor countries was the new feature included in a reformed International Wheat Agreement.

In spite of limited success two things stand out. The first is that the experience of some ten years of consultation, confrontation and negotiation over agricultural protectionist policies has shown that progress is probably possible. The meat and dairy products working parties in the Kennedy Round were finally overcome more by the time factor than by any particular insoluble difficulty. Hopefully internal Common Market difficulties, of a nature similar to those encountered in the past by the USA as a result of generous domestic support policies, will lead the Community in years to come to more reasonable attitudes. Recent reports of conflict within the French Government over agricultural policies also seem to point in this direction. In Europe generally a constantly falling agricultural population and rising agricultural production are causing a pincer movement in favour of higher productivity. Within a generation or so it is likely that many of the structural inefficiencies of European agriculture will have disappeared, that specialisation will be widespread and that the conditions for two-way trade in agricultural products will exist between Europe and the rest of the world.

A second conclusion that can be drawn from the Kennedy Round experience is that no future multilateral tariff bargaining will be able to exclude agriculture *per se* once again. In the words of Sir Eric Wyndham White, when Director-General of GATT: "One thing was made abundantly clear at the very outset of the Geneva negotiations; that is, that significant trade negotiations can no longer leave agriculture on one side."[13]

[13]Wyndham White, "Agriculture within World Trade," Address to Congress of the International Federation of Agricultural Journalists, Heidelberg, September 12, 1967.

The implications of negotiations held until now are that tariffs are minor issues when it comes to agricultural trade and that what must be negotiated is the domestic production and support policies that distort the trading picture. It is therefore less a question of simply establishing regional or universal freer trade and more one of taking each broad agricultural sector and agreeing on a single code of support policies adapted to the special needs of each particular branch of agricultural production. Only after this is done will it be possible for a rational system of world trade in agriculture to develop. One could also conceivably agree to a certain amount of geographical specialisation in agricultural production depending on aptitudes and sectoral requirements.

The Kennedy Round has clearly shown up a major obstacle to further progress in the direction of freer trade. Unlike the disparities issue and some of the non-tariff barriers it is a real difficulty that will remain with us for some time to come. It is an area for study and investigation, since further progress in freer trade in industrial goods depends in large measure on some degree of harmonisation of the level of agricultural support accorded to farmers in industrial countries. In the absence of such harmonisation arguments for industrial protection will continue to bear weight. Furthermore, the agricultural exporters of the world—in particular the USA and Canada—are likely in the future to make industrial tariff concessions dependent upon the maintenance, and if possible growth, of their agricultural export markets. If one remembers that the USA is an essential part of any further progress in freeing world trade, the crucial nature of the agricultural problem becomes apparent.

3 BEYOND THE KENNEDY ROUND

As we have shown, the world has been groping for twenty years now for greater freedom in trading arrangements. In a broad sense the creation of regional trading groups such as the EEC and EFTA is as much part of this trend as the trade liberalisation within the OEEC and the successive tariff negotiations within GATT.

Now that the Kennedy Round is over and the tired negotiators are taking a well-earned rest, the question that many people are asking themselves is—what next? It is clear that the world can slip back as well as move forward—but it is certain not to remain stationary. In this paper, though we must unfortunately always keep the possibility of regression at the back of our minds, we shall be mainly concerned with the various means of continuing progress that are at present at our disposal.

The world can proceed to the goal of free trade—and in 1968 one need no longer hesitate to state this as being our ultimate objective —in one of two broad ways. Firstly, by multiplying regional free trade arrangements, broadening the scope of their memberships or creating new ones; secondly, by gradually reducing tariffs on a multilateral basis and on the MFN principle (that is, without discrimination towards third parties). The possible variants of these two broad methods are innumerable. The purpose of this section is to examine some of the variants that are currently being discussed, or have been discussed in the past, in order to weigh the advantages against the disadvantages of each and to clarify the alternatives now before us. It must be pointed out from the start that our viewpoint is not that of any one country, but rather that of the world's trading community as a whole. Our yard-stick for measuring the virtues of this or that proposal will be in how far it serves the interests of that trading community and its ultimate goal of free trade. Our purpose is to discuss proposals of real practical significance, and if it is felt that some of them demand too much in the way of rational behaviour from governments, then it should be remembered that the whole trade liberalisation movement since the end of the last war is, in itself, an impressive monument to rational behaviour. Since 1958 the Common Market has been tarred with the inward-looking brush, but its performance in the latter part of the Kennedy Round has shown that it is prepared to negotiate. The UK is one of the most protectionist developed countries in the world, yet three times in the past ten years (1956–57, 1961 and 1967) it has attempted to achieve complete area free trade with much of Europe and already in 1959 entered into a free trading agreement with some of Europe's most competitive nations. The USA has long been regarded as a protectionist country, yet it fathered the GATT, passed the monumental Trade Expansion Act of 1962 and is actively preparing to take a new initiative early in 1969.

The fact is that twenty years of trade liberalisation have taught governments (and, incidentally, business) that the removal of protective barriers does *not* lead to widespread distress, unemployment and social unrest. Strangely enough, it has been found to lead to increased trade (imports as well as exports) and enhanced efficiency . . . just as those ivory tower academics said it would.

Regional Approach to Freer Trade

Regional free trade is very fashionable at the moment and it is sometimes thought that it can be an answer to our problems all on its own. Although, however, the regional approach towards freer trade has much to recommend it, it must always be remembered that it means discrimination against someone—temporarily at least. Because of this, regional free trade should not be thought of as an end in itself and sufficient to our long-term needs or aims.

But there is no doubt that an excellent case can be made for the proposition that when tariff reductions on a non-discriminatory basis are for various reasons blocked the formation of a customs union or a free trade area is justified.

In the past, when the world's trading system was organised by a network of commercial treaties each containing the most-favoured nation clause, the only generally permitted exception to the principle of non-discrimination was the freedom to enter or form a customs union. When the GATT was drawn up in 1947 the time-honoured customs union reservation was included in the draft and, at the request of a number of under-developed countries, free trade areas were also included as they believed that a customs union would be too difficult for them to administer should they wish to avail themselves of the customary exception to non-discrimination.

In the mid-1950s, when no further progress appeared to be

possible in the field of tariff reduction on a non-discriminatory basis, six European countries decided to form a customs union; in 1959, after an attempt had been made to heal the trade discrimination breach in Europe that this implied, seven other European countries formed a free trade area and were joined in 1961 by an eighth. No doubt inspired by these examples of economic integration, other regional trading groups soon followed in other parts of the world, notably in Latin America and in Africa.

In 1965 and 1966 the Kennedy Round was bogged down in a number of seemingly insoluble problems, some of which we have already described. It seemed at the time as though the EEC was doing what it could to prevent a successful outcome to the negotiations in order to preserve the virginity of its common external tariff, and hence the purity of the Community as such. In the 1950s it had been the inability of the USA to negotiate that obliged the Europeans to find a regional solution to their tariff problem. In the 1960s it seemed as though the USA would be forced to seek a regional solution to trade liberalisation because of the apparent impotence of the Brussels commission. The internal EEC crisis engendered by France in the night of June 30, 1965, over the agricultural question threatened to break up the *ménage à six* and paralysed its power to negotiate in Geneva. Under the circumstances it is not surprising that people began to occupy themselves with regional alternatives to the Kennedy Round.

Proposals for a free trade area among like-minded industrialised countries began to appear in 1965 in the form of papers and speeches by private individuals and independent men of politics. In 1966 they reached print in the form of a policy statement by the Canadian-American Committee of the National Planning Association in the USA and the Private Planning Association of Canada (both un-official bodies) in a succinct 17-page document entitled "A New Trade Strategy for Canada and the United States." The idea received sufficient attention for the Joint Economic Committee of the US Congress to request a study of its implications.[14]

The proponents of a free trade area among industrialised countries all agree that whatever the membership might be to begin with, the

[14]Theodore Geiger and Sperry Lea, "The Free Trade Area Concept as Applied to the United States", in "Issues and Objectives of US Foreign Trade Policy" (Subcommittee on Foreign Economic Policy, Joint Economic Committee, US Congress, US Government Printing Office, Washington D.C., 1967).

long term objective would be to include all developed and some less developed countries and thus achieve an effective system of world free trade.

It is generally agreed that to begin with the present EFTA countries would be part of the system and that it would probably include the USA, Canada and some other European, Asian, Latin American and Commonwealth countries. This concept of an open-ended, Atlantic-based free trade area is being referred to in Britain as a North Atlantic Free Trade Area (NAFTA), because of the prospective initial membership, it otherwise being recognised to be something of a misnomer in view of the possible participation of Japan, Australia and others.

A necessary condition for the fulfilment of even part of the NAFTA plan is that a sufficient number of trading countries should quite genuinely believe that tariffs are a thing of the past and that free (or freer) trade is a "good thing". As we have already attempted to show, it is not so much the belief that is lacking at present, but a technical means of achieving the objective. A free trade area is in fact nothing more than a technique whereby those countries believing that tariffs are indeed a "barbarous relic" of the past may with impunity bypass those countries or groups that still find them of some use.

It is interesting to note that the proposed NAFTA commitments are intended to be kept to the minimum necessary for the establishment of effective regional free trade.

Thus it is a free trade area that is proposed and not a customs union. Of the two, the customs union is generally considered to be the higher form of life in spite of the fact that it is really far less viable than a free trade area (a frequent biological observation). Because a customs union does not leave its members free to pursue an independent foreign commercial policy (the external tariff is the same for all) it implies a minimum common political will. A free trade area, because it leaves its members full sovereignty in trade relations with the outside world, is far less exacting and indeed does not imply a specific political commitment. It is because of the easy-going atmosphere of a free trade area that it is thought that the USA could become a member of NAFTA without upsetting the political balance of the developed world. This aspect of the problem will be discussed below.

In order to conform to GATT rules, a free trade area, like a

46

customs union, must cover "substantially all trade" within the area. Like many phrases in the GATT, this one is vague and it has yet to be given a clear interpretation. But it is this phrase that allows GATT to keep an eye on EFTA, the EEC and other regional arrangements. EFTA in fact does not extend free trade to agricultural products (there are a few odd exceptions like melons, which are treated like industrial products) and it is estimated that this excludes about 10 per cent of total intra-area trade. In NAFTA proposals agricultural goods are also excluded to begin with. This does not mean that the free trade area *per se* is incapable of doing something for agricultural trade. In fact EFTA deals with it in a pragmatic and not very publicised way (it is not entirely blameless from a GATT point of view) through a series of bilateral treaties which link up EFTA's two main agricultural exporters (Denmark and Portugal) to the main agricultural importers. The result is that an effort is made to see that trade in agricultural goods increases at least as rapidly as trade in industrial goods through a series of quota arrangements.

Whether such an arrangement would have to be negotiated into NAFTA remains to be seen, but there is no doubt that many of the potential non-European members would be reluctant to allow free access to their markets for industrial goods unless they received in exchange guaranteed access to their partners' presumably growing markets for agricultural produce. This would be the case, in particular, of Australia, New Zealand and some Latin American countries. The USA and Canada would of course prefer to include agriculture, but might conceivably be prepared to leave it out at first for the sake of achieving industrial free trade among as wide a number of industrialised countries as possible, including the EEC. NAFTA including the EEC as a member would be able to do nothing about agriculture on a global basis (for the present at least). On the other hand, it might be able to do something about it bilaterally, as EFTA has done. A NAFTA arrangement that did not include the EEC could find an area solution to agriculture if the weight of the area's agricultural exporters were roughly in balance with that of the agricultural importers: but even EFTA, which includes one of the world's largest single food importers, the UK, has its agricultural problems and continues to deal with them bilaterally.

When the EFTA convention was drawn up it was intended to keep to the bare minimum of necessary commitments for the fulfiment of the free trade area objective. But it nevertheless included a number of "rules of competition" which were intended to guarantee the expected benefits against possible erosion, either by private or by public interests. What EFTA does is to prohibit any non-tariff barriers to trade which are found to "frustrate the benefits expected from the removal or absence of duties and quantitative restrictions on trade between member states" (articles 13, 14, 15, and 16). NAFTA participants would probably also have to agree on a code of good behaviour that would deal with the non-tariff barrier problem in much the same way.

An interesting feature of current NAFTA proposals is that it is proposed to offer less developed countries the same conditions of access to the NAFTA market as they would have if they were members, without asking for anything in exchange. Such one-way preferences are not entirely absent from existing EFTA arrangements. One of EFTA's members is Portugal, a less developed country. The Stockholm Convention has made special provision for the case; it permits Portugal to raise tariffs until 1972 for infant industry protection and while granting Portuguese exports free access to the markets of the other members, the convention allows for a very much longer period of tariff dismantlement with respect to imports, running to 1980. This flexible type of arrangement would, incidentally, allow one to adapt transitional periods to the needs of various countries that might wish to be founding members of NAFTA while not being in a sufficiently strong position to participate fully from the start.

When talking of an open-ended, Atlantic-based free trade area it is of course the question of membership that is all-important. Unless this is known in broad terms it is impossible for a country to evaluate with any degree of accuracy the advantages and disadvantages of participation or, for that matter, of non-participation. In the abstract one can point to a number of attractive features of NAFTA. There is, for instance, great attraction in the inevitability of the inter-zonal tariff reductions leading to zero positions at the end of an appointed transitional period, when compared with the spasmodic and uncertain nature of multilateral tariff negotiations. Indeed, it is strongly felt by some that even multilateral MFN negotiations should, in future, find some automatic mechanism for tariff reduction with which to guarantee some kind of result and to negotiate only the way of getting there. There is also the feeling that area free trade will bring with it a manageable dose of free trade conditions—

import competition and export opportunity—and that in this manner industry can be relatively painlessly acclimatised to the idea and practice of free trade on a wider basis. There is of course the inestimable advantage that the free trade area technique allows members to retain their commercial sovereignty *vis-à-vis* the outside world. There is also the universal faith in the "dynamic" effects of integration and the benefit to efficiency they bring to the industry of member countries. And there is, finally, the discrimination one must suffer if one is left out. All these considerations, in the abstract, would encourage a broad membership for NAFTA.

But when NAFTA is criticised as being a non-starter, it is for political and not for economic reasons. Indeed, there are as yet no economic grounds for criticising the realism of the plan, for no one has as yet undertaken the extensive research necessary to determine whether a particular country would gain or lose from participation (the purpose of the The Atlantic Trade Study series of papers is to examine this question from the British point of view).

The broad assumption as to the possible membership of NAFTA is that in addition to an unspecified number of European countries, it would include the USA, and it is here that the criticisms concentrate. It is argued that the proposal for an open-ended, Atlantic-based free trade area does not correspond to the present political relationship between Europe and the USA and that it would find little echo in most European countries. It is said that the indubitable trend to asserting increased independence from the USA, so obvious in France where it has found its most extreme expression, but also in existence in other continental European countries, would run counter to any proposal that would create a "special relationship" with the USA. The European "isolationists" are not all birds of a feather. To leave aside those whose anti-American attitudes defy analysis because of their primitive origins, opinion ranges from an unrealistic minority hypnotised by the vision of Europe as a "third force" through to a more widespread group which simply desires complete withdrawal from world power politics. The European neutrals, for instance, wish to maintain the credibility of their chosen foreign policy by taking steps to make sure that the USA is given no better treatment than anyone else. For these countries any particular link with the USA, however purely economic in intent and effect, is inevitably a political issue that few wish to face. As for the remainder, they are increasingly sceptical of US policies in Asia, US nuclear defence policies and the like. While they wish to remain under the overall protection of the USA—indeed they have no choice, not even France—they wish to disassociate themselves as much as possible from policies over which they of course have no control and with which they are not in full agreement.

The great days of Atlantic co-operation, when the East-West conflict was in full swing and when the opponents faced each other across Europe, are gone now and have been replaced by a far more complicated type of relationship. Today there is no question in continental Europe of following the USA politically, come what may, although there is quite a large body of moderate opinion which supports the Atlantic view of things. While EFTA in fact does show that countries can go a long way in collaborating in economic matters without political implications, the example is not entirely applicable because Britain, after all, is not the USA. And if EFTA has shown that politics can be left out of economic integration, it has also shown that one large partner can have an overwhelming effect on the course of events within the group.

If some detractors of NAFTA say that the continental European countries would not play ball with America, others claim that the USA itself would never contemplate the discrimination that a free trade area implies. Its interests are universal and would not permit, for instance, inferior treatment of the EEC should the latter find it impossible to join NAFTA.

Furthermore, it is said that the one-way concessions proposed for the benefit of the less developed countries would not work in practice and that as one of the major aims of US foreign policy is nowadays to find a solution to the problems of the less developed, membership of NAFTA would be out of the question as it would inevitably discriminate against them.

Professor Jacob Viner has made the telling observation that great powers enter economic integration for political reasons and small countries do so for economic ones.[15] The USA, for whom foreign trade represents relatively so little, would enter a free trade area for political reasons—for instance to strengthen the unity of the Western

[15]This would explain Britain's schizophrenic attitude to European economic integration. Trailing clouds of imperial glory, she has frequently acted politically when she should have seen to her economic interests. Even when political and economic interests were felt to coincide it was clearly the political aim that was uppermost in the attempts to join the EEC, causing a dangerous minimisation of the negative economic consequences and too much blind faith in the positive ones.

world, to promote the Atlantic partnership, or to draw part of Asia (Japan) more firmly into the European and American ambit. The question thus becomes one of determining whether NAFTA would further or hinder these broad aims, and here the case can be made either way.

Assuming that some type of market access could be negotiated for the less developed countries, the crucial question is that of whether the EEC would become a member. If it does, there is no question of "splitting the West" and the American aim of strengthening the unity of the Western world would not be impaired. If, however, as is feared, the EEC opts out, and NAFTA comes into existence without it, then the "unity of the Western world" objective appears to be seriously compromised. But we have already said that the free trade area solution to tariff problems is one that is justified when progress, for one reason or another, is blocked in the GATT forum. If, for example, progress is blocked because the EEC wishes for the time being to maintain its common external tariff at present levels then the US aim of strengthening the unity of the Western world is similarly frustrated.

It therefore becomes a question of whether one should wait passively for the EEC to join the general pursuit of free trade or whether, at some risk, one should take steps towards that goal without them. Neither alternative is wholly attractive, but of the two the second has a distinct advantage. If a free trade area were to face an EEC with very few outsiders besides the under-developed, the pressure on both sides to reach agreement would be enormous, and more might be achieved by a temporary split than by years of heavy multilateral negotiations. This argument may seem erroneous to those who have seen the abysmal lack of success of EFTA in doing the same for Europe. We are dealing here though with'an organisation that lacks leadership of any kind whatsoever: the only possible leader abdicated mentally in 1961. Furthermore, EFTA is small whereas NAFTA, if it included the USA, would have enormous weight and corresponding powers of attraction.

Early in 1967, when the outcome of the Kennedy Round was still highly doubtful and it looked as though the procrastination of the Community might be fatal, the discussion of the pros and cons of NAFTA need have gone no further than this. But with the completion of the Kennedy Round[16] and the partial implementation of its provisions, the full extent of the protectionist opposition on both sides of the Atlantic, and the urgent need for some free trade counter-offensive, has become apparent.

The advocates of protection do not of course argue from a theoretical position, stating that protection is better than free trade. Instead they use arguments specific to each particular situation. In France protectionist measures have been justified in debate by the economic disruption caused by the May, 1968, disturbances, though many observers had wondered long before what action France would take in order to offset the effect of the Kennedy Round concessions, together with EEC free trade, on her deteriorating balance of payments. In the UK, French quantitative restrictions are observed with envy; there are many who would like to impose similar measures in order to alleviate the British Government's stringent deflationary policies. In the USA more than a hundred protectionist motions have been put before Congress, proposing measures ranging from quotas to subsidies.

The revival of protectionist forces in countries like France and Britain, while of course disturbing, is unlikely to have a disastrous effect on world trade. Protectionist measures probably will not be long-lived if all other major trading countries maintain the pressure for their removal. This is one lesson that Britain appears to have learnt from the experience of her 1964 surcharge. Furthermore, a country imposing trade restrictions, or introducing export subsidies, opens itself to retaliation in its major export markets.

Unfortunately, such comforting arguments break down when one deals not with medium-sized powers, such as France and Britain, but with a giant the size of the USA. If America turned protectionist it would change the whole post-war trading structure. She is the world's largest trading nation and comprehensive import restrictions would affect half the world's trade at one blow. But perhaps more important, the climate of trade relations between countries would be most adversely affected.

During 1968 the Johnson Administration's courageous defence of its liberal trade position in the face of the powerful demands for protection to be afforded to many sectors of US industry has been

[16]The present version of this paper is different in places from the original. The changes, such as in the remainder of the passages discussing the free trade area approach, are the result of taking a new look at a situation in perpetual motion.

the saving grace of a dangerous situation. How President Johnson's successor will act remains to be seen. In the USA it is disturbing to observe the extent to which protectionism for balance of payments reasons is invoked by economists and others (either in or near government) who are neither real protectionists nor stand to gain personally from such a policy. This attitude is not difficult to explain. America's European creditors have been so insistent that the USA should put an end to the dollar flow that it seems to Americans as though Europeans would be prepared to put up with import restrictions in order to achieve this end. Wherever the truth of the matter lies, it is indeed alarming to find well-informed and disinterested people willing to sacrifice the present level, and rate of growth, of world trade for a doubtful form of monetary stability based on physical restrictions.

In order to stop the development of protectionist trends on both sides of the Atlantic, the arguments of the protectionists and well-meaning dollar-defenders must be countered with a very strong representation of the opposite case. Business everywhere would lose in a contraction of world trade. It looks very much as though the world economy will head in this direction unless a newer, suitably dramatic and positive move is shortly made towards the further liberalisation of international trade. The revival of protectionist ideas since the conclusion of the Kennedy Round is so marked that if no definite advance is made the world economy will almost certainly move back. Like Alice, the major trading nations must run in order to stay in the same place. The extent of the mutual interdependence of intricate industrial economies must be emphasised and if possible formalised. Under the circumstances, an open-ended, Atlantic-based, free trade association would be the most, and perhaps the only, effective means of stemming the protectionist tide and maintaining the present level of world trade.

Besides this pressing argument in favour of a broadly-based free trade association, others have emerged since the end of 1967. Now that it is clear to all that British entry into the EEC is a long-term proposition at best, Britain's desire for wider markets can only find expression across (and perhaps beyond) the Atlantic. Within the EEC there are certain problems (such as agriculture and the associated overseas territories) which surpass the frontiers of the Six and which demand a wider theatre for their solution. People of independent thought in the Community appear to be talking more freely about the possibility of a wider free trade association among industrialised countries which would permit them to maintain the Community while giving them a broader base for dealing with their growing difficulties in certain specific sectors. Finally, if it really seemed as though the EEC might regard the NAFTA idea favourably, the smaller EFTA members would not hesitate to support it.

In short, developments since the end of the Kennedy Round suggest that even if the political difficulties surrounding the NAFTA idea remain considerable, they seem to be giving away slightly to the calculable economic advantages, while from a purely intellectual point of view, NAFTA seems to be the only idea of sufficient stature with which to successfully confront the rapid growth of protectionist feeling.

NAFTA, though, is certainly not the only alternative at present being discussed.

Conditional Most-Favoured-Nation Clause

We have shown how, when the universal method fails, countries turn to the regional solution sanctioned by GATT to further their freer trade objectives. But another solution has been proposed, this time in discordance with existing international agreements. In December, 1965, when it seemed as though all further progress in the Kennedy Round was to be blocked by the inability of the EEC to negotiate, two members of the US House of Representatives, Mr. Henry S. Reuss and Mr. R. F. Ellsworth, suggested to the Joint Economic Committee of Congress that the USA should continue to negotiate tariff reductions among more willing partners, and not pass the reductions on to those who did not reciprocate. On the face of it this seems to be a perfectly reasonable solution to the recurring problem of what to do with the laggards and it in fact was traditional US trade policy until 1923. But apart from the fact that it would require a GATT waiver (meaning a unanimous vote), it would establish a dangerous precedent of discrimination in world trade.

There is a good reason why the principle of non-discrimination should be the GATT's most sacred tenet. While each country individually would like nothing better than to enjoy preferential treatment in its export markets, it is equally anxious to see that no rival obtains such favoured treatment. If he does so, the reaction of the country discriminated against is to punish the offenders by discriminating against *them* in their turn. The inter-war period showed us that nothing could be more disastrous than the discrimination engendered by discrimination, leading to bilateralism, quantitative controls and preferences. A new leaf was turned after the war when GATT set itself the objective of eliminating discrimination among its members. The technique by which this was achieved was the *unconditional* MFN clause.

The unconditional MFN rule, carefully nurtured by GATT for over twenty years now, has brought its members unquestioned benefits. Though natural reluctance to give one country or another a "free ride" may have reduced the level and extent of certain concessions from time to time, in fact GATT's multilateral forum keeps such free rides to a minimum. As a result every negotiated concession is automatically passed on to all contracting parties whether they participated in the negotiation or not. Should this principle be once seriously disobeyed the whole system of tariff concessions negotiated since the war could be unravelled like so much knitting by trade warfare. This need not necessarily happen, but it is a risk that must be taken into account when one abandons the principle of non-discrimination. But it is also true that the principle of unconditional MFN needs a minimum of genuine good faith on the part of all trading countries. The main negotiators in the Kennedy Round, for instance, became increasingly irritated by the attitude of some of the white Commonwealth countries and Japan who frequently sat on the fence waiting for concessions to be passed on to them without offering anything in exchange. The question of whether to apply conditional MFN treatment to these countries was seriously considered during the Kennedy Round. It seems as though a change of heart on the part of Australia, New Zealand, Canada and Japan will be necessary in the future if the principle of unconditional MFN is to be maintained.

The problem may arise once again in the near future if the US Congress introduces and passes protectionist legislation. Will the other participants of the Kennedy Round take this lying down and write off three years of arduous negotiations as a dead loss? There is in fact a possibility that they may decide to apply the Kennedy Round results among themselves while "waiting" for the USA to come around. The European chemical agreement mentioned earlier is only one example of what might occur. It would indeed be an irony of history if the story of the League of Nations were repeated. Would it be followed now, as then, by an American retreat into

55

(trade) isolationism? After twenty years of efforts in the opposite direction it would be almost inconceivable. We hope that it is no ostrich instinct that leads us to think that such a retreat would be politically unthinkable for the USA and that reason will in the end prevail in Congress.

Kennedy Round II?

Clearly, another way in which the world could take further steps in trade liberalisation would be to repeat the Kennedy Round in a few years' time. If all goes well, the tariff cuts negotiated in Geneva from 1964 to 1967 will be fully implemented by 1972. Leaving aside the disturbing possibility that protectionist forces in the USA and elsewhere might cause some back-slipping, what are the prospects for a successor to the Kennedy Round once its results have been digested?

Common sense and previous GATT experience suggest that the results might be very disappointing. The reason is that negotiators have probably now reached the "hard core" tariffs which are unlikely to yield to conventional approaches towards liberalising trade. The universal type of trade negotiation, if at all successful, would probably be so shot through with exceptions that the effort required to reach agreement would far exceed the will to do so. These considerations are reinforced by the feeling that multilateral trade negotiations are subject to diminishing returns in the short and medium term and that little less than a generation must separate two really successful tariff "rounds".

Previous GATT experience also suggests that a new approach to tariff reduction can yield impressive results the first time it is used, but that subsequent "rounds" prove disappointing. When GATT was first put into operation with the 1947 round of tariff negotiations, the method of *multilateral* tariff bargaining was as revolutionary as the linear approach adopted a decade and a half later. It was a marked improvement on the old bilateral system of tariff negotiation that, after 1880, had begun to yield diminishing and later negative returns, bringing the world to the incredible impasse of the 1930s. Yet in spite of the fact that the multilateral item-by-item type of negotiation was so successful the first time around, or perhaps because of this, it proved impossible to repeat the experience satisfactorily.

If it is hard to measure the "height" of a tariff how much harder it is to measure the value of a tariff concession—and in fact not even the GATT's Secretariat has attempted to do so. The table which follows is not intended to be anything but a guide to illustrate the fact that the significance of the four tariff rounds that followed the 1947 negotiations, taken together, was probably less than the first one considered alone.

ESTIMATED RESULTS OF GATT TARIFF NEGOTIATIONS

Negotiation	Value of Trade Covered	Number of Concessions Made
Geneva 1947	$10,000m*	45,000
Annecy 1949	n.a.	5,000
Torquay 1951	n.a.	8,700
Geneva 1956	$2,500m	n.a.
Geneva 1960-61 (Dillon Round)	$4,900m	4,400
Geneva 1964-67 (Kennedy Round)	$40,000m	n.a.

At pre-war prices.
Source: GATT Secretariat, Geneva.

According to this very rough guide, the first round of 1947 still looks very good, even if compared with the results of the Kennedy Round. In fact the value of world trade has increased by some 360 per cent from 1947 to 1966 ($55,000m to $200,000m) which indicates that the two rounds are probably on a par with one another, although many of the Kennedy Round tariff cuts go deeper.

One can probably argue that the reason why the tariff rounds of 1948, 1951, 1956 and 1960–61 produced so little was because the USA was not under one of its most dynamic Administrations and because European countries were bent on regionalism. But it must not be forgotten that the new system itself had disadvantages. Item-by-item negotiation was lengthy and onerous and it encouraged countries to give away as little as possible of their "bargaining strength"—as measured by the supposed height of their tariff. When it was replaced in the Kennedy Round by the linear approach to tariff bargaining the breakthrough seemed terrific. It meant that the principle of reciprocity, though it of course continued to apply in theory, should have been eroded in practice. For if all countries cut their tariffs by an equal amount it is highly probable that some countries will gain more than others in the process. The important fact to retain, however, is that it would be unlikely that a country could actually lose, especially if provision were made for exceptions to the general cut. Theoretically, the linear approach to tariff bargaining makes it unnecessary for a country to maintain a tariff higher than it otherwise would simply for bargaining purposes, since the commitment to reduce tariffs is the same for all. If the linear form of tariff reduction were to be applied successively one of the great stumbling blocks of past negotiations would be overcome—the maintenance of useless tariffs for no better reason than that no one offers anything for their abolition.

The linear form of tariff reduction, though, as practised in the Kennedy Round differed from theory in more than one respect, and indeed adopted many of the aspects of the item-by-item type of negotiation. Far from being a way of by-passing the old bargaining process, the Kennedy Round was the lengthiest and most onerous in all GATT's history. The disparities issue showed that the old desire to retain tariffs for bargaining purposes was far from dead, and a linear 50 per cent cut was not achieved.

This is not to denigrate the results of the Kennedy Round, which were impressive, but to make the rather obvious point that where there is a will, there is a way: but if there is a way and no will to apply it one gets a "second best" result. The Kennedy Round, for all its success, achieved a "second best" result, and that with difficulty. Yet it *was* revolutionary in comparison with previous GATT negotiations because it had a set target—the 50 per cent linear cut in industrial tariffs—and this in itself was a powerful incentive to the negotiating parties not to fall too far short of it. The "target method" could be used again with profit on condition that the target was pitched high enough—in other words, at the elimination of industrial tariffs. Anything less would inspire no one and achieve little. Since the world is probably not yet ready to accept such a target as being the basis for a successor to the Kennedy Round, and targets would be put at a disappointingly low level, one must remain sceptical as to their possible use, especially if attempted too soon.

Tariff Harmonisation

If we stay within the traditional GATT framework and try to improve on the system of linear tariff cuts used in the Kennedy Round, we must discuss the issue of tariff harmonisation. It has been suggested that before we can go any further in multilateral commercial negotiation we must achieve some kind of tariff harmonisation and that this limited goal should be our next step. The argument is that present tariff disparities make it impossible to apply the linear method of tariff reduction in practice. In fact, as we have seen, the Kennedy Round was negotiated successfully in spite of the disparities issue. But it is interesting to dwell a moment on the implications of tariff harmonisation as a possible next step, in order to judge its validity.

The most recent example we have of tariff harmonisation is the EEC's common external tariff. It is no mean achievement. It is a pure study in the politics of economics. It was simply decided that the Community's outer tariff should be the unweighted average of the tariffs of all six member countries, and that was that. When the harmonisation of tariffs, however, is advocated as being a reasonable prelude to further linear tariff negotiations, it is not intended that the process should be pushed, as with the EEC, to the extreme case of tariff equalisation. At the start of the Kennedy Round, the Community proposed a measure of tariff harmonisation to deal with the disparities problem but, as we have already seen, it proved difficult to agree on a formula which could identify a disparity. Current proposals for tariff harmonisation are, of course, very much tied up with the disparities issue and find more echo in continental Europe than in the USA. Tariff harmonisation seems not only unnecessary in the light of the Kennedy Round experience, but also impossible to achieve in practice because it demands unrequited concessions on the part of high tariff countries.

The Sector-by-Sector Approach

The sector-by-sector approach is currently being discussed as another means by which tariff erosion may be pushed a little further. Some[17] consider that it is a blind alley, and not a very long one at

[17]See, for instance, John W. Evans, "US Trade Policy: New Legislation for the Next Round" (Council on Foreign Relations, Harper and Row, New York, 1967).

that. Others, notably Sir Eric Wyndham White[18], have thought that this approach may be the only one able to yield results in the immediate future and while the Kennedy Round is still being "digested".

This approach would be different both from the old item-by-item type of negotiation and from the linear method used in the Kennedy Round. It would consist in taking clearly defined products—such as steel, automobiles or refrigerators—and attempting to reach free or freer trade within each "sector". The question of whether or not this approach could yield appreciable results would depend mainly on how sectors would be defined. Defined narrowly, the approach would indeed yield little; generously interpreted, it could be of significance. If it could generate its own momentum, and if successful negotiation in one sector inspired negotiations in further sectors, it is conceivable that a free trading network could be built up by a process of gradual accumulation.

There are four possible types of sector-by-sector tariff reductions, two of which would require a GATT waiver, and two of which would be in accordance with GATT principles.

We have an example of a sectoral agreement which at one time required a GATT waiver—the European Coal and Steel Community (ECSC). Here tariffs were reduced to zero on two specific product groups, but on a discriminatory basis—hence the need for a GATT waiver. It is also possible to imagine a sectoral agreement that would not go as far as the ECSC: an agreement that would reduce tariffs on a discriminatory basis by something less than 100 per cent. Neither of these alternatives is satisfactory viewed from the world at large. If tariffs are maintained *vis-à-vis* third parties it is an open question whether the quantum of protection in the world has increased or not. ECSC experience has shown that even for the parties to the agreement sectoral tariff elimination on a non-MFN basis is fraught with difficulties, notably of overproduction.

What is now being discussed, however, is sector-by-sector tariff reductions on a MFN basis. This approach has the virtue of conforming to GATT rules. Once more, one can divide sectoral tariff reductions into two broad groups: one, where the tariff reductions

[18]Wyndham White, "International Trade Policy: the Kennedy Round and Beyond", Address to the Deutsche Gesellschaft für Auswärtige Politik, Bad Godesberg, October 27, 1966. On the other hand, in a letter to *The Times*, July 5, 1968 (signed with others), Sir Eric came out in favour of "a broadly based free trade association".

are limited to less than 100 per cent; the other, where free trade on a MFN basis is achieved.

This first alternative was used in the Kennedy Round whenever things became sticky, sometimes successfully and sometimes without result. The chemical sector, for instance, was negotiated separately and now forms an agreement distinct from the general protocol. But an attempt to reach a separate agreement on aluminium failed at the last minute. Commodities were negotiated multilaterally by sector only when it was found that bilateral negotiation would yield no result. For instance, no separate protocol was needed for steel because it was considered that this was essentially a bilateral problem to be solved between the EEC and the UK. While the USA and Japan reduced their steel tariffs by about 50 per cent without discussion, the UK and the EEC had to reach agreement to reduce the disparity between them as well as the actual tariffs before the matter could be settled. Indeed the net result of the Kennedy Round on steel is more one of harmonisation than of reduction, and tariffs are now low. Pulp and paper were at one moment considered for sectoral treatment.

The lesson of the Kennedy Round for this type of sector-by-sector tariff reduction is that there is really little point in pursuing it unless an effort to achieve free trade in a given sector is made. As with the possibility of Kennedy Round II, discussed above, further tariff cuts of, say, 50 per cent would inspire nobody to action. The effort of negotiating on this partial basis (let alone the problem of Congressional approval) would be too great and the returns too small. To achieve free trade in a given sector is another matter and would at least be clear and unambiguous. Would it be possible? There are several possible avenues open to the sector-by-sector approach, some of which are being actively pursued at present.

Nuisance Tariffs

There appear to be a few sectors where the Kennedy Round has reduced tariffs to the point where their protective effect can be considered negligible and where their continued existence is due more to inertia than to the desire to maintain them for their nuisance value. In such cases, there is reason to hope that a concerted effort to eliminate tariffs altogether would meet with success. Indeed, the arguments for *not* doing so seem to boil down to the you'll-never-get-Congress-or-the-Commission-to-agree type of ob-

c*

jection with which every proposal for progress is invariably confronted.

The Canadians proposed free trade in aluminium during the Kennedy Round, but the EEC (read France, alias Pechiney) would have none of it. If one assumes that the other producers and consumers of aluminium would have been prepared to discuss the idea, one could say that never have so many been held back by so few—in this case, one. Although the Kennedy Round itself has come to an end, negotiations on aluminium are nonetheless in progress, as we write, and are not yet completed.

As is well known, the USA proposed a formula for achieving sectoral free trade in a number of products at the very start of the Kennedy Round. Congressional authority to eliminate tariffs altogether on those products in which the USA and the EEC combined accounted for over 80 per cent of world trade was in fact a variant of the sector-by-sector approach to free trade. Being a general formula, it of course included a rather odd series of products at the time when it was thought the UK and others would join the EEC, some of which would have been easier to negotiate than others. Generally speaking, however, the products it would have covered had the EEC succeeded in enlarging its membership were of a technical nature and included a good portion of heavy industry type products.

Dominant Supplier Authority

If the sector-by-sector approach is to be reactivated in the future, the dominant supplier formula could be used to break up the problem of finding suitable sectors into manageable portions. The 80 per cent guide-line might point to some thirty product categories, of which some would be retained as likely candidates for tariff elimination. At some later date the guide-line might be widened to include products in which "Atlantic" trade would account for, say, 70 per cent of total world trade, and so on. This type of approach would not be as systematic though as it might seem. It would make negotiation on a likely product in, say, the 50 per cent "class" wait upon perhaps frustrating negotiations in other "classes". Furthermore the formula gives precedence to those products that are of interest to the industrial countries of the world, and as such is not designed to contribute anything to the trade problems of the under-developed. Finally, although the "dominant supplier" concept as devised by Congress in the Trade Expansion Act has its *rationale* in GATT practice—item-by-item negotiations were conducted among "principal suppliers" and their results passed on to other contracting parties—it is probably unwise to strait-jacket the sector-by-sector approach in a pre-conceived and rigid formula.

A more flexible and pragmatic means of finding suitable sectors for tariff elimination would be preferable, involving down-to-earth research in various fields. It is of course outside the scope of this paper to enter into such detail, but it is possible to distinguish three broad categories where the sectoral approach to free trade might be both desirable and possible : one, products which have a high modern technological content; two, products that are already internationally produced and traded in quantity; and three, semi-manufactures or investment goods that are themselves the inputs of other industries.

Industries with High Technological Content

With the first group what makes or breaks a firm is not the protective tariff but the new idea, the inspired invention that gives it a momentary lead over its competitors. In industries where the technological frontiers are constantly being extended, no tariff will save an inefficient firm because what determines the direction of trade is less price than performance.

There is a great deal of confused thought at present concerning the "technological gap" between the USA and Europe. It is felt, with some justification, that certain sections of American industry are more competitive than those in Europe because of their technological superiority. Unfortunately the instinctive reaction of many Europeans is to advocate protection on these grounds. This of course only makes matters worse and incidentally encourages American firms to jump the tariffs by buying up their inefficient European counterparts. Some people even go so far as to advocate the exclusion of American investment in sectors where advanced technology is all-important and propose a European "technological community" which, behind protective walls, would soon gather strength and equal American technology in power and progression.

This is pure nationalism, admittedly of a new kind. But even if it is tied to the idea of "Europe" it is none the less reprehensible, first because it is a facet of wholly undesirable anti-Americanism and, secondly, because nationalism, European or otherwise, is to be deplored. Unfortunately this does not do away with the problem.

Since the new nationalism hides behind economic arguments to make its case, one is justified in bringing the economic arguments that count against it. In the first place, it is said that unless Europe pools its supposedly scanty technological resources it will become progressively inefficient and incapable of competing with American products. But what reason is there to believe that Europe will succeed in closing the "technological gap" by keeping the Americans out? Indeed, the only possible consequence of excluding technologically advanced American products (which are usually not consumer goods but industrial inputs) would be to penalise European technology, thus causing a further deterioration of its supposedly inferior competitive position and a progressive relative impoverishment of Europe as such.[19]

The only way to deal effectively with the "gap" (such as it is) is to bring the Americans *in*. Why should European industry suffer the cost of a pains-taking repetition of what the Americans have already done years ago? Europe should open itself completely to the benefits of American financed research, and consider itself fortunate that it does not have to foot the bill. The answer of the nationalist is that this would be an open invitation for a wholesale American takeover of European industry. This argument lacks logic, for what at present encourages American investment in Europe is the desire to avoid the tariff discrimination caused by the EEC's and EFTA's internal free trade. In the absence of tariffs between Europe and America in goods with a high technological content, there would probably be less American investment in Europe and more trade in the goods in question. This would mean that technologically advanced pieces of machinery, new industrial products—in short, new inventions of all kinds—would be available to European industry on the same terms as to American industry, thus putting the two on an equal footing. To believe that American firms would not sell their inventions to Europeans on the same terms

---

[19]The true picture is of course far more *nuancé*. In some respects European technology is in advance of American and its competitive position is by no means as weak as the new European nationalists would have us believe. The strength of the American protectionist offensive at the end of the Kennedy Round is surely indirect proof of this.

as they do to other Americans is to think that businessmen are as concerned with nationalism as politicians. Goods and patents cross frontiers continually and businessmen are inspired by nothing more mysterious than the profit motive. To impose a tariff or other restriction on their movement is simply to tax the potential user.

Products Internationally Made and Traded

In short, the logic of the economic argument lies wholly in favour of eliminating all restraints on technologically advanced goods in order to close the "technological gap" and to raise the efficiency of European industry. If this simple truth could once penetrate this area could become an ideal one for the sector-by-sector approach.

Apart from the special case of the "products of tomorrow" there are numerous and growing industries which are becoming more interested in gaining access to foreign markets than in preventing others from entering their own—as witness the "economies of scale" arguments in favour of regional economic integrations. More often than not, a certain amount of osmosis either way has taken place in spite of the existence of tariffs. The products we have in mind are likely to be finished goods for the most part—automobiles, washing machines, appliances—and unlike the case for techno-logically advanced goods just discussed, they will probably not be industrial inputs themselves. The case for tariff elimination here is more directly concerned with the advantageous consumption effects this would have on a fairly wide range of consumer products and the increased managerial efficiency that would result from brisker competition.

One can generalise and say that products which are commonly produced, exported and imported all at the same time by a number of countries are excellent candidates for tariff elimination. And if one comes to think of it, this means quite a few products. All that will occur is that more will be traded and greater product specialisa-tion will take place, to the benefit not only of the community, but also of business interests themselves. Japan is frequently cited as being a major problem in this respect. She cannot be excluded from free trading arrangements. Yet for many European *and* American industries she appears in some sectors all too competitive. One way of dealing with the Japanese case is to arrange for voluntary export restraints (already used openly in the Cotton Textile Agreement). This practice is more justified than it would seem at first sight. For

Japan is highly protectionist in many respects and uses a wide range of non-tariff barriers to restrict trade. Negotiated export restraints could be played off against these non-tariff barriers.

Semi-Manufactures

There is no doubt that the logical way to attack protectionism is from the bottom up. A paper producer has a right to expect tariff protection from his government if the latter obliges him to buy his pulp at prices that are themselves the result of protective measures. The solution would be to free trade in pulp and leave the paper producer with no justification for protection. Tariffs on unprocessed raw materials are, almost without exception, nil or negligible. But tariffs on processed raw materials are frequently deceptive. They appear low, but in fact they are high in relation to the value added in the course of transformation. Indeed, in many industrialised countries the processing of raw materials is heavily protected and mighty forces in favour of tariffs have developed over the years. So however logical it may appear to attack protectionism from the bottom up, it might in fact be impossible to achieve. Yet the sector-by-sector approach offers a way out of this difficulty in that it divides the opposition. When one negotiates across-the-board tariff reductions, as in the Kennedy Round, there are some interests that are bound to be hurt and it is a matter of chance whether those who stand to lose will have greater weight than those who stand to gain. But when one negotiates free trade for a specific semi-manufactured product—say aluminium—though one may indeed invoke the wrath of protected aluminium producers, one may nevertheless count on the support of all firms that use aluminium as an input. For these firms have an interest in being able to buy aluminium at the lowest possible market price in order to improve their competitive position, both at home and abroad. But the support of these firms for free trade in aluminium would probably fade away if free trade in their particular product lines was also part of the deal. Thus it is easier for governments to overcome protectionist forces at home if they tackle them one by one, and here the sector-by-sector approach offers an answer. For the purpose of discovering likely sectors that could be the object of this approach to free trade, one might add that the more "basic" an input is, the more industries to which it contributes, the more likely it is that internal support for free trade in that product will outweigh the opposition.

Playing one pressure group off against another is a technique not entirely foreign to governments engaged in trade negotiations. The chemical agreement that emerged from the Kennedy Round is an example. In fact the linch pin of the whole agreement—Congressional approval for the abolition of ASP—depends on whether the American automotive industry, in conjunction with tobacco and canned fruit, will outbid the chemical interests.

When we discussed the possibility of forming NAFTA we found some potential difficulties which had to be taken into consideration. The sector-by-sector approach has the advantage of not being subject to such political objections. Free trade would be built up slowly among the major trading partners of the negotiated commodities. The signatories of one agreement would not necessarily be the signatories of another. With the growth of the system, free trade would spread both country and product-wise. But as free trade would be negotiated on a MFN basis there would be no problem of discrimination which, under certain circumstances, can be shown to have political implications.

It could be argued that the sector-by-sector approach does not take into account the interests of under-developed countries, especially in view of the three product areas suggested above as suitable for such a course. It is true that if free trade in a given sector is achieved it is difficult to see how preferences could be given to the under-developed countries within the sector. On the other hand, there is by definition no discrimination against them and new investment, moreover, would be dictated on the basis of comparative advantage, provided a minimum of political stability could be guaranteed. American investment in steel, it might be recalled, has been attracted to Italy and German investment in electronics has migrated to Portugal, to say nothing of intra-area investment due to free market access to rich industrial markets.

The sector-by-sector approach, then has two advantages over the free trade area approach; it "divides the opposition", making it easier for governments to take action (should they wish to) and it is free of political implications.

But these advantages are unfortunately outweighed by serious drawbacks. In the first place, the process might be agonisingly slow. For centuries now countries have bargained one concession off

67

against another and the sector-by-sector approach, because it is by definition dealing with one product or group of products, reduces the scope for the balancing of "concessions". There might be a few sectors where a balance could be achieved within the sector (perhaps steel) but this would get us nowhere fast. What is needed for the sectoral approach to succeed is the realisation by governments that tariffs themselves impair the competitive position of their industries and reduce the consumer welfare of their populations. If this were once accepted there would be less talk about reciprocity and a good deal more progress. One must admit, however, that under present circumstances it is not realistic to expect such a development.

Secondly, the sectoral approach would not have the discipline of the free trade area, where free trade in substantially all products would have to be achieved according to a precise timetable. In the absence of a commitment to negotiate on "substantially all" sectors, the approach might peter out before it achieved anything. Free trade in a few sectors only would, moreover, be trade diversionary. For unprotected goods would wherever possible be substituted for protected ones. But if there *were* a commitment to negotiate from A to Z, then one of the advantages of the sectoral approach—that of dividing the opposition—would be forfeited.

Thirdly, the sectoral approach is open to the objection that in practice there will always be one major trading partner which will refuse to play the game, and this will bring us back either to the free trade area approach or to conditional MFN.

Finally, and most important, in the post-Kennedy Round atmosphere of growing protectionism, what could have been an asset—the flexibility of the sector-by-sector approach—becomes a liability. It permits governments to give in to protectionist demands while presenting an outward appearance of adherence to free trade through concessions on unimportant issues.

4 NEED TO COUNTER PROTECTIONISM

We have seen how industrialisation and increased production over the past 150 years have brought with them a desire—not to say necessity—to trade. Few people perhaps realise that nineteenth-century free trade was preceded by a period where protection of domestic industry was achieved by a total prohibition of imports, where tariffs existed for revenue purposes almost exclusively, and where trade flows were frequently determined by the permission, and not only the ability, to trade. Seen in this light the past 150 years show a trend towards increasingly freer trade. This long-term evolution has been overshadowed by a short relapse of two decades within living memory, active sectoral interests which, throughout the period and in spite of the trend, managed to obtain protectionist advantages and some economic doctrines that stressed the advantages of a national policy over an international one.

In commercial policy matters, the world does not stand still. We are either in a period of progression or in one of regression. At the moment we are moving forward, and this has been realised by protectionist forces in all the industrialised countries. Voices are to be heard in the USA and EEC that we should do nothing for the time being and should wait for the results of the Kennedy Round to be digested. Yet in the absence of any positive move forward, it is highly likely that back-sliding will take place, given the *perpetuum mobile* of human affairs. And the back-sliding, once started, might be all the greater because of the impressive degree of trade liberalisation that has been achieved in the past two decades.

In this connection, one of the more subtle "let's rest a while" arguments is that the satisfactory results of the Kennedy Round have reduced the tariff problem to perfectly acceptable proportions, that the division of Europe into two trading blocks is no longer acute now that the dividing wall has been halved, and that the USA no longer faces insuperable discrimination in its European markets. This argument overlooks the fact that the most protective element of a tariff is probably to be found in the last few percentage points. When one emerges from a period of rising protection and achieves tariff reductions, the first cuts will simply take some of the stuffing out of inflated positions, intentionally built in for negotiating purposes. Successive reductions will get to the hard core only with time. Apart from this, the lower a tariff becomes, the greater is the intangible expense in time and effort of passing customs in relation to the duty paid. It may be no accident that EFTA trade began to expand significantly only when the last 20 per cent cut was made in intra-area tariffs in December, 1966. Similarly, significant trade creation and re-allocation of factors on a world basis will probably be prevented until the present barriers to trade are largely eliminated.

It must furthermore be remembered that the Kennedy Round was not a tariff negotiation only, as all previous GATT negotiations had been, but was the first real *trade* negotiation. Besides tariffs on industrial goods, non-tariff barriers were discussed and in the case of agriculture one went as far as to discuss national support policies as well. Wherever the truth may lie in the tariff issue, it is obvious that at least in these last two fields further action needs to be taken, and that the simple idea that protection equals tariffs cannot be entertained.

Finally, in so far as governments desire a continual rise in productivity, an assurance that their industry is to remain competitive, a possibility of exploiting economies of scale, an enjoyment of the benefits of trade and specialisation and of the fruits of research the world over, the course of wisdom is to move further down the road to free trade. Since countries are reluctant to make unilateral tariff reductions however desirable they may be from a domestic point of view, it is essential that the discussion should be continued.

Further Progress

Firmly convinced of the need to continue our efforts to achieve free trade, the central purpose of this paper has been to discuss the various means of further progress at present at our disposal. We have discussed the regional approach, the possibility of another Kennedy Round, the conditional MFN approach, and the sector-by-sector approach on a MFN basis. We discussed them roughly in order of decreasing familiarity, and in order to bring the threads of our argument together in our conclusions, we shall now put them into a more logical sequence.

A Second Kennedy Round is an approach that at present has the most adherents in the USA. There is a tradition of renewing trade legislation at regular intervals for the purpose of allowing the Administration to negotiate tariff reductions under the vigilant eye of Congress. Just as the Reciprocal Trade Agreements Act was renewed many times before it was replaced by the Trade Expansion Act, so it is felt that there is no reason why the latter should not be renewed with equal fidelity. It is more than likely, however, that the negotiating leeway will get smaller and smaller, as it did in the 1950s. This approach is probably the most un-inspiring of all and allows protectionist forces on both sides of the Atlantic full play. The argument that successive renewals of the Trade Expansion Act is all that Congress will allow is no longer convincing because the USA is now faced by a trading block as large as itself which, while still in its infancy, was able to force a monumental change in the USA's traditional trade policy. In fact, the USA rose to the challenge in a very stimulating manner and there is no reason to suppose that it cannot do so again, even if the challenge comes from a different quarter—say EFTA or the Commonwealth. If we admit that the USA is capable of taking an adventurous view of trade policy, then a second Kennedy Round would be too humdrum. But it is there to fall back upon should the more ambitious schemes fail.

The Conditional MFN Clause approach is one that arises from the one just discussed. It is a mutation of the MFN bargaining which states that if some countries wish to reduce tariffs faster than others they should neither be held up by the laggards nor be obliged to give them a free ride. We have pointed out earlier that this apparently facile solution embodies a risk far greater than the questionable benefits it would bring to the world's trading community, and that it should, for this reason, be rejected. If one wished to return to a high level of protection, no quicker road could be chosen; trade negotiations would lose much of their multilateral nature, become increasingly bilateral and rapidly break up the present world trading system.

The Sector-by-Sector Approach is simply another way of seeking free trade among the industrialised—and industrialising—countries of the world. If completely successful, this approach would in the end achieve the same result as an open-ended, free trade area, but by a different means. It is a question, therefore, of choosing the means best suited to the present situation.

If the regional approach has distinct advantages over the first two —Kennedy Round II and conditional MFN—so the sectoral approach has certain advantages over the regional. But at the same time it resurrects the old drawbacks of prevarication and delay. The main advantage of the sectoral approach seems to lie in the fact that it is less exacting than NAFTA and avoids its political implications. It gives governments greater negotiating leeway than any other solution but, as we have seen, such flexibility can be as much of a liability as an asset when protectionist lobbies are gaining and not losing strength. Under present circumstances it therefore seems that the sector-by-sector approach would be painfully slow, subject to default on the part of one or more major trading countries and capable of providing no more than a partial solution to the problem of protectionism.

The Free Trade Area Approach avoids the diminishing returns of a second Kennedy Round, the bilateralism of conditional MFN, and the prevarication of the sectoral approach. The set timetable of the free trade area, as well as the pre-arranged goal of zero tariff positions, make it impossible to exclude protectionist strongholds from the system. Similarly, the inclusion of the major industrial countries would avoid any narrow bilateral bargaining. Objections to this solution take the form of emphasising the political difficulties on both sides of the Atlantic and pointing out the discrimination that is implied against the less developed countries. The problem of the less developed has not been given much attention in this study. The reason is that whether it is by trade, aid or a combination of both, an international solution to the problem of the poor depends upon agreement among the rich. Presumably, if they agreed on a free trade area among themselves they would also be able to agree on how to help the less developed. The crucial point is that they must first reach agreement among themselves as to the basic system of world trade they desire before anything of substance can be achieved for the Third World.

Free trade among industrialised countries, our ultimate goal, is not going to be achieved overnight. If any single conclusion can be drawn from this study of the various means of achieving it, it is that success depends upon the widest possible participation on the part of the industrialised countries of the world. Britain, as one of the world's major trading countries, has responsibilities in this connection. It is therefore important that she should begin to look beyond the immediate issue of her relationship to the Europe of the Six and, in her own national interest, realise that her future lies not only in Europe but also in the world at large.

Part III

WORLD POLITICS AND
TRADE STRATEGY

by

Lionel Gelber

1 A COUNTERVAILING INITIATIVE

No army, wrote Victor Hugo, can withstand the strength of an idea whose time has come. This might well be so when the idea is one that fills some deep human need or when it magnifies the scope of men or renders society more just. Yet the free world has been obliged to repel "waves of the future" such as Fascism and Nazism and against the onrush of Communism it is still on guard.

Even so, there have been some crucial ideas whose power could not be withstood when their time came. One was the post-war upsurge of ex-colonial peoples. The time has also been propitious for ideas of another type—for those that have as their embodiment the United Nations (UN), the North Atlantic Treaty Organisation (NATO) and the European Economic Community (EEC).[1] These were only inevitable though in the sense that specific crises had to be met. It is in the same sense that today a realignment of industrial powers is called for. With the need to maintain the impetus of trade liberalisation, particularly with the recrudescence of protectionism on both sides of the Atlantic, support has been growing for a multilateral free trade area approach to the problem, which in addition might afford developing countries greater access to industrial markets.[2] For so constructive an idea the time may come sooner than has been supposed and in more ways than one.

Expansion of international trade would be the purpose of such a fresh initiative. Although non-political in character it might nonetheless exert a very concrete political effect. If that is so its rationale

[1] In mid-1967 the European Economic Community, the European Coal and Steel Community and European Atomic Energy Commission were merged. As a single entity it is now officially called the European Communities. But throughout this study use will continue to be made of the more familiar abbreviation, the EEC, or such terms as the Common Market, the Six or simply the Community, when referring to the countries that collectively comprise the new Europe.

[2] The most feasible and closely-argued proposition along these lines was put forward in May, 1966, by the Canadian-American Committee, which is jointly sponsored by the National Planning Association in Washington and the Private Planning Association of Canada. See "A New Trade Strategy for Canada and the United States" (Canadian-American Committee, Washington D.C. and Montreal, May, 1966).

would be political as well as economic. Nor could anything be politically more significant than the identity of those who might get the project off the ground.

Making a Start

Under the various proposals mooted[3] the industrialised nations of the North Atlantic are not the only participants envisaged. From the political standpoint, however, the concept will be to the advantage, first of all, of Britain and the United States. Together with Canada they can best set the new movement on its course. The founding nucleus may thus be dubbed a North Atlantic Free Trade Area (NAFTA) until a neater and more all-inclusive title catches on. But the idea's title-deeds, not its title, are what should matter. In these the entire free world has a stake.

By its make-up NAFTA would act as a magnet attracting others from the more distant corners of the earth. When it is actually formed the EEC might well decide to adhere. Scandinavian members of the European Free Trade Association (EFTA) would probably follow Britain's lead, if only for economic reasons. Despite Soviet disapprobation, Austria, one of the neutral members of EFTA, has been negotiating for associate membership of the Common Market, while Switzerland prefers to abstain completely from the Treaty of Rome and Portugal is not ready yet for full free trade with even her EFTA partners. Like the Nordic countries, Ireland—with whom the United Kingdom has a separate free trade agreement—would also be inclined to do as Britain does. Indeed, such are Irish-American ties, there is nowhere she would be more at home than in an Atlantic-based free trade area of which the USA is a sponsor.

[3]Senator Jacob Javits, of New York, was one of first to introduce the idea of a multilateral free trade area to a legislative assembly. See his speech, "The Second Battle of Britain", *Congressional Record*, US Congress, Washington D.C., Vol.111, No. 148, August 12, 1965, pp. 19421-25.

The free trade area method for liberalising trade was developed by Professor H. Edward English, now of Carleton University, Ottawa, in "Atlantic Trade Policy: The Need for a New Initiative", *Moorgate and Wall Street*, London, Autumn, 1965. For a fuller version see English, "Transatlantic Economic Community" (Private Planning Association, University of Toronto Press, Toronto, 1968).

In addition see Paul Douglas, "America in the Market Place" (Holt Rinehart and Winston, New York, 1966). There was also an article by Ralph I. Straus, "A Proposal for New Initiatives in U.S. Foreign Trade Policy", *Orbis*, Foreign Policy Research Institute, University of Pennsylvania, Philadelphia, Spring, 1967.

Then across the Pacific there are Australia and New Zealand, two Commonwealth countries which, by every fibre of their national being, belong in any association between Britain, the USA and Canada. It would be highly desirable for them, as for their partners in the Atlantic, that Japan should also belong and for wider purposes than economic co-operation.[4]

A Positive Step

One other preliminary comment may be made. Though the new Europe has flourished, the yard-sticks for determining its stature are not merely economic. The most salient fact about Western Europe is that, as the main focus of power in the West, history has passed it by.

After World War II the American taxpayer primed the pump for the economic recovery of Western Europe. He may claim credit for a lot of the success that the Europe of the Six has since enjoyed. This he does not always get. There is, all the same, much in Western Europe's recent past that raises doubts about its future behaviour. Exponents of British membership of the EEC have taken it for granted that the free world would be better off if, by pooling resources and building a counterpoise to an American super-power, Western Europe was to carry more weight, both politically and strategically. That may be though to blink the tragic record of modern Europe and to ignore current trends. A European counter-poise that hampered American leadership might, on the contrary, detract from the security of the Western world. About the change such a Third Force could do even US observers have been mute.

There have been many who deplored the UK's earlier reluctance to sign the Treaty of Rome before Mr. Harold Macmillan's Government finally sought membership of the Common Market in 1961-63. These people, found in all three political parties, fear that she may have missed the boat. But to miss what may have been the wrong boat is no misfortune and, in any case, if the ultimate destination is the maintenance of a free world order, another boat might be an altogether better one to take. It may appear negative to contend that integration in a European union is something for the British

[4]About the desirability of Japanese membership see Chapter 5, Page 147 below.

people to avoid; that, unless Britain wants to abandon an individual role in world affairs, she ought to reject Europeanisation. On the other hand, it would be a positive step to espouse a world-wide venture that would create new unities without destroying old ones and from which even non-participants could reap benefits. Beyond Europe lies most of what is alive and dynamic in the West. It is with all that is energetic in the world overseas that Britain must align herself if, as she revives flagging energies, she is to reassert a political identity of her own.

But for Britain to reject Europeanisation would not be to reject Europe. On the contrary, left to exercise an individual role, she could develop closer political, financial and commercial relations with other European countries, both inside and outside the EEC. If membership of a broadly based free trade association, affording greater access to the American mass market, serves to strengthen the British economy, London's voice would carry greater weight with her European neighbours as it would in world councils. Working through existing institutions—the Organisation for Economic Co-operation and Development (OECD), the General Arrangements to Borrow (better known as the Group of Ten), the International Bank for Reconstruction and Development (the World Bank) and NATO, to name but a few—the revitalised capacities of British diplomacy could bring a moderating influence to bear in the maintenance of world order and stability.

There is no need to define in detail the purposes of an individual British role. It could take several different forms. Drawing on her EFTA experience, however, Britain could play a leading part in the pragmatic development of a flexible and world-wide free trade association that might be the most dramatic and effective counter to a deleterious drift into protectionism. Drawing on Commonwealth experience, she could work for the adoption of a worthwhile scheme of temporary tariff preferences for developing countries, thus correcting a bias in the present system of international trade against Third World interests.

The political case for a new trading arrangement must therefore be stated in its own right. It has not been. As an alternative to the Common Market, Westminster has dismissed the NAFTA idea as "second best", as a position on which to fall back if Britain again knocks unavailingly on the doors of Brussels, as an expedient for contingency planners to study but keep on ice.[5] The UK cannot treat it in this fashion, however, and expect Washington, with protectionism and isolationism stirring again, to take up the cudgels for it. The USA has had her hands full with a war to wage in South-East Asia, with the arms race more ominous than ever, with the woes of American Negroes to assuage and with so much in her cities to clear out and renovate. Washington may yet be disquieted by the manner in which the new Europe uses its collective strength. For Britain to augment that strength has nonetheless been American policy since the East-West contest first materialised.

So Washington, too, must think again. What the USA has still to perceive is that Britain cannot be Europeanised in some major spheres without being Europeanised in others. It is all of a piece. The long-standing American thesis has been that the UK, on joining the EEC, could check measures which derogate from American leadership and undermine Atlantic co-operation. When Britain alters her status, though, she might, *nolens volens*, only serve to further such measures.

At present there are no institutional fetters upon the British Government when it co-operates abroad with others. After joining the EEC the British people might enjoy less autonomy; eventually, as a subordinate unit, Britain might have to act against her own will and Washington may not like it when she does.

This may seem no moment, when Britain is paring down overseas commitments, to insist upon the degree to which the USA should still be concerned with the perpetuation of an individual British role. The more events of late have paved the way for Britain's Europeanisation, the more it is incumbent upon the USA, as leader of the West, to look again at what this would entail. But if the British economy could prosper in a free trade area designed to embrace most industrialised countries the British people might no longer feel compelled to take a Eurocentric view of their destiny.

Even before the Gaullist veto of January, 1963, when the Kennedy Administration was doing its utmost to assist the Macmillan Government achieve Britain's entry into the Common Market, it was clear from a political angle that there ought to be a counter-

[5] *Parliamentary Debates (Hansard)*, Official Report, House of Commons, H.M. Stationery Office, London (hereafter simply cited as *Hansard*), Vol. 746, No. 916, May 9, 1967, cc. 1294-95; *ibid.*, May 10, 1967, cc. 1509-13 and 1630.

vailing American initiative.[6] By launching a multilateral free trade area the USA might do more than promote the liberalisation of trade. Such an area could help avert inroads on the power structure of the West. And the preservation of that power structure is, for the USA, a condition of American primacy.

[6]In *The Statist*, London, March 9, 1962, the present writer pointed out that "a strictly North Atlantic regional approach" was then improbable. Warning on political grounds against policies being followed by London and Washington, he argued that a "loose" arrangement would be better for Britain and the West and suggested that the United States should urge one.

"A countervailing American initiative" was later advocated in a talk to a parliamentary group in the House of Commons, London, on November 26, 1962, the text of which was subsequently published in the *Monthly Bulletin*, Commonwealth Industries Association, London, December, 1962.

The same points were raised in a pamphlet published in London some weeks after the first Gaullist veto. The problem was again discussed from a politico-strategic angle in an article, "Anglo-American Imperatives", *Orbis*, Summer, 1963.

The political case for "a countervailing American initiative" was restated in Lionel Gelber, "The Alliance of Necessity" (Stein and Day, New York, 1966; Robert Hale, London, 1967).

2 NEW TRADE STRATEGY AND THE NEW EUROPE

Now that Britain has again been rebuffed in her efforts to join the Common Market, more attention is being paid to NAFTA proposals.[7] But many still cherish a hope, more likely an illusion, that the door will be unbolted automatically when President Charles de Gaulle is no longer in office. They rather fancy that factions as diverse as French industrialists and France's Communist Party will then give Britain the nod; that West Germany, which could become first in the new Europe, will be less ambivalent. On this issue, however, any sort of obstruction from across the Channel might be regarded, from the standpoint of the Western alliance, as a blessing in disguise. The reason why should be evident when the full consequences of British membership of the EEC are set out in terms of present day politico-strategic realities.

The theme here is the political case for an open-ended, Atlantic-based free trade area. But recent proponents of British entry into the Common Market have also laid store on its political aspects, though without clarifying what these would be. It is therefore with the implications of what they have been saying that this analysis should begin.

Britain and the EEC: Political Motive

In May, 1967, when Britain again applied for membership of the EEC, Mr. Harold Wilson, the British Prime Minister, informed his television audience that "the political argument is stronger". Shortly after, before the Western European Union, Mr. George Brown, the Foreign Secretary at the time, added this further gloss: for Britain, he announced, "the balance of economic advantage" would be a "fine one."[8]

---

[7]There have in fact been *three* rebuffs. For a brief account of the attempt to form a Europe-wide free trade area, over which the first was incurred, see Gerard and Victoria Curzon, "Options after the Kennedy Round", Part II in this volume.

[8]*The Times*, London, May 9, 1967; *ibid.*, July 5, 1967. Mr. Brown had long urged the entry of Britain into the Common Market and it was after he became Foreign Secretary that she made her second bid. When he resigned from office in March, 1968, he confessed that he had known fairly well what the outcome would be. See

What nobody seemed to notice, or acknowledge, was that these official utterances knocked most of the Common Market campaign, as it had been conducted for a number of years, into a cocked hat. After all, it was to alleviate Britain's economic difficulties that public men and opinion media, industrialists and financiers had been advocating British membership. But from what Downing Street has most recently said it may be inferred that Britain will be no worse off economically when she withdraws her application. If after such a withdrawal she is better off, what others deem a defeat will in fact constitute a deliverance.

Much, at any rate, was left unexplained when the House of Commons debated the second Common Market bid. Mr. Wilson summed up his Government's aim as the creation of a strong Europe that could "exert far more influence in world affairs than at any time in our generation". Mr. Edward Heath, Leader of the Opposition, concurred: "The main objective in the negotiations is political, I believe. It was in 1961."[9] Almost at once, however, bipartisan agreement nearly broke down over what entry by Britain into the new Europe would signify in so vital a realm as defence. The economic consequences have been scrutinised from many angles, and not always with favourable results, as the Prime Minister's own testimony showed.[10] About the political consequences, though, the English-speaking peoples have, from start to finish, been fed with wishful generalities.

Even if economic reasons had outweighed political ones, the Europeanisation of Britain would have had the most serious political effects. Westminster now declares that the reverse is true; that political reasons outweigh economic ones. All that can be done here is to suggest what the political effects might be and how they would affect each other. Throughout this political analysis there is, expressed or unexpressed, one further consideration. It is for others to demonstrate whether participation in NAFTA, as compared

George Brown in *The Sunday Times*, London, March 17, 1968. The issues must still be evaluated in the light of the policies he did much to frame.

[9]*Hansard*, Vol. 746, No. 195, May 8, 1967, cc. 1094 and 1100; *ibid*, Vol. 746, No. 196, May 9, 1967, c. 1296.

[10]Mr. Wilson conceded in Parliament that the effect on Britain's balance of payments of membership of the EEC could be minus £500m on current account at the end of a five-year transitional period. See *Hansard*, Vol. 746, No. 195, May 8, 1967, c. 1081. This followed a widely-read assessment by *The Times* on May 1, 1967, that the cost to the balance of payments could be between £400m and £800m.

with membership of the EEC, would furnish Britain with a balance of economic advantage that would be more than fine. But it is to the former that the balance of political advantage must be assigned if an individual role for Britain should still be preserved.

An Organic Process

What might extinguish an individual role for Britain, as a member of the EEC, may not be what the Treaty of Rome prescribes, but an organic process that the treaty has set on foot. On the plane of formal legislation there has been no further progress towards a political union. The Community has nevertheless evoked and speeded up a criss-cross of economic forces that only federalising measures will eventually be able to regulate. If participants are to gain from the dynamic effects of economic integration, policies must be harmonised in both the fiscal and monetary spheres—especially if the new Europe is to have a common currency. Involved here are important political implications. For the determination and super-vision of common economic policies pre-supposes the existence of a supranational, decision-taking authority. The EEC cannot move ahead in economic domains without moving ahead elsewhere as well.

Economic integration and political unification are, in other words, opposite sides of the same coin. The questions they raise have not featured much as yet on the Community's agenda. With the completion of the customs union phase, however, these questions will be pressed to the fore when the Six embark on the second stage of the Common Market's development, that of integration. In fostering the free exchange of goods and services across borders, it must contrive rules to which all subscribe, together with an ever more elaborate administration, if it is to get things done. At the centre, in short, there will have to be governmental powers, ones which transcend the sovereign powers of member governments. That is how the USA had to make the most of her opportunities. Like her, the EEC cannot act as a single state without possessing the attributes of a state; and it is as a state that it must act more and more.

Champions of the new Europe have, besides, enunciated political aims that only a single, overall statehood could accomplish. These would modify the power structure of the West. An experiment in supra-nationalism, according to some, may not be the same as federal union. But this is a distinction without a difference. Those that take a Eurocentric view of Britain's destiny are, by the sheer logic of their own political credo, federalists in spite of themselves.

None of this will occur if the Common Market disintegrates. Its members could then individually join a multilateral free trade area. But the Six are not likely to fall apart. On the contrary, they have been weaving themselves together in an ever tighter economic fabric. While they may resist its ensuing political grip, they cannot do so for long. Within the Community, President de Gaulle upheld the sanctity of the nation-state. The future, however, is more than even he could manipulate.

That is something for British public opinion to ponder. For there is a dispute over the degree to which, if Britain signs the Treaty of Rome, the Council and Commission of the EEC may encroach upon the sovereignty of the Queen in Parliament. A political union cannot be forged without thus encroaching more and more. This is rudimentary. Some believe Britain can protect her autonomy through a veto on change. It is change, though, that others are after when they talk about making the institutions of the Community more democratic.

Then there are those who equate membership of the EEC with membership of other international undertakings such as the UN, NATO, the General Agreement on Tariffs and Trade (GATT), EFTA, the Organisation for Economic Co-operation and Development (OECD), the International Monetary Fund (IMF) and the International Bank for Reconstruction and Development (the World Bank). But these bodies are restricted to specific functions and in this respect NAFTA would resemble them. The EEC, on the other hand, is not subject to such a restriction. As it evolves a total commitment will be extorted. Germane here, moreover, is the fact that under Article 240 the UK's signature to the Treaty of Rome would be irrevocable. Britain could not resign from the Common Market. Nor would a veto serve against so incessant an erosion of sovereignty. Its use might only stultify the well-being of an organism with which her own fortunes were bound up.

At this juncture the danger appears remote. There is no drive towards organic unity. Mr. Wilson may have allayed misgivings when he assured the House of Commons "that the federal momentum towards a supra-national Europe, in which all issues of foreign policy and defence, for example, would be settled by majority voting, for the time at least has died away".[11] But "for the time at least" may be a fairly short period of time. It is the duty of governments to look ahead.

The drive towards a federal Europe has been impeded by the same obstacle as British entry into the Common Market. To outwait President de Gaulle has been, for the European lobby in Britain, the obvious tactic. That is what the federalists of Western Europe have also been doing. They have not given up. The UK's participation would do most though to accelerate an organic process from which Britain must shrink if there is any ambition to keep an individual role. For the larger the scale of economic integration the more it may take command.

Should this be so, the British could learn too late what they have let themselves in for. The motive for UK membership of the EEC may be a political one. Those who proclaim it, however, seem to assume that Britain could always pick and choose between the political consequences of Europeanisation. In fact, she could do nothing of the kind if, on being Europeanised, she ceases to be a free agent. As long as Britain clings to the control of defence and foreign policy she may retain an individual role in world politics. But components must abandon so cardinal a feature of sovereignty if a political union is to work.

Defence and Foreign Policy

These are fundamentals that demand a more thorough ventilation than most opinion media, British and American, have been disposed to allow. Mr. Heath touched a sensitive nerve when, as the House of Commons debated Britain's second Common Market application, he adverted to the topic of defence arrangements. In response the Government front bench itself was more prone to scold than elucidate.[12]

For the defence of Europe, Britain—accepting primacy by the USA in the West—has stood behind the Atlantic Alliance. She has opposed the amalgamation of the British nuclear deterrent with the French *force de frappe* lest it become the strategic core of a Third Force that would probably be anti-American, bound therefore to bedevil NATO and even to imperil the peace. To placate President de Gaulle, Mr. Heath nevertheless summoned up the apparition of

[11]*Hansard*, Vol. 746, No. 195, May 8, 1967, c. 1093.
[12]*Hansard*, Vol. 746, No. 196, May 9, 1967, cc. 1297-1300.

just such a separate European deterrent. It is one that will indubitably arise if Britain should ever be merged with a European union.

The Conservative leader may have rendered a service if by spilling the beans, Europeanisers in the Wilson Government were discouraged from attempting a deal with the French along the lines he had set forth with so much missionary zeal. Then and later his proposition might have offended the Bonn Republic when Britain was seeking West German support in Paris as well as at Brussels and it might also have offended the Soviet Union when the treaty against the spread of nuclear weapons was still being negotiated by Lake Geneva.

Bipartisan agreement, despite this flurry, survived. So did a certain dialectical inconsequence, a sort of political make-believe into which the advocacy of the European cause had lapsed. The objectives of the new Europe, as boosted and extolled by the Labour Government and the Conservative Opposition, have been very high sounding. They belong though to the sphere of defence and foreign policy. For Britain to achieve them in the company of EEC partners the management of defence and foreign policy must pass into the hands of a conjoint European authority superior to national governments. She cannot will the end without willing the means and if the end is dubious it should not be willed.

The question Britain has raised is thus a far-reaching one. Though it is constitutional first of all, it must from the outset affect still graver issues. The European school of thought in Britain, like Gaullists and non-Gaullists across the Channel, expect the new Europe to play a part on the world stage as great as that played by other super-powers. But the EEC cannot play that part until it has been unified to a similar extent.

An American Prototype

It is as a representative democracy that the Community hopes to enlarge the scale of things. The USA, rather than the USSR, is therefore the super-power that Western Europe must take as its example. It has long been patent that the new Europe can only combat Americanisation by emulating an American prototype economically.[13] If the effort is mishandled, however, it could have

[13]This point is discussed more fully by the writer in "A Marriage of Inconvenience", *Foreign Affairs*, Council on Foreign Relations, New York, January, 1963, pp. 316-318. It is dealt with again in Gelber, "The Alliance of Necessity", *op. cit.*,

a political fall-out that many, on both sides of the Atlantic, might greatly regret.

Differences in circumstances will also be patent. Although the EEC may unify itself on a vibrant American model its starting point cannot be the same. Between most pioneer economies in the New World there was a single language; among the advanced countries of the Old World, variations in culture and history are profound. Even so, the American federal union underwent a Civil War that nearly tore it apart. Today, however, economic integration can proceed at a faster tempo in Western Europe than it did at first in the USA.

Not only has there been the Federal Constitution—tested by conflict and re-interpreted by the Supreme Court—to weld together the states of the American Union. Much was done by railways and telegraph lines as towns and cities sprang up from the wilderness. All the same, more than a century passed after the Declaration of Independence before the advent of corporate bigness, symbolised by Andrew Carnegie and the United States Steel Corporation, clinched these Herculean endeavours. Now that the EEC has removed internal tariffs the new Europe will not have to wait that long. For political unification, the Community has an economic infrastructure that is, as it were, pre-established and geographically more compact. No organic process can wipe out all that distinguishes one ancient European people from another. But it will override inexorably and thus remould.

Bigness is the American label for a phenomenon that has not been solely American. What will further accelerate the pace of integration in Western Europe is an attempt to imitate super-powers technologically in order to vie with them politically. That is another reason why, as compared with an Atlantic-based free trade area, it is essential to ascertain beforehand what Britain would be joining. Europeanists aver that only through economic unity with European neighbours can Britain's own economic requirements be met. Nothing, however, will do more than such unity to speed up a merger that would be irreversible, politically as well as economically.

In the last quarter of the twentieth century a free hand for the UK cannot be what it was in the last quarter of the nineteenth

---

pp. 31-34 *et seq.* The point is treated as a recent discovery in Jean-Jacques Servan-Schreiber, "Le Défi Americain" (Denoël, Paris, 1967).

century. Even then, "splendid isolation", no longer splendid, had to be renounced. Now, within a vast array of commitments, Britain still has her individual role. But it is one she may progressively and finally have to abandon on merging with European neighbours. For as the EEC moves from a customs and economic union to a political and federal union, overall sovereignty must reside within that entity. Member states would have to obey it in every sphere of governance. Neither Massachusetts, nor Ontario nor New South Wales possesses external ties. There is no way either in which a British component of a close-knit European union could retain any.[14]

Overseas Affinities and the British Role

In short, the prerequisites for an individual role would have vanished. Britain has been the pivot of the Commonwealth and chief ally of the USA. With the British economy out of joint, her role may now be a more modest one. But for Britain overseas affinities have been sources of strength. Those sources of strength should be conserved more than ever—not dissipated—when the British economy is under stress. No violence would be done to the historic overseas affinities of the British peoples in a multilateral free trade area. These would be the very stuff of a NAFTA initiative that revolved at first around the USA, Canada and the UK. Without those overseas affinities to sustain her, Britain is less likely to be a potter of the new Europe than clay in the potter's hands.

Misjudgement about these questions has not been confined to London. American policy-makers have also gone astray. It has been their contention that if Britain joined the EEC she could prevent the new Europe from hiving off from the West in a self-regarding Gaullist vein as a Third Force. They would thus have to predicate the continuance of Anglo-American friendship. Yet that is one of the overseas affinities Britain would have severed on becoming an integral part of a European union. Washington has fancied that the British might guide the new Europe along safe paths. But they might have little strength for doing this after they have cut

[14]Not even Quebec, if Canada is to remain Canada, may be an exception to this rule. German *Lander*, like Swiss cantons, have sovereign powers. The former, if the federal government consents, may sign treaties with other countries. But these prerogatives are relics of which no practical use is made.

themselves off from overseas sources of strength. Rather it is they who would be dragged along.

That has been a point missed not only by his critics but by President de Gaulle himself. Of the rival Soviet and American hegemonies, it is the latter that he sought to cut down to size. He could have done this by wresting the UK from the USA's side. Europeanisation would diminish Britain. The General feared instead that the Europeanisation of Britain would diminish France. He thus handed back the initiative in the West to the USA—if, that is, she is prepared to seize it. By providing Britain with an alternative to membership of the EEC, the NAFTA project would revalidate American leadership. If such a proposition offers Britain an opportunity, it offers one to the USA as well.

A Comedy of Errors

Seldom in high politics can there have been such a comedy of errors. But it has also been a cautionary tale. When President John Kennedy proposed an Atlantic partnership he assumed that its West European and North American pillars would bolster the power structure of the West and not deepen the gulf between them. By his animus, all the same, President de Gaulle illustrated how deep that gulf could be; how, when aggrandised, the new Europe might twist American policy against itself. With his second veto on British entry into the Common Market, President de Gaulle seemed as exasperating as ever. Unintentionally, he had done the West a good turn.

From every angle this has been the most ironic of spectacles. There is still much to straighten out. Even if Britain had ceased to act as a Trojan Horse for the USA she might still have earned a Gaullist blackball. For as part of the EEC she would bring in other countries with her. Denmark, Norway and Ireland applied when she did. These new members, together with other small ones, might line up behind Britain rather than France. President de Gaulle was thus for the enlargement of the new Europe in theory. But he could not be in practice lest it slide from his grasp. As a result of this dichotomy he was never able to follow through. For the new Europe must be enlarged if there is to be a Third Force that could intimidate the USA—if, in the post-Gaullist era, Gaullist concepts are to achieve full-bodied expression. Nor could those concepts achieve full-bodied expression without the power structure of the West being impaired.

Both Washington and London should accordingly have been asking what the new Europe would be like if enlarged by Britain's inclusion. There is no sign that either of them have done so.

At Westminster a strange mystique had cast its spell over both the Labour Government and the Conservative Opposition. By enhancing the status of the new Europe, their spokesmen assured Parliament, a British participant would somehow enhance its own status. "I believe", said Mr. Brown, as Foreign Secretary, "that Europe, *and through Europe this country*, will have a renewed strength and influence."[15] But if, on being Europeanised, Britain loses any independent status of her own, she will have less influence, not more. This is a possibility that has never been mentioned. Nor have the political infirmities of countries with which a merger would ensue once Britain signed the Treaty of Rome. The new Europe can exert more weight in world affairs when, through accepting British membership, it becomes less circumscribed. On the other hand, if European unity is purchased at the expense of Atlantic unity, Western Europe itself will not be more secure.

Isolationism for Britain?

Britain, it is true, might retain an individual role by means other than a NAFTA arrangement. She only has to maintain the *status quo*. Economically this would allow her to continue Commonwealth tariff preferences and, with them, the importation of low-cost foodstuffs. EFTA, too, might carry on, provided Paris and Bonn do not entice Scandinavian members away. But a multilateral free trade area, initiated by North Atlantic countries, would furnish a still wider grouping in which, as Britain toughens up flabby economic sinews, her political ones could be toughened up as well. What the British people must not do is take a wholly insular view of their destiny and so jib at all external ties. This is what some in official quarters almost suggest in hankering after a policy of "going it alone". Such British neo-isolationists might feel that, for Britain, Japan could be a prototype.

Doubtless there are analogies. The Japanese are also a thickly-populated island people for whom overseas trade is the life-blood. With her industrial infrastructure Japan is making more of a mark than Britain herself. But in the world arena the Japanese posture is rapidly changing. For one thing, the foreign policy of Japan has not

[15] *Hansard*, Vol. 753, No. 3, November 2, 1967, c. 345. Italics inserted.

been the same as that of orthodox fence-sitting neutrals like Switzerland or of didactic, militant neutralists like India. Through her security pact with the USA, she has been in a class of her own. The auguries now are that with US collaboration she will do more, rather than less, to reinforce the common defence. Other industrial countries will want Japan to join them in the proposed free trade area that would span both the Atlantic and the Pacific. It is for a bigger role that the Japanese are being cast.

From Japan, therefore, British neo-isolationists may garner few crumbs of comfort. The fact is that Britain cannot keep an individual role by drawing in upon herself. That role must instead be replenished and if other sources of strength are required they will mostly be found in an outward-looking grouping of developed countries.

The political consequences of two contrasting dangers may thus resemble each other. Isolationism for Britain would signify a degree of under-commitment that must turn the clock back. She would thwart herself no less through the amount of over-commitment which EEC membership would demand. Here, moreover, is another brand of isolationism that might pin her down. For a Third Force, if Britain augments the size of the new Europe, will simply constitute a collective isolationism writ large. Under no brand of isolationism, whether it be her own or that of the new Europe, can Britain's scope be adequate.

Through Europe's Back Door?

There is one hypothesis by which some may justify the snubs Conservative and Labour Governments have invited from Paris and Brussels. They would treat British efforts to join the EEC as a sort of try-out, an historic episode that could not be shirked and had to be gone through with before any alternative course could be pursued. It is true that, in the political psychology of the British people, abstract logic has not been conspicuous. There are occasions when what they do is determined by events, at home and abroad, over which they have no control. As a rule, though, it is by trial and error that they make up their minds. Not that there would be anything tentative about Europeanisation or that it might be deemed pragmatically as a mere experiment. The road which President de Gaulle blocked is one upon which Britain could never retrace her steps. After his second veto there were nevertheless proposals to win entry into the Common Market through the back door. How good were they?

The drawbacks to some kind of probationary or transitional membership of the EEC are, at bottom, the same as the drawbacks to full membership. There is nothing to be said for a halfway house when the entire journey may be ill-advised. As an end in itself, however, associate membership may seem more innocuous. There would be no commitment of a constitutional nature. Britain could thus reconcile European ties with ties beyond the new Europe. No such reconciliation would satisfy those who take a Eurocentric view of Britain's destiny. "We would be passengers on the train", remarked Mr. Brown in May, 1967, "but the driving would be done by someone else and we should not even be able to decide where we wanted to go."[16]

Europeanisation is what would deprive Britain of the ability to decide where she wanted to go. Without her, the new Europe might have less steam. From that train, however, she could, as an associate member, jump off. But even to associate membership there is a serious objection. If an open-ended, Atlantic-based free trade area is the most auspicious of targets, on both political and economic grounds, nothing else should deflect Britain from it.

Prospects for Democracy in Western Europe

Britain has proclaimed her economic qualifications for Common Market membership. About the political qualifications of the EEC's own members she has been more remiss. It has, for instance, been the postulate of those of a Eurocentric persuasion that when she adheres to the Treaty of Rome the British view of Europe's destiny would prevail. But what if it did not? That is the sort of question most British opinion media have allowed nobody to discuss. A change in Britain's constitutional status might not only curtail her capacity to manage events; it might leave her at their mercy. Britain will be trapped if, after she joins, the new Europe gets out of hand. In a free trade area that reaches out to the Antipodes she would not only stay institutionally untrammelled; she would still be consorting with the most robust democracies in the modern world. About the prospects for democracy in Western Europe there is less certitude.

Among the Six it is France and West Germany who call the tune while Italy is bigger than Belgium, the Netherlands and Luxem-

[16] *Hansard*, Vol. 746, No. 197, May 10, 1967, c. 1513.

bourg. If Britain merges with them she will not be merging, in the main, with mature democracies but with ones whose record in the last generation has scarcely inspired confidence. History has much to teach. The political impulses of Germans, French and Italians have affected British foreign policy for centuries. Upon the European-isation of Britain these would also permeate her domestic affairs and any escape hatch from them would have been sealed.

Trends in the Bonn Republic

West Germany, to be sure, has been living down the multifarious horrors of the Nazi era. But in the Bonn Republic there is again a conflict between representative democracy and those authoritarian traditions of which the roots among Germans run deep. When the Christian Democrats and the Social Democrats formed a coalition government the task of opposition fell to a party as small as the Free Democrats. More sinister, in the eyes of those who remember how the Weimar Republic collapsed, has been the unrest among German students and the growing polarisation between extremes of Right and Left. About 50 per cent of younger West Germans would favour an authoritarian form of government according to recent sociological surveys.[17] No serious effort has been undertaken to teach the war guilt of Nazi Germany and of it most students are unaware. During World War II and during the period of Allied occupation, it was hoped that any post-war German regime would make a whole-hearted attempt at the political re-education of German youth. Little that was whole-hearted seems to have been done. Ultras on the Right and Left might be headed off by doing away with proportional representation—an electoral system with a heavy toll among European democracies. The Communist Party has been declared illegal and many feel that if it were re-instated watch could be kept upon it. Unabashed, however, neo-Nazis comport themselves within the law.

Already there have been portents of what could happen to the Bonn Republic if, as the post-war German boom subsides, an economic depression recurs. In the Ruhr, miners have been waving the red flag, while it is to the disgruntled of all classes that the

[17]See, for instance, Regina Schmidt and Egon Becker, "Reaktionen auf Politische Vorgange: Drei Meinungsstudien aus der Bundesrepublik" (Institute fur Sozial-forschung, Johann Wolfgang Goethe-Universitat, Frankfurt, 1967). Also see *The Times*, April 8, 1968.

National Democratic Party appeals.[18] When militants of the far Right win seats by crying for the acquisition of Germanic territories beyond the frontiers of 1937 there are tremors on both sides of the Iron Curtain. Hitlerism, sanitised and in mufti, could again be on the march.

That is a nightmare which the conservative and socialist parties seek to banish by attaining, with the support of the Western alliance, a reunification of the two Germanies within prescribed boundaries. If Moscow accepts this, a new German Reich will have to accept Polish jurisdiction over the Oder-Neisse lands. But the fulfilment of German nationalism within narrowed borders may still be too much for Russia and other East European countries to stomach. West Germans will thus have a grievance not unlike the one against the Versailles *Diktat* which the Weimar Republic nourished and the Nazis exploited with such iniquitous ease.

None of this is without bearing on Britain's course. After the second Gaullist veto on her entry into the EEC, West Germany remonstrated less than other members lest France retaliate by recognising East Germany and so put German reunification out of court. If only because of the *rapprochement* between Paris and Moscow, Bonn has to have its own *rapprochement* with Paris.

It is the Russian standpoint though that should be noted here. Hitherto the USSR has preferred the domination of the Common Market by President de Gaulle to the domination of Western Europe by a greater Germany. Tomorrow, after de Gaulle, Moscow may have to pursue the same policy in another manner. It is in the light of politico-strategic realities such as these that the British people should ask whether they want to be riveted to irredentist German claims, as they would be more intimately than ever once the UK joined the EEC. The enlargement of the new Europe through Britain's inclusion has been depicted by Mr. Wilson as a step towards a *détente* with Russia.[19] But just as the West may be more

[18]Herr Willy Brandt, chairman of the Social Democrats, would make a good Chancellor, it has been reported by the Bonn correspondent of *The Times*, yet the fact that he "resisted the Nazis, left Germany in 1933, and took Norwegian nationality for a time when deprived of his German citizenship by Hitler in 1936, is bitterly held against him by many Germans, who are quite ready to accept as Chancellor a former member of the Nazi Party, and a head of state whose past has been the subject of many questions". See *The Times*, London, March 22, 1968.

[19]*Hansard*, Vol. 746, No. 195, May 8, 1967, cc. 1095-96. Chapter 3 below will deal, among other topics, with politico-strategic realities that may not only govern

united when the new Europe is small, so a small Germany might be a prerequisite for a settlement between Russia and the West.

Foreign Policy and Political Philosophy

As for France and Italy, they may yet be riven between extremes of Right and Left. A former President, Signor Antonio Segni, has been charged with complicity in a recent abortive military *coup d'état* against the Italian Republic. In France a fifth of the electorate supports the Communist ticket while in Italy more than a quarter does so; indeed, with collaboration between the Italian Communist Party and the Proletarian Socialists, one third of Italian voters are now pro-Communist. A Centre-Left coalition had, for some years, dished any Popular Front between the Italian Communists and neutralists of the far Left. But in both Italy and France the pusillanimity of the Centre is a painfully familiar story.

In all this there could be a moral for Britain. She has problems of her own to solve. She cannot solve them by enlarging the sphere of much in the West that might de-stabilise. The process of Europeanisation—when she has lost overseas sources of strength—may only de-stabilise Britain. And so on these grounds, too, the focus of British activity should lie elsewhere. It is in a wide free trade area that Britain might now do best.

Foreign policy and political philosophy are not the same thing. They nevertheless interact. Among devotees of representative democracy are to be found, for instance, the most Atlantic-minded of Europeans. That correlation is no accident. It is one, moreover, that London and Washington should take into account when planning ahead.

A crisis in French democracy restored General de Gaulle to office. Upon his departure, another had been foreordained. Neither will it be easy for his successors to lift the French ban on British entry into the Common Market. In a government consisting of Gaullists, the Centre and the Right, French industrialists would still be heard from. In a Popular Front the Communist segment, eager for France to desert the Western alliance, will also insist that Britain disentangle herself from the USA. But there has been no secret about the hurdles Britain must still surmount. More enigmatic is the

---

a settlement between Russia and the West but also determine the fate of the two Germanies.

mentality of those who burke what the UK would have to face if those hurdles could be surmounted.

Gaullist Revolt against the West

Europeanists have assumed that the processes of European integration will be orderly ones. They may not be. If, after de Gaulle, major components prove unable to govern themselves in a democratic fashion, Britain, by merging with them, will have been asking for trouble. Apart from Germany and Italy, France has always failed to achieve a fixed midpoint between authority and anarchy. On this score the record of the past three decades is not reassuring. The English-speaking peoples let down France after World War I. They cannot be blamed, all the same, for the fatuity with which the Third Republic bungled its own defences against yet another German invasion. After the English-speaking peoples liberated France from the Third Reich and erased the Vichy dictatorship, the Fourth Republic also faltered. The Fifth Republic was tailored to suit the idiosyncrasies of President de Gaulle. It could hardly outlive him. Never in France has there been a major constitutional change without some upheaval.

There was a sudden reminder of this during the spring of 1968 when a student rebellion and nation-wide strikes shook the Gaullist regime on the home front. Until then the French people had been in one of their more apathetic or compliant moods. A year before, as a matter of fact, Britain had applied for membership of the Common Market just when the President, after circumventing the National Assembly, began—under a cloak of legality—to govern by decree. The Paris correspondent of *The Times* was astounded at "the relative mildness of the reaction to a move which would be tantamount to a *coup d'état*" if it had occurred in Britain.[20] No less astounding was the relative mildness of the British reaction. After all, the UK would be affected by what the French did if ever committed to them constitutionally. Most British opinion media did not, however, seem to care. They were intent, before the second Gaullist veto, on putting across a Eurocentric line at any price. Even after that they still pegged away.

Nor is this all that has been disconcerting. Britain could not merge governmentally with European neighbours and not be involved more than she is now with their own particular objectives in

[20] *The Times*, April 28, 1967.

the field of foreign policy. Reunification with East Germany is the *arrière pensée* of the Bonn Republic. Among the French, this has had its counterpart in the Gaullist revolt against the West. On joining the EEC the British people would have been compelled either to rally to that revolt or else incur the added strain of struggling against it within narrower European confines.

It will take more than the exit of the General to do away with Gaullism. For he has made articulate what others will still feel after he has gone. Nor is that so only in France but elsewhere in Western Europe. And here one fact may be significant. More French voters have acquiesced in the Gaullist revolt against the West than in the domestic accomplishments of the Gaullist reign.

Their levity has been staggering. Since World War II, France has dwelt under the American nuclear umbrella and, in order to bolster local NATO forces, there have also been substantial contingents from the USA, Britain and Canada. Early in August, 1967, all the same, a French opinion poll announced that, as between the USSR and the USA, 57 per cent of French voters thought their country should not take sides. During March, 1968, 56 per cent were again reported to endorse Gaullist foreign policy.[21] The assistant editor of *L'Express*, the Paris weekly, has stated that "two-thirds of the French approve of General de Gaulle's foreign policy."[22] There has been no reversal of alliances. But when neutralist sentiment thus takes hold, the Western orientation of France cannot be what it was. Nor would Britain, on being Europeanised, have the means to renew it. If anything, her own orientation is what may instead be altered.

Opinion polls are of course far from conclusive. When the British Government applied for entry into the Common Market, they should have wanted evidence of a more widespread resistance to Gaullist foreign policies than there has been, but nothing was said. There were some outcries against them in France. The General could shrug these off though because, at the grass-roots, the largest portion of public opinion has been with him.

[21]Dispatches from Paris in *The Guardian*, London, August 8, 1967, and in *The Times*, August 27, 1967. Also see the *International Herald Tribune*, Paris, April 8, 1967.

By December, 1967, more than one-quarter of the French population was reported to believe that the USA represented a military danger to Western Europe. See the *International Herald Tribune*, December 11, 1967.

[22]Marc Ullmann, "What Chances for Britain in Europe?" *The Times*, May 11, 1968.

That raises awkward questions for the future. France began her modern alignment with the English-speaking peoples in the days of Delcassé and the *Entente Cordiale*. Only during the Vichy interlude did she back away from the West. World War II might have been averted, however, if after World War I the US Senate had ratified an Anglo-American treaty of guarantee that Woodrow Wilson and David Lloyd George had signed with Georges Clemençeau. But since World War II the USA, Britain and Canada have been making amends. The North Atlantic Alliance, with the USA now in the van, bestowed upon the French that for which they had pleaded so long. In spite of this, President de Gaulle—by evicting NATO from the soil of France—sabotaged the machinery through which the alliance may be implemented. In doing that, moreover, he gave West Germany a higher military status within the Western alliance —a gratuitous concession which turned much of modern history upside down.

And there are others among the traditional axioms of French statecraft that Gaullist France violated without effective dissent. Western Europe will be less secure if the Cairo-Moscow axis obtains control of the Middle East. But after the Arab-Israeli war of June, 1967, it was towards that axis rather than towards the West that President de Gaulle had leaned.

NATO, Canada and French Statecraft
Then, too, there is the manner in which the President of France flouted the comity of the West by doing what he could to egg on the break-up of Canada. He would never have permitted the Bonn Republic to meddle in the affairs of Alsace-Lorraine as Gaullist France has meddled in the affairs of French Canada. Not for centuries have the French evinced solicitude for the well-being of their kinsfolk across the Atlantic. Among the latter General de Gaulle and the Cross of Lorraine aroused scant enthusiasm during World War II. It was the isolationist spirit of Quebec, the in-difference of many French-Canadians towards the fate of Western Europe and the free world, that did most during the conflicts of 1914-18 and 1939-45 to alienate them from their English-speaking compatriots. Later it was as a pawn in his own neutralist game that President de Gaulle addressed himself to Quebec.

It would weaken the security of the West if an independent French-speaking state in North America took its cue from a European Third Force. There is a link between the North American Air Defence Command (NORAD), the early warning system that Canada and the USA have built against an attack from the north, and the NATO system across the Atlantic. Hitherto, for hemispheric defence, the two North American members of the Western alliance have had complete access to the land and air of the province of Quebec. They might still have this, however, if Quebec became a sovereign nation, only on her own terms. Furthermore, when Canada and the USA built the St. Lawrence Seaway they never anticipated that they would have to negotiate transit rights with another littoral power. The foodstuffs, arms, munitions and industrial products that passed from the ports on the Great Lakes up the St. Lawrence during the two world wars were vital for the defence of the West. They could be again.

It is thus with a united Canada that the USA can best act against the adversaries of the West. But President de Gaulle was less worried about the adversaries of the West than about an American leadership which holds them at bay. Canada has been a key segment of that Anglo-American factor on which so much in the free world has depended. If a blow at the one would be a blow at the other, it was part of a wider Gaullist design.

This is not an issue Britain can ignore. Her own interests are ill-served when in Western Europe, Canada and the Middle East a French ruler thus flouts the comity of the West. Britain has been seeking a closer attachment with those, in France and the Common Market, who—despite vapid, feeble gestures of protest—had let the General get away with it all. The fact that he could get away with it for so long has revealed much, albeit inadvertently.

After M. Pierre Mendès-France extricated France from Indo-China, President de Gaulle capped the work of French de-colonisation by evacuating Algeria and staving off civil war within the borders of metropolitan France. But without the vigil that the USA and the rest of NATO maintained, he could never have altered the regime at home with impunity or striven unmolested against his own allies abroad. Communist voters are anti-Western by definition. But the General, by misreading the signs and hewing to his own rigid preconceptions, had also persuaded another considerable body of French opinion that France can down-grade or dispense with safeguards that others have tendered. It is not only with a political volatility such as this that Britain, on becoming a member of the EEC, would have to conjure year in and year out. If it went further, it would drag her along.

Lessons for Britain

Not that the rest of Western Europe is responsible for what President de Gaulle has done. Even among the Gaullists of other countries the antics of their celebrated mentor must have caused dismay. By vouchsafing a reprieve from Europeanisation he had, nevertheless, given Britain another chance to examine what EEC membership could entail. The price of Europeanisation would be a close-knit union with, among others, three peoples as politically unpredictable as the West Germans, the French and the Italians; with major components of the new Europe that are less staunchly committed than Britain herself to representative democracy and even the well-being of the West. This is not a price Britain could have paid at the best of times. If these were the best of times Britain would never have contemplated so rash a gamble.

Nor will traditional methods be of any avail for meeting such dangers. The conjecture has been that within the EEC, rather than from without, Britain would operate as a corrective to whatever is unruly or domineering. That, too, is why lesser members—the Italians, the Belgians, the Dutch and the Luxembourgers—have had so constant a predilection for British membership. Most other new recruits would also gravitate towards Britain. Against the ascendancy of the French and West Germans there could thus be an inner equipoise.

Britain must still put first things first. She may have had to sacrifice much of her standing in world affairs. She is not obliged though to forfeit it entirely so as to ensure the domestic tranquillity of the new Europe. By the total loss of an individual British role it is the West as a whole that would be set back. If there is no enlargement of the new Europe its political transgressions would, after all, do less harm. It is not by plunging in that Britain can do most to regulate the new Europe but, in some degree, by holding aloof.

There is yet another point. Western and Central Europe were the hinge of world politics until World War II. They are so no longer. When Britain ruled the waves she either had the European balance of power as a protective device or did what she could to restore it. Since World War II, however, there has been no European balance of power. It is a different sort of balance that furnishes security and to which Britain has been contributing. If she is to go on doing so she must, as always, look beyond Western Europe. Only by drawing upon overseas sources of strength, something an Atlantic-based free trade area would enable her to do, can Britain still exert a free hand on her own side of the Atlantic as well.

In a Eurocentric view of Britain's destiny there is thus one abiding defect. It forgets that her affinities are dual ones; that she is at once a European and an extra-European power. But while integration with the new Europe would debar extra-European affinities, there would be room in a free trade grouping for many varied types. Nor is it only Britain that may discern in the wider horizons of a NAFTA arrangement an inestimable boon. The USA, as leader of the West, should do the same.

Would the murder of the two Kennedys and Martin Luther King turn others away from the USA and vindicate Third Force tendencies? Memories are short. In the twentieth century it was the war of 1914-18, a European conflict that began with a political assassination, which did most to decivilise the modern world. Tens of millions died thereafter under Communist, Fascist and Nazi dictatorships. These enormities were European, not American, in origin. Only a society as free as the American can diagnose its own ills in the light of day and as long as it enjoys that right the qualities that make for leadership will persist.

3 AMERICA, THE GLOBAL BALANCE
AND BRITAIN

The USA will have to take up the idea of an open-ended, Atlantic-based free trade area if it is to get anywhere and such would be its political merits that these alone should impel her to take it up. Against the Europeanisation of Britain she has, first of all, the power structure of the West to preserve. Even on that score this new project would be no mere salvage operation. Then, too, a multi-lateral free trade area will transcend regional or other particularisms. If it only did that it would rate as a forward step.

Nor is this the only reason why a new economic alignment of industrial powers would have virtues that are more than economic. By its sheer world-wide extent, it would also correspond to the politico-strategic realities of the age.

No politico-strategic reality is as decisive as the scale on which world contests are waged nowadays. Pearl Harbour started the war in the Pacific but, as in 1914-18, the Germans still had to be subdued on the Western and Russian fronts. Nobody, however, could restore a European balance of power that Europeans themselves had destroyed. A global balance has superseded it: one which, in the era of nuclear weapons and long-range war technology, the USA has done most to uphold; one also in which Western Europe, with an American guarantee as the basic feature of its security, is today but a key sector.[23] There are, moreover, not only bigger dimensions with which the West must reckon. Western Europe is dissatisfied with the redistribution of power within the West.

By taking the lead the USA, with others at her side, has either

---

[23]The shift from a European balance was mentioned by the writer in *Foreign Affairs*, January, 1946, then enlarged upon in "Reprieve from War" (Macmillan, New York, 1950), in "America in Britain's Place" (Frederick A. Praeger, New York, 1961; Allen and Unwin, London, 1961) and in "The Alliance of Necessity", *op. cit.* But according to an article in *International Affairs*, London, July, 1967, this concept was first stated in 1955 by a German historian. The author of this article has frankly admitted that his assertion (that this concept was first stated by a German historian) was incorrect. Though *International Affairs*, a journal issued under the auspices of the Royal Institute of International Affairs, was requested to publish a correction of this error, it has to date failed to do so.

stemmed the main outward thrusts of adversaries or, where peripheral thusts have been attempted, hemmed them in. Yet the very endeavours that blocked enemies of the free world have, as it were, unleashed the discontent of those—allied and neutralist—who have benefited from American endeavours. Some of that discontent may have been justified. Western Europe would all the same resent disparities of power even if it had less to complain about.

As leader of the West, moreover, the USA also has a lot to complain about. It would be naïve for her to expect gratitude from beneficiaries: what she does for others she does as much for herself. Blunders are unavoidable when she must defy the map on so vast a scale. The magnitude of her task is nevertheless without precedent. The root cause of friction may be the way West Europeans have glossed over that primal fact.

Global Balance and American Primacy

Europe the protected and America the protector do not have the same frames of reference. What the USA does must fit into a global pattern; that, however, which magnifies her scope may even reduce the number of options that are open to her. It is, on the other hand, the essence of a Gaullist foreign policy that the new Europe now has more options than were open before it had recovered from the ravages of World War II. Yet a Third Force, even though premised on the ability of Western Europe to go it alone, must also still count on reinsurance by the USA.

The North Atlantic Alliance was not set up to provide free rides, but some of its signatories are riding at half-fare and Gaullist France has even been loosening the rails. For the moment other members of the North Atlantic Alliance do not agree with the French that the Soviet threat to Western Europe has virtually evaporated; that American preponderance is worse than anything Russia might still do. But when the EEC moves from an economic to a political union, its innate Third Force tendencies are bound to reshape it. These will be less bold if Britain stays out. The majority of West Europeans, all the same, still want the Atlantic nexus to continue. Nothing is more likely to ensure its continuance than British participation in an Atlantic free trade area. On both sides of the Atlantic this is nonetheless an issue over which even the Atlantic-minded have been confused.

Meanwhile, differing emphases between the USA and Western

Europe make part of the background against which a new economic grouping of industrial powers would be formed. In putting the political case for a NAFTA arrangement it may therefore be well to discuss those differences somewhat further.

Western Europe and East Asia

After World War II the USA could not allow the European sector to go under lest the entire global balance shift against her. Western Europe, however, has not been as ready to acknowledge that for its own sake Asian segments of a global balance must also be defended. Local circumstances have not been the same in Asia as in Western Europe. Apart from Russia, a rival of the West, and Japan, not yet re-militarised, there have been no advanced industrial states on the rim of China with which to organise the security of the more vulnerable Asian theatres. With a few others the USA has done what she could.

The affairs of Europe and Asia have been interacting for many years. After Imperial Japan defeated Tsarist Russia in 1905 the latter turned back to the Balkans where, as she clashed with the Hapsburg Empire, World War I finally erupted. Though there had again been military campaigns in the Middle East, it was Pearl Harbour which transformed World War II from a European into a global conflict. But it was the Korean War which first demonstrated how far-reaching might be the repercussions of conflict when long-range weapons are employed. If the USA had invaded Manchuria or bombed targets on Chinese territory, Russia, the ally of China, could have hit back at Britain, the ally of the USA, from Soviet bases in East Germany. No one could be sure either that Russia, aided and abetted by the Communist parties of France and Italy, would not push beyond the Iron Curtain if the USA were to be bogged down in an Asian land war.

What, as a matter of fact, the Korean crisis did for Europe was to bring West Germany into the North Atlantic Alliance and hasten her rearmament. In the 1960's it was again the shadow of China looming over non-Communist Asia that induced the USA to assist South Vietnam against North Vietnam. Once again Washington felt an Asian sector of the global balance had to be held.

There was no joy in the USA over the Korean War but the American intervention against North Vietnam has been even less popular. As always, it was the innocent among the Vietnamese,

North and South, who suffered. From elsewhere in South-East Asia, however, a number of countries have joined with the USA. So have Australia and New Zealand. They greet anything that might retard China's regional domination. Even for India, neutralism has lost its savour. Harassed by Chinese encroachments from Tibet, she has been less censorious of the USA than she was during the Korean War. What might also be noted is that the USA could again fight a land war in the Far East without putting Western Europe at risk. Turmoil in China may not last. Tension between Moscow and Peking is likely to do so.

The Cuban missile crisis of 1962, moreover, had left its mark. North Vietnam has procured her supplies from Russia and China, but China would emerge as victor, *tertius gaudens*, if Russia and the USA should ever let themselves collide. The Soviet Union might compete with the USA in South-East Asia and, from the Middle East, press the West harder than ever. The Russian course has all the same been one of audacity tempered with caution.

Long-range Weapons and the Strategic Interlock

Such forbearance has had its origins, of course, in the new war technology. The dimensions of world contests have not only been magnified; they also have their ominous nuclear phase. The European sector of the global balance is as safe as American underpinnings make it. What it feared during the Korean War was that when the USA fights in Asia, a strategic interlock—spanning continents—might engulf Western Europe in a nuclear holocaust. And yet the new Europe cannot improve matters by building a deterrent of its own. Should it ever use one, all other deterrents, big and small, might come into play. With nuclear furies unloosed everywhere, the last state of Western Europe would be worse than its first.

A treaty against the spread of nuclear weapons has been signed —on the principle, no doubt, that it is still good sense to lock the stable door, or try to close it, after the more restive horses have been stolen. China and France now have their own nuclear weapons, and some neighbours of China might build deterrents against her unless super-powers provide security guarantees. But it is difficult for the super-powers to provide these when they themselves could upset any nuclear equilibrium by building anti-missile systems and by devising ever more deadly weapons. The outlook would be darker still if nuclear dissidents acquired weapons by which they might embroil super-powers against each other.

Until there is an accord between nuclear colossi, mankind will have to live dangerously. It is the desire of the British people to reduce hazards in this most hazardous of all spheres. Here, nonetheless, the Europeanisation of Britain could also have an unsettling effect while membership in another sort of grouping would at least leave things as they are.

Britain's Europeanisation and a European Deterrent

Over nuclear issues NATO has adopted better consultative procedures between the USA and her Atlantic allies. But if, *après de Gaulle*, a European political union evolves, it will have the French deterrent at its disposal. Britain could not merge with such a union without the British deterrent also being ceded. This was perceived by Mr. Heath, the Conservative Opposition leader, while the Prime Minister, Mr. Wilson, only observed that such a step would dash hopes of a *détente* with Eastern Europe.[24] Both of them have promoted Britain's Europeanisation. What this would entail from the standpoint of politico-strategic realities they have yet to spell out.

In a close-knit political union the means of defence must belong to the union as a whole. The upshot will be an amalgamation of deterrents under the control of a European supra-national authority. Such an amalgamation may not technically contravene the treaty against the spread of nuclear weapons, although the USSR might disagree. There will be one deterrent where there would have been two. Even so, the Bonn Republic, as a component of a European union, would also have commensurate access to any European deterrent. Not that either France or West Germany could get a lone finger on the trigger. Each of them, however, has nursed ambitions that might de-stabilise when, if there is to be a *détente* between Russia and the West, stability should be the goal.

East European countries shrink from the rebirth of a greater Germany. The West will not elicit their goodwill by creating a European deterrent to which Bonn might have access. At first

[24]*Hansard*, Vol. 746, No. 196, May 9, 1967, cc. 1297-1300, and interview with Mr. Heath, *The Sunday Times*, October 15, 1967. For further discussion of the proposal for an Anglo-French deterrent between Mr. Heath and the Defence Secretary, Mr. Denis Healey, see *Hansard*, Vol. 760, No. 74, March 5, 1968, cc. 241-42 and 356-59.

glance the USSR would cheer on a Third Force that could detach the new Europe from American leadership. But Moscow would probably have reservations about this if it gave the Germans more latitude.

There is, in addition, yet another angle from which the British people should canvass such European contingencies. The grim exigencies of modern war technology, as well as a political community of interest, have made it prudent for Britain to co-ordinate the British deterrent with the overall American deterrent. There could be no co-ordination of that kind if Britain were to be Europeanised. It is as a member of an Atlantic free trade area, and not as a component of a European union, that she could still pursue foreign and defence policies of her own.

Nor is this all. A deterrent as stupendous as the American can do without a British supplement. But the USA upholds a nuclear equilibrium on behalf of the West and for any in the West to disturb it would be supreme folly. That equilibrium would be disturbed if the British removed their deterrent from the American ambit only to fortify a European deterrent with it. (Over this the USA herself could be at fault. Under a 1958 agreement she furnishes Britain with assistance in the development and production of nuclear weapons. If Washington lets that agreement expire, the upshot can be a post-Gaullist nuclear deal between Paris and London from which a European Third Force might take off.) If nuclear dissidence is a danger, it will not vanish when, through such a transference, a European deterrent is formed. Derogating from American control of Western deterrents, it could only deepen the split within the West.

Russia, a Third Force and the Power Structure of the West

It would also deepen the split between Russia and the West when, as nuclear dissidence mounts, a settlement is more and more urgent. The remedy for super-powers might be a bilateral settlement between themselves. The more the new Europe is enlarged, and Britain's inclusion would do most to enlarge it, the more the Big Two may have to get things done on their own. Western Europe would like to mitigate disparities of power between itself and the USA. Dabbling in nuclear politics will only make them more acute.

The British people are, besides, still among those who regard the unity of the West as the one sure base from which to reach a settlement with Russia. It was President de Gaulle himself who, despite lip-service to the enlargement of the new Europe, did not in fact allow it to be enlarged; who, by thus preserving for the West the foundations of unity, also left Gaullism with a smaller arena than it might have had if, after he has bowed out, it again makes a stir. What must be condemned root and branch is the mischief he wrought by his hostility towards American leadership and the misjudgements about the East-West contest by which he rationalised that hostility. But even this could be of use if it teaches Washington that, with Britain abstaining, the new Europe may not so readily get out of its depth; that when it has limits there will be more and not less unity in the West. Through membership of an Atlantic free trade area, Britain might still serve common purposes on the European shores of the Atlantic as well.

For Europe, at all events, the Kremlin may have hit upon an ingenious new tactic. Without the American presence, Western Europe would have been as exposed to coercion after World War II as Asian sectors of the global balance. Now, however, it is by hanging back that Soviet policy may do best. In the long run the Kremlin might frown upon Third Force tendencies. But when it lets Western Europe relax it also gives those tendencies a chance to ripen and bear fruit. For less unity in the West this is not a big price to pay.

Yet Russia has not only stationed many units of the Red Army just behind the Iron Curtain but keeps a vast array of missiles trained on Western Europe. As with Czechoslovakia again, she can try to impose her will on Western Europe on the spur of the moment. She might have been tempted to do so as recently as 1962, if, after the Berlin crisis of 1961, Russia could have erected missile bases in Cuba. An American hegemony kindled the wrath of President de Gaulle. Over Western Europe and Cuba, the USA has staved off Russian efforts to disable the inner citadels of the West. Outlying ramparts might prove less firm. Since 1962, moreover, with China on the rampage, with North Vietnam and Egypt a drain on the Soviet economy and with a power vacuum to fill in the Middle East and adjacent waters, Russia anyway would have been busy elsewhere. That is how Gaullist tenets have sounded so plausible. And for the interim, the Kremlin is not inclined to discourage them.

About this the British people should make no mistake. The existing power structure of the West is what enables Western

Europe to take it easy. What could impair that power structure are Third Force propensities which, fanned rather than engendered by President de Gaulle, will outlast him. Britain might want to combat them, but on becoming a member of the EEC she would have less and not more capacity to do so. They may, when she has given up her individual role, simply sweep her along.

Britain and German Reunification

There is not only the likelihood, furthermore, that, upon Europeanisation, Britain will be swept along over issues that, by severing her from the USA, could undermine her own security. Over other issues, too, she may discover herself fettered when unfettered is what she dearly wants to be—with one of these being the future of the two Germanies. Not that this can be decided before Russia and the West settle other outstanding questions—an eventuality that seems remote when the Soviet Union is still trying to outmatch the West. Even now, however, it is evident that without some compromise between the two camps no settlement can ever be brought off. But the new Europe may be more uncompromising over German reunification than over other issues and if Britain were a component of a European union she would have to do as it does.

Signatories of the North Atlantic Alliance have endorsed the reunification of West Germany with East Germany. It is, nevertheless, among fellow members of the Common Market that the Bonn Republic can now drum up most support for that aim.

Here is another example of the sort of thing that, upon Europeanisation, Britain may be letting herself in for—the sort of thing membership of an Atlantic free trade area would save her from. The EEC has done much to end Franco-German enmity and, together with the Atlantic Alliance, ensure that West Germany turns to the West rather than the East. This is a job that can be done without undoing, as British participation in the Common Market might undo it, the power structure of the West.

West Germany might hold her allies in the West to the letter of their bond. Yet if they cannot redeem it, she would be wise to release them. The bulk of German-speaking peoples may wish to dwell together again, but their right to self-determination has been at odds with the right of smaller neighbours to self-determination. Nor in a nuclear age can even West Germans want it to take precedence as a goal over the need for a settlement between Russia and the West. The plight of East Germans should not be exaggerated, not everybody who speaks English or French has the same allegiance. If the Bonn Republic can do without Austria it can do without East Germany as well. The fate of East Germany is, after all, no more bitter than that of other Russian client states. What would relieve strain throughout the Soviet imperium is that settlement between Russia and the West which the demand for German re-unification may defer.

All the same, it would only irk West Germans if fellow members of the Common Market were the ones who did most to win Bonn over. This must become a more intimate partnership than NATO or the proposed free trade grouping of industrial countries. The path to economic co-operation within the EEC has been rugged enough. When political co-operation has yet to be devised, other partners will be the last to rile Bonn over so delicate an issue. But under a NAFTA charter, Britain would not be subject to the same restraint. Not that either she or the USA can do as they please. Bonn is the only one that can rid the North Atlantic Alliance of its pledge to German reunification. Britain might want to impress upon West Germans the politico-strategic realities of the situation. This, after she had joined the EEC, would be more and not less difficult to do.

France, the Bonn Republic and Russia

In that sense, too, the UK can do for France what the French, despite Gaullist presumption, can no longer do for themselves. France got nowhere when, in 1958, President de Gaulle proposed a triumvirate with the USA and Britain—a rank for the French that others in the Western alliance would never accept. It is not improbable that, as between West Germany and Britain, the General would still have preferred to go hand in hand with the latter. But he could never have built a Gaullist Europe without assistance from the Bonn Republic, and unless he had given German reunification the stamp of approval he could never get that assistance. President de Gaulle propitiated Warsaw and Moscow by recognising the Polish annexation of the Oder-Neisse lands. Concurrently he vexed them when, over the reunification of the two Germanies, he collaborated with Bonn.

For sheer virtuosity this was an exceptional feat. When Bismarck walked a similar tightrope, he had more than Gaullist France has had to offer others. Without the Russian ban on German reunification, however, not even the General could keep it up. East Germany is in tutelage to Moscow and when Moscow forbids the reunification of the two Germanies it is fortunate for France. A greater Germany would, after all, take the place in Western Europe to which France herself aspired. There might still be a Third Force, but the Germans and not the French would be in the driver's seat. The French have said that, by their *rapprochement* with Russia, they can put in a word for Bonn at Moscow. Through that traditional French expedient, nevertheless, France might also reinsure herself against the resurrection of a greater Germany. Paris, moreover, is not the only capital that veers and tacks. Washington must do the same.

The USA has also had to press for German reunification. That has been Bonn's reward for having adhered to the West, but it cannot go on being rewarded forever. West Germany now has nowhere else to turn. When Russia is the one that sticks to the division of Germany, Bonn can scarcely plot with Moscow against the West in the manner of Rapallo or the Nazi-Soviet Pact. And Russia will not relent when, as leader of the West, the USA does most to negotiate a settlement with her.

A settlement with Russia is what the British people seek. But over the German issue, as over nuclear issues, the new Europe has had objectives of its own. Other, more global, considerations must govern the world policy of the USA. It is in conjunction with the USA rather than the new Europe that Britain can still further the peacemaking which she hopes will lie ahead.

About the German problem one feature should be specially noted. Bonn is thinking in terms of Western and Central Europe. For Moscow it is Eurasian, even global, elements that are paramount. Generally, if Russia and the West reach a settlement, the two rival camps may still have to maintain counteracting systems of power. These should enforce agreement and not prolong antagonism. But until they call off other activities—direct and indirect—that prolong antagonism, there can be no overall agreement to enforce. Under the Soviet concept of peaceful coexistence, Russia persists in her endeavour to supplant a free world order with a Communist one. By subsidising "wars of liberation" she may also undermine the outer defences of the West. Such a pursuit of power through ideology is something the Soviet Union will have to repudiate before there can be a durable peace. What Russia might ask in return is that the West jettison a policy that could render the Soviet imperium less secure. The reunification of the two Germanies has become such a policy.

It was not always so. For some years after World War II, Moscow might have allowed the two Germanies to establish a loose, neutralised, all-German confederation. NATO had stationed armies and aircraft on the soil of West Germany. These it would have had to withdraw if the Bonn Republic were neutralised. The effect of such a neutralisation could always be descried. In the global balance, its own European sector would shift against the West—with Russia scoring at last.

For the Soviet Union, moreover, President de Gaulle might have revived so tantalising a prospect. After all, he had ejected NATO from French territory, despite the extent to which Western Europe still has to rely on an American guarantee. Like Russia he clamoured for a complete evacuation of the European continent by American troops. Moscow, however, will not brook the domination of Western Europe by yet another German Reich. A Third Force, enlarged by British participation, could split the West. But the accession of East Germany to West Germany might also enlarge the new Europe. There can be no such enlargement as long as twenty Russian divisions keep a German client state within the Soviet grip and that is where, politico-strategic realities being what they are, East Germany will now stay.

The Impact of China

About this, two miscalculations account for impolicy in the West. First of all, there has been a failure to grasp the damage that might be done by a Eurocentric view of Britain's future role. Secondly, though, the interaction of European and Asian affairs has had political consequences to which more heed should have been paid. By her resurgence China may not only push the Soviet Union, reluctantly yet inexorably, towards a settlement with the West. That resurgence is what also inscribes, as a major Russian item on the agenda for world settlement, the perpetuation of the German *status quo*.

It will not add to the comfort of the Soviet Union as a Eurasian power if so populous a neighbour as China extends her sway over East Asia, South-East Asia and South Asia. Boundary disputes would have sufficed to estrange them from each other. But a schism in ideology sharpens an historic feud. While the Asian pot is boiling, all quiet on the Western front, territorially at any rate, may therefore be the Russian motto. China exists. A greater Germany does not. Against the rebirth of a strong German neighbour on the European frontier of the Soviet imperium, Russia can still put her foot down. She is resolved to keep it there.

It is unlikely, moreover, that Moscow will yield if Bonn clubs together with Peking. This would constitute pressure, reminiscent of Rapallo and the Nazi-Soviet Pact, against Russia herself. It would also be another German betrayal of the West. But a threat to Russia on two fronts is what makes the resurrection of a greater Germany so repugnant to the Soviet Union. All it might do now is give a further spurt to any *rapprochement* between Russia and the Western alliance.[25]

In terms of the global balance, it is no bad thing when the Soviet Union rules out German reunification. The West, too, is against the expansion of China. If the re-emergence of a greater Germany distracted Russia from the affairs of East Asia only Peking could rejoice. The two super-powers, Russia and the USA, have been on opposite sides of the barricades in Vietnam and the Middle East. But in Hanoi, at least, there has thus not been a Chinese monopoly. In 1966, when the Soviet Union mediated between India and Pakistan, Russia and the West had the *status quo* of South Asia as a common interest.

Recent turmoil in China does not mean there is no longer a Chinese threat to Asian regional security—to Asian sectors of the global balance. The Soviet Union itself did not become as formidable as it now is overnight. But China has reawakened and even if she lapses into governmental chaos, even if her regime totters, those among the Chinese who have mastered the latest war technology would be as adept as ever. Adapting their skill to her pan-Asian goals, China may browbeat her neighbours more than she has. Unless

[25]An attempt by the Bonn Republic to build up Communist China against the Soviet Union is a contingency that, despite the alarm sounded in Moscow, has not been unforeseen. It was dealt with in Gelber, "The Alliance of Necessity", *op. cit.*, p. 150.

Altered circumstances render improbable a Sino-German agreement along the lines of the one which Hitler and Stalin concluded. The present writer had warned against a Nazi-Soviet Pact in *The Fortnightly*, London, March, 1938—two weeks before the fall of Austria, six months before Munich, a year and a half before that Russo-German accord precipitated World War II. Most of this analysis was reproduced in Gelber, "Peace by Power" (Oxford University Press, New York and London, 1942).

the two super-powers are going to let her do so unopposed, they themselves will have to sink their differences on the perimeter of China. But they may not get together, there or elsewhere, if the stumbling-block of German reunification slows them up.

Russia, Western Europe and a Greater Germany

It is into the wider ramifications of world politics that the German problem must fit. No progress will be made, though, if an enlarged Europe only pins Britain down and, by disuniting the West, foreshortens the West's negotiating capacity.

Russia and the West, to be sure, have had more than German reunification to set them apart. All the same, it is the one issue over which Western Europe, as such, may delay or speed up a settlement between the two camps. Germans might reject one of the politico-strategic realities that, in two successive world wars, they did most to bring about. Now they will have to adjust themselves to it and when they do so they may, as a concomitant, let their own allies off the hook.

Then there are the barriers between Western Europe and the Soviet client states of Eastern Europe. Britain, with the rest of the Western alliance, would like to see those barriers razed. But East European countries go along with Russia in keeping the Germanies divided. This, for them, is—after all they have been through over the centuries—the question of questions and one that drab party dictatorships keep alive, despite the way the USSR has dragooned East Germans, Hungarians and Czechoslovaks. Russia is on top and, by its German policy, the West does not exactly incite Soviet client states to break away.

For London (as indeed for Washington) the route to Eastern Europe is thus politically the same as the route to Moscow and it does not pass through the Common Market. Advocacy of German reunification in the West does its bit to postpone a settlement between the West and Russia. When, too, it deepens the sense of dependence on their own Muscovite overlord among the countries of Eastern Europe, it also further postpones that very emancipation of the Soviet imperium which, with her allies in the West, Britain has always favoured.

Here again a closer tie with German demands is the last thing for which the British people should hanker. But elsewhere as well, many are apprehensive over what these demands would entail. For even if a greater Germany could be affiliated with the West, it would swamp the Common Market economically and overawe any political union that evolves within it. Nor could Britain serve as an offset if, after she has shed overseas connections, the new Europe might only swallow her up.

Some have averred, however, that a greater Germany would be safe for her neighbours if the countries of both Eastern and Western Europe banded themselves together in either a loose-knit or a tight-knit community. But no such pan-European nostrum is in sight and mankind cannot wait for a settlement between Russia and the West until anything so Utopian crops up. The idea of a free trade area, on the other hand, is far from Utopian. Use therefore may be made of it to crown any *détente* between industrial countries that are still at variance ideologically and politically. An application from Yugoslavia to EFTA could presage such a trend.

It is within the Bonn Republic itself that the one practicable solution for the German problem must be found. West Germans are not the first people in history who have had to adapt themselves to a lower rank. It would be futile for them to rebel against politico-strategic realities for which other peoples bear less of the onus than the Germans themselves.

A few general observations may be apposite. The quest for the reunification of the two Germanies implies that all who speak the same tongue must invariably cherish the same political loyalty. This is the sort of German imperialism by which the Nazis, with their racial doctrine, were debased. It is a more civilised French version that President de Gaulle tried to invoke against Canada. A greater Germany, moreover, would not even inherit the mellowing sanction of age. The life of its predecessor was brief, lasting only from 1871 to 1945. The goal should be a further lightening of yokes everywhere in the Soviet imperium. A settlement between Russia and the West will be the signal for that. Irredentist German claims are not the sole obstacle. But the sooner the Bonn Republic cuts its losses, the sooner the Soviet Union will have to make concessions on other issues which, for the sake of peace, it ought to make.

One further comment about the Bonn Republic may be added. The country will have to clarify its place in world councils before Britain should be mixed up with it more closely than she now is as a member of the North Atlantic Alliance. The new Europe, after all, will not need a British counterpoise against the advent of a greater

Germany if the German *status quo* gets its assent. In any rational scheme of world order, it is better for the Bonn Republic to waive the unattainable than for Britain, on being Europeanised, to forfeit an individual role.

Third Force versus the Unity of the West

Europe had to have a British stabiliser when that continent was the hub of world politics. While the new Europe can still do much, there has been—with the post-war configuration of power—a change of venue. The West must look elsewhere for a lead. A global balance is what it now has to uphold. In the making of policy there would be a reflection of global criteria when like-minded countries establish a new economic grouping which would have its anchorage in the North Atlantic but which may also stretch around the earth.

It is, then, not only on grounds of trade that this project would be a progressive one. On political grounds, if the West is to be governed with wisdom, it should sweep all before it. In principle even President de Gaulle was for the enlargement of the new Europe. Infinitely more important was the way he illustrated how, when enlarged, it could tear the West asunder. In the Atlantic partnership that President Kennedy envisaged, Western Europe and North America were to be twin pillars upon which the Western edifice would rest. What he may have been trying to head off was a constellation of power in which the new Europe would be a wholly separate luminary. This was one of those dangers though against which scant warning could get through to the British public. The overwhelming majority of UK opinion media—press, radio and television—were out to implant on Britain a Eurocentric outlook. Any serious public debate of its political consequences would appear to have been taboo.[26]

When, nevertheless, Britain made her second bid for entry into the Common Market, political objectives—vague, lofty and self-deceptive—were played up. These were to be achieved, according to Mr. Wilson and Mr. Heath, within the Western alliance.[27] But

[26]Normally the intellectual Establishment, British and American, tries to arouse the political Establishment, Right and Left, from dogmatic slumbers. But that could not be done when these two Establishments, over a topic like the Europeanisation of Britain, had become bedfellows.

[27]*Hansard*, Vol. 746, No. 195, May 8, 1967, cc. 1089-97. *Ibid.*, Vol. 746, No. 196, May 9, 1967, cc. 1282-1301.

if Britain could have been Europeanised, the new Europe must in the nature of things have spoken for her, even if she abhorred what it had to say. In Washington, all the same, it had been assumed that, on joining the EEC, Britain would serve as a brake upon disruptive Third Force tendencies. During 1967, as a matter of fact, she was preparing herself to facilitate them.

There were bipartisan hints of this when Britain applied for membership of the Common Market. Mr. James Callaghan, later Home Secretary but still addressing the House of Commons as Chancellor of the Exchequer, favoured such a move because—like the USA and the USSR—the EEC, he felt, was becoming a "great power bloc". Although the Leader of the Opposition did not then employ such phraseology, he did advocate an amalgamation of the British and French nuclear deterrents which would be the strategic core of any Third Force. Mr. Heath may have wanted the EEC to redress the balance between Western Europe and North America within the framework of the West. Yet Gaullist France, with whom he proposed strategic integration, had already defected from NATO.[28] On both front benches Third Force propensities were implicit rather than explicit. None who toyed with the Europeanisation of Britain could elude them.

They could be detected again at Scarborough when, in October, 1967, the Labour Party endorsed the British application for membership of the Common Market. The American intervention in Vietnam had provoked a demand for severance from the USA. Downing Street would permit no such step. When, however, Mr. Brown, as mouthpiece for the Government, inveighed against the polarisation of world politics between the two super-powers, he could not help but intimate that a third super-power may be the solution.[29] If it is

[28]*Hansard*, Vol. 746, No. 196, May 9, 1967, cc. 1282-1311.

It was, moreover, the contention of one Conservative ex-Minister, Mr. Duncan Sandys, that, with Britain, Europe—as one of the giants—would be entitled to a seat at the top table. (*Ibid.*, No. 195, May 8, 1967, c. 1124.) Mr Sandys, with other Conservatives, was subsequently to denounce the British withdrawals from East of Suez. But as a veteran Europeanist he had himself to impeach first of all. On this point, see Chapter 4 below.

[29]Reports from Scarborough in *The Guardian* and *The Times*, October 6, 1967.

Mr. Brown, like a number of British opinion media, struck a less Gaullist note after the second British endeavour had been spurned, after further British attempts to appease President de Gaulle petered out. On retiring to the back benches, the ex-Foreign Secretary wrote about "an enlarged Europe as part of the Atlantic Alliance". (See *The Sunday Times*, March 17, 1968.) But what would an enlarged

the solution it is one that, smashing the Atlantic nexus into smithereens and demolishing the power structure of the West, could also cripple Britain's own security.

Veto and Aftermath

On this theme even the Prime Minister was soon to blow hot and cold. In November, 1967, Mr. Wilson had declared at the Guildhall:[30]

> "I yield to none in my support for the great institutions of the Western alliance, for continuing friendship with the government and people of the United States. But there is no future for Europe, or for Britain, if we allow American business, and American industry so to dominate the strategic growth-industries of our individual countries, that they, and not we, are able to determine the pace and direction of Europe's industrial advance, that we are left in industrial terms as the hewers of wood and drawers of water while they, because of the scale of research, development and production which they can deploy, based on the vast size of their single market, come to enjoy a growing monopoly in the production of the technological instruments of industrial advance. . . . this is the road not to partnership but to an industrial helotry, which, as night follows day, will mean a declining influence in world affairs, for all of us in Europe."

That though was too ill-assorted a compound of motivations—the political with the economic, the pro-Western and pro-American with the strictly Gaullist—to go down with the Elysée Palace. Within a fortnight the second French veto had been pronounced and the Prime Minister thereupon undertook to rebut the General's argument point by point.

It was, however, a British rebuttal of Gaullism by a sort of nascent, muted British neo-Gaullism. The President of France had reiterated his concept of the new Europe as "a counterweight to the immense power of the United States". At this, in his speech of November 29, Mr. Wilson did not demur. He seemed piqued rather by Britain's exclusion from such a counterweight. "What

---

Europe be like? What if it weakened rather than strengthened the Western alliance? These were the questions that European trends should have raised.
[30] *The Times*, November 14, 1967.

matters here", exclaimed the Prime Minister, "is not words but action."[31]

Mr. Wilson had proposed technological co-operation as a step towards British entry into the Common Market. Such a course has long been advisable whatever Britain does. But technological co-operation between Britain and European countries must not be such as would derogate from political co-operation in the West or rob Britain of her individual role. The Labour Government and the Conservative Opposition were both pro-American. Anti-American sentiment had nevertheless always lurked among those who took a Eurocentric view of Britain's destiny.[32] By the autumn of 1967, it looked as though Mr. Wilson's quarrel with President de Gaulle had been accentuated by the General's refusal to let Britain join him in his quarrel with the USA.

This was overdoing it. About the balance of payments the Prime Minister was quick to remind the French that "not all the cards are held on this side of the Atlantic". On a still graver topic he had no similar rebuke to utter. The American "domination" which President de Gaulle had denounced was not only economic and monetary but that of an alien "political system". Were there also shackles here for Britain to throw off? About these the Prime Minister kept mum.

Americans themselves have been perplexed by the economic impact of the USA on other countries. It sounded, however, like an echo from Moscow or Peking, Cairo or Belgrade when the General described the manner in which the USA had underpinned the security of Western Europe as the imposition of an alien political system. If there had been such an imposition, a Third Force might resist it. But what President de Gaulle derided as an alien political system also happened to be a power structure on which Britain still relied. To omit that point from any itemised British refutation was like the proverbial attempts to write "Hamlet" without the Prince of Denmark. It was omitted.

All the same, President de Gaulle had again suggested some other kind of trade arrangement with Britain when he shut the door upon her once more. After he met with the West German Chancellor, Dr. Kurt Kiesinger, during February, 1968, Bonn itself read too

---

[31]For reports of President de Gaulle's press conference and Mr. Wilson's reply, see *The Times*, November 28 and 30, 1967.

[32]Gelber, "The Alliance of Necessity", *op. cit.*, pp. 57, 66 and 163-184.

much into what they had recommended. But at the plenary session of the Franco-German talks, President de Gaulle even declared that, economically and politically, the new Europe may derive great advantage from British membership of the the EEC—though for such membership, according to him, Britain was still ineligible. It might be, as the Paris correspondent of *The Times* surmised, that right-wing extremism in the Bonn Republic had softened the General's attitude towards Britain.[33] Extremism on the Left, as manifest in German student disaffection, may have evoked no similar alarm if only because it was so anti-American while French student riots had not yet tarnished the Gaullist image.

Another objective, moreover, could be accomplished by a commercial arrangement between the Common Market and applicants for entry. London and Washington might be less likely to form a multilateral free trade area if Paris and Bonn offered Britain a quasi-European alternative of their own. Through it she might be lured politically from the American fold without being admitted into the new Europe itself. Not that this would be a device for reducing discrimination against American exports—a sore point in Washington, but scarcely one in Paris and Bonn. Then, too, though pending British withdrawals from East of Suez did not make Britain as Eurocentric as France, they were a move in that direction. After prolonged discord, London might thus get a pat on the back from Paris. There could also be a sop to Bonn and less docile capitals of the Common Market that would pacify them without France being dislodged from her rule of the roost.

But only Bonn had been pacified. Italy, the Benelux countries and the Common Market's own Commission thereupon proposed various methods either for skirting the French veto or for at least bringing about more co-operation with Britain. The British, however, had been holding out for full EEC membership while Scandinavian members of EFTA were less prone to do so. The maxim that half a loaf is better than no bread might still carry the day.

About one topic Paris and Bonn were in perfect agreement with London and that was the priority of politics over economics. When they conferred in February, 1968, President de Gaulle and Chancellor Kiesinger had reiterated the desire of the French and West German Governments for an enlargement of the EEC that would

[33]Dispatches from Paris in *The Times*, February 17 and 21, 1968.

make it an organised, independent and active factor in the world equilibrium.[34] Then in the Bundestag, a month later, Dr. Kiesinger added his own rider—one that should have given the free peoples of the West as much pause as any exposition by the aged oracle of the Elysée.

At the outset the Chancellor appeared to be on the side of the angels. He spoke up for the entry of Britain into the Common Market. When he referred to strong ties with the Atlantic Alliance and the USA it was not Gaullism à la Paris. His primary objective, all the same, was German reunification within a united Europe and, when he put this first, Dr. Kiesinger, as a champion of the West, sounded less than sturdy.

Not that he gibed, in the style of the Master, at the power structure of the West as an alien political system. But he did say that neither the Bonn Republic nor a united Europe could seek their future in what he called an *Imperium Atlanticum*—a concept of suzerainty for which they must create their own substitute.[35]

A Soviet imperium, with its client states, has been one thing. Quite another is that power structure which the USA has upheld—one, moreover, to which West Germany herself is so indebted. Yet Gaullist misnomers in Bonn raised few eyebrows elsewhere. Public men in Britain had themselves been dallying with Third Force notions while, from current American anxieties, these must have seemed pretty remote.

Even more remote, when Moscow prohibits it, is the reunification of the two Germanies. What Dr. Kiesinger had nevertheless divulged was the vacillating nature of Bonn's commitment to the West—with Bonn adhering as long as expedient but with an adherence that springs from no deep-seated inner conviction, as the Chancellor himself portrayed.

The fact is that West Germany still wants more from the Western alliance than she can get. It renders her secure; about reunification there is nothing her allies can do. The dream of a greater Germany may grow dim as a result. When it does, the ties between Bonn and the West could sag. Gaullism had distorted French policy; West Germany might also adopt it. A Third Force would thereupon be in the making, although unless Britain participates it must still fall short and if an Atlantic-based free trade area should be formed there

[34] *The Times*, February 17, 1968.
[35] *The Guardian*, March 12, 1968.

will be less reason than ever for Britain to participate.

Meanwhile, Britain might touch up her economic credentials. For Common Market membership, though, her political ones may still be suspect. A familiar predicament thus recurred. London still wanted to eat its cake and have it too. Despite pressure from within his own party, the Prime Minister had again refused to dissociate Britain from the American war effort in Vietnam while the US Treasury, with an eye on the health of the American dollar, had been steadfast in support of the devalued pound. Nor had the Commonwealth been liquidated. The ante-room of the Common Market was therefore as far as Britain could intrude. Her more inward-looking European policies did not find entire credence in Paris when outward-looking British interests were still so palpable.

Britain, the New Europe and US Policy

Ultimately this has also been a trial of strength between France and the USA, one that the latter could lose by default. If the USA were to lose she would have only herself to blame. London has burned no bridges to Washington; reasserting itself through a countervailing free trade area initiative, Washington can yet keep Third Force tendencies within bounds. American and British policy-makers may feel that a second Gaullist veto had merely protracted an impasse. What they have been given is a breathing-space in which to take stock afresh.

It will not be easy for them to do this. Britain would have to abandon further efforts to get into the Common Market before Washington may revise American policy. But until Washington has had second thoughts about these issues, London itself might waver. Yet American policy across the Pacific cannot be reappraised without there also being a reappraisal of American policy elsewhere. As 1967 drew to a close the US Secretary of State, Mr. Dean Rusk, indicated that "a European caucus", or a European Defence Community to which Britain should belong, could still bank on American sympathy. Then on February 7, 1968, President Johnson signed a statement that called for "a strong and democratic Western Europe as an equal partner with the United States. . . ."[36] But if

[36]Dispatches from Washington, *The Times*, December 8, 1967; and *International Herald Tribune*, February 9, 1968.

President Johnson signed this statement after meeting with M. Jean Rey, President of the EEC Commission—a body whose *modus operandi* is somewhat at variance with representative democracy as this is understood in the West.

Western Europeans wonder whether the USA will co-operate with them as an equal partner, it is no less legitimate for others to wonder whether the new Europe can be both "strong and democratic" concurrently.

A partnership there must be, but it is bound to be lopsided when disparities of power are so huge. NATO cannot eliminate them. The decentralisation of nuclear controls is still fraught with peril. It is a settlement between Russia and the West that will do most to restore the comity of the West. The West, though, cannot negotiate from strength if that strength is sapped by its own dissensions.

The global contest has entered a new stage. Here super-powers vie with each other more than ever; there, it is alleged, they might set up a Russo-American condominium. And by sitting with them at the top table the new Europe could not do much about such a double hegemony. The USA must still underwrite the security of any European union. On being enlarged, through the accession of Britain, the new Europe might only hinder its own American guarantor. Even as a single entity it could not fend for itself and only those that fend for themselves can enjoy the highest rank.

The West still has its power for peace to preserve. A Third Force will, however, detract from the power of the West when it equates American preponderance with attempts to undo that preponderance by a rival camp. Then, too, if the West dissolves into competitive regional segments, Britain could not alternate at will between Atlantic and European attachments. On being Europeanised she must not only do as the Europeans do but, sustained as she has been by a web of overseas ties, it would be out of character for her to do so.

On the other hand, nothing could be more appropriate for her than a free trade grouping with a centre of gravity that lies beyond Europe. The British people have not been told all that awaits them in the EEC and what, as claimant for a seat at the top table, awaits the new Europe among the titans of the earth. It is tragic that events should have narrowed their scope just when the dimensions of world politics have been broadening out. But a Eurocentric view of their destiny does not only go against the grain. It diverts Britain from that quest for a middle stance between primacy and decline through which, for her own sake and in the interests of the West, she may still keep an individual role.

As for the USA, the heavier her global burdens the more she needs to share them with others. By sponsoring a NAFTA arrangement she could not only avert a shift in the power structure of the West that might be so adverse. Across the length and breadth of the free world she could renew old links or forge new ones on wider fronts.

There is, nevertheless, the fear that the USA would crush other participants economically. Somehow, if she is to reap political dividends from such a project, she must also make it a viable one for them. Intervention in Vietnam has been more cruelly onerous than the USA could ever have anticipated. A free world order has still to be maintained and she is still doing the most to maintain it. The fundamentals of post-war leadership by the USA are as valid as ever. And a new economic grouping of industrial powers could help her to reaffirm them.

4 OPEN SOCIETIES AND THE OPEN SEA

If Britain ever had to choose between Europe and the open sea, according to a Churchillian dictum that President de Gaulle once quoted, she will choose the open sea. This, too, could be a rationale for British membership in an open-ended Atlantic-based free trade area that a later generation might well mull over. By the late 1960s, however, it was the French Head of State himself who, by stone-walling on British entry into the Common Market, did much to remind the British people of where, with their own political apti-tudes and seafaring traditions, they really still belong. Europeanisa-tion for Britain might be singularly inopportune, above all, if it coincided with a fresh, sinister era in the maritime phase of the struggle, at once so old and yet so new, between open and closed societies.

East of Suez: Britain Pulls Back

Nevertheless, it is to the European theatre that—under a series of cuts in government expenditure, first announced on July 18, 1967 and then, after the devaluation of the pound sterling, on January 16, 1968—Britain is henceforth to devote most of her defence efforts. Commonwealth countries that have counted upon a British presence East of Suez will no longer be able to do so. Nor can the USA. East of Suez is a region in which a British power apparatus has been a major prop of the global balance. When Britain dismantles that apparatus the USA, willy-nilly, must shoulder additional burdens across the Pacific. But when Russia is making an attempt to outflank the European sector of the global balance from the Middle East and from Europe's own encircling seas, there may also be additional burdens for Britain to bear nearer home.

So far any re-planning can still be undertaken within a NATO and Anglo-American framework. This could alter all the same. It may be that disengagement East of Suez was the price that the Wilson Government had to pay before the pacifist wing of the Labour Party would vote for other budgetary cuts. It may be that some who have taken a Eurocentric view of Britain's destiny also contrived a strategic pull-back in consonance with that view. That, at any rate, was the impression conveyed by Britain's Foreign Secretary of the day. "We have faith in this continent of ours—Europe", Mr. Brown informed Parliament. If Britain, according to him, was to exert world influence she must first sign up with the EEC, not abstain from it.[37]

No such goal is within reach. There will be a change in Britain's defence posture. But in the autonomy, and therefore in the status of the UK, there can be no similar change as yet. The Prime Minister explained that Britain will "retain a general capability based in Europe—including the UK—which can be deployed overseas as, in our judgement, circumstances demand, including support for UN operations".[38] Britain's role may now be more restricted geographically. It remains an individual one and it will have to remain that way if Britain is to retain "a general capability" of her own. As long as a British defence posture is as flexible as that which the Government visualised it will, though based in Europe, be thoroughly incompatible with Britain's outright Europeanisation. With membership of a loose free trade grouping it would not be incompatible at all.

Could a permanent British presence East of Suez ever be restored? The Conservative Opposition declared that they will again try to maintain one if they get the chance. The Labour Government expressed doubt that this would be practicable.[39] It would indeed be difficult, after the British power apparatus is liquidated East of Suez, for Britain again to intervene on a large scale beyond the European theatre. The Soviet Union might rule the air and sea routes of the Middle East while, for circumnavigating Africa, even the ports of South Africa may be closed to the ships of the Royal Navy. Nor would there be means of supply on the spot when British mobile, amphibious forces arrive. As a formula for British action, nonetheless, "general capability" could still pass muster. As such, it is one that Washington, as well as London, should explore.

A lesser role for Britain is better than no individual British role at all. Over this issue, however, Opposition indictments of the Govern-

[37]*Hansard*, Vol. 757, No. 45, January 24, 1968, cc. 434-38.
[38]*Hansard*, Vol. 756, No. 39, January 16, 1968, c. 1581.
[39]*Hansard*, Vol. 756, No. 40, January 17, 1968, c. 1821. *Ibid.*, Vol. 756, No. 41, January 18, 1968, cc. 1990 and 2078. *Ibid.*, Vol. 757, No. 45, January 24, 1968, c. 428. *Ibid.*, January 25, 1958, cc. 633-634.

ment rang hollow. They might differ over ways and means. But it was a Conservative objective that, *au fond*, Labour Ministers were carrying out. Even when cuts had to be made in public expenditure, the Opposition front bench did not ask for the cancellation of Anglo-French projects like Concorde—a supersonic aircraft, more costly than the British presence East of Suez—or the Channel tunnel. For Gaullist France would never have let Britain into the Common Market if these projects were cancelled. The fulfilment of that quest would be worse than its non-fulfilment. But for its non-fulfilment the price already has been exorbitant.

During an ensuing debate there was one moment of truth. "In Europe", said Sir Alec Douglas-Home on behalf of the Conservative Party, "the Government's aims are reasonably defined. They are, of course, inherited policies; they are not their own."[40] The political consequences of those aims have never been reasonably defined. That Labour Ministers inherited them from Conservative predecessors is, all the same, beyond dispute. The Opposition tried to draw a tenable line between the Government's bid for entry into the Common Market and Britain's recessional from East of Suez. No such line could be drawn. In a broadcast to the Australian people, Mr. Harold Macmillan, as a former British Prime Minister, lashed out at the British withdrawals. Mr. Heath, who had deputed for him when Britain first negotiated for entry into the Common Market, was as full of reproaches.[41] Yet these two public men were the very ones who had done most to foster the Europeanisation of Britain before the Labour Party even held office. The chickens have been coming home to roost but it is to a bipartisan roost that they have been coming.

Britain's Role and American Interests

About all this one point should be made. Britain still has leeway. She might now concentrate strategically on the European theatre. She has not been Europeanised politically. Power in the West, as seen from Washington as well as London, is again being redistri-

---

[40]*Hansard*, Vol. 757, No. 45, January 24, 1968, c. 417.

[41]For Mr. Macmillan's broadcast, see *The Times*, March 4, 1968, and for Mr. Heath's speech see *Hansard*, Vol. 760, No. 74, March 5, 1968, cc. 235-253.

Although President de Gaulle had been flouting the comity of the West on a number of fronts, Mr. Heath seemed to admire French policy for moving "into the outer world again".

buted. No structural damage, despite a damaging change in strategic emphasis, has been done as yet.

Certainly it is not too late for the USA to stop the rot—if, that is, she feels an even more drastic British drop-out should be averted. And it is through a NAFTA arrangement that she could do this.

What has been transpiring in Washington and London is plain enough. Each has been trying to ride two horses at once. Not everybody in Britain that has taken a Eurocentric view of her destiny has been a last-ditch, hyper-actuated Europeaniser; they merely have assumed that Britain could be Europeanised without having to sacrifice an individual role and, with it, such vehicles as the Commonwealth and Anglo-American friendship. Nor should American policymakers have been astonished by impending British withdrawals from East of Suez. These steps have always been among the strategic corollaries to that merger between Britain and the new Europe which, for so many years, Washington itself has urged with so much ardour.

In July, 1967, President Johnson had expressed the hope that Britain would still maintain her position in the Indo-Pacific theatre. If the USA did not find utility in an individual British role, the President could not have spoken as he did. Nor would there have been so much discomfiture at lower levels when in January, 1968, the Government announced that British withdrawals from East of Suez would be even speedier and more complete. As an ally, nevertheless, Britain could not be let go. Over Vietnam there had been no misunderstanding. On the Prime Minister's next visit to Washington, President Johnson told Mr. Wilson that the American people were still backing Britain.[42]

This should not have been surprising. A major British presence East of Suez may vanish beyond recall. But in the European theatre itself an individual British role will still serve other, inter-related American interests. The case for the perpetuation of that role is as cogent as ever. Rather than stifle it, a multilateral free trade area would leave it unencumbered and in play.

Even now, moreover, there can still be a degree of minor strategic co-operation between the USA and Britain within a Commonwealth set-up East of Suez. This might be oblique first of all. In forging a

[42]Dispatches from Washington, *International Herald Tribune*, July 19, 1967; *The Guardian*, February 10, 1968.

joint air defence system, Australia, New Zealand and Malaysia will have assistance from Britain if they collaborate with Singapore to keep that island's great naval port, together with the Malacca Straits, within the ambit of the West. Nor could there be a regional showdown without the USA, shunning fresh burdens in the Orient as she may, supporting this common effort—with the US Navy making use of the Singapore naval base. Beyond the South East Asia Treaty Organisation (SEATO) there may be no fresh American security pledges on the Asian mainland. The USA, nevertheless, also has her compact with Australia and New Zealand and that is more solid than ever. Malaysia and Indonesia have buried the hatchet. Eventually the new economic Association of South-East Asian Nations (ASEAN) might even seek a neutralisation of South-East Asia with Communist China as one of its guarantors. But if members of ASEAN (Malaysia and Singapore together with Indonesia, Thailand and the Philippines) could thus trust Peking the entire region would be comparatively secure.

This is the point that must be considered when there is talk about an equilibrium for East Asia, South-East Asia and South Asia organised by the countries of the region themselves. Western Europe, after all, is backed by North America. Still, if Japan, India and Australia had nuclear weapons of their own, they might offset the local nuclear supremacy of China. Japan, however, is not ready for that step psychologically, while it might be more of a financial load than India and Australia can bear. The treaty against the spread of nuclear weapons has had a cool reception. Washington, Moscow and London have made joint proposals about guarantees for the security of some Asian countries. Meanwhile, it is the US Navy that keeps the length and breadth of the Pacific under surveillance. It has its patrol in the Persian Gulf. An American naval force in the Indian Ocean is no longer inconceivable.

There, too, Britain still has a number of atolls or islands and one or more of these could be the site of a conjoint undertaking between London and Washington. In traversing that theatre, Polaris submarines and other American warships may need a centre for supplies, refuelling and communications. An Anglo-American staging post in the Indian Ocean could have a dual convenience. First, it might furnish a link between the Asian mainland and strategic facilities which Australia has been putting at the disposal of her American ally. Secondly, it could meet a hazard to regional security if the Cairo-Moscow axis bars the air-space of the Middle East to overflights by the military aircraft of the West.[43] An alternative route may yet have to be mapped out across or around Africa. It is through an Anglo-American staging post on a British foothold in the Indian Ocean that this could be done.

India herself might still be a trifle schizophrenic about such an enterprise. Under Nehru she had revelled in a pre-Gaullist Gaullism of her own: a self-righteous creed of non-alignment that was more averse to the West than to the East. Nowadays, as her feud with Pakistan over Kashmir simmers on, India also has to cope with a threat from China. What would give her relief is an accord between Russia and the West over the *status quo* in East, South-East and South Asia. Until there is one, she may be more apt to placate Moscow than welcome defence activities by the West in her own vicinity.

On the other hand, India never knows when she may have to appeal, as she contemplated doing in 1962 and 1965, for Anglo-American air cover during a Chinese scare. She has been loath to sign the new treaty against the spread of nuclear weapons without a guarantee by the chief nuclear powers, East and West, against Chinese nuclear blackmail. It is through a few minute British possessions in the Indo-Pacific theatre that the USA, for one, could expedite the enforcement of any American guarantee. On both sides of the Atlantic there are those, rendered secure by American preponderance, who will vociferate against measures taken anywhere to implement American power. But if the South Asian sector of the global balance is turned against the West, India would face ruin.

The Commonwealth

What will the Commonwealth be like after the British disengagement East of Suez? It is a group of nations that could never have emerged if the seas had not been kept open for open societies. Today among most of its Afro-Asian members, as among members of the UN, few live up to a heritage of law and public life that the British passed on. Even so, imponderables of the Commonwealth have not only conserved ties with the West. They have made the political standards of open societies those towards which a number of less open ones may still aspire. Intangibles such as these cannot

[43]Problems raised for the free world by the Cairo-Moscow axis will be sketched below.

figure on a chart of statistics. Sceptics may ridicule them. But they still do count between the English-speaking peoples. It is for the latter to make the most of them elsewhere.

The Commonwealth had nevertheless lost much of its cohesion before Britain, renouncing a world-wide role, adopted an individual one within narrower Occidental limits. There would not be any-thing left if a British pivot let itself be converted into an outer island province of a European union. As things are, the Commonwealth can still endure—if, that is, British and overseas partners desire it to do so. What may change, with the contraction of British power, is the underlying pattern of that entity. Some Canadians have wondered for years whether, with equality of status between members, Britain's traditional function as the main funnel for Commonwealth affairs has not been outmoded; whether members must have a British clearing-house to keep in touch with each other. Perhaps they can do without one. If they can, a polycentric Common-wealth is what will have to persevere if the Commonwealth is to persevere at all.

Defence and Anglo-American Co-operation

Then from the standpoint of defence, there is the future of Anglo-American friendship itself. The British withdrawal from East of Suez has not been the first occasion when some—the wish often being father to the thought—have registered its demise. But the Anglo-American factor is not only rooted in history. Until Britain is Europeanised it can still be reactivated as necessity ordains. As a key ally Britain does not rank as high as she once did. Her residual power may still be relied upon even under altered circumstances. Britain is now going to concentrate, strategically, on the European theatre. But politically she is not yet of the new Europe in any Third Force sense. Among current trends that is a primordial fact on which the USA, as leader of the West, may capitalise more than she herself yet comprehends.

It is what Britain may contribute to a European Third Force which would either make one feasible or endow the new Europe with the capacity to undo the power structure of the West. Against that danger, however, the USA can sponsor the formation of an Atlantic free trade area—one by which no enlarged, semi-neutralist aberration, within or beyond the Western alliance, would get command of British defence resources.

These resources have been described in part by the Defence Correspondent of *The Times*:[44]

"Even after the cuts we will still be spending twice as much on defence as Italy, and about a quarter as much again as either France or Germany. We will have more and better aircraft, over a wider range of capability and fire power—with a front line force of about 500 compared with about 400 for the others.

Our ability to use these, and any other forces outside Europe, will be greater than any of our neighbours', since we have tanker and transport aircraft and naval logistics on a scale not remotely contemplated by the others.

Our navy will outnumber Germany's by four to one, Italy's three to one, and France's nearly two to one. We will have at least 10 nuclear submarines; France will have four; the rest of Europe none. The army, though only half the size of the others in Europe, is acknowledged to be the best equipped, and for its size certainly the most effective in political as well as military terms."

Lacking from that survey, all the same, was any mention of aircraft carriers which would enable British aircraft to operate at sea. France has two. But with the Fifth Republic's virtual defection from the Western alliance these must be eliminated from strategic planning for the West. If most British aircraft carriers are phased out, the Royal Navy will have to get air cover from the US Navy. Not that there is anything very novel about this. NATO has depended on the USA for tactical atomic weapons and, in long-range aircraft, Britain will eventually have to depend on her for conventional strike and reconnaissance. There will simply have to be more of such interdependence in weapons when, within European waters, Britain joins the USA and others to keep open the open seas.

In other respects Mr. Denis Healey, Britain's Defence Secretary, addressing Parliament, could still claim much for the defence resources of Britain. The British Army, though smaller than others, is the only full-time professional one in the West, while the Chieftain is the most powerful of all tanks. When Britain has withdrawn entirely from East of Suez, the Royal Navy, among the navies of the West, will still be second in size and striking power to the US

[44]Charles Douglas-Home, "New Strategy for Defence", *The Times*, January 24, 1968.

Navy. As never before, moreover, NATO now has its southern flank to reinforce.[45]

By May, 1968, there could be an announcement of specific plans for the European redeployment of British defence resources. These will be twofold. NATO is having assigned to it a mobile British task force stationed at home but with its own air transport and an amphibious British force stationed in the Mediterranean and other European waters. Flexible response has superseded massive retaliation in NATO doctrine. The new British defence posture will tally with it.

Britain's residual capacity is thus not to be scoffed at. The question for Washington, as well as for London, is how it will be employed. The USA has felt that Western Europe should do more to stand on its own feet. Now that she may have to fill the gap left by the British withdrawals from East of Suez, she might curtail somewhat the American presence in the European theatre. But if an enlarged Europe were anti-American in orientation, Western Europe itself—with American leadership undercut—would be less secure.

The course Washington should chart seems plain. Britain will have to retain an individual role if she is to withhold British power from a European Third Force. As long as British power is still available for co-operation with the USA in the European theatre, there will be less to distract America when she must do more in other menaced theatres. It is a policy for keeping British power available that Washington should now pursue.

There is another salient reason for ensuring that nothing be done to preclude Anglo-American co-operation in the defence of the European theatre. France's defection from NATO enhanced the status of the West Germans. A shrinkage of the US presence in Europe would boost it still further.

None of this will smooth the West's path towards a settlement with Moscow. Still less would a *détente* with Russia be possible if the Bonn Republic shared in the control of tactical nuclear weapons, although the use of such weapons enters into NATO plans. One conclusion will be evident. The USA must still work with Britain if she is to exercise freedom of manoeuvre in any global redeployment and, too, in her overall diplomacy if a settlement with Russia

[45]*Hansard*, Vol. 757, No. 46, January 25, 1968, cc. 624-29.

is ever tackled. But the British cannot work with the USA unless they also exercise freedom of manoeuvre and some foresight about this is what the European policy of the USA now requires.

As long as the USA must take the lead in maintaining a global balance, she cannot detach herself or let herself be detached from the European sector of that balance. She must therefore beware of the extent to which the British withdrawal from East of Suez merely grooms the UK for all-out participation in the kind of Europe that would be inimical to American interests. It is a new free trade grouping of industrial nations, one that will provide Britain with an alternative to joining the EEC, which might give the USA the sort of reassurance she must have about the continent of Europe when she is so fully pre-occupied with other global fronts.

The security of Western Europe cannot be envisaged apart from the security of the maritime approaches to it. On distant sectors Britain will now do little. In the European theatre itself, nevertheless, there is, with her naval power, more for her to do than ever.

The *Pax Britannica* left a lasting impress when it furnished a shelter behind which great overseas democracies came of age and great overseas dependencies girded their loins against Britain herself. When the primacy of the West shifted across the Atlantic it was still the English-speaking peoples who kept the sea lanes open. A free trade area that is widely dispersed must have free access by sea to the far corners of the earth. As a small highly industrialised island that lives by trade, Britain must still want to do all she can to ensure such access. Industrial nations are not the only ones that have a stake in this. Unless the sea lanes are kept open, under-developed countries will also be cut off from the outer world. But there, too, a serious problem has arisen.

NATO's Southern Flank

The global contest between Russia and the West has a new locale. That new locale is the open sea. Such has been the risk of nuclear confrontation with the USA that, since the early 1960's, Western Europe and the Western Hemisphere have been off-bounds for major Soviet ventures. Russia may nonetheless try to outflank free societies by defying their capacity to keep open the open seas—by acquiring leverage of one sort or another for rending their historic maritime life-lines.

Hitherto the southern flank of NATO had not been deemed a

vulnerable one. But so big has been the increase in Russian sea-power that the West will now have to be more alert than ever from the Baltic and the Western Mediterranean to the waters of the Middle East and the Indo-Pacific theatre. It is through the further-ance of wider global objectives, to boot, that Soviet patronage of Arab states may also pay off.

What could not be as lucrative was the *sacro egoismo* of Gaullist France. For President de Gaulle, balked by American leadership and mortified by Anglo-American friendship, was pro-Russian and pro-Arab at a juncture when, for the defence of sea as well as land frontiers, France and the Western alliance are again so inter-dependent.

The Western Mediterranean is not a zone upon which Russia has traditionally fixed an expansionist eye but, after Soviet penetration of the Eastern Mediterranean, she may do so. Since the days of the Truman Doctrine the US Sixth Fleet has been predominant through-out the Mediterranean and, in order to supplement its ceaseless vigil, NATO has mustered an inter-allied destroyer squadron—one that will be deployed permanently in the Atlantic both as a standby and as a model for a counterpart NATO force in the Mediterranean. Between the Atlantic and the Mediterranean, moreover, the Western alliance has always had Gibraltar at its disposal. After the inhabi-tants of that famous Rock have voted to stay under the British flag there should not be any change. But now—unless Britain retrocedes Gibraltar to Spain—Madrid, despite its accord with Washington, may bar warships of the American fleet from Spanish ports. Yet Spain herself could be less secure when she thus wreaks her malice on the USA. Still worse has been the self-destructive behaviour of the French.

France also has a Mediterranean frontier to defend. Under the Evian Agreement of March, 1962, she did not have to cede her Algerian naval base at Mers-el-Kebir until 1977. But it has already been handed over. Russia is the second among naval powers and paymaster of the Arab cause. She can procure the use of Mers-el-Kebir even if its sovereign rights remain with Algeria. This may not occur at once. Soon, nevertheless, the Russians might steal a march on the West in the Western Mediterranean. And if they do that, France will have only herself to thank.[46]

[46]Britain, according to President de Gaulle, could not be deemed genuinely "European" as long as she holds on to such remnants of a British presence in the

What should perturb the West even more is the accelerating pace of Third Force tendencies in all French military dispositions. Though France has had 70,000 troops stationed in West Germany, these may not always serve the Western alliance; nor has the Bonn Republic itself been as candid with the French as it ought to have been. Typical of what was going on, when the living standards of French workers and farmers have been so low, were proposals for a French inter-continental missile system and a French orbital bomb. For now France is to be prepared *à tous azimuts*—at all points of the compass. As a twentieth century throwback to the strategy of Louis XIV and Marshal Vauban, the French General Staff have been drawing up plans for the defence of France, not only against the adversaries of the West but, like some latter-day Ishmaelite, against her own allies. Such wilful neutralism could be a European Third Force in embryo. It is a gauge no less of French political immaturity. For public disapprobation has been scant and none of the French High Command has resigned.

In a Popular Front, moreover, Communist ministers would never let France resume her ties with NATO. She may spend less on arms. Against the West she would still be in revolt.

Little has been said about this in British opinion media. Among some there is the belief that Third Force tendencies will cease when, as President de Gaulle dismounts from the saddle, Britain gains admission to the Common Market. Among others, Third Force tendencies are apparently deemed proper when Britain herself can direct them.

And these are issues that cry out for reassessment by the USA herself. It was President de Gaulle who prolonged Britain's vocation as a bastion of the West by debarring her from the Common Market. But she must also withhold her weight from the new Europe if, after the General has departed, it is not to extend his own Third Force aims. It is through a wider, looser trade grouping that the USA, by offering Britain an alternative to Europeanisation, might yet counter a larger post-Gaullist Gaullism. Not that Gaullist irrationalities were the same as the self-defeating ineptitude which culminated in Vichy—in a regime against which General de Gaulle

---

Mediterranean as Libya, Cyprus, Malta and Gibraltar (See C. L. Sulzberger, *International Herald Tribune*, February 2, 1968). And that was news from Paris which Moscow, as well as Madrid, as the General must have realised, should have been gratified to get.

himself, from exile in Britain, first earned renown. They were at variance though with the politico-strategic realities of the age. France herself can bicker with the West only because she has its power structure to keep her safe. Meanwhile, Russian naval moves in the Mediterranean might affect the European sector of the global balance. In addition, Soviet moves of another kind, with the Middle East as their centre, may now alter the picture East of Suez.

Middle East and Global Contest

Control of the Middle East, that crossroads of three continents, has long been a key to the control of Europe. Today, however, when major contests have global dimensions, it might furnish access to even more distant regions. During her Victorian zenith, it was Britain that excluded the Russians from the Middle East and thus from an Indo-Pacific theatre in which her Indian Empire and other British dependencies were situated. Under President Truman the USA took Britain's place in the Mediterranean without abasing Britain herself. But President Eisenhower and John Foster Dulles must have made the Kremlin exult when, shaking the Western alliance, they reinstated Colonel Nasser. Americans may rue the day that the USA thus gave the Cairo-Moscow axis a new lease of life. For it is in the very regions from which Britain has been retiring that Russia, with ten-league boots, has been striding forward.

Soviet policy in the Middle East must be distinguished from the action Moscow has been taking in East, South-East and South Asia. When Russia poured arms and supplies into North Vietnam, she was not only attempting to match the support South Vietnam gets from the USA. She was also trying to deny China a lien on North Vietnam and the entire region. Similarly, in South Asia, Delhi has looked to Moscow as well as to Washington and London whenever there has been a flare-up in the chronic frontier strife on the Himalayas between China and India. Yet when Mr. Kosygin mediated between India and Pakistan in 1966, he had Russian ambitions in the Middle East as a goad. The last German Emperor, William II, preened himself on being the Protector of Islam and the Kremlin might do the same. (Moslem wards overlooking how badly religion fares in the Soviet Union while the Soviet Union overlooks the severity with which some Moslem peoples treat native Communists.)

Moscow thus has new friends in Rawalpindi as well as old ones in

Delhi to cultivate while the Pakistani capital itself cultivates both Peking and Moscow. Pakistan wants to wrest Kashmir from India. Like the USA and Britain, the Soviet Union is against any change in the territorial *status quo* of South Asia that China may impose. In the Arab world, however, the Chinese rivals of the USSR are still a *quantité négligeable*: there Russia and the West are competing more than ever. In the Middle East it is the *status quo* that the Cairo-Moscow axis has been trying to subvert.

Russia did not lose out either when the Israelis again trounced the Egyptians during the Six Days War of 1967. For Egypt is even more beholden to her and, too, as the British pull back, the gates to the southern half of the Arabian Peninsula stand ajar. Before the Egyptian fiasco in the Yemen, Cairo might have had a stepping-stone to the conquest of oil-rich territories on the Persian Gulf. Now the Soviet Union itself can supplant her. Not only may Russia draw oil from the oil principalities of the Persian Gulf for her own expanding industries. A political stranglehold on the region would also give her one on oil supplies for Britain, most of Western Europe and Japan.

There are other politico-strategic prizes in the region towards which Russia might gaze. She is now entrenched at the Red Sea port of Hodeida and in Somalia, across the Red Sea, she has an African foothold that may grow. Britain and Egypt, moreover, had scarcely withdrawn from the southern half of the Arabian peninsula before the Soviet Union took under its wing both the Republican faction in the Yemen and the new Republic of South Yemen. Not that this could be a success at once. But the Arab lands to which Moscow has ministered are the ones with empty coffers and today South Yemen is more impoverished than most.

For so militant a crusader against imperialism as Russia, here is empire-building in the grand style. South Yemen contains the former British naval base and airport of Aden. From there Russia would not only be able to police traffic through the Suez Canal, the Persian Gulf and the Gulf of Aqaba. She would also have broken through to the Indo-Pacific theatre at last.

As for the Israelis, they must want to banish any danger that, from scattered islands at the mouth of the Red Sea, the Yemen will menace traffic to and from the Gulf of Aqaba. In the port of Eilat, Israel has a door of her own, through the Indian Ocean, to Africa and the rest of Asia. But as Russia gets Aden into her clutches she will have acquired an outlet of quite another sort. For that is where Soviet policy in the Middle East and Soviet aspirations in the Indo-Pacific theatre might intersect.

The Six Days War may thus have repercussions that will be felt far beyond the Middle East. During the Suez crisis of 1956-57 Egypt could still hold the West to ransom by closing the Suez Canal. The use of giant oil tankers which circumnavigate the Cape of Good Hope has since been limiting Egypt's ability to do that. Shortly, too, oil from Iran will flow through an Israeli pipeline from Eilat, on the Gulf of Aqaba, to Ashdod on the Mediterranean. Egypt may thereupon vie with Israel by building an oil pipeline of her own, parallel with the Suez Canal, from Suez to Alexandria. The longer route for ordinary commercial traffic between the Occident and the Orient has, nevertheless, added to other shipping costs, something a straitened British economy can ill afford.

Britain, moreover, has had an agreement with South Africa under which British naval vessels could be berthed and fuelled at the Simonstown base or use other South African ports. After the Wilson Government, as a reprimand for white racism in South Africa, renewed their embargo on the sale of arms for defence to the Republic it may be that this agreement will be disregarded.

Washington, on the other hand, will have noticed how supplies to North Vietnam from the Soviet Union that did not go by rail across Chinese territory have also had to be shipped around Africa— a long haul Russia did not anticipate when she equipped Egypt for another assault on Israel. The US Administration will also have noticed that as long as the Suez Canal is bottled up, the USSR cannot make the most of any naval facilities she acquires on the Red Sea and perhaps, at a later date, on the Indian Ocean at Aden. Even Siberia might be less secure. Men and arms for Soviet East Asia could best move through the Suez Canal if a Chinese foe should ever bomb the trans-Siberian railway.

The Suez Canal may be blocked as long as Israel, by her occupation of the Sinai Peninsula, holds its left bank. Until Egypt consents to the use of that maritime artery by Israeli shipping—until, that is, there is a peace treaty between Cairo and Jerusalem—Israel will not voluntarily evacuate the Sinai Peninsula. President Eisenhower and John Foster Dulles, with Dag Hammarskjold, as UN Secretary-General, to assist them, were in a hurry to have the Suez Canal cleared. President Johnson and Mr. Rusk were less impatient.

Never have world politics been so intricate. And here again, when there is a global balance to maintain, issues that are seemingly unconnected may in fact be connected profoundly. Britain, the USA and Canada, to cite another instance, will not go along with South Africa when, under her *apartheid* policies, she discriminates against Africans; that country may therefore have to purchase arms for defence from France. Unlike France, though, the South African Republic has been against the ascendancy of the Cairo-Moscow axis in the Middle East and for the preponderance of the West everywhere else.[47]

More immediate is the pit that some countries of South Asia have dug for themselves. Economies as underdeveloped as those of India and Pakistan could do without the additional costs of transit round the Cape. But they had pandered to that sabre-rattling by Egypt which was to bring about the second closure of the Suez Canal. Though Asian countries detest *apartheid* they must, as during the Suez episode of 1956-57, again use South African ports—a privilege which South Africa, so as to avert a world-wide economic depression on which Communism might batten, grants them once more. South Africa would only play into the hands of Russia if she denied the use of port facilities to her non-Soviet opponents. And this is important if, ensconced in Aden, the Red Fleet should ever assail Western shipping round the Cape.

It is, nevertheless, a strange quirk of fortune that two African countries at odds with the West should be seated at two essential points of oceanic contact—Mediterranean and Indo-Pacific, Indo-Pacific and South Atlantic—between open societies. In no other respect, of course, can those two countries be bracketed together. Egypt's concept of world order is, for the West, a malign one. It is not South Africa, however, that is against the West; rather, it is the West that is against South Africa. But above all, in keeping open the open seas, her stake and that of open societies is the same.

Soviet Diplomacy and Soviet Naval Expansion

In the meantime, Soviet diplomacy is pushing forward at another extremity of the Indo-Pacific theatre—on its Asian land approaches.

[47]Anomalous, too, would be the monetary aspect of a *rapprochement* between France and South Africa as well as between France and the Soviet Union. As major gold producers, South Africa and the Soviet Union had much to gain from the Gaullist crusade against the American dollar and the British pound.

The West has had a northern tier of three Islamic countries, namely Turkey, Iran and Pakistan, as a buffer to encroachments from the north. With these the Russians have been mending fences and yet they play no favourites. In the Indo-Pacific theatre the USSR also extends its influence through naval co-operation with India. Delhi's purchase of four Russian submarines may be followed by Soviet assistance when India builds naval bases against Pakistan and China. Nor would a breakthrough at Aden hamper Russia in giving such assistance. But what in turn has preceded all these developments is the outburst of Russian naval activity on the other side of the Suez Canal, in the Mediterranean.

Although Russia now has a naval base on the White Sea she has been restricted by her land-locked Eurasian confines to warm-water ports. Under the Montreux Treaty of 1936, Russia must notify Turkey in advance when Soviet warships use the Straits between the Black Sea and the Mediterranean. But, as the main outpost of NATO in the Eastern Mediterranean, Turkey has been somewhat restive—though she may be less so when, under a new treaty, US bases and American personnel yield the privileged status they have had. The despatch of a Red Fleet to the Mediterranean does more than strengthen Russian diplomacy in the Middle East. From that inland sea which is the Mediterranean, the open sea may lay open as never before to Russian sea-power.

In the Mediterranean the Soviet Union has long made its presence felt. For a number of years, Russian vessels have dogged and even interfered with ships of the American Sixth Fleet. Nor is it unlikely that tactics as daring as these did much to embolden Egypt when, in the spring of 1967, she again took to the warpath against Israel. Now, as recompense for Russian support, the Soviet Navy has obtained at Alexandria and Port Said in Egypt and at Latakia in Syria the kind of naval facilities that the American Sixth Fleet has been getting from Spain, France, and NATO allies elsewhere in the Mediterranean.[48]

These though are not trends which all Soviet-oriented peoples can applaud. Yugoslavia would still be one of Moscow's client states if, as a Mediterranean country, she did not come within the geographic ambit of the West. While she also has been one of Egypt's mentors, she may be as worried as NATO itself by the

---

[48]Moscow would also like Cairo to grant land facilities to the Russian Air Force.

Russian naval presence in the Mediterranean. NATO, on the other hand, would be handicapped if Malta turned neutralist and the Soviet Fleet thus gained access to Maltese naval facilities. That island is a key to communications between the Western and Eastern Mediterranean and to the regional maritime strategy of the West. Britain, the USA and NATO, with the American Sixth Fleet patrolling the Mediterranean and the Royal Navy about to be concentrated in European waters, cannot neglect Malta.

The expansion of Russian sea-power, as part of a wider design, may thus impinge on the global interests of the West at a number of highly sensitive points. In two world wars the Germans tried to clinch victory by employing submarines that would sink all vessels transporting supplies and troops from North America to Western Europe; by splitting open societies from each other. Moreover, when Russia herself reeled back under the Nazi onslaught, Britain and the USA braved German undersea warfare and brought succour at a terrible cost in men, shipping and supplies. But the Soviet Union has now taken a leaf out of the German book. Today it can deploy a larger number of submarines than the West.

Then, too, in the absence of base facilities, navies can now be more self-sufficient. The US Navy has its fleet trains and Britain has her Royal Fleet Auxiliaries. The Russians have tankers and tenders with which to keep at sea, far from home, the vast Soviet array of oceanographic ships, fishing fleets and merchant marine—all with a para-military use—as well as outright men-of-war. There may even be landings by a Soviet marine corps.

Russia is also branching out in naval air-power. She will soon have three helicopter assault carriers for use in more distant corners of the earth. During the autumn of 1967, moreover, the reverberations were enormous when an Egyptian patrol boat, armed with Soviet missiles, out-gunned an Israeli destroyer. Never before had a warship been sunk by surface-to-surface missiles fired from another vessel. Hitherto it was only with a torpedo that a vessel of lower tonnage had destroyed a warship. The Soviet Union has supplied nearly forty of these missile-launching ships to Arab countries on the Mediterranean.[49]

To match them the Israelis have been building similar patrol boats and so have the Americans. Politically the threat which such

[49]*Revue de Défense Nationale*, Paris, January, 1968, quoted in *The Guardian*, December 29, 1967.

weapons pose is a complicated one. The West could also be menaced at sea if lesser antagonists fought "wars of liberation" with small Russian missile-launching ships. The global balance maintains peace as super-powers shrink from a head-on clash in the nuclear and conventional spheres. But some of its protégés could help the Soviet Union outflank the West if, like Egypt, they learn to handle the latest weapons. Here again, though, Russia could outsmart herself. For there can be retaliation in kind or from the air when, as now, Soviet targets are so dispersed. If, in addition, China has protégés with which to play that same game, it is Russian vessels that could bear the brunt.

About their resurgent naval power the Russians have been less than reticent. Not since the days of German maritime aspirations under Emperor William II has a rival of the West been so assiduous in preparedness at sea. During the Cuban missile crisis of October 1962, it was a display of US naval power that constrained Russian ships to turn back. They were not likely to invite a repeat performance. Within five years the Commander-in-Chief of the Soviet Navy, Admiral Sergei Gorshkov, could boast that the West no longer claims undivided supremacy at sea.

Strategic mobility, according to Admiral Vladimir Kasatonov, the Deputy Chief, is what the Kremlin is after. Qualitatively the Soviet Union has acquired a new strategic function by mustering nuclear fire-power in waters that were once the undisputed preserve of the "imperialists"—of Britain and the USA together with France. Out of its nuclear missile fleet, Admiral Kasatonov has also observed, Russia has developed a strike force that is not only global but self-contained.[50]

America, Britain and Russia's Challenge at Sea

For the West this is a state of affairs that could transform the world scene. It cannot demur when Russia shows the flag in regions where it has long been pre-eminent. But neither would the message thus imparted be an innocuous one. Ever since World War II the West has maintained a global balance from fulcra that are maritime as well as territorial. Now Russia, so formidable as a Eurasian power on land, has been generating a capacity—like that which Britain and the USA have had—to intervene at will on other world fronts.

[50] *The Times* and *The Guardian*, July 31, 1967.

That raises two possibilities. On the one hand, if the cold war is renewed, so may undertakings like the Soviet effort to establish missile sites in Cuba—though now with less risk of a climbdown. On the other hand, if Russia and the West should ever negotiate a settlement, the bargain Moscow may attempt to drive in the 1970's might be harder than any it could have driven in the 1960's. Overall deterrents will still rule out war. But it may be less easy for the West to shape or reshape the peace.

Such, too, are politico-strategic realities with which the English-speaking peoples must conjure when they examine prospects for a free trade grouping that (with others) Britain, the USA and Canada ought to set going. A choice between Europe and the open sea is not one that Britain can make. In British calculations there must be room for both. They cannot, moreover, overlook the threat that open societies now face on the open seas. It is no hour therefore for Britain, of all countries, to lock herself in as a mere adjunct of continental land-power; to foreclose totally on her own overseas affiliations; to constrict the radius of British action irretrievably. The financial strain of these years should pass away. But the British people will frustrate themselves irremediably if, as during the 1930's, they again misjudge their own interests.

For Britain, with one foot in Europe, with the other foot beyond it, resiliency is all. Through a middle stance, between primacy and decline, she can still do much. Only by retaining an individual role can she do it. Only in a multilateral free trade area, projected by Atlantic countries and sustained as it must be by the open sea, can she play a part that is economically, politically and strategically congenial.

For the USA, too, such a new trade initiative could be more of a boon than she yet perceives. If the EEC is enlarged, its Third Force propensities might undermine the power structure of the West. It cannot be enlarged unduly if an Atlantic free trade area precludes the Europeanisation of Britain. But the USA also has a challenge to meet on the open sea and a loose combine between most open societies—economic in substance, maritime in form—will range them with her. A closed society, prowling the oceans, may try to interpose itself between them; a realignment of major trading nations can do a good deal to bind them together. Britain, like Barkis in "David Copperfield", must be willin' to join one. She may be willin' if, in a more nubile mood, the USA again takes the lead.

5 ACROSS THE PACIFIC

One canard about the NAFTA idea must be scotched at once. It
has not been conceived as a rich man's club, a cabal of opulent,
developed economies against the poor and underdeveloped. That
is the kind of stigma that might be fixed upon it by some, on both
sides of the Atlantic, who have either taken a Eurocentric view of
Britain's destiny or who cannot discard a Eurocentric view of the
free world as a whole. Yet in such a project there would be much of
which developing countries could approve.

Developing Countries and NAFTA

British membership of the EEC would have spelled the end of
Commonwealth tariff preferences. These must also disappear, after
an interval, if Britain, Canada, Australia and New Zealand join a
multilateral free trade area. But that grouping will not shelve the
well-being of developing countries, Commonwealth and others. It
is by working together, and not by drifting apart, that industrial
nations might devise economic opportunities for others less
developed.

Through collaboration in a broad free trade area the developed
countries can furnish developing countries with preferential access
to their markets. With the prospect of worthwhile outlets for their
infant industries, the developing countries, in turn, will have no
excuse for engaging in uneconomic import substitution. Low-cost
imports should present less of a problem to developed countries
when adjustments are in any case being made to meet increased
competition within the free trade area. The ensuing expansion of
international trade should brighten the financial outlook and leave
industrial nations with more funds to allot for development aid.[51]

A poser in semantics recurs. The proposed free trade grouping
should extend beyond the geographic limits of the Atlantic community. But there are not only specific reasons, politico-strategic
as well as economic, for Britain and the USA to take the first steps

[51]See David Wall, "The Third World Challenge: Preferences for Development"
(The Atlantic Trade Study, London, January, 1968).

towards the formation of such a project. Unless they start it off, the movement towards a free trade area will not be started at all.

Developing countries could become associate members. Full membership will mainly be for countries bordering on the North Atlantic that, by the accidents of history, have the requisite industrial qualifications. If anything is to be done, the founding group that launches this project must not be unwieldy in size or have a composition that is more likely to retard than expedite. The perpetuation of economic privilege by an Atlantic-based free trade area is what some doctrinaires in the West will declaim against. The provision of fresh economic stimuli is what developing countries themselves may desire most.

Japan, Australia and New Zealand

Stress should be laid, at this point, on the membership of Japan in what, for want of a better designation, is being called a North Atlantic Free Trade Area. Politicians, economists and publicists may wrangle over the degree to which it will pay her to join a free trade area with some of the other industrial countries. But she has common interests with them in the politico-strategic domain and these should tell. A new grouping of industrial powers will have more amplitude in all domains if it numbers on its roster an Asian nation as industrially outstanding as Japan.

This would also ease matters for the Antipodes. By antecedents and culture, Australia and New Zealand belong to the Atlantic community. Geographically they are part and parcel of the Indo-Pacific theatre. Exciting new discoveries of minerals, oil and natural gas will brace Australia's capacity as a buttress of the free world. It would not only be good for world trade but politically remunerative if an Atlantic-based arrangement linked up with the Pacific through the inclusion of Japan, Australia and New Zealand. All three have security pacts with the USA. When Britain put entry into the Common Market ahead of Commonwealth trade preferences, Japan as well as the USA loomed larger for Australia and New Zealand in the field of trade and investment. There should be no laments in Washington, London or Ottawa if such economic ties furthered other broad interests for the West as a whole.

The map has decreed that Australia and New Zealand must carry a larger share of defence burdens in South-East Asia. Contingents from those two Commonwealth countries served with

British forces during the confrontation between Malaysia and Indonesia while, in South Vietnam, they fought side by side with American troops. Until now it would have been awkward for Japan to follow suit, for her to assume a proportionate share of regional defence burdens. It may soon be even more awkward for her not to do so.

A New Course for Japan

After World War II the cold war was quick to supplant the wartime coalition of victor great powers. Nor was there anything uniform about the manner in which, beyond the Soviet camp, victors and vanquished got along with each other. Italy returned to the comity of the West at once, the East-West contest spurred on the establishment of the Bonn Republic and the rehabilitation of West Germans, while Japan went her own way. But for Japan, as for the others, it was behind the shield of American preponderance that, with a minimum of military expenditure, recovery could proceed.

Japan has not been attracted since World War II by the accoutrements or glamour of super-power. Under her constitution, the country may not despatch an expeditionary force abroad—though the USA might be now the last to insist upon the observance of a restriction that General Douglas MacArthur imposed. The question is whether she can trust herself, or others will trust her, when she brings her full weight to bear. From her corner of the earth Japan could do as much as a European Third Force to destabilise the global balance if neutralist factions, at once so rabid and so vocal, ever got the upper hand. A cry of Asia for the Asians might speed up the quest for Chinese markets. But this cry has also meant Asia for the Japanese and other Asians will not have forgotten that.

The shadow of a greater Germany still broods over Eastern Europe. Similarly, over vast tracts of the Far East, the shadow of a greater Japan has been slow to lift.

Yet Japan has few irredentist ambitions—a fact that may make it less hard for some of her former victims to accept her as a good neighbour. Nor, if anything went amiss, would membership with Japan in a loose economic grouping have the same political consequences for others as membership in a tight-knit union with post-Gaullist France or the Bonn Republic. The Japanese are not as advanced politically and socially as they are industrially. From that angle, too, it would be profitable for Japan, as for everybody else in the free world, if she were aligned with an Atlantic-based free trade area in which more seasoned democracies set the tone.

Such an alignment could also mark a change in other aspects of Japanese policy. After World War II, Japan tried to be all things to all men. About the resurgence of China, for instance, she was less worried than the USA. But then so was Nehru's India until Indian frontiers on the Himalayas were breached. When the Americans intervened in Vietnam, the Japanese Government endorsed what they had done—much to Moscow's indignation and in the teeth of popular dissent. Tokyo, after all, is within closer range than Moscow or Washington to Chinese hydrogen bombs.

Eventually, despite any treaty against the spread of nuclear weapons and as the trauma of Hiroshima and Nagasaki fade away, Japan may want to produce a deterrent of her own. Until she does, she will be more dependent than ever on the overall American deterrent.

That introduces a further ambiguity. For the American deterrent gets some of its regional strength from American installations on Okinawa—a Japanese island that Japan wants the USA to hand back. But the USA will have to retain military rights on Okinawa before its return to Japan will be safe.

There is ambiguity, too, in the attitude of Japan towards Russia, a country she defeated in the Russo-Japanese War of 1904-05 and warded off until her own defeat brought World War II to a stop. The Soviet Union chides Tokyo periodically for seeking to regain Japanese islands that it occupied at the termination of World War II. Even so, Moscow may propose that Japan, with her dazzling industrial proficiency, develop the natural resources of Siberia—industrial access to Eastern Europe being dangled before Tokyo as additional bait. China, however, regards as her own some of the territory thus earmarked by Russia for development by Japan. In general, an agreement of this kind with the Soviet Union might signal the end of Japanese efforts to run with Chinese hares while hunting with hounds from the two other major camps.

But Russia and the West, as the two other major camps, are also at odds. Japan may or may not grab the chance to develop the natural resources of Siberia. What she dare not do is jeopardise her mutual security pact with the USA. In 1960, after this had been signed, the Opposition toppled the Government. Since then the war in Vietnam has exacerbated anti-American feeling and it will be tough sledding in 1970 when the treaty has to be renewed.

But since then, too, Communist China has acquired nuclear weapons and, as Japan takes due cognisance of that sombre fact, it should predispose her towards the West not less but more than ever. Nor can she relish the Soviet bid for global sea-power. The Japanese are, after all, shipbuilders and shipowners, exporters and importers of the first rank. Most of Japan's oil is shipped in by the biggest of tankers plying the Straits of Malacca from the Persian Gulf and the Arabian Peninsula. Unless those vessels can pass, unhampered, to and fro, Japanese industry would grind to a halt.

It may be that, in the British withdrawal from East of Suez, there have been two lessons for Japan. The first of these would be a regional one. Japan will have to build herself up as a naval power. The revision of her security pact with the USA must enable her to bear a fair share in policing the sea lanes of the Indo-Pacific theatre. But the second lesson may be more than regional. As never before, Japan should be conscious of her own stake in a free world order. The life of the nation is governed by the endeavour of open societies to keep open the open seas. A project as flexible as a multilateral free trade area would be in accord with that endeavour.

It may also be in accord with the concept of "an Asian-Pacific sphere of co-operation" that Mr. Takeo Miki, Japan's Foreign Minister, has been elaborating. Japan is ensuring sources of supply for the long run on all sides of the Pacific. Increased trade with Pacific countries will result and with that increase further complementary efforts along the lines of a wider free trade area could multiply. Japan is also expanding her trade with the Occident. But she is more and more aware of a regional responsibility as a rich industrial power for the economic well-being of East Asia. There might be, through membership of a multilateral free trade area, a fertile synthesis between these two objectives.

Membership would be no less thorny an issue for Japan than it would be for others. Steep economic obstacles will have to be surmounted. Such an undertaking could never surmount them if political impulses of considerable potency did not lie behind it. Regionally, too, it will be better for developing countries if, through a free trade area spanning the Atlantic and the Pacific, Japan leans more and more towards the West.

The joke, if she does, would be upon those who have looked

askance at the NAFTA idea. Rather than act as a rich man's club, this project might set for all its members a higher level of generosity towards the less rich. And if it did that it would be fulfilling one of its own aims. On many counts a new far-flung trade initiative could do for the free world much that must be done and that can be done in no other way.

6 A GREAT AND GREATER CONTEXTURE

In the end, if an American initiative is what must start a new grouping of industrial trading nations, there should be some assurance that the British will respond with alacrity. But qualms over the domination of their economy by the USA could make them hesitate. It will be for technical experts to dispel British qualms or set them in perspective. Their exploitation by those who have taken a Eurocentric view of Britain's destiny is nonetheless grotesque. For nothing has been more calculated than Europeanisation to ensure her submergence.

NAFTA and American Primacy

American preponderance does, all the same, put some US allies in a quandary, disuniting the West even while underpinning the West's own security. If the USA were not pre-eminent technologically, the free world might have ceased to be free. The new Europe must Americanise itself technologically if it is also to stand on its own feet against an American guarantor.[52] Whatever magnifies the dimensions of world contests renders acute disparities of power in the realm of defence and diplomacy. Disparities are no less acute in the realm of industrial production, overseas trade and foreign investment.

It was because of these, moreover, that Mr. Brown, as Foreign Secretary, dismissed the NAFTA idea as a practical alternative when Britain applied for membership in the Common Market. For such a grouping "inevitably would be dominated by its one superpower member. Our ability to influence, not only world affairs but the very organisation of our own economy, would in these circumstances compare unfavourably with what we might expect to be the case were we in an enlarged European Community."[53]

[52]This point is dealt with in Chapter 2, Pages 88-89 above.
[53]*Hansard*, Vol. 746, No. 197, May 10, 1967, cc. 1512-13.
After the second Gaullist veto and the resignation of Mr. Brown from the Foreign Office, the Prime Minister again denied that a North Atlantic Free Trade Area is "a realistic present alternative to membership of the European Economic

Mr. Brown might have hammered this home as a debating-point. As a half-truth it calls for scrutiny. It is of no avail if a helmsman averts shipwreck on Scylla only to founder on Charybdis. With the loss of overseas ties, something which joining the EEC must entail, Britain will have lessened her own capacity to play a major part within the new Europe itself. An Atlantic-based free trade area, on the other hand, would not subject its members to an organic process; upon its members it would make few institutional demands. Although there would still be the problem of economic predominance by an American mammoth, it is not one from which Britain can escape behind the walls of the Common Market. Within them. as within Britain's own island frontiers, a number of American industries are already entrenched.

There are no certain answers, but paradox is rife. In his Guildhall speech before the second Gaullist veto, Mr. Wilson cited the computer industry as one that should be organised on a European scale. Yet the very industry for which the Prime Minister had expressed solicitude was less than avid for an exchange of know-how with the French. Nor does Britain have to be Europeanised so as to achieve economies of scale; a NAFTA arrangement could, under equitable safeguards, offer these, too. Like his spokesman, Lord Chalfont, the Prime Minister had warned against an American take-over.[54] For the West, if the new Europe took over Britain, it would be still worse.

During the spring of 1968 there was one event that might have indicated how, and on what, sights should be set. More than private business was involved when a handful of American and British companies enabled the Lockheed Aircraft Corporation to order Rolls-Royce aero engines for its giant new air buses. For by this deal Britain had not only shown that she could hold her own in the field of the most advanced large-scale technology. She had done so without mortgaging her political independence across either the Channel or the Atlantic.

This seminal transaction will not raise balance of payments

Community". See *Hansard*, Vol. 761, No. 86, March 21, 1968, cc. 596-99. But how "realistic" has been, or might be, the bid for the entry of Britain into the Common Market? There may be a very different situation when policy-makers and legislators in Washington have studied the politico-strategic, as well as the economic, case for a multilateral free trade association.

[54]Compare the Guildhall speech, *The Times*, November 14, 1967, with *The Guardian*, November 15, 1967. For Lord Chalfont see *The Times*, October 10, 1967.

difficulties. A complex resale plan is to take care of them. Trade between the American and British economies, in other words, can be a two-way street. And it is on such a principle that NAFTA must repose.

Before this deal there had been another good omen. Britain found herself in a more favoured category than members of the EEC when, on January 1, 1968, President Johnson announced measures to reduce American foreign investments.[55] It may be that when American investors have bought out British firms they also supplied British investors with funds for setting up or expanding other British industries. The wry fact is that, even if the new Europe could have been aggrandised by the accession of Britain, it would still seek the American investments it decries and to which, like Britain, it owes so much.

Common Market countries are likely to feel the pinch as American capital investments are curtailed. American corporations may have used some of the US trade deficit to purchase European industries. But after all the American gold drain has not been a conspiracy by Washington and Wall Street, Detroit and Pittsburgh, Philadelphia, Chicago and Los Angeles, against the American dollar. Much of it can be traced back to American foreign aid—to assistance without which, among other regions, Western Europe itself might have recovered from World War II with less speed or been Communised before it could recover. Prodigious also has been American military expenditure on wars in Korea and Vietnam as well as on the defences of the West all the world over. If there were no American primacy, those in the West who rail against it would soon be singing another tune. Its credits and debits figure on the same balance-sheet. American strength cannot have a political impact abroad without having an economic one as well.

For such a state of affairs there is no precedent. Two world wars and their grim sequel, the East-West contest, have accelerated the growth of the American economy. Without the technological exuberance that the USA has generated, the free world—at one

---

[55]That category gave Paris a chance to jeer at this further proof of exceptional ties between the English-speaking peoples—of how un-European the British still were.

Economic cutbacks also made Britain withdraw in April, 1968, from European space programmes under which European telecommunication satellites were to be built.

stage or another—might have succumbed. Yet undue American control of their key industries or basic resources, by embittering allies, fans Third Force tendencies that could disrupt the West. Britain, all the same, might only widen the breach by drawing away from the USA. Whatever is done must be done in conjunction with Washington. But the opportunity for doing this is one that the USA will have to furnish. She must not let it slip by. Though a wide trans-oceanic free trade area requires an American initiative, altruism is not what should prompt the USA. Common interests may be served.

The New Europe and Britain's Role

Not that any such project would be arrayed against the Common Market. On the contrary, the hope is that the new Europe would participate. Nor will NAFTA want to discourage the EEC from setting its own house in order technologically. Britain, however, is under no obligation to help the Common Market do so when the price for her, and thus for the rest of the Western world, would be excessive. Europeanists seem to have presupposed that she is.

Across the Channel, as a matter of fact, this has been a perfectly intelligible presupposition. Architects of European unity like M. Jean Monnet and M. Paul-Henri Spaak, and anti-Gaullists like M. Pierre Mendès-France and M. Jean-Jacques Servan-Schreiber, may not over-estimate the status of the new Europe in contemporary affairs. But it is their natural bent to take a Euro-centric view of Europe's own destiny. By the same token a view of Britain's destiny that is Eurocentric is also their *métier*. Vistas from London, however, and from Washington, too, must be more spacious and it is in the light of these that NAFTA proposals should be judged.

Canada and the USA

Nor is the choice before Britain one between being Americanised or being Europeanised. Rather it is whether the UK wishes to keep an individual role. Europeanisers have purveyed the myth that membership in NAFTA would convert Britain into the fifty-first state of the American Union. But in one respect at least they are misinformed. As a candidate for Americanisation, Britain does not begin as high on the list as some or all of Canada. What the history of Canada has demonstrated is how, despite propinquity, even the hemispheric sway of her great neighbour can be resisted.

No other foreign community has been as steeped in the American way of life as the English-speaking sections of Canada. In no other advanced country has the embrace of American technology been so all-enveloping. Yet even where the Canadian economy is little more than a branch establishment of the American economy, it is a branch establishment with a difference.

Canada, after all, retains an identity of her own and, since the days of the Battle of Britain, has functioned in world politics as a middle power. Americans may learn at school and college about bitter frontier disputes with neighbours to the north. It is Canadians themselves, however, who will have revived the old American dream of annexation if, as they let their country fall apart, a few of the ensuing fragments seek entry into the American Union. Inner rifts, not pressure from without, are what could break up the Canadian Confederation—those between French-speaking and English-speaking Canadians as well as the sectionalism which results when a vast semi-continental expanse is at once so underpopulated and so heterogeneous.

On the other hand, such is the mesh of trade and investment that whatever rivets together the Canadian and American economies may also rivet together Canada herself. Then, too, there is the hemispheric defence of North America, something that also gives the USA a vested interest in the Canadian *status quo*. English-speaking Canada has been permeated unremittingly by all that Americanises. From the standpoint, though, of the USA, the North American scheme of things—economic, demographic and strategic —should remain intact.

With this question of an American takeover, then, Canada has had more experience than any other advanced'country and from that experience there is much for Britain to glean today. Before World War I, when the Canadian electorate rejected a proposal for reciprocity in trade between the USA and Canada, the industrialisation of the Canadian economy had not got far. So great has been the amount of American investment in Canada since 1911 that a north-south free trade pact could arouse trepidation even now. But an open-ended Atlantic free trade area would be multilateral and not bilateral in composition. Its sheer diversity would make it less of an economic and political gamble for those who take part.

Britain is not as exposed as Canada to Americanisation in depth.

What either—as a member of a new free trade grouping—loses on the swings, it may gain on the roundabouts.

There has, nevertheless, been a recent American threat to Canadian independence of another, adventitious kind. When President Kennedy broached his programme for an Atlantic partnership, he himself could not have foreseen all that it implied. Washington had been eager to assist Britain's first bid to join the EEC. According to the Kennedy blueprint there were to be two pillars, one in Western Europe and one in North America, with the European pillar enlarged by the Europeanisation of Britain. Yet only through the merger of Canada with the USA, a consummation from which Canada had long recoiled, could the North American pillar of the new Western edifice be rounded out.

In a multilateral free trade area there would be no such hazard. For this project would not only enable Britain to perpetuate an individual role: it would do the same for Canada. Nor, as long as her attachments are oceanic as well as hemispheric, would Canada have to speak entirely with an American accent. For a number of years she treasured the hope that, as a counterpoise to a pervasive American influence, she could also turn to the Commonwealth. Now, if Britain is swallowed up by the new Europe, continental regionalism will be the vogue on both sides of the Atlantic and, in coping with the USA, Canada will stand more and more alone.

A project through which contingencies as dismal as these may be averted is one that Canadians should do their utmost to foster. They have their stake in the established power structure of the West. An Atlantic free trade area would do much to preserve it. In the proposed initiative Canada should therefore be glad to join the USA and Britain as one of an inaugural trio. Economically a NAFTA arrangement may or may not be as profitable for her as for some of its other members. In terms of her own political status it would be.

USA and World Order

As for American attitudes, even those who pooh-pooh the idea on economic grounds may have to acknowledge its politico-strategic cogency. From one angle the spectre of American supremacy is what haunts critics in Britain and Canada. A vision of foreign imports swamping the most lucrative of markets is, from another, what frightens American protectionists. On economic grounds, however, US participation in a NAFTA scheme should displease neither the American consumer nor the American exporter. Over its domestic effect, protectionist and anti-protectionist may skirmish. For the USA, as leader of the West, this project could be an epoch-making instrument of policy and should be so treated.

Such a new Grand Design would be timely. The war in Vietnam will have left scars. Nor could the USA be self-immobilised by race war at home without shaking the foundations of world order; without enemies of the West taking heart. A school of American neo-isolationists has supervened. There are also many unreconstructed American internationalists who contend that the USA is over-extended and ought to retrench. With a far-seeing new initiative, however, she could reaffirm her true place in the free world and human affairs.

There is not only disenchantment over the way things have gone in South-East Asia. Western Europe has been one of the main beneficiaries of American preponderance. Brickbats from that quarter have nevertheless been more plentiful than bouquets. And now restrictions have had to be put on American investment in Western Europe. But the Marshall Plan served the USA after World War II as an economic milestone on the road from political isolationism. Along that same road the NAFTA plan might become yet another economic milestone.

The issue should be restated. There is more than an individual British role to save. If it goes, the international post-war American role may go as well. For nothing will do as much as European isolationism to make the USA lose patience with trans-Atlantic allies and revert to a political isolationism of her own.

Not that a Third Force, after the new Europe has been enlarged by the absorption of Britain, would shove the USA back into her shell. Even NATO might linger on precariously. But, under the old classic American isolationism, it was only within the Western Hemisphere that the USA intervened. A fresh brand of American isolationism could not thus delimit itself. After the war in Vietnam, the USA will have wounds to lick. Even so, when there is a global balance to uphold, the security of the European sector will still be a vital American interest. A policy of America First has long been obsolete. While Britain may adopt a policy of Europe First, this does not mean that one of Asia First is on the cards for the USA. What it does mean, if a Third Force emerges, is that there will be still less teamwork in the West, that coalition diplomacy will be at a discount.

West Europeans have wanted a bigger say in the conduct of world affairs. But coalition diplomacy has had to reflect inequalities between allies that the politico-strategic realities of the age have bred. Without it, nevertheless, American action might have been more unilateral than it has been. If the new Europe, swayed by Third Force tendencies, goes it alone, so will the USA.

The resurgence of China, antagonism between super-powers elsewhere, the perils of the arms race, ferment among intellectuals and the quest for reform in Eastern Europe, the inability of the Soviet Union to restrain nationalism among client states while subsidising it against the West farther afield, competition between guns and butter on the Russian home front: all these, taken together, might still push Washington and Moscow towards a *détente*. But if, on being enlarged, the new Europe impairs the structure of power in the West, the USA may retort by enlarging her own power structure. Nor would this be Fortress America as she might have envisaged it before Pearl Harbour. There can be no return to the hemispheric, unilateral imperialism of the past. When world contests have global dimensions, a super-power like the USA has to operate on a global scale. That is why, with a global balance to maintain, she must still underwrite its European sector. But the allowances she makes for the susceptibilities of the new Europe are not likely to be more frequent than before.

This, then, is a turning-point for the USA as well as for Britain. Setbacks in South-East Asia and in the monetary field may again illuminate the limitations of American power. All the same, these cannot obscure what the USA has achieved as the prime custodian of a free world order. World War II might never have broken out if the English-speaking peoples, despite the ordeal of World War I, had not taken world order for granted. It must in fact still be shored up without surcease.[56] The West can be strong when that is done in a co-operative spirit. Through its power structure it has the means for unity. But if it is to preserve the one it must preserve the other.

The decision, moreover, rests with Britain first of all. It is her Europeanisation that might give Third Force tendencies a fillip. Yet

[56]This point is dealt with by the writer in "The American Role and World Order", *The Yale Review*, Yale University Press, Summer, 1967. See also Gelber, "The Alliance of Necessity", *op. cit.*, pp. 15-45.

here the decision rests with the USA as well. For if she lends herself to an open-ended, Atlantic-based free trade area the British people will have less cause than ever to take a Eurocentric view of their future. Not that the security of the West is the sort of question that may be set forth in the prospectus for a new trade grouping of industrial countries. But politically it would be at the heart of the entire project.

The Anglo-American Factor

There would be something else. A loose oceanic free trade arrangement might perpetuate conditions in which Anglo-American friendship can endure. That it should endure, despite the manner in which it has been misconceived and misrepresented, is still imperative.

Anglo-American friendship has of necessity undergone a sea-change. In American counsels the rank Britain enjoys may, for the moment, only be commensurate with the size of her contribution to world order, with the pre-concerted weight she can bring to bear. Nor will that weight amount to as much as it once did when, under cover of financial stringency, the Europeanisation of British strategy has preceded the Europeanisation of Britain herself. Yet if Britain pulls herself together economically she may do so along other lines as well. Countries like France, West Germany and Japan have sprung back from defeat in war. It may be that Britain, unvanquished in war, will not defeat herself even now beyond recall. An individual British role, if Britain is Europeanised, could be lost irreparably. Options for her would no longer be open. But through participation in an Atlantic-based free trade area they still would be.

And so they still would be, as far as Britain is concerned, for the USA. In Anglo-American friendship, variability is the one element that has never varied. But no other ally of the USA has had Britain's range or quality. It is too soon for Washington to write her off.

In detail history may never repeat itself and yet, as great issues recur, it should teach us how to handle them. Before the second veto by President de Gaulle on British entry into the Common Market, Lord Chalfont, the British Minister for European Affairs, said that henceforth Britain's relationship with the USA "will be Europe's relationship".[57] As a forecast this assertion was premature.

[57] The Times, October 10, 1967.

What it implied was that, as a separate factor in world politics, Anglo-American friendship would be no more. Nothing, though, did as much during the first half of the twentieth century to preserve a free world order. In the second half, it may still have value.

A few basic truths about Anglo-American friendship will therefore be relevant here. Winston Churchill and Franklin Delano Roosevelt did not invent that prime factor. It took its modern shape at the turn of the century and was to outlast them. Nor has there been anything unusual about disparities of power between the USA and Britain. The Anglo-American framework lacked symmetry before the leadership of the West crossed the Atlantic. It was only when Britannia ruled the waves that, unmolested, the USA could build herself up and, as she acquired most of her strategic outposts, move to the fore. No ethnic homogeneity prevails, all the same, within or between the English-speaking peoples. There are Anglo-Saxons in the Gaullist lexicon but nowhere else. It is nevertheless reassuring that Britain and the USA, together with Canada, Australia and New Zealand, should cherish those affinities in the spheres of language and literature, law and government that have expedited what Churchill described as a special relationship. What has made it special is a flair for putting those affinities to good use.

That use may no longer be world-wide. But seldom in the plenitude of power has the USA wanted to act alone. It is not in the interest of the free world that she should. Among allies none can do in unison with her what Britain may yet be able to do once her economy has been restored and her independence revivified. Anglo-American friendship has long had a habit of making professional mourners look silly. If they would study its history they might learn why. The relationship between Britain and the USA is now a grossly disproportionate one. It could still have a utility, if its potential remains, that might prove unique. Unless Britain keeps her individual role, there can be no Anglo-American potential. In an Atlantic free trade area she may keep it.

Political Case for NAFTA

The case for a new trade alignment is thus a many-sided one. A countervailing NAFTA initiative could add to the general well-being if it is organised for the transaction of business in its own specific field. Simultaneously, and not without some judicious premeditation, it could also conserve political assets that nothing can replace.

"Do not entertain so weak an imagination", Edmund Burke admonished Parliament before the American Revolution began, "as that your registers and your bonds, your affidavits and your sufferances, your cockets and your clearances are what form the great securities of your commerce. Do not dream that your letters of office, and your instructions, and your suspending clauses are the things that hold together the great contexture of this mysterious whole."

As yesterday, so today—the securities of commerce have to be put in a broader context. But now there is an even greater contexture of like-minded nations to hold and be held together. The chief Western democracies are not the only ones with a stake in a free world order. Towards a further liberalisation of international trade, however, they must make the first effort. It is from an American initiative, supported by Britain and Canada, that others such as the EFTA countries may take their cue. And if they all combine for trade it might be more than trade that impels them.

Politics, rightly understood, keep breaking in. The West is more than the Western alliance and the free world is more than the West; a new multilateral free trade grouping would serve all three. Such a project must cut across geographical regions. But so do the foundations of peace. Existing equilibria within the West are what enable the West to uphold existing equilibria on a global scale. And a NAFTA arrangement would not only reinforce these economically. It might curb political dislocations within the West as well.

Nor is this all. It could, by its advent, refresh the atmosphere. There has been a plethora of formulae for the reconstruction of the West. Here is a project that may revitalise and renew. Gathering together a number of countries with economic vigour and getting its impetus from them, the drive for a wide-ranging free trade area might give an impetus to others in turn. And if it does that its time will have come because it suits the needs of the time.

Part IV

BRITAIN AND THE FREE
TRADE AREA OPTION

by

Maxwell Stamp

and

Harry Cowie

1 BRITAIN'S POST-WAR TRADE POLICY

There has been a reluctance to examine the basis of British commercial policy in the post-war world. Perhaps this can be explained away by the pragmatic posture which some policy-makers like to adopt when confronted by broad issues of this kind. Not always has this been so. Nineteenth-century free trade policy was based on a comprehensive doctrine of economic thought which sought to justify this course of action, in terms of the benefits it bestowed on not only Britain but also on the world at large. It was then recognised that a nation which sought to base industry on overseas trade, as well as on domestic consumption, must give top priority to a commercial policy allowing industry to import freely. Such a policy would assure the cheapest supplies of raw materials and foodstuffs and at the same time create purchasing power abroad for the import of products of British factories.

Even the inter-war years witnessed a conscious effort on the part of government in Britain to create a commercial policy which would answer the needs of the time. In the 1920s and 1930s the system of international trade which had been founded on free trade was severely cut back through crisis measures taken during World War I to establish infant industries; and immediately after the war to protect national markets from outside competition and the threat of unemployment. Britain, along with other countries, adopted a system of duties or tariffs on imports of other countries' products. The British duties were extended by other Commonwealth countries in the Ottawa Agreements of 1932. The system of Imperial Preference did provide a partial answer to the problems of the time by maintaining the level of Commonwealth trade, and assisting Commonwealth countries to develop during a period in which Britain's imports from other sources fell by about one-half in value.

Imperial Preference encouraged the emergence of the sterling area, by which Commonwealth countries kept their reserves in London. This system played an important part in enabling Britain subsequently to finance the 1939-45 war effort. The other side of the medal was the cost to efficiency in Britain arising from the reduction of competition in the home market consequent upon the protective and preferential measures of the 1930s.

Whether or not one agrees with these policies, namely free trade in the mid-nineteenth century or Imperial Preference in the 1930s, at least they were attempts to formulate a commercial policy based on what was regarded at the time as Britain's best interests. By contrast, in the post-war world of the 1940s and 1950s such efforts as there have been to formulate a trade policy that corresponded to real British interests have been either puny or half-hearted reactions to initiatives, such as the European Economic Community (EEC),[1] which have fundamentally been devised to deal with the trade problems of other countries.

Probably the root cause of Britain's failure to devise an effective commercial policy in the post-war world lay in the fact that although the United Kingdom emerged from World War II with the prestige of victory and the trappings of a great trading power, resources were in fact depleted and the country was heavily in debt. At first the extent of the relative loss of trading power was not evident either to the British Government or to the British people. For the prostrated state of European competitors allowed the UK to enjoy an artificially large share of world trade. The urgency of adapting policies, or the need for devising new ones, was thus not realised for some time.

Multilateral Approach

Britain's relative weakness was also disguised by the important role London played alongside Washington in shaping the International Monetary Fund (IMF), the International Bank for Reconstruction and Development (the World Bank) and the International Trade Charter. The British again were prominent in the setting up of the General Agreement on Tariffs and Trade (GATT), a typically English organisation insofar as it is a prime example of how the provisional becomes permanent. The GATT was intended to be a temporary arrangement until the International Trade Charter could be drawn up and ratified. When the United States

[1]In mid-1967 the European Economic Community, the European Coal and Steel Community and European Atomic Energy Commission merged. The new entity is entitled the European Communities. But throughout this study we continue to use the more familiar abbreviation EEC, the term Common Market or simply the Community when referring to the countries that collectively comprise "the new Europe".

failed to ratify the Charter, the GATT continued in existence as the main instrument for lowering tariffs on world trade.

The British Government recognised that an international body that could help to prevent competitive tariff wars could be an important medium through which to raise the level of world trade. For example, in the 1947 White Paper on the Geneva Tariff Negotiations it was pointed out that:

"The United Kingdom, owing to its peculiar dependence on a flourishing export trade, stands to gain as few other countries do from a revival of multilateral trading conditions and the outlawing of protective restrictions of imports and exchange of the kind which strangled normal trade in the 1930s."

Fundamentally the GATT sought to promote multilateral trade, first by committing members not to raise existing tariffs or margins of preference. Secondly, members undertake to extend any negotiated tariff-cuts to all other members under the most-favoured-nation (MFN) clause. This is the principle of "non-discrimination". The MFN obligation does not apply to special arrangements, such as Imperial Preference, that were in existence before the GATT was signed. All the same, the Commonwealth preferential arrangement did come under fire from the Americans during the GATT negotiations and Britain agreed not to grant bigger and better preferences to other Commonwealth countries, even on a reciprocal basis.

There were two important exceptions to the principle of non-discrimination allowed for in the GATT. These were the formation of free trade areas and customs unions, provided "they do not raise barriers to the trade of other contracting parties with such parties". In other words, the common tariff set up round a customs union, and the arrangements in a free trade area, must not be more restrictive in incidence than the general incidence of the duties and regulations of commerce which applied previously to countries not participating in the customs union or free trade area.

In fact, although Britain was willing to take a leading part in reducing tariffs in the post-war world, the world-wide tariff negotiations under GATT, of which there have been six rounds, including the so-called Kennedy Round, did not lead to dramatic reductions in tariff levels. This has had a particularly unfortunate effect on Britain, who found herself with one of the highest tariffs in the Western world but at the same time was psychologically unable to negotiate away this seemingly important ace. One might have expected policy-makers to have realised after the fifth round that the high UK tariff was more of an embarrassment to British industry —through its cost-raising effects—than a magic key to use for opening doors to rich foreign markets. In that case it might have been expected that a policy of unilateral cuts in the British tariff would have been forthcoming, as they were, for instance, from West Germany in 1956-57. These cuts could have been made *de facto* and not *de jure* if special importance had not been placed on the negotiating value of a high British tariff. As far as is known, however, no proposals for a policy of this kind have been made by a post-war President of the Board of Trade.

It would therefore seem that, although Britain may have wished to pursue a commercial policy which would achieve a multilateral reduction in tariffs through the channels of the GATT, an attachment to high tariffs as a bargaining counter prevented her from taking the lead in this direction. Instead it was the formation of the EEC that prompted a new initiative for multilateral negotiations for reducing tariffs. And that initiative came from the Americans in the shape of the Trade Expansion Act of 1962 which prepared the way for the Kennedy Round. It did not come from Britain. The result has been a further decline of British influence on decision-taking in international trade policy. In the Kennedy Round the most important decisions were made by the EEC and the USA with the UK adopting a rather protectionist stance over certain issues (like iron and steel), ill attuned, it seemed, to a declared policy of seeking to lower world-wide tariff barriers.

The Regional Response

Soon after World War II it became clear to Britain and the USA that the multilateral institutions which had been set up to deal with world problems did not provide an adequate answer to the problems, in particular, of European recovery. This was partly because the IMF and the abortive International Trade Organisation were primarily designed to cope with the problems that might arise from another American or world slump. Neither the IMF nor the World Bank, moreover, had the powers to create sufficient credit or extend sufficient aid to get the devastated economies of Western Europe on their feet again. If anything, the British were more aware than the Americans that regional institutions would have to be formed to deal with these problems. At first the USA was reluctant to support European institutions that did not include the Soviet Union. The United Nations Economic Commission for Europe was established on this basis and hence its field of action was circumscribed from the start.

By 1947 it was evident that neither Britain nor continental Europe had sufficient resources to pull themselves up by their own bootstraps. In a famous speech General George Marshall, the US Secretary of State, proposed on June 5, 1947, that the European countries could draw up a recovery programme with the financial support and help of the USA. Sixteen West European governments accepted this invitation and in the following year the Organisation for European Economic Co-operation (OEEC) was created to co-ordinate the programme. The British Government played a leading role both in its creation and in ensuring that the organisation was not a supranational one. Britain was not willing to be bound by majority decisions taken by the OEEC which might fetter her in other parts of the world. She was anxious to set about restoring the free movement of goods in Western Europe so long as it did not limit her freedom of commercial policy elsewhere. Indeed, it was as a result of a British initiative that the system of quantitative restrictions on trade was gradually liberalised. On the other hand, a proposal in the original OEEC convention that the contracting parties promise to "continue the study of customs unions or analogous arrangements such as free trade areas" was quietly dropped.

The Common Market

Had Britain taken the lead in proposing a free trade area, or perhaps a customs union, there would probably have been a favourable response. Arrangements could have been made to accommodate the special problems and interests involved in Commonwealth connections. Failure to do so may be regarded in retrospect as a cardinal error on the part of the British Government. The opportunity was not seized partly because Britain was still the dominant economic power in Western Europe. Whitehall was wary, moreover, lest drawing closer to Europe should weaken the special relationship with the United States. If, on the other hand, the initiative had been seized, and the leadership in Europe retained, British influence might have been strengthened.

The absence of any UK lead left the way open for other arrangements. For some time the smaller European countries had been pressing for larger markets. In 1948 the Benelux customs union was formed between the Netherlands and the Belgium-Luxembourg economic union. Then in 1950 M. Robert Schuman, France's Foreign Minister, proposed a coal and steel pool which would "internationalise" the Ruhr by removing barriers to trade in these products between France and Germany and between them and other West European countries. Britain was asked to join. Although the decision might have gone the other way if Sir Stafford Cripps, then Britain's Chancellor of the Exchequer, had not been abroad recuperating from illness, the Labour Government eventually decided that it could not take part in a scheme that might cut across its own plans for these basic industries, only recently nationalised. Once again there was a failure to assess the proposed scheme in terms of its potential and Britain's long term economic prospects.[2]

The European Coal and Steel Community (ECSC) was established in 1952 and membership was composed of the six continental countries of France, West Germany, Italy, Belgium, Holland and Luxembourg (the Six). The architect was M. Jean Monnet. He believed that European unity could be achieved only through functional co-operation and looked, therefore, to the ECSC as a pilot scheme for complete European integration.

At Messina in June, 1955, the European movement's next step was to set up a committee under M. Paul-Henri Spaak, the Belgian Foreign Minister, to investigate ways and means of extending the ECSC into a general scheme for removing trade barriers and establishing an economic community. Once again the British Government was represented at these talks. Once more though the UK observers were withdrawn when it became plain that the scheme involved the establishment of a customs union under the umbrella of a supranational authority. Perhaps the British decision was taken on the grounds that it was unlikely that the Six would be able to agree on or ratify such an ambitious project. After all, it was only a short time before that another attempt at European unification, namely the European Defence Community, had crumbled after the French National Assembly had failed to ratify the treaty. But the Six confounded their critics by translating the Spaak Report into the Treaty of Rome which was signed on March 25, 1957.

The Treaty bore the marks of national bargaining. Negotiating

[2]William Diebold, "The Schuman Plan: a Study in Economic Co-operation, 1950-1959" (Oxford University Press, London, 1959).

from a position of relative weakness, the French Government was able to win extensive concessions especially regarding overseas territories. Based on the experience of the ECSC, the Rome Treaty was a framework document that set forth statements of intent rather than a series of laws or rules. Even so, it laid down the steps for the complete dismantling of trade barriers between members, the establishment of a common external tariff, and a common commercial policy under the supervision of a supranational European Commission that would have powers to make proposals to a Council of Ministers in which decisions would be taken by a majority vote. The goal was a Common Market, a European Economic Community.

A Europe-wide Free Trade Area

The UK Government reacted swiftly to this new situation by proposing a Europe-wide free trade area that would include both the Six and the other OEEC members. Tariffs and other trade restrictions would be removed between members of the free trade area. But whereas the Six would have a common external tariff, Britain and the other members would maintain their national tariffs towards third countries. Whereas, furthermore, the Common Market would include trade in agricultural products, the proposed free trade area would be restricted to non-agricultural products.

There can be little doubt that if it had come off the Europe-wide free trade area would have afforded the UK a means of taking advantage of the benefits of free trade in industrial products in Western Europe without having to forego traditional policies of importing foodstuffs and raw materials from the cheapest sources abroad or having to make more than minor modifications to the system of Commonwealth preference. Although the negotiations sometimes came close to success, they ultimately foundered on the rock of Franco-British rivalry. The French Government, which had succeeded in striking a good bargain in the Rome Treaty, recognised that the entry of Britain and the Scandinavian countries would result in diluting the benefits that France and her overseas territories could hope to gain from the EEC. In addition, the view was widely held in France, and to some extent among the rest of the Six, that Britain should not be allowed the free trade benefits of the Common Market without also adopting the far-reaching commitments to a common tariff, a common agricultural policy and other common economic policies. There was, too, a protectionist element in the French thinking. At the time of the negotiations France had not carried out her successful devaluation and still supported the commodity prices of her overseas territories at above world levels. These factors made them reluctant to enter a free trade area that would allow the more competitively priced products of the UK and the rest of the Commonwealth to reduce the potential market for the products of the franc zone.

The breakdown of negotiations for a Europe-wide free trade area was quickly followed by talks among the industrial federations and the employers' organisations of the Outer Six—Austria, Denmark, Norway, Sweden, Switzerland, and the UK. These organisations, and particularly their large member companies, had by then examined the pros and cons of free trade in Western Europe and decided that the advantages far outweighed the disadvantages. The Swedish, Swiss and Austrian governments were also anxious that an alternative trading arrangement should be devised if European-wide free trade was not possible in order that their industries (which suffer from exclusion from the EEC) should have access to a wider market. The British Government was not very enthusiastic. It would, after all, involve offering tariff free entry to the large and protected UK market in exchange for access to comparatively small low-tariff countries. Nevertheless, the UK decided to promote the European Free Trade Association (EFTA) as a means (1) of keeping the other continental countries out of the orbit of the Six; (2) in order to increase their relative bargaining power; (3) because these countries were important in trade terms to the UK; and (4) to demonstrate that a free trade area was a feasible proposition.

EFTA has been a relative success. It has at least proved the point that it is possible to remove all tariffs and quotas between countries of disparate size and stage of development (Portugal was an unexpected addition to the Outer Six) without having to establish a large supranational institutional framework. The Stockholm Convention, which provided the basic plan for EFTA, is a short document of twenty pages by sharp contrast to the bulky Rome Treaty. Secondly, the scheme relies to a very large extent on agreement among members that problems can be solved as they arise; so far this has been enough, although EFTA itself has been subjected to considerable strains, notably the UK application in the autumn of 1964 of an import surcharge without proper consultation. Thirdly, the convention is "evolutionary" in character and can therefore be adapted to changing circumstances without re-negotiation. This provision could be important if the EFTA countries were to decide to take part in a wider Atlantic arrangement. Fourthly, EFTA has demonstrated that it is possible to have free trade in industrial products without harmonising agricultural policies so long as there is give and take between members regarding exactly what does qualify as a non-agricultural commodity.

The USA and European Integration

The success of the Marshall Plan confirmed the view of the supporters of European integration in the US Administration that their policy should be geared to establishing an integrated Western Europe that could stand unsupported. They recognised that European economic integration would involve discrimination against the USA. But this was regarded as a price worth paying for political unity. During the summer of 1951 the State Department came to believe that the political unification of Europe was something that the USA should encourage more actively and began pressing quite hard in this direction.

At the same time, though, some American experts recognised that the position of the UK was quite different from that of countries across the Channel and that what was needed was a continental European union within an Atlantic framework. There was a reference to an Atlantic Community in the Truman-Churchill communiqué of January 9, 1952. This might have led to fruitful discussions if the British Government had been able to advance positive proposals. Instead, the next British move was limited to proposing a reduction in the functions of the OEEC and shifting them to the North Atlantic Treaty Organisation (NATO). This the Americans, quite rightly, opposed. It is interesting to note that some Atlantic proposals were put forward by the US Mutual Security Agency at this time culminating in the so-called Green Book. These proposals involved tying sterling, the dollar and another unit, expected to evolve from the six-member European Defence Community, in order that international liquidity could be increased and expansion fostered. The proposals also involved setting up a multi-billion dollar stabilisation fund, to be called the Atlantic Reserve System, as well as an Atlantic Economic Board to co-ordinate trade and other policies affecting currency relationships. Membership in both the reserve system and the economic board was to be limited at the outset to the USA and the UK with only ultimate provision for the projected European Community. The Green Book did not get support from the US Treasury, which was opposed to measures on an Atlantic basis that seemed to cut across its desire to return to fully convertible currencies and the pre-1914 world trading order. They are, nonetheless, an indication of the kind of Atlantic proposals which might have provided the basis for official discussion at that time if the British Government had been reasonably receptive.[3]

More generally, the US Administration threw its weight behind supranational European integration. The ECSC was actively encouraged. In August, 1952, Mr. Dean Acheson, the US Secretary of State, said: "It is the intention of the United States to give the Coal and Steel Community the strong support that its importance to the political and economic unification of Europe warrants." American support for the Rome Treaty, though, was not quite so open because ratification of the treaty occurred at the time of the Suez crisis. But there was undoubtedly strong American support behind the scenes. The same support was not forthcoming for the Europe-wide free trade area proposal which to American eyes did not possess enough political attractions to justify the additional discrimination against US exports that would result. EFTA, too, earned the scarcely concealed disapproval of Washington. By this time, the British Government was actively considering entering the Common Market itself, provided American support could be obtained.

Early in 1960 the possibility of British membership of the EEC began to be studied in Whitehall. According to one well-informed source, a top-level committee chaired by the Permanent Secretary of the Treasury, Sir Frank Lee, came to the conclusion that Britain should seek to join the Six, first, for fear of political instability among the Six which could lead to the disintegration of the EEC; secondly, because the EEC could become the main partner of the USA, with a consequent loss in relative standing for the UK not only with the USA but with the overseas Commonwealth; thirdly, because it was felt that if Britain joined the EEC it would be possible to establish a real Atlantic partnership; and fourthly, because it was believed

[3]Max Beloff, "The United States and the Unity of Europe" (The Brookings Institution, Washington, D.C., 1963).

that membership would stimulate Britain's economic growth.[4]

Political considerations therefore largely determined the decision taken in Whitehall and by the Government. Further, there can be little doubt that when Mr. Harold Macmillan, Britain's Prime Minister, went to Washington for talks with the newly-elected President John Kennedy, it was precisely in terms of common political interests that Britain's entry into the EEC was discussed. The Americans wanted Britain to join in order to provide an element of stability in European politics and to ensure that the pre-eminence of the Atlantic alliance was not overlooked. After this meeting Mr. Macmillan came away with the full knowledge that the USA regarded British membership of the EEC as an essential first step towards the building of an Atlantic Community.

Trade Expansion Act of 1962

Britain's decision to apply for membership was regarded by the US Administration as the end of one act and the opening of another in a Grand Design. US policy became concerned with the repercussions of an expanded EEC. The objective of the Kennedy Administration from the outset was to bring the rest of the non-Communist world into a system of generally freer trade and payments which would have two centres of power, namely the USA and a European Community that would include Britain. President Kennedy proposed, and Congress accepted, the Trade Expansion Act by which the Chief Executive was granted unprecedented authority to negotiate multilateral tariff reductions of up to 50 per cent on an across-the-board basis and, too, to abolish tariffs on commodities where the USA and the EEC together represented "80 per cent or more of aggregated world export value". This initiative was supported by Congress and business opinion in order to promote the Grand Design for an Atlantic Partnership as well as to counter the possible threat of increased discrimination resulting from British accession to the Rome Treaty.

The Kennedy Round that followed took much longer than anticipated and proved less sweeping than allowed for under the Trade Expansion Act. President de Gaulle's veto in January, 1963, meant that the "80 per cent" clause fell by the way. Without

[4]Miriam Camps, "Britain and the European Community, 1955-63" (Royal Institute of International Affairs, Oxford University Press, London, 1964).

Britain's entry into the EEC the clause applied only to a few commodities.

Veto of Britain's Entry

Britain's 1961-63 effort to join the EEC was deemed as a turning point in history. Its failure left the Atlantic alliance (with the doubtful exception of France) without a strategy for the West. The possible factors which led to Britain's application being vetoed therefore need to be briefly recalled.

It is sometimes suggested that the British Government made a tactical error in not accepting earlier in the negotiations the main obligations of the Rome Treaty. This is perhaps true. But having previously raised many objections to he treaty, Britain could hardly begin bargaining by offering to sign the EEC's "Constitution". In any case, the veto was only exercised when it became obvious that the British Government was determined to make whatever concessions it thought necessary to join the EEC. The French negotiators, it would seem, never really believed that Britain would be prepared to pay the price of entry. When they realised that the British were determined to join there was no alternative but abruptly to break off the talks.

In other words, President de Gaulle clearly regards Britain as a rival to French domination of the European Community. The Labour Party Conference coming out in October, 1962, against Britain joining Common Market, except on impossible conditions, may have been a contributing factor. For by this time it seemed unlikely that the Conservatives would be returned at the next General Election. Again, the Nassau agreement on defence may well have been final proof for President de Gaulle to denounce Britain as an American "Trojan Horse" in Europe. What undoubtedly remains is the existence of a power struggle between Britain and France. And it cannot be said with certainty that this struggle will be resolved when President de Gaulle departs. Membership of the EEC by Britain and other EFTA countries will require extensive changes in the arrangements caused by the Rome Treaty. These resulted from long hard bargaining and the Six are understandably reluctant to go through the whole process again. Relations between the ten or eleven that would belong to such an enlarged EEC must inevitably be different (and for some perhaps less advantageous) than existing relations between the Six. For instance, the industries of the present members, together with the EEC Commission, have drawn up their plans in terms of a Community of Six. British entry would therefore introduce an element of uncertainty into a Common Market which is rapidly solidifying. Is it not a little naive, moreover, to believe that the Europeans are going to welcome the British on the grounds that they will introduce a degree of political stability and prevent the Community from drifting too far from the Atlantic alliance on questions of East-West relations, disarmament and attitudes to the developing countries?

The EEC has demonstrated that it is capable of running its own affairs. But its methods often differ from the ways of the Anglo-Saxon countries. The Common Market is, to quote Professor Walter Hallstein, the first president of the EEC Commission, not just in business but in politics. It would be a great mistake to believe that the course of the EEC will now necessarily run parallel to the American Grand Design. If Britain achieves membership of the EEC, the Government will have to work out what strategy it would prefer the Community to follow in trade relations, besides other areas of activity, with the USA and the rest of the outside world; if, on the other hand, Britain is again barred from membership what will have to be prepared is a studied alternative strategy for international economic policy.

2 TARIFF AND TRADE PATTERNS

Failure to formulate a successful trade policy since World War II is symptomatic of Britain's inability to adjust to the changed circumstances. The years after the war confronted Britain with an enormous challenge. Whereas the USA and Russia had emerged from the hostilities with a vastly increased productive power, Britain had consumed a considerable portion of her assets, especially overseas assets, and was consequently relatively the poorer. The National Institute of Economic and Social Research has calculated that during the two world wars, and the years immediately following, the US national income grew at an average annual rate of 4 per cent while the national incomes of the UK, France and Germany remained unchanged. Large gains were also made during the war years by neutral countries, particularly Sweden and Switzerland, and semi-industrialised Commonwealth countries, such as Canada.

Between the two world wars the European countries managed to achieve a higher rate of growth of gross national product (GNP)

ESTIMATES OF GROSS DOMESTIC PRODUCTS IN INDUSTRIAL COUNTRIES (At 1955 prices in US $'000 million)

	1899	1913	1929	1937	1950	1955	1964
USA	59.0	97.0	168.0	171.0	294.0	362.5	477.0
Canada	3.4	7.2	10.3	10.1	20.0	24.8	34.7
EEC	46.1	60.0	74.9	78.2	100.6	136.1	215.0
of which							
France	14.0	16.0	25.0	22.4	32.4	40.0	62.5
W Germany	20.5	27.2	28.4	32.4	33.7	51.9	85.0
UK	34.0	42.0	42.0	50.0	54.7	63.5	81.9
Continental EFTA	8.0	10.6	13.9	17.8	25.9	30.8	46.2
Japan	2.8	4.8	9.1	12.9	11.1	16.5	40.1
	153.3	221.6	318.2	340.0	506.3	634.2	894.9

Source: Bela Balassa, "Trade Liberalisation among Industrial Countries" (McGraw-Hill, New York, 1967).

than the USA. This trend has continued in most large European nations since 1950, but not in the UK. Britain's rate of growth in the period 1950-60 was only 2.7 per cent, compared with 3.2 per cent in the USA and over 4 per cent in all the other major industrial countries. These rates of growth of GNP were reflected in growth of exports which in almost every country were higher than national income, again except in the UK, which managed in 1950-60 to achieve an annual growth of exports of only 2.4 per cent, as contrasted with 16.9 per cent in West Germany, 14.1 per cent in Italy and 10.8 per cent in Japan. In the years 1960-65 the UK accomplished a slightly higher rate of growth of GNP of 3.3 per cent, and an export growth rate of 3.7 per cent; although an improvement, these rates were still almost half those of industrial competitors.

TRENDS IN TRADE AND OUTPUT IN
INDUSTRIAL COUNTRIES
(Average percentage rate of growth)

	GNP		Imports		Exports	
	1950–60	1960–65	1950–60	1960–65	1950–60	1960–65
Canada	4.0	5.5	4.7	5.9	3.8	7.7
France	4.5	5.1	6.4	8.8	6.0	7.0
W Germany	7.8	4.8	17.2	10.5	16.9	6.5
Italy	5.7	5.1	12.0	9.3	14.1	12.7
Japan	8.9	9.6	15.4	13.1	10.8	15.7
UK	2.7	3.3	4.3	2.8	2.4	3.7
USA	3.2	4.5	5.4	6.4	5.3	6.4
Total	4.3	4.8	8.1	7.3	6.6	7.2

Source: "OECD: Economic Growth 1960-70" (Organisation for Economic Co-operation and Development, Paris, 1966).
Note: Exports and imports are shown here on a "national accounts basis"; that is, including services and factor incomes from abroad.

Declining British Share of Trade

Britain's relative position in international trade has tended to decline with her declining share of world trade and production. The British share in the combined gross domestic product of the industrial countries declined from 13.3 per cent in 1929 to 10.8 per cent in 1950 and 9.1 per cent in 1964. Her share of the combined exports of rich nations has been falling even faster in recent years.

SHARES OF INDUSTRIAL NATIONS IN THE
EXPORT OF MANUFACTURES (in percentages)

	1950	1955	1960	1965	1966
USA	27.3%	24.5%	21.6%	20.5%	20.3%
UK	25.5	19.8	16.3	13.5	13.0
W. Germany	7.3	15.5	19.3	19.2	19.5
France	9.9	9.3	9.7	8.8	8.6
Italy	na	3.4	5.1	6.8	6.9
Japan	3.4	5.1	6.9	9.4	9.8

Source: *National Institute Economic Review*, National Institute of Economic and Social Research, London.

From 1950 to 1960 the British share of manufactured exports of the industrial countries fell from 25.5 per cent to 13.0 per cent. In the same period the US share has fallen from 27.3 per cent to 20.3 per cent. The largest relative increases have been registered by West Germany and Japan. Their shares have more than doubled. To some extent these statistics only reflect that the USA and UK built up very large shares of international trade in the immediate post-war years which would inevitably have declined as the other industrial countries regained pre-war positions. But the table above also indicates that the Common Market countries and Japan have achieved substantially faster export growths in the years 1950-66 than the UK.

Changing Pattern of Trade

Britain's "classical" pattern of trade, established in the period 1860-1930, was triangular in nature, consisting of an export surplus with the primary producing countries and an unfavourable trade balance with industrial Europe and the USA. This pattern was advantageous to the UK as the export surplus on trade with the primary producing countries was sufficient to cover the deficit on trade with the industrial countries and leave substantial funds for investment overseas. By 1913, through triangular trade and successful investment overseas, Britain had reached a position where investment income more than covered the trade gap, even though imports from Europe and North America were more than double exports to these continents.

In the inter-war period the balance of payments deteriorated. In the 1930s some overseas disinvestment occurred. Net income from overseas investment fell by nearly half between 1927 and 1932. The protectionist measures introduced in 1932 were envisaged as a means of reducing the balance of trade by as much as was necessary to keep the balance of payments at a level that would not endanger sterling. Imperial Preference was generalised in 1932 in an effort to shield Commonwealth exporters to Britain from the trade-restricting effects of these measures and sustain primary imports from the Commonwealth. Insofar as the UK bore most of the burden of the preferential arrangements in the 1930s, the result was to curtail Britain's ability to run an import surplus with continental Europe and North America.

TRADE IN MANUFACTURES BETWEEN INDUSTRIAL COUNTRIES
(At 1955 prices in US $'000 million)

	Intra-European		Intra	Intra-Continental	
					Japan/
			Intra	Europe	Europe
	UK/	Intra-	North	North	& North
	Continental	Continental	America	America	America
1899	2.00	1.50	0.16	1.24	0.20
1913	2.64	3.08	0.54	2.08	0.45
1929	2.29	3.77	1.56	2.78	0.64
1937	1.45	2.39	1.09	2.13	0.76
1950	2.27	2.96	2.49	2.63	0.30
1959	2.50	8.50	3.98	5.76	1.60

Source: Alfred Maizels, "Industrial Growth and World Trade" (Cambridge University Press, London, 1963).

Since the last war strenuous efforts have been made to reorientate British trade away from developing countries towards industrial ones. By the end of the 1950s Britain was clearly losing heavily through a large share of her trade being directed to the semi-industrialised countries, whose imports were growing considerably slower than those of Western Europe and North America. In the 1950s trade between the continental European countries was expanding at a rate of 5½ per cent per annum. By contrast, British trade with continental Europe was increasing at less than 1 per cent. Indeed, trade between Britain and Western Europe was no higher in 1959 than in 1913, whereas intra-continental trade had more than doubled.

According to one expert the severe contraction that took place in UK trade across the Channel was largely a result of the general rise in tariff levels and the introduction of trade restrictions in the 1930s.[5] As earlier indicated, these restrictions managed to support Commonwealth trade at a time when world trade was declining. This respite though was bought at a high price. For British exporters tended to look more and more towards sterling area markets and to neglect more dynamic ones. This remained the case after the war, at least until 1954, when the UK was still supplying 84.9 per cent of the manufactured imports of New Zealand, 71.4 per cent of Australia's and 52.8 per cent of South Africa's. With Australia and New Zealand these shares were higher than in 1937.

By 1966 the industrial areas were taking 55.5 per cent of UK exports against 42.5 per cent in 1956. The share of Western Europe in UK exports has risen in the last ten years from 26.3 per cent to 33.6 per cent and the percentage increase registered by exports to the EEC and EFTA has almost been identical at 123.2 per cent and 124.0 per cent respectively. The share of British exports taken by Commonwealth countries has fallen from 45.9 per cent in 1956 to 30.7 per cent in 1966 (including South Africa). UK exports to the USA have out-performed even EFTA figures, the percentage rise during the decade being 156.6 per cent. The adverse balance on trade with the USA, at current prices, has consequently fallen from £165.6m. in 1956 to £97.2m. in 1966.

Despite such developments the UK has maintained a very large export trade with the overseas sterling area and other primary producers. In 1966 these markets took 41.6 per cent of British exports. They also accounted for 40.6 per cent of UK imports. Commercial policy in Whitehall cannot afford to ignore this very important sector of British trade.

[5]Alfred Maizels, "Industrial Growth and World Trade" (Cambridge University Press, London, 1963).

The first lesson that can be drawn from trends in world trade is that Britain has a very real interest in, and can derive big advantages from, freer world trade. The attempt to maintain Commonwealth trade and the British home market in the 1930s may have made some sense in the inter-war years, but it makes little sense today. Trade is growing fastest between members of either continental Europe or the North American continent. Britain has much to gain from the lowering of trade barriers that would help to establish stronger links with those fast-growing regions. It seems likely that there are powerful factors in current economic development which have an expansionist impact on trade. These factors are at present playing a more important role in North America and Western Europe. They include, first, improvements in communications such as jet air transport, containerisation, liner trains, motorways and long-distance telephone services. A second important factor is the broadening of consumer and business tastes that has developed from television and increased international travel. Technological change is resulting, thirdly, in larger scale units of production and distribution. Then there is, fourthly, the development of international companies which are spreading "know-how" and modern management techniques.

These developments suggest that trade between industrial nations will continue to expand at an historically high rate. Britain is faced with the problem that much of this trade expansion will take place in either the EEC or the North American market. It is accordingly in British interests to ensure that there are the fewest barriers possible to prevent UK exports from competing in these two large common markets on the same terms as the products of the member countries.

It might have been thought that the Kennedy Round has reduced tariffs to negligibility. But they are still high enough to be a serious impediment to trade. For not only are the tariffs on some important manufactures quite high. Even apparently low tariff rates can represent significant protection of domestic producers. Economists have pointed out that what matters in this connection is not the rate of the tariff on the final product, but the rate of protection that that tariff affords to value added in domestic industry: and this "effective" rate of protection may be substantially higher than in the nominal rate of duty.

An arithmetical example may help to show how this conclusion is reached. Suppose a product has a world price of \$1.00 of which \$0.66 represents raw materials and \$0.33 the value-added by foreign producers. Assume imports of the product are subject to a tariff of 10 per cent. The domestic producer can therefore incur a maximum expenditure of \$1.10 to produce the item. How much more can he spend on value-added than the foreigner?

	Foreign Product	Domestic Product
Domestic market price	1.10	1.10
Price to producer	1.00	1.10
Cost of materials	0.66	0.66
Price chargeable for value added	0.33	0.44

The excess of domestic over foreign value added is \$0.11, which on a percentage of foreign value added is 33 per cent. This is the effective rate of protection afforded by the 10 per cent nominal tariff rate in this example.[6]

Commonwealth Preference

An obstacle to freer trade for the UK has been the system of Commonwealth preferences. Successful at a time when world trade was declining, the system has not maintained, when world trade is expanding, the British share of Commonwealth trade or the Commonwealth share of the British market. This is partly because the level of preference has been falling. It has been estimated that the average margin of preference on all imports into the UK was 10-12 per cent in 1937. This margin had fallen by 1948 to 6-7 per cent.[7] Much of this fall was due to rising prices. For the average prices of UK imports nearly trebled between 1937 and 1948, thus reducing the *ad valorem* incidence of specific duties. By 1957 the average margin of preference had declined to 5½ per cent. According to another study, carried out by the Board of Trade, the average margin of preference had risen by 1963 to 7.2 per cent, accounted for by a

[6]Harry G. Johnson, "Trade Preferences and Developing Countries", *Lloyds Bank Review*, London, April, 1966.
[7]Donald MacDougall and Rosemary Hutt, "Imperial Preference: Quantitative Analysis", *Economic Journal*, Royal Economic Society, Oxford, June, 1954.

substantial increase in the relative importance of manufactured goods (which get a higher preference) imported from the preference area.[8]

On the other hand, when account is taken of the "effective" tariff rates (that is, the much higher rate of protection on the portion of value-added), a 7.2 per cent average margin of "nominal" preference could be significant. This margin of preference will furthermore tend to rise as Commonwealth countries become able to send more and more manufactured goods to the British market. A margin of preference of this order could be extremely important to the industries of developing Commonwealth countries.

The margin of preference that British exports receive in other Commonwealth countries has also been declining on balance since 1932. In 1961 about one half of UK exports to the Commonwealth preference area, the Board of Trade study showed, entered duty free. Slightly more than half of Britain's exports enjoyed some margin of tariff preference: the average margin on all exports was $6\frac{1}{2}$-7 per cent. Comparisons with earlier studies indicate that the value of preference to British exports has declined during the post-war period, but not as fast as in the years 1937-48. The margins of preference Britain enjoys are above average in the Canadian, Australian and New Zealand markets where in 1961 margins of preference (on all imports from the UK) were 8 per cent, 10 per cent and 17-18 per cent respectively. In any case the economic growth of the older Commonwealth countries, in which Britain receives the most significant preferences, has been very considerable, contributing to the diversification of Commonwealth trade. Commonwealth exports are ten times their pre-war level and imports have expanded 12 times. If the pre-war proportions of these trade flows were assigned to the UK, the country would have to absorb about £3,100m annually of Commonwealth produce and to supply in return about the same amount of manufactured goods. Some decrease in the UK proportion of exports to the Commonwealth was therefore inevitable.

One of the problems posed then by British membership of the Common Market is that the adoption by Britain of the EEC common external tariff would convert the present preferences

[8] R. W. Green, "Commonwealth Preference: Tariff Duties and Preferences on United Kingdom Exports to the Preference Area", *Board of Trade Journal*, Board of Trade, London, June 11, 1965; and Green, "Commonwealth Preference: United Kingdom Customs Duties and Tariff Preferences on Imports from the Preference Area", *Board of Trade Journal*, December 31, 1965.

enjoyed by certain Commonwealth exports to Britain into an anti-Commonwealth preference for EEC goods. This problem does not present itself so severely in a free trade area (such as EFTA) which would allow the UK to maintain preferential margins, although, of course, they would have to be extended to other members, thereby reducing the effective Commonwealth preference. If tariffs within the free trade area, however, were reduced only gradually the margin of preference could be temporarily maintained by reducing tariffs against Commonwealth and developing countries at a faster rate than against the industrial members.

Professor Harry Johnson, now of the London School of Economics, has suggested in another context that there is a case for extending preferences to all developing countries, on the following grounds:[9]

    (a) that the developed countries have accepted a real obligation to assist the development of the developing countries;

    (b) that, nevertheless, they are for various reasons unwilling to increase their foreign aid programmes substantially; and

    (c) that any massive move towards trade liberalisation is not politically feasible in the near future.

In these circumstances, Professor Johnson argues "that an increase in aid given in the disguised form of trade preferences would be a desirable second best and could be sold to the public of the developed countries where a direct increase in aid could not".

Towards an Industrial Free Trade Area

Britain has a strong interest in removing trade barriers. She would gain easier access to the most rapid areas of trade growth. Export growth is closely connected to general economic growth. Freer trade would provide British manufacturers with much needed competition and at the same time allow industry to take advantage of considerable economies of scale. A greater degree of specialisation would be fostered which would in turn raise productivity. These factors, especially the dynamic factors, are difficult to quantify, but would certainly be very important to the British economy. They would provide, through market forces, the larger units and the increased specialisation which the Government is trying to encourage through bodies such as the National Economic Development Council.

[9]Johnson, *op. cit.*

Britain stands to benefit greatly from sharper and more intense competition, which can be a powerful agent in making the UK economy more efficient and by breaking the vicious circle of inflationary wage and price rises that have plagued the economy since the war. This is rightly advanced as a major reason for the British attempt to enter the EEC; but *a fortiori* it is a reason, too, for entry into an even larger trading group.

In the post-war period Britain has supported, as already described, multilateral agencies, such as GATT, in the movement towards freer trade. London has felt inhibited though in taking the initiative in more far-reaching schemes of regional integration because of the significance attached to world-wide trading links, Commonwealth connections and the special importance of the Atlantic alliance. The successful establishment of the EEC has forced Britain to undergo an agonising reappraisal of her future role in the world. Two successive governments have decided that it would be to the advantage of the UK to join the EEC.

Should the second attempt to join come to naught, it is necessary that Britain should have an alternative arrangement for arriving at freer trade. The analysis of the changing pattern of trade in this section suggests that the ideal solution would be international free trade between the industrial nations, coupled with special arrangements for the developing countries. For various reasons it seems unlikely that this ideal arrangement can be obtained through the traditional style of negotiation in the GATT.

The Role of GATT

Evidence suggests that the Kennedy Round has taken the MFN approach to tariff negotiations about as far as it can go. Sir Eric Wyndham White, as Director-General of the GATT, was quoted by *The Times* as saying on May 16, 1967: "The Kennedy Round is probably the last of the major pure tariff exercises. The next stage may come," he suggested, "in establishing free trade among major international industries."

Sir Eric had already suggested that the role of the GATT must change after the Kennedy Round. In an address at Bad Godesberg in October, 1966, he spelt out that future tariff negotiations would have to be of a different kind:

"I see progress in the field of tariff reduction as being best sought through the promotion by the major industrialised countries of a free trade arrangement covering, (a) the consolidation of all existing duty-free items, (b) the 'nuisance' duties I have earlier referred to, (c) certain sectors of industrial activity which are ripe for a move towards free trade, and (d) additional sectors or products on which duties could be eliminated from time to time through negotiation or agreement, or by unilateral action."

He said then that in his opinion arrangements of this kind should be negotiated in the GATT and the benefits extended through the MFN clause to other GATT countries. But as he also admitted, the successful results of international co-operation in this field will not be achieved if negotiations are limited to tariff and other trade barriers. In today's world co-operation in technology and research and development are also necessary. For these and other reasons it would appear that the future of trade liberalisation lies in the direction of wide free trade areas.

Possible Types of Trading Patterns

A free trade association can be confined to a few countries or it can be open to any country, anywhere, which wants to join. There is thus a wide range of possibilities, ranging from an association between the UK, the USA and Canada alone, through a similar association including EFTA or also including the EEC to one including all the industrialised nations of the world with special "associate" arrangements for developing countries.

It will be convenient to call the USA, Canada and EFTA (including the UK) grouping the North Atlantic Free Trade Area (NAFTA). When the EEC is also included this will be stated.

Initial progress would probably have to be made on the basis of certain "founder members" agreeing rules. These might well be the USA, the UK and Canada. But provision would certainly have to be made for the extension of the area to others at a very early date.

From the UK point of view there would be considerable advantage in a free trade area with the widest possible membership. The inclusion of the USA and the EEC would be highly desirable. Tariff-free access to these big, wealthy markets would give British industry the best chance to expand and specialise in the products in which UK manufacturers possess competitive advantages. If Britain is to abandon the policy of maintaining a protected home market, the biggest possible export opportunities might as well be sought in return. One disadvantage of such a wide, tariff-free area is that it would not be possible to accord significant preferences on manufactures or raw materials to developing countries or to the Commonwealth. But there would inevitably be a long transitional period—perhaps as long as fifteen years or even more—to enable businesses to adapt to the new rules of the game with minimal disruption. In this period it would be possible to continue to give, or even to increase, preferences to developing countries without demanding reciprocal concessions.

Participation in a free trade area would involve for Britain much less disruption to the existing pattern of her economy or political life than would membership of the EEC. Food could still be imported from the cheapest markets, thus avoiding the rise in the cost of living which would follow acceptance of the EEC's common agricultural policy. Britain would not have to "surrender sovereignty" or be obliged to clear so many matters with, say, the French before action could be taken. Consultative mechanisms would of course need to be developed. Harmonised policies, too, would have obvious advantages. But EFTA has demonstrated that a free trade area can operate successfully without an elaborate bureaucracy or the surrender of sovereignty.

On the assumption that Britain is or can become reasonably competitive, so that industry should not be overwhelmed by competition either from continental Europe or the USA, a free trade area, as wide as possible, but certainly including the USA, Canada and EFTA, has much to offer. But is it feasible? Examined next are some of the studies that have already been made into the different aspects of an Atlantic-based free trade area.

3 PROPOSALS FOR A NORTH ATLANTIC FREE TRADE AREA

The various NAFTA proposals were originally a response to the challenge President de Gaulle presented to the West when he vetoed Britain's 1961 application to join the EEC. At that time it appeared that the Common Market would be an inflexibly protectionist block in world trade and that those other countries desiring freer world trade would have to pursue that objective by negotiating special arrangements among themselves. The unexpectedly successful conclusion of the Kennedy Round has dispelled the worst of these earlier fears, but at the same time it has opened up the possibility of a further substantial move towards full free trade among industrial nations. Whether the members of the EEC would be prepared for this further step is at present extremely problematical; consequently, contemporary exponents of the NAFTA scheme see it as a means whereby those nations that wish to move ahead may do so without being blocked by the unwillingness of the Common Market countries to join in and yet without jeopardising the chance of their eventual participation.

Why a free trade area? If North Atlantic countries want free or freer trade why is it necessary to use this form of economic organisation? First, as already mentioned, it would seem unlikely that another multilateral negotiation like the Kennedy Round can again be mounted. In GATT negotiations the rate of progress has been determined by those major trading nations least willing or able to offer meaningful concessions. As a recent paper prepared at the request of the subcommittee on foreign economic policy of the Joint Economic Committee of the US Congress has pointed out:[10] "The unconditional application of the MFN principle has committed the multilateral approach to proceed like a wartime convoy, at the speed of its least active participant. Otherwise such a country would have been given through the operation of the MFN principle, a 'free ride'."

[10]Theodore Geiger and Sperry Lea, "The Free Trade Area Concept as Applied to the United States", submitted to Subcommittee on Foreign Economic Policy, Joint Economic Committee, United States Congress, Washington, D.C., July 28, 1967.

The success of the Kennedy Round means that another multi-lateral negotiation would be confronted with the hard-core problems such as textiles and the question of non-tariff barriers. Indeed, the Kennedy Round may well have made non-tariff barriers more significant obstacles to trade than tariffs themselves. Like the mountains at the bottom of the sea, non-tariff barriers have not been so important while trade has had to navigate against a raging sea of tariff protection, but as the level of the sea comes down, the peaks of non-tariff barriers are likely to show more above the surface. It is highly probable that non-tariff barriers will be resorted to more and more by governments as tariffs are removed under the Kennedy Round agreement. The GATT, however, has never had a very strong mandate in the field of non-tariff barriers and it is un-likely that negotiations in the GATT will be able to deal with them adequately. A free trade association, on the other hand, would be well placed to adopt measures to control the discriminatory effects of regulations and practices that affect the free flow of goods and services. Even EFTA, for example, which intentionally limited the degree of economic integration among its members, found it necessary to establish some "rules of competition" in order to prevent tariffs being replaced by non-tariff barriers.

Sovereignty

Although "rules of the game" are necessary, a free trade area, as has been demonstrated by EFTA, does not involve a pooling of sovereignty and the derogation of national powers to a supranational authority. This would be of great importance in any arrangement involving the USA. Professor Max Beloff, of Oxford University, has, among others, emphasised the point:[11]

> "It would seem to be the conclusion to be drawn from the fifteen years of history since the announcement of the Marshall Plan that the arguments about Atlantic unity tended to be circular ones. It was intellectually realised that many of the most important problems could not be resolved except on an Atlantic scale, but it was also felt that public opinion in the United States was so wary of any direct challenge to national sovereignty that only inter-governmental solutions were possible."

[11]Beloff, *op. cit.*

A free trade area thus seems the only arrangement, apart from a multilateral approach through the GATT, in which the US Congress would be likely to agree to American participation. It is interesting to note that the proposals that have been put forward from time to time to free trade on a North Atlantic basis have been worked out in terms of a free trade area and not a customs union or economic community.

In September, 1957, Mr. Peter Thorneycroft, Britain's Chancellor of the Exchequer, proposed in Ottawa what he described as an "adventurous proposal", namely the establishment of a free trade area between Canada and the UK. This proposal was a response to calls for a closer trade association with the UK that Mr. John Diefenbaker, the Canadian Prime Minister, had made earlier that year. The fact that Mr. Diefenbaker's Government was only a minority one made the position too delicate for this "adventurous proposal" to be entertained. To quote the correspondent of *The Times*: "Acceptance of a free trade area would have landed him (Diefenbaker) in all kinds of problems especially in districts where textile interests were calling loudly for protection. . . . Neither side wants to turn the idea down. Britain forced the issue to see how strong are the intentions of the Canadians on Anglo-Canadian trade."

The weakness of Mr. Thorneycroft's initiative, if it might be so called, was that it contained nothing for Canada. The country already enjoys free entry into Britain, but does not concede free entry to the UK. This argument is complicated by the fact (1) that British exports are given a substantial preference over other Canadian purchases abroad; (2) that many Canadian secondary industries with high wages and short production runs are not competitive with British exports there; and (3) that Canadian imports into Britain are not competitive with British home producers.

From the outset it has been greatly doubted whether the proposal was seriously intended. Details do not seem to have ever been spelt out. Instead, the incident has remained a sensitive point in the history of Anglo-Canadian relations.

Canadian-American Free Trade Proposals

While the Thorneycroft proposal was not pursued by either side, it did encourage groups in Canada to consider the problem of freer trade. In 1957 the Canadian-American Committee was established to investigate, on a private basis, problems arising out of the growing interdependence between Canada and the USA Sponsored by the Private Planning Association of Canada, based in Montreal, and the National Planning Association, in Washington, its membership is about evenly divided between Canadians and Americans and consists of 57 business leaders, 12 labour leaders, four heads of agricultural organisations and four university presidents.

The committee began by instituting a series of studies on the particular problems in the trade and other economic relations between the two countries. These researches gradually led to a consideration of the possibility of free trade between them as a general solution to these problems. In 1963 the various possible characteristics of a scheme for bilateral arrangements between the USA and Canada were examined in a paper, "A Canada-US Free Trade Arrangement". This study assessed the possible scope and nature of a free trade arrangement by systematically examining a wide range of practical choices. A second paper, "A Possible Plan for a Canada-US Free Trade Area",[12] published in 1965, narrowed down the alternatives to a plan for a Canada-USA free trade area. The hypothetical plan was based on a consideration of the several European projects, especially EFTA and the decision there not to allow exceptions in the coverage of non-agricultural products. This last was because of the difficulties that had arisen in the abortive Nordic customs union project where exceptions were attempted. The plan opted for a free trade area (rather than a customs union) as defined by GATT rules, on the grounds that:

"The arrangement would not attempt to create a closer economic union for its own sake. Accordingly the arrangement should not, beyond what is necessary to serve its basic purpose, interfere with the partners' freedom of action or with the normal operation of their private enterprise economies. The arrangement should also avoid interfering with the outside commercial relations of the two partners."

Canadian participation in the Commonwealth preference system was also cited as a factor indicating a preference for a free trade area over a customs union. In addition, it was pointed out that a free

[12]"A Possible Plan for a Canada-US Free Trade Area" (Canadian-American Committee, Washington, D.C. and Montreal, February, 1965). See also Sperry Lea, "A Canada-US Free Trade Arrangement: Survey of Possible Characteristics" (Canadian-American Committee, October, 1963).

trade area would offer the fewest difficulties in expanding member-ship to include other countries. The coverage of agricultural products would be limited, at least at the beginning, even though no exceptions would be allowed with non-agricultural products. But the plan did commit the partners to study the Canadian-American agricultural situation and, by a set date, to reach a basic agreement. Certain shock absorbers to ease the difficulties of adjustment to free trade were also provided for, particularly in the case of Canada. These included a prolonged transitional period for the removal of trade barriers protecting Canadian raw materials and manufactures. It was envisaged, for example, that the USA would make five annual cuts of 20 per cent on tariffs over 5 per cent whereas Canada would make ten annual 10 per cent cuts. Where competition could be drastically increased provision was made in the plan for adjustment assistance in the form of low-interest loans, and rehabilitation grants to workers and farmers to learn new skills and move to new jobs.

With membership of the proposed free trade area covering Canada, the USA and Puerto Rico (which is within the US customs area), it was laid down that:

"The free trade area would neither include nor affect tariff preferences involving the United States or Canada with other countries—namely the US-Philippines arrangement or the Commonwealth preference system."

On the other hand it was assumed, as a matter of basic principle, that the aim was to further the practice of freer trade throughout the world, rather than to create an inward-looking North-American trade bloc. Consequently paragraph 5 of the plan stated:

"While the free trade area would initially apply only to Canada and the United States, these two partners may subsequently negotiate with other independent countries concerning full or associate membership, or with other free trade groups concerning possible links or mergers with them."

Economic Integration

The committee regarded the degree of economic integration as the most complex area of decision. Appropriate steps would have to be taken, the plan's authors pointed out, to control the dis-criminatory effects of non-trade regulations affecting freely traded products. In general, however, the question of economic integration was approached cautiously. Steps were shunned that were not proven necessary. Some rules of competition were stipulated, based on EFTA experience. The partners would be expected to identify a number of obviously discriminatory government aids and settle on means of dealing with them before the founding date. The relevant paragraph in the plan said:

"The partners will take appropriate steps to control the discriminatory effects of such government aids to freely traded products as:

(a) measures resulting in assistance to exports to the partners.

(b) measures manifestly and artificially giving domestic production a competitive advantage over the production of similar products in the partner country.

(c) national transport policies resulting in rates or conditions manifestly favouring domestic products.

(d) measures favouring government procurement of domestic products over products originating in the partner country."

What the committee had in mind particularly was the special tax advantages which apply both in Canada and the USA with regard to shipbuilding. Here it was suggested that action should aim to equalise the degree of subsidisation as between the two countries. Another area of discrimination assumed to require inter-governmental agreement was that of preferential treatment of domestic producers in public procurement policy; here it was suggested that a common "Buy North American" policy might be adopted.

Provided for in the plan was the temporary imposition of restrictions against imports and capital flows. As a measure of last resort, these could be applied:

"(a) only after consultation with a partner, at which time the cause and possible remedies of the difficulty will be investigated and defensive measures other than restrictions on trade and capital will be carefully considered; and

"(b) only when the member imposing such restrictions agrees to do so for a specified temporary period and to refrain from treating its partner less favourably than any outside country."

Institutions proposed in the plan are designed solely to serve the Canada-USA free trade area and like the EFTA institutions are as simple as possible with a minimum supranational element. This was thought necessary, first, in order to allay Canadian fears of political absorption by the USA and, secondly, to satisfy the prerogative of the US Congress to approve or reject American foreign trade policy.

The plan provided for a council which would be the executive board meeting at two levels, normally that of the heads of permanent delegations and periodically that of cabinet ministers. As there would only be two members, majority voting was excluded and instead it was proposed that all council actions would require the agreement of both parties. A secretariat was envisaged but the plan implies that the council would be best able to determine organisation and procedures. An appeals board was also suggested, comparable to the examining committees of the EFTA convention, undertaking impartial appraisals of complaints. The plan provided as well for a Canada-US investment bank which could, if necessary, help to finance the investment and readjustment needs of industry.

Although the plan aroused only mild curiosity in the USA, the rigorous examination of the problems made it an interesting prototype for any future Canadian-American scheme. In Canada interest has been far more intense. The plan stimulated considerable comment there, providing a realistic basis for the Canadian Liberal Party's 1966 resolution which called for a North American free trade area.

Meade, Ohlin and Javits Proposals

Meanwhile, various other plans for a wider free trade area were being ventilated. In 1962 Professor James Meade, of Cambridge University, suggested that all the industrialised countries of the North Atlantic should together reduce their restrictions on imports from each other and from the rest of the world. In this way could be overcome the problems that would arise for the Commonwealth countries if Britain joined the EEC. Also ensured would be that the Common Market was itself outward looking. He saw the arrangement as a general agreement on tariffs and other trade barriers between an enlarged EEC and the USA.[13] But Professor Meade argued, too, that the arrangement was a viable alternative for Britain if satisfactory terms were not obtainable from the EEC.

In 1964 Professor Bertil Ohlin, leader of the Swedish Opposition at the time and a distinguished economist, in a speech to the Netherlands-Benelux Committee, reported in *The Financial Times*,

[13]James E. Meade, "UK, Commonwealth and Common Market: A Reappraisal" (*Hobart Paper* 17, Institute of Economic Affairs, London, 1962).

talked on November 12 of private discussions on a free trade area covering North America and EFTA in the event of the Kennedy Round breaking down. No more than a preferential area was foreseen at the beginning. But to satisfy GATT rules it would be necessary to work towards a free trade arrangement. More recently Professor Ohlin has elaborated on his views on preferential trading arrangements between EFTA and North America, arguing that it would be unnecessary to harmonise policies under such a scheme. For the main problem is to maintain full employment consistently with relative wage-price trends necessary to preserve balance of payments equilibrium under fixed exchange rates, a problem which faces governments anyway.[14]

In a famous speech on August 12, 1965, Senator Jacob Javits proposed on Washington's Capitol Hill that the USA should consider forming a free trade area with Britain that could be extended to Canada and then, on a reciprocal basis, to other EFTA countries, the EEC and eventually to all members of the OEEC's successor, the Organisation for Economic Co-operation and Development (OECD). His concern was to help Britain, as a vital member of the Western alliance, in her economic difficulties and, too, to look to the interests of underdeveloped countries. Senator Javits said the objective should be free trade in manufactured products among industrial nations by the end of twenty years. Associate membership should be offered to the developing countries with right of access to their markets after a transitional period in which they would be allowed to retain infant industry protection. He suggested, in addition, that there should be financial support for Britain during the transitional period, perhaps exempting her from the US interest equalisation tax in order to encourage the provision of long-term American private capital to modernise British industrial plant.

Later in the year, on November 8, the liberal Republican from New York elaborated on his proposal in London, calling for a wider free trade area. He said that if membership of the EEC could not be obtained, Britain should:

". . . consider phasing into a trade partnership with the USA, Canada and other industrialised countries. To be practical, such an alternative must be prepared in advance, or it will not be

[14]Bertil Ohlin, "Some Aspects of Policies for Freer Trade", in R.E. Baldwin *et al.*, "Trade, Growth and the Balance of Payments: Essays in honour of Gottfried Haberler" (North Holland Publishing Company, Amsterdam, 1965).

available when it is needed. . . . The USA must now indicate the degree of support it is prepared to give to the UK and to the 'Five', should a reconstituted EEC be necessary; and make it abundantly clear what it is willing to do in case the UK makes a *bona fide* attempt to join the EEC and fails again. This US alternative, which I proposed last August, may now be restated in the light of subsequent events as a proposal for a treaty of free trade and economic co-operation with the UK, other EEC and EFTA nations, Canada, New Zealand and Australia, and other industrialised countries of the OECD which agree to adhere to the new rules of trade of the free trade area."

The Javits speech was not an official trial balloon. It was an indication though that if the multilateral approach to freer trade appeared no longer workable, an important section of American public opinion was willing to contemplate and to recommend a new approach towards the freeing of world trade on the part of the USA. Departure from the traditional attachment to the principle of non-discrimination was no longer unthinkable.

A New Trade Strategy

During this period the Canadian-American Committee decided to consider the extension of the free trade area plan into a wider trade strategy. In May, 1966, a statement, entitled "A New Trade Strategy for Canada and the United States", was published.[15] Mr. Sperry Lea, the American research director of the committee, has described the work as motivated by a desire to think seriously about all plausible alternatives to the multilateral approach including a free trade area among willing countries. Of the strategy he has written:[16]

"This should not be seen as an act of retaliation against the EEC (which would be childish and counter productive) nor as a second best approach to be considered anon (which might well prove to be too late) but, rather, as perhaps the most sensible approach which the United States and Canada could take in the future."

The statement reviewed post-war trade negotiations and stressed several new challenges, among them the possibility that after the

[15]"A New Trade Strategy for Canada and the United States" (Canadian-American Committee, Washington D.C. and Montreal, May, 1966).
[16]Geiger and Lea, *op. cit.*

200

Kennedy Round the multilateral approach would cease to be appropriate; the difficulties, as well, confronting the Atlantic Community, especially the UK, and, too, the need to better meet the interests of developing countries.

Political goals, the statement observed, have become the primary considerations shaping US trade policy. Four were discussed: first, the reinforcing of the Atlantic alliance, with special attention to Britain's economic position; secondly, the strengthening of bonds between all developed countries, thus accommodating Japan, Australia and New Zealand in any Atlantic-based trade arrangement; thirdly, the assisting of economic growth, and thereby political stability, in less-developed countries; and fourthly, the channelling of US co-operative efforts through existing international institutions. Regarding US trade performance, the statement broadly assumed that the absence of a workable freer trade policy would mean a declining access to certain foreign markets for American exports.

With Canada the Committee agreed that although the political aims were important economic factors remain paramount:

"Foremost among the economic considerations are (a) the need to achieve the freest possible access to foreign markets for Canada's primary and related processed goods; (b) an expansion of the potential market for Canadian manufactured goods in order to permit increased specialisation (c) to allow access to imported goods that are lower in cost and better in quality."

Despite the different emphasis put on trade policy by the international interests of the USA and Canada, significant areas of common ground could be identified. A free trade area, under GATT rules, was subsequently found to be the most practical way of accommodating the two countries' policy objectives.

"Following the Canadian and American desire to broaden, rather than narrow, economic co-operation among all developed countries, such a free trade arrangement would need to have the widest practical initial or imminent membership and a sincere intention to embrace all industrialised countries, including those that might initially decline membership but might find it possible to join later. To be consistent with Canadian and US policy, the arrangement would also need to incorporate the objective of easing the trade problems of developing countries. In one proposed method the developed countries would extend free access to their markets without expecting full reciprocity until industrial progress in the developing countries made it possible for them to reduce their own trade barriers."

Outlined then were the broad principles on which a wider free trade area could be based. Those set out in the committee's North American plan still generally applied. On membership the committee specified that the free trade area should be based "on the principle of opening membership . . . to all eligible industrialised countries, and of extending some special 'one-way' trade privileges to all developing countries." The EEC, the EFTA nations, Japan, Australia and New Zealand are mentioned as countries that would clearly qualify for participation. Problems were nonetheless recognised:

"Under present circumstances, the participation of the EEC countries as a unit would probably be delayed while the economic and political problems accompanying the formation of their full customs union were being resolved. Likewise, the special geographic position and development policies of Australia and New Zealand might make them reluctant to participate for the time being. The unique character of some Japanese trade controls could introduce a special problem for Japan.

"In view of the uncertainties and special problems of some of the prospective members of a broad free trade association, it would seem most appropriate for Canada and the United States to establish a nucleus for the larger grouping by encouraging at the outset the participation of the United Kingdom and its EFTA partners."

The Committee's statement has left the ball in Britain's court. For as Mr. Lea has recently pointed out, "despite interest in some American circles, and a Canadian interest, a positive American response could only come after a positive expression of British interest".[17] The purpose of this paper is therefore to discover what the British interest in NAFTA might be.

[17] Lea, "Americans for Free Trade", *The Round Table*, London, January, 1967. This article discussed the development of interest in the free trade area concept in the USA. For a parallel account of interest in Canada see Roy A. Matthews, "Canadians for Free Trade", *The Round Table*, London, April, 1967.

4 EFFECTS OF NAFTA ON BRITAIN

Although a major post-war goal of British commercial policy has been the maintenance of British influence in the Atlantic alliance, little consideration has been given in the UK to the implications of an Atlantic free trade area. Too often when proposed it has been dismissed without study as either impractical, a non-starter for want of American support, or likely to be economically disastrous, leading to Britain's absorption by the USA.

Serious study in North America has shown, as already related, that the NAFTA proposal, in the context of American and Canadian trade policy, can be considered both practical and desirable. American official opinion, it is true, remains to be convinced. US trade policy is largely determined, though, by political objectives. Strengthening of the British economy is to the fore in this respect. The implications of a NAFTA arrangement for the UK therefore become a factor in the equation.

To Washington it must seem the British do not believe NAFTA, or something similar, would be economically advantageous for they have given it neither much consideration nor support. But this does not necessarily follow. It has been a habit of British Governments to fail to appreciate the longer-run implications of the first steps towards freer trade arrangements in Western Europe and then to find themselves anxious to join at a later stage.

In this section an attempt is made to assess the economic consequences for the UK of membership of NAFTA. The members of what might be a new grand design are assumed, in the first place, to be the USA, Canada, the UK and other EFTA countries. It is perhaps unlikely that the EEC would be interested in joining in the early stages. The common external tariff is widely regarded there as a necessary protective wall behind which there is a greater chance of integrating the Six into an economic union. Furthermore, the French Government is unlikely, it would seem, to agree at present to participation in a free trade area with the USA. Other countries—Japan, Australia and New Zealand—might well join a free trade area along the lines of the NAFTA proposal. Indeed, the Pacific countries have already given some consideration to a

Pacific free trade area which might include the USA and Canada. For purposes of this part of the analysis, the members of NAFTA are assumed to be only the North Atlantic countries outside the EEC.

Secondly, it was assumed that NAFTA, like EFTA, would be restricted, again in the first place, to largely industrial commodities and basic materials. The main method of providing agricultural protection is not so much tariffs as price support schemes and other internal subsidies. While there would be a strong case for the inclusion of freer trade in farm produce as an objective of the free trade area, and some agricultural undertakings might be a necessary condition of American support for the NAFTA idea, it would probably not be possible initially to include agricultural products and foodstuffs, except, as with EFTA, in a few special cases. Such a programme, and the further steps towards a more general freeing of agricultural trade, would be of great interest, of course, to temperate-zone foodstuff producers; indeed, it could make the difference between Australia and New Zealand joining or not. Even so, while recognising its importance, we have considered that the first step would probably be the formation of an industrial free trade area and accordingly restricted this study to that subject.

Relative Heights of Tariffs

The classical case for free trade is based first on the gains involved in the opportunity to sell commodities on better terms than would be possible in the absence of tariff reductions and, secondly, on the benefits that accrue from the opportunity to consume lower cost imports in place of more expensive domestic goods. There are other effects from free trade: the so-called dynamic effects, which take account of changes in production methods and economies of scale resulting from the increased size of the market. But the classical case is real enough and provided a useful starting point for our analysis.

To establish the relative heights of the tariffs of possible member countries was the first task. Various tariff comparisons have been made in the last few years. They have all been superseded by the Kennedy Round. For this study's purpose it was therefore decided to first compare post-Kennedy Round tariffs. This was a major undertaking. American and Canadian tariffs are not classified the same as those in West European countries, including the UK, which have all adopted the Brussels Tariff Nomenclature (BTN). We were assisted, however, by the various keys and concordances that were prepared by the British, American and Common Market authorities for the Kennedy Round. These have made it possible for the first time to compare accurately item-by-item the tariffs of the UK, the USA, the EEC and Japan.

Calculating unweighted arithmetical averages for all BTN groups corresponding to the Standard International Trade Classification (SITC) divisions permitted an assessment of the relative heights of the tariffs of the main industrial countries as they will be when the Kennedy Round reductions have been completed in 1972.[18]

The following table of industrial tariffs after the Kennedy Round indicates that the leading industrial countries will by 1972 have average tariffs in a range between 7.0 per cent and 12 per cent. At 11.2 per cent the average US tariff will be the highest, followed by the UK at 10.2 per cent, Japan at 9.8 per cent and the EEC at 7.6 per cent. The actual UK level of protection is lower, though, than would be implied by these figures because of the very low level of preferential duties levied on manufactures coming from the Commonwealth preferential area. Duty paid by Commonwealth countries will average only 1.2 per cent.

What is striking about this tariff comparison is the relatively low level of the rates that can be looked forward to once the Kennedy Round has been carried out. Only on textiles and clothing will the average rates in most industrial nations be in the range 15-25 per cent. Some individual items will still be heavily protected. These will be offset by many low rates. The average industrial tariffs of the major trading nations will be in a range considered low in pre-Kennedy Round days. Abolishing duties altogether now seems a practical proposition. The difficulties and advantages must not of course be under-estimated. For the magnitude of the flow of trade between the developed countries means that the reduction of even relatively low duties could make a considerable difference to international trade.

Examined next are the two static effects of trade liberalisation:

[18]It would have been interesting to have been able to calculate effective tariff rates, as explained on Page 185. The input-output tables required, however, to calculate value added coefficients are not sufficiently detailed to have allowed us to do this. In any case, it seems probable, from Professor Bela Balassa's original work, that the *relative* tariff levels would be the same whether using nominal or effective tariffs since we are comparing highly industrialised countries at similar stages of development. This being the case we decided to restrict this study to the nominal tariffs as they will stand in 1972.

INDUSTRIAL TARIFFS AFTER THE
KENNEDY ROUND (1972)
Comparison of average tariffs by SITC divisions
(Per cent *ad valorem*)

SITC		US	UK (MFN)	UK (Pref.)	EEC	Japan
51	Chemical elements & compounds*	9.4	8.8	0.2	6.8	9.1
52	Crude chemicals	3.9	6.0	0	2.2	3.3
53	Dyestuffs and Colouring materials	11.8	6.9	0	6.9	7.2
54	Medicinal & Pharmaceuticals	10.3	7.8	0.4	6.7	9.0
55	Essential Oils & Perfumes	7.8	10.6	0	6.1	10.5
56	Manufactured Fertilizers	4.6	4.6	0	3.0	2.5
57	Explosives	4.7	8.3	0	7.3	11.3
58	Plastics	10.5	6.4	0	7.5	9.5
59	Other Chemicals	8.8	6.4	0.4	6.0	9.6
5	**All Chemicals**	9.2	8.1	0.2	6.4	9.0
61	Leather manufactures	7.8	9.7	0.3	5.8	14.4
62	Rubber manufactures	6.9	8.5	1.8	5.7	7.7
63	Wood & Cork manufactures	8.2	7.5	0	7.3	9.0
64	Paper & Board manufactures	8.9	12.6	0	11.0	8.6
65	Textile Yarn & Fabrics	18.6	16.3	7.3	10.5	10.9
66	Non-metallic Mineral manufactures	10.5	9.1	0.03	6.5	7.6
67	Iron & Steel	8.7	9.0	0	7.2	8.9
68	Non-ferrous Metals	12.2	7.4	0	6.3	11.4
69	Other manufactures of metal	12.7	11.5	0.05	7.9	10.6
6	**Manufactures classified by materials**	12.3	12.0	1.2	8.0	10.0
71	Machinery—Non-electric	5.8	8.8	0.4	5.7	9.4
72	Electrical machinery	8.1	10.4	0.7	7.9	9.5
73	Transport equipment	7.2	10.5	2.5	8.5	9.7
7	**Machinery & Transport equipment**	6.7	8.8	0.8	6.8	9.5
81	Sanitary, Plumbing, Heating	14.9	11.5	0	9.0	8.8
82	Furniture	10.1	12.5	2.1	8.1	11.9
83	Travel goods	13.0	17.5	0	11.3	15.0
84	Clothing	22.6	19.9	9.2	11.8	16.5
85	Footwear	11.8	19.6	2.7	10.7	10.8
86	Professional & Scientific instruments	15.4	13.6	2.1	8.6	11.8
89	Miscellaneous manufactures	10.9	8.9	1.3	7.4	8.5
8	**Miscellaneous manufactured articles**	14.7	10.5	2.6	8.5	10.5
5–8	**AVERAGE TARIFF ON MANUFACTURES**	11.2	10.2	1.2	7.6	9.8

*Assumes abolition of ASP (see Page 235)

the trade creating and the trade diverting effects. These are, respectively, the amount of new trade that will be created for the UK, and the amount of non-member trade that will be captured by the UK in the North American markets.

Trade Creating Effect

The direct effect of NAFTA on member countries would be trade creation arising from the removal of tariffs over a period of years. To measure the trade expansion that would follow the dismantling of tariffs it was necessary to assume an elasticity of import demand. For finished manufactures we assumed, on the basis of studies by various economists, that a 1 per cent fall in import prices resulting from the reduction in tariffs would lead to an increase in imports of 3.5 per cent in the USA, 3.1 per cent in Japan, 2.68 per cent in the UK, and 2.06 per cent in Canada.[19] With semi-manufactures the 1 per cent fall in the tariff would lead, we assumed, to a 1.38 per cent increase in the USA, 1.42 per cent in Japan, 1.06 per cent in the UK and 0.82 per cent in Canada.[20]

The extent of changes resulting from NAFTA would also depend on the level of trade at the time tariffs were removed. Two variants were applied. First, we analysed the trade creating effect of dismantling tariffs in NAFTA using 1965 trade figures. Secondly, we projected current trade figures to 1972 in an effort to relate post-

[19]R. J. Ball and K. Marwah, "The US Demand for Imports 1948-58", *Review of Economics and Statistics*, Harvard University Department of Economics, November, 1962.

[20]The elasticities used in this study are more conservative than in similar studies made by Professor Bela Balassa in "Trade Liberalisation among Industrial Countries" (Council on Foreign Relations, McGraw-Hill, New York, 1967) in which the US import demand elasticity used is 4.12 compared with 3.5 in our study. The latter figure was used in order to base our study on the same elasticities of import demand as used by Professor R. G. Hawkins, of New York University, in his study of the economic implications for the USA of a broadly based industrial free trade association, published by New York University Press in November, 1968. As the ratio of domestic production to imports is much higher in the USA, the American elasticity of import demand is substantially higher than the UK and may well be higher than 3.5, in which case our study has *under-estimated* the rise in UK exports to the USA under a NAFTA arrangement. The use of the Balassa elasticity of US import demand would increase our estimate of the resulting increase in UK exports to USA by over 17 per cent.

We cannot therefore accept the critical statement, "North Atlantic Non-Alternative", made in *The Economist*, London, March 30, 1968, that our study "depended on some startling optimistic assumptions about the response of demand to price changes". See our letter in *The Economist*, April 6, 1968.

Kennedy Round tariffs to the trade figures of the year in which these duties will be operational. We also tried to allow for any price rise in the UK and Canada that would follow increased exports resulting from NAFTA by assuming, on the one hand, that prices would absorb 25 per cent of the tariff reduction and, on the other hand, that export prices would remain unchanged. This method establishes a fairly wide band of price changes in the UK and Canada, but assumes that since US exports only account for a small proportion of industrial production it would be possible for American industry to produce a reasonably substantial rise in exports without increasing prices.

The Anglo-American Trade Balance

The first important conclusion that emerged from the analysis was that, on the basis of exchange rates ruling prior to sterling's devaluation in November, 1967, Britain's balance of trade in manufactures[21] with the USA would improve quite substantially in NAFTA provided British export prices could be held down. We calculated that, compared with 1965, under NAFTA the UK would be able to export $243m. more manufactured goods to the USA, but in return would only increase imports of manufactures by $186m. This means the trade balance with the USA would improve by as much as 30 per cent. On the other hand, if the greater effort meant a price rise in Britain amounting to a quarter of the amount by which tariffs are reduced, with no corresponding American rise, the UK would only be able to export $182m. extra manufactures to the USA, slightly less than the total increase in American exports to the UK.

Returning to the assumption that UK prices did not rise, relative that is to prices in the USA, the trade groups that would particularly benefit from the dismantling of US tariffs would be clothing (+$17.08m.), textile yarn and fibres (+ $13.89m.), motor cars, aircraft and other transport equipment (+ $62.16m.), non-metallic mineral manufactures (+ $21.25m.), machinery (+ $32.76m.), professional and scientific instruments (+ $9.85m.) and electrical machinery (+ $9.17m.).

The extent of increases in UK imports from the USA stemming from NAFTA would depend on the relative height of the UK tariff and the quantity of imports at the time of the removal of the tariff (assumed in this instance to be the same as the 1965 level). According

[21]See Table 4 on Page 252 for a definition of "manufactures" as used here.

to our analysis, the largest increases would come in machinery (+ $64.54m.), electrical machinery (+ $26.78m.), professional and scientific instruments (+ $19.10m.), transport equipment, including cars and aircraft (+ $18.18m.) and paper and board (+ $11.57m.).

It has not yet been possible to use elasticities to calculate trade flows either in total or for individual categories between now and until the Kennedy Round reductions have been implemented in 1972. We have considered it useful, however, to give some indication of the possible position in 1972 by projecting the trends between 1960 and 1965. During this period the cuts arising from the previous so-called Dillon Round of GATT negotiations were being introduced and it is probable that the average annual rate of reduction will not be very different in the 1965-72 period from that which was actually achieved in 1960-65. Under this head also it appears likely that by 1972 Britain would have improved her balance of trade with the USA if NAFTA is introduced. We calculated on this basis that UK manufactured exports to the USA would increase by $454.0m. and UK manufactured imports would rise by $412m. As UK manufactured imports from the USA have been rising more rapidly in the period in which we based our projections, namely 1960-65, the improvement on the trade balance by 1972, on the assumption that this trend continues, would not be as favourable as it is at present. But even on these assumptions, the UK would derive some benefit from further trade liberalisation with the USA. On the other hand, if UK prices rose by 25 per cent of the tariff reduction and American prices did not rise, British manufactured exports to the USA would only increase by $340m., or $72m. less than the estimated increase in US exports to the UK. This emphasizes the importance of keeping down the relative level of British prices.

The UK-Canadian Trade Balance

The UK should gain relatively from the direct effect of free trade with Canada. In incidence, the UK preferential tariff on manufactures is considerably lower than the Canadian preferential tariff on UK manufactures. Unfortunately it was not possible to make the same detailed comparison of the Canadian tariffs with the UK and other tariffs. No key exists relating one to the other. Using previous tariff comparisons, and adjusting the figures for reductions in the

Kennedy Round, it was nonetheless possible to arrive at tariff averages for the main SITC groups for both the Canadian MFN tariff and the preferential tariff.[22] On this basis, Britain should be able to lift exports of manufactures by $49m. provided export prices remain stable. This would represent an increase of slightly more than 10 per cent of the 1965 total. Canadian manufactured exports to the UK, enjoying either free entry or low tariffs, would only increase fractionally as a result of NAFTA: by $2.6m., we estimate, if export prices remain stable; and by about $1.9m. if a rise in Canadian export prices absorbs one quarter of the tariff reduction effect. If UK export prices go up by the same amount, the country could expect to gain less, but still substantially more than the Canadians, namely about $36.8m. Even this figure would represent a 13.6 per cent increase in the favourable trade balance on manufactures which the UK enjoyed in 1965 with the Canadians.

On the basis of our projected trade figures for 1972, the UK would fare marginally worse, but could still expect to achieve a net increase in exports of almost $40m., given stable export prices. The UK exports which should do best, on the basis of 1965 trade figures, would be machinery (+ $13m.), transport equipment (+ $7.5m.), electric machinery (+ $5.5m.) and clothing (+ $2.2m.).

Trade Diverting Effect

Implementing NAFTA would not only create trade between members. It would divert some trade away from third countries to member ones. British exporters, for instance, would benefit from tariff free entry to the American market, whereas EEC exporters would continue to pay the US tariff. This trade diverting effect could be important on account of the size of the export trade of the EEC with North America. In 1965 the Common Market exported $2,901m. manufactures to the USA and $429m. to Canada. About 10 per cent of EEC exports to North America might be deflected as a result of the tariff differential. This calculation is based on a low elasticity of substitution of 1 and it should be noted that American economists have estimated that the elasticity of substitution between

[22]"Atlantic Tariffs and Trade", (Political and Economic Planning, London, 1962).

USA and European exports in third markets was about 2.5.[23] If a similar elasticity applied to UK-EEC exports to the US the diversion effect would, of course, be much bigger than has been allowed for here. Nevertheless, even on fairly conservative assumptions, we calculated that the UK would deflect $261m. of EEC exports from the US market and $43m. from the Canadian market. On similar assumptions the UK could capture about 10 per cent of Japanese trade in North American markets, if Japan were not in NAFTA. Britain should be able to gain almost as much Japanese trade in the USA as could be captured from the Europeans—say about $225m. This would, of course, provide a strong motive for Japan to join the free trade area.

TRADE CREATION EFFECTS OF NAFTA
(Export Prices Constant)
US $ million

	USA	Canada	Total
UK Exports	243	49	292
UK Imports	186	3	189
Net Balance	+ 57	+ 46	+ 103

The trade diversion effect of NAFTA, at least as far as the UK is concerned, could be more important than the trade creating effects. If we assume that UK trade with other EFTA countries would not be directly affected by NAFTA, as the tariff barriers have already been abolished, then the trade creating effects, as far as the UK is

[23]An elasticity of substitution of 1.0 is low compared with estimates of substitution of 2.5 between US and European exports in third markets made by Arnold C. Harberger in "Some Evidence on the International Price Mechanism", *Journal of Political Economy*, University of Chicago Press, December, 1967. We used this conservative measure of trade diversion in order to allow for the factors which we have not been able to quantify in this study. For example, Britain would also lose a small share of her existing markets in EFTA to the USA and Canada under a NAFTA arrangement (including the EFTA markets). It was not possible to repeat for all the EFTA countries the calculation of tariff averages for trade groups. Professor Balassa, *op. cit.*, has made some calculations on the basis of the average Swedish tariff *before* the Kennedy Round agreement. These showed that the resulting effect on UK exports would probably be small because the EFTA tariffs were generally low. The USA would also capture a share of the UK preferential market in Canada and likewise the Canadians could divert some British exports from the US market in a NAFTA scheme. We have estimated, as shown later in this chapter, that a North American free trade area could result in a diversion of $103m. of UK exports to North America although the effect of a NAFTA arrangement would obviously be considerably smaller.

concerned, would be as set out below (on the assumption that UK and other export prices are constant).

On the alternative assumption that export prices in Canada and the UK would rise by 25 per cent of the amount of the tariff reduction, with no rise in US export prices, the net balance would be reduced from $103m. to $31m.

TRADE CREATION EFFECTS OF NAFTA
(Export Prices Rises in UK and Canada)
US $ million

	USA	Canada	Total
UK Exports	182	37	219
UK Imports	186	2	188
Net Balance	− 4	+ 35	+31

The trade diversion effect could be larger. As already seen, the UK could win trade away from the EEC in the North American market totalling $304m. and from Japan, in the same market, totalling $248m. The total trade diversion effect could therefore be $552m. compared with an increase in British exports through trade creation of $292m. With Japan as a member of NAFTA, however, the trade diversion figure would fall to $304m. and the total increase of British exports, through trade creation, would be $317m.

The combined trade creating and trade diverting effects of NAFTA (on the assumption that Japan was not a member) would amount to $844m; that is 8 per cent of all British manufactured exports and almost a 56 per cent increase in British exports to North America compared with the 1965 figures. Assuming export prices remained stable, the UK balance of trade with USA and Canada would improve by $657m.; if they rose by 25 per cent of the tariff reduction, the trade balance with North America would improve by $583.5m.

Comparison with UK in EEC

The devaluation of sterling in November, 1967, has made UK export prices more competitive in world markets. British shipments to the USA, for example, increased by 40 per cent in the second quarter of 1968 as compared with the same three months of 1967. As long as this advantage is maintained, Britain should benefit even more from a NAFTA arrangement than indicated in the calculations of this study, which necessarily have had to be based on pre-devaluation trade statistics.

What would be the trade creating and diverting effects of the UK joining the EEC? On the same assumptions, the trade creation effect would be slightly larger if Britain joined the EEC than if she joined NAFTA, despite the fact that the average tariff is lower, because the UK has a larger export trade at present with the Common Market than with North America. UK exports would increase by $316m. against an increase to North America of $292m. On the other hand, British imports from EEC countries would rise by $286m. with the removal of the UK tariff on Common Market manufactures. This figure would be almost $100m. greater than the comparable increase in British imports from North America as a result of NAFTA. Furthermore, the trade diversion effect to the UK's advantage would not be nearly as large as in NAFTA. We estimate that the UK, assuming the same elasticity of substitution, would take $165m. trade in manufactures away from the USA and $26.3m. away from Japan as a result of joining the EEC. The total trade diversion, on Britain joining the Common Market, would therefore be considerably smaller than trade diversion in NAFTA. It seems likely, moreover, that the UK would lose more to the EEC in Britain's "preferential" EFTA markets than the USA would take from Britain's preferential markets in Canada. Even ignoring the latter factor, it would appear that the direct effects of joining the EEC would not be as advantageous as joining NAFTA. (See Table 5 on Page 253.)

EEC AND NAFTA COMPARED
(Increase in trade resulting from UK membership)
US$ million

UK	NAFTA	EEC
Export Increase (trade creation)	292	316
Export Increase (trade diversion)	552	191
Import Increase	189	286
Net Change	655	221

While this comparison is restricted to trade in manufactures, membership of the EEC would involve Britain in such other commitments as the common agricultural policy and greater mobility of capital movements. Both these factors could be costly to the balance of payments, at least in the short run. NAFTA on the other hand could be restricted, at least initially, to trade liberalisation. Certainly, on the basis of the above assumptions, the NAFTA proposal would seem to hold out greater advantages for British exports than the EEC.

We also examined the direct effect of removing tariffs on the Anglo-Japanese trade balance in manufactures. In 1965 the total UK manufactured exports to Japan at $113.4m. were slightly higher than the $112.3m. imported from there. The lowering of tariff barriers between Japan and the UK would lead to an almost equal increase of trade both ways. British exports to Japan would increase by $25.2m. and Japanese exports to the UK by $24.8m., assuming constant export prices. But if export price rises absorbed one quarter of the tariff reduction, the trade increase for both countries would be smaller: about $18.9m. in British manufactured exports to Japan and $18.6m. in Japanese exports to the UK.

British machinery exports should do best, especially non-electric machinery, which could rise by $11.5m. on the basis of constant export prices. British chemical exports could rise by 15 per cent. Transport equipment and professional equipment should do quite well, although in these sectors the imports of Japanese goods could also be greater.

As might be expected, the Japanese could look forward to a net gain in exports of clothing and footwear. But we calculate that on the basis of existing trade flows the gain would be fairly modest, although Japan limits existing exports of cotton textiles to the UK. Japanese clothing exports would rise by $4.65m. and footwear by $1.58m. On the other hand, British exports of textile yarn and fabrics would rise by $2.09m. against an increase of Japanese exports to Britain of $1.66m. The UK should also benefit from the removal of the quota and other non-tariff barriers which extensively protect the Japanese market. This might decisively tilt the balance in Britain's favour.

North American Free Trade Area

It is possible that if the UK shows no interest in the NAFTA proposal, the USA and Canada may decide to "go it alone" and establish a free trade area, perhaps along the lines of the Canadian-American Committee's plan. Canadian economists have pointed out that in purely economic terms there is a strong case for Canada entering a free trade arrangement with the USA alone. Professor

Ronald Wonnacott, of the University of Western Ontario, points out:[24]

"The key to the future for Canadian manufacturing is success in getting on to a commercial footing with US industry. This holds true of the above free trade schemes which includes Canada and the US. However, it may be easy for Canadian industry to manage this adjustment if only Canada and the US eliminate tariffs. If Europe and Japan are included there is no guarantee that Canada will not be by-passed in the process of international rationalisation. The Canadian advantage *vis-à-vis* the US is in terms of lower wage costs, but if the free trade area includes other countries with even lower wages they might well pre-empt many of the major activities that otherwise are located in Canada."

The prospect of a North American free trade area, without Britain, must be taken seriously, if only because of the success of the Canadian-US automotive agreement which virtually eliminates tariffs on cars, buses and components between the two countries. Historically, Canadian cars have been comparatively expensive, due to tariffs forcing manufacturers there to produce a large number of models for a limited market. The agreement now allows Canadian manufacturers to undertake longer, more economic production runs to serve the whole North American market. General Motors of Canada, to quote a case in point, announced plans in 1966 to export about 75,000 cars and trucks to the USA during 1967, the first ever to be sent over the border by GM of Canada. There are signs that the agreement, made in 1965, is beginning to equalise production costs in the two countries, one of the main factors responsible for past price disparities.

The automotive agreement is being suggested as the basis for similar agreements in other sectors. For besides removing duties, the automobile companies agreed with the Canadian Government that they would (1) maintain the existing ratios of Canadian production to Canadian sales, (2) make certain that a 60 per cent Canadian value is added to components, labour and overheads, and, (3) expand Canadian production by $260m. beyond normal growth by 1968.

[24] R. J. Wonnacott, "Trade Arrangements among Industrial Countries: Effects on Canada" (Studies in Trade Liberalisation, Johns Hopkins University Press, Baltimore, 1967).

British industry has not been happy about the agreement. It removed, after all, the substantial advantage that Commonwealth preference afforded UK car exports. (The preference remains *vis-à-vis* other non-Commonwealth countries, the main competitors in Canada where British cars are concerned.) But a North American free trade area in all manufactures and industrial materials would be a far more serious matter for British exporters.

A North American free trade area would inflict serious damage on British trade with Canada and the USA. Assessing the extent of this damage in quantitative terms is very difficult. The preferential tariff on UK exports to Canada averages about two-thirds of the MFN rate, but exceptions abound and such important items as cars and footwear enter duty free. US transport costs are considerably lower than British ones and it is difficult to estimate the relative importance of this compared with the tariff preferences.

It would not be unreasonable to assume, however, that the US might capture 10 per cent of British exports to Canada and that Canada might capture 5 per cent of British exports to the USA. Implied here would be a loss of $50m. in British exports to Canada and $53m. to the USA. The machinery sector would probably be hardest hit. Chemical and iron and steel exports would also suffer. Needless to say, the actual loss of British trade might be considerably bigger than these educated guesses suggest.

Relative Labour Costs

The Canadian-American Committee's study highlighted the relative labour cost advantage that Canada enjoys over the USA. According to Professor Wonnacott the Canadian advantage represents a total cost advantage of 7-8 per cent in the labour intensive leather and clothing sectors.[25] At the other extreme, the Canadian cost advantage is as low as 1-2 per cent in the petroleum and, too, in the pulp and paper industries where wages account for only a small proportion of total costs.

This line of reasoning also applies to the comparative cost advantage which could hold good for Britain where average hourly wages are considerably lower than in either Canada or the USA (For comparisons see Table 2 on Page 248.) These costs include not only direct wage costs (such as time earnings and piece rates plus shift and overtime rates) but also all indirect wage costs including

[25]*Ibid.*

216

social security benefits, paid holidays and training costs. The table is based on statistics prepared by the Swedish Confederation of Employers,[26] supplemented by data for Canada obtained from the US Bureau of Labour Statistics.[27] Total wage costs in the UK

1965 TRENDS IN PRODUCTIVITY AND WAGE COSTS IN MANUFACTURING INDUSTRY
(Value in US$. Index 1960 = 100)

	Average Hourly Wage Costs		Output/Man Hour		Wage Costs/Unit Output	
	Value	Index	Value	Index	Value	Index
USA	3.20	119	4.44	120	.72	99
Canada	2.15	109	3.64	115	.59	105
France	1.29	147	1.74	125	.74	118
W. Germany	1.52	163	2.36	129	.65	126
UK	12.0	132	1.38	115	.87	115
Japan	.45	173	.72	147	.62	118

Sources: Swedish Employers Confederation, Bureau of Statistics: "Direct and Total Wage Costs for Workers".
US Bureau of Labour Statistics: *Bulletin,* 1518, June, 1966.
National Institute Economic Review, Statistical Tables, May, 1967.

compared with North America and Western Europe are the lowest, the table shows, in the following industries: chemicals, beverages, building materials, mining, foodstuffs, paper, and shipyards. They are the second lowest in the following: textiles, rubber, engineering, construction, clothing, iron and steel, and road vehicles.

Labour costs are of course the most decisive in manufacturing industry, accounting in the UK for about half of all inputs. Although labour costs in Britain are lower, labour productivity is considerably lower than in the USA or Canada. Wage costs per unit of output

[26]"Direct and Total Wage Costs for Workers, 1957-65", Swedish Employers Confederation, Stockholm.
[27]*Bulletin,* Number 1518, United States Bureau of Labour Statistics, Washington, D.C., June, 1966.

were rising faster in the UK than in the USA or Canada in the period 1960-65, but not as fast as in West Germany, France or Japan. The potential gains from trade creation under NAFTA will depend to quite a large extent, as already discussed, on whether the UK can prevent export prices rising under the extra pressures of higher demand for exports or internal inflationary policies. This will depend in turn on whethe relative wage costs per unit of output can be prevented from rising in Britain more quickly than in the USA and Canada.

Non-Tariff Barriers

So far this chapter has been concerned with customs duties and levels of trade. But non-tariff barriers also loom large and will loom still larger as tariffs are lowered under the Kennedy Round agreement. A detailed study of this question has been made by Mr. William Kelly,[28] of the US Department of Commerce. We have drawn on it heavily. Non-tariff barriers take many forms and include quantitative restrictions and state trading, government buying, arbitrary methods of customs classification and valuation and anti-dumping legislation. Whereas the effects of removing tariffs can be assessed on certain assumptions, non-tariff barriers are not so easily quantified.

North American non-tariff barriers seem, on the whole, more restrictive on trade than those used in the UK or other EFTA countries. Coal is an exception. Many West European countries severely limit imports of US coal. The UK, for example, has prohibited imports of coal from non-Commonwealth countries since 1958. The US, though, provides an outstanding example of preferential buying through the well known "Buy American Act", examples of which are quoted later in this study (see page 234). In practice, the British Post Office and other government departments and nationalised industries follow similar "Buy British" policies. Investigation would probably reveal similar discrimination by European governments and state agencies. The USA and Canada have also different customs classification and valuation systems which have a very noticeable restrictive effect on trade.

The notorious American selling price, which applies to certain chemicals, is examined in a later section (see page 235). Canadian

[28]William B. Kelly, "Non-Tariff Barriers" (Studies in Trade Liberalisation, Johns Hopkins University Press, Baltimore, 1967).

valuation practices are almost as complex. The Minister of National Revenue, to take the most familiar aspect, may determine the value of goods for duty purposes if they "prejudicially or injuriously" affect the interests of Canadian producers; and he is free, apparently, to establish any value, although this provision does not apply to the British preferential tariff. Japan maintains quantitative controls on a wide range of imports, both to protect certain domestic industries and, too, to bargain for the removal of restrictions by other countries.

Given the importance of non-tariff barriers erected by other countries, Britain should gain substantially from the removal of non-tariff barriers in a NAFTA arrangement. While the coal industry would suffer as a result of American imports, the economy as a whole would gain.

The experience of Scotch whisky in the US market provides an interesting example of the effect of non-tariff barriers. This is one case, in fact, where the effect of the non-tariff barrier concerned can be readily converted into a tariff equivalent.

Whisky is among the traditional British exports which at present face considerable discrimination in the American market. Most distilled spirits, including whisky imports into the USA, are bottled abroad at less than 100 per cent proof, therefore paying excise tax and duty on a wine gallon basis. Nearly all spirits produced domestically are taxed on a proof gallon basis when they are withdrawn from bond. This results in a tax differential in favour of the domestic product. To illustrate, a gallon of imported Scotch whisky bottled at 86 per cent proof pays an excise tax of $10.50 (based on wine gallon assessment), whereas a gallon of bourbon whisky bottled after dilution to 86 per cent proof bears a tax of $9.30. In addition, the imported whisky pays a duty of $1.20. In effect the wine gallon basis of assessment results in a levy on the water content in the imported product of $1.61. It is estimated, on the basis of 1964 imports, that the additional revenue to the US Treasury resulting from this basis of assessment is around $60m.

In recent years there has been a shift from bottled to bulk imports largely for this reason. Whisky exporters, as it happens, prefer not to ship in bulk because there is a prestige value in foreign bottled goods and they are better able to control quality if they do the bottling themselves. Also the value added in the bottling and labelling of the spirit abroad is lost in bulk exports.

Dynamic Effects

The gains to the UK economy in extra trade if Britain was to pursue the NAFTA proposal could be considerable provided relative costs could be kept from rising. But there are other effects of trade liberalisation, what economists call the dynamic effects. These include the increase in the size of the market open to manufacturers which leads to cost reductions through economies of scale, increased specialisation and improved methods forced by increased competition. This aspect of increased trade is not new to economic thought. Adam Smith pointed out in "The Wealth of Nations" that:

> "The greatest improvement in the productive power of labour and the greater part of the skill, dexterity and judgement with which it is anywhere directed, or applied, seem to have been the effects of the division of labour . . . this division must always be limited . . . by the extent of the market."

Even so, it is only in recent years that economists have placed much stress on the dynamic effects in the theory of trade liberalisation. Professor Bela Balassa, of Johns Hopkins University, has drawn attention to the relationship between large-scale economies and market size. In his most recent work he has pointed out that on these grounds Britain should benefit from freer trade. He writes:[29]

> "In general, it would appear that the gain from economies of scale is inversely related to the size of national markets. In relative terms, the exploitation of economies of scale following the liberalisation of trade would therefore provide the largest gains to small countries. Still, indications are that countries of the size of the UK can derive considerable benefits from economies of scale following the liberalisation of international trade."

The long runs necessary to achieve full advantage from mass production can only be achieved if the market is sufficiently large. In theory exports can provide an indefinite enlargement of the market. But in practice manufacturers do not usually consider exports as an adequate substitute for a large home market. Exports tend to be highly precarious. They do not provide the requirements of a market—stability and uniformity of product—on which mass production can be safely based. Indeed, one of the most important

[29]Balassa, *op. cit.*

arguments underlying the economic case for British membership of the EEC has been that the Common Market could not then be suddenly closed off to British exports for political or balance of payments reasons, thus enabling manufacturers to plan accordingly. This point is actually far more valid as an argument for joining NAFTA, since Europe, even after tariffs have been removed, will not be a very homogeneous market, natural differences—widely differing local tastes and other market imperfections—being likely to remain for many years. It could be a long time before Europe can be said to be a "home market" for Britain, in the event of membership being achieved, even if the Community does evolve into a true economic union. NAFTA, on the other hand, would give British exporters access to the vast US market free of tariff and other trade barriers. And the American market exhibits a remarkable level of demand for homogeneous products and would therefore provide British industry with the right kind of economic climate for taking full advantage of economies of scale. The increase in total US imports between 1964 and 1965 was just over £1,000m., almost double the total of British exports to the USA in 1965. Such is the size of the American market that although total imports amounted to £7,000m. in 1965 this represented only 3 per cent of GNP in the USA.

There are several ways in which increasing the size of the market, and thus the size of the economic unit, could lead to increased efficiency in British industry. First, certain industries and companies can realise economies of scale by building larger plants. These are particularly crucial in technologically based industries such as petrochemicals, where labour costs have been shown to rise by only 20 to 30 per cent and capital costs by only 60 to 70 per cent as output doubles.

Secondly, a larger market permits a higher degree of specialisation within an industry. The motor car industry is frequently cited in this connection. For instance, the specialised production of components in separate plants in the USA has allowed greater economies of scale to be reaped in electrical and ignition systems, radiators and heaters, steering wheels and transmission equipment. Until 1914 almost all the world's cars used German magnetos. Even in 1915 British aircraft still used Bosch magnetos acquired through Switzerland. The British market, it has been remarked, has not been big enough to encourage the growth of specialist producers of equipment

H*

—who themselves might have created new possibilities of progress.[30] Professor Balassa has also pointed out that generally the cost advantages from vertical specialisation produce a situation where material costs are 10 to 25 per cent lower in the USA than in Western Europe because American producers can draw on a vast network of specialised suppliers who enjoy economies of scale.

Thirdly, a larger market permits the lengthening of production runs for individual commodities. This horizontal specialisation has been cited as accounting for a considerable part of the differences in productivity between America, on the one hand, and Europe and Canada on the other. Higher productivity in USA compared to Canadian textile plants has been explained by the fact that American firms can concentrate on a single fabric while Canadian establishments often produce 5 to 100 types of fabric. The Canadian-American Committee's plan for a free trade area in North America drew attention therefore to the productivity gains that industry in Canada would achieve through greater specialisation as one of the main reasons for Canadian participation in a free trade area.

Toning up the Economy

Another dynamic effect of trade liberalisation is the intensified competition that results from the lowering of tariff and other trade barriers. An argument that is often used regarding the benefits of British membership of the Common Market is that this would give British industry a "salutary jolt". The argument, however, would apply even more strongly to participation in a NAFTA arrangement. For American industry, in general, is more competitively minded than its European counterpart. Various explanations have been suggested. Professor Tibor Scitovsky, of the University of California, has pointed out:[31]

> "Much of European industry was established on a small scale at a time when the advantages of large-scale production were not yet known; and this has created vested interests and a tradition that are among the main obstacles that stand in the way of a transition to the now more economical large-scale production in a few plants. . . . Also with the smaller scale

[30]C. F. Carter and B. R. Williams, "Industry and Technical Progress" (Oxford University Press, London, 1957).
[31]Tibor Scitovsky, "Economic Theory and Western European Integration" (George Allen and Unwin, London, 1958 and 1962).

of national industries and markets in Europe, personal relations are closer and feelings of solidarity are greater among competitors. . . . Hence the prevalence of cartels in Western Europe: and the price rings. Common Market organisations and gentlemen's agreements are frequent even in uncartellised industries."

Whatever the reasons, European industry certainly tends to be more cartel minded than competitive in outlook. There are consequently many areas where the Common Market's formation has not resulted in price reductions commensurate with lowered tariffs. This is apparently the case also in EFTA where the secretariat has recently made an investigation into the situation and reported that there was little or no evidence that the lowering of tariffs had brought down prices, although it was admitted that price increases had not been so great as they might otherwise have been. American industry, by contrast, believes in a more effective form of competition. Anti-trust legislation, the influence of the frontier, and pioneering traditions have played their part. The USA is consistently pioneering the important innovations in research, management techniques, advertising and so on. If Britain wants the advantages of a competitive environment she is far more likely to achieve them under the NAFTA plan than within a Europe that is cartel minded and less competitive.

Mr. Michael Shanks, a former industrial adviser to the Department of Economic Affairs, has argued that Britain would only be competitive with the USA in industries possessing a high labour-capital ratio. In other words, the comparative advantage that Britain enjoys over the USA lies in only one thing: the cheaper cost of labour. He argues that "the USA by contrast would greatly increase penetrations of the British market in high-technology, capital intensive industries—computers, electronic capital goods, scientific instruments and the more sophisticated types of machinery scientific instruments and the more sophisticated types of machinery".[32]

But this thesis is not supported by recent trends in British exports to the USA or by empirical studies. For the most rapidly growing items of UK exports to the USA during the last decade have been aero-engines and machine tools. According to our calculations, the

[32]Michael Shanks, "NAFTA: The Mirage in the West?", *The Times*, London, December 4, 1967.

UK industries that would benefit most from trade liberalisation are capital intensive ones, such as transportation (+ \$116m.) and iron and steel (+ \$96m.). These findings are supported, moreover, by the views of business economists as expressed in a survey conducted by Maxwell Stamp Associates, the results of which are summarised in Chapter 5 of this study.

Mr. Shanks argues that the best way to close the technological gap is to exclude American exports, but the only possible consequence of keeping out American technology (which takes the form of an industrial input) would be to penalise British technology. There is only one long run "protection" against American industry, namely the ability to compete through specialisation and efficiency; and these two factors depend to a large extent on greater UK access to the American market and greater opportunities for joint contracts with US companies.[33]

Economic Growth—NAFTA and EEC

Yet another dynamic effect of joining a larger market might be to accelerate Britain's rate of growth. Often it is suggested that Britain should adhere to the Rome Treaty because the EEC is "the most dynamic market in the world". The implication is that the rate of growth of GNP in the Six has been high in recent years and therefore Britain can expect to benefit from a free trade relationship with countries enjoying higher rates of growth than the UK. That the EEC itself was responsible for accelerating the growth of GNP in member countries, or that if it did the effect was lasting, has never been demonstrated satisfactorily.[34] West German growth, for instance, declined from an average of 9.3 per cent in the period 1950-55 to 4.8 per cent in 1960-65; in 1966, GNP there actually declined. The growth of some countries outside EEC (such as Japan) has also been exceptional. At the most the EEC can only be claimed as one of the factors responsible for growth performance.

Growth depends, first, on the rate of expansion of economic capacity and, secondly, on the change in the degree to which capacity is utilised. The first is more fundamental depending, as it

[33]Harry Cowie, "Why NAFTA Makes Sense", *The Times*, December 11, 1968.

[34]Alexander Lamfalussy, Economic Adviser to the Banque de Bruxelles, was one of the first to raise serious doubts about the presumed role of the EEC's formation in the growth performances of member countries. See his article, "Europe's Progress: Due to Common Market?" *Lloyds Bank Review*, London, October, 1961.

does, on the rate of growth of working population and of output per employed person. According to the OECD the USA will experience a very rapid increase in working population, rising from 111.2m. in 1965 to 136.30m. in 1980.[35] This increase is almost double what is expected in Italy (the West European country with the fastest-growing working population) and almost four times the increase expected in West Germany.

The Canadian working population is also forecast to increase even more rapidly than that of the USA. In the years 1965-70 the Canadian working population will rise, it is projected, by an average 9.2 per cent a year against 6.6 per cent in the USA and only 2.3 per cent in West Germany.

1965-80 ESTIMATED INCREASE IN WORKING POPULATION

Average per cent increase

	1965-70	1965-80
Canada	9.2	na
USA	6.6	22.8
Italy	4.4	13.2
Sweden	3.5	10.6
UK	3.4	10.2
France	3.4	11.6
Germany	2.3	4.8

The rapid expansion of working population in North America will tend to be reflected in a faster rate of economic growth. Using official statistics of working population, we made estimates of employment in 1977 and prepared projections of GNP for 1972 and 1977 for NAFTA and the EEC. In the absence of any adequate basis for estimating changes in productivity beyond 1970, we assumed that the forecasts of output per person made by the OECD would be achieved. The OECD figures were adjusted for the forecast trend in hours worked and the anticipated effect of economic and social policies, but they take no account of trade liberalisation. The results are shown in Table 1 on Page 247.

Even on the assumption that unemployment in North America will

[35]"Demographic Trends, 1965-80" (Organisation for Economic Cooperation and Development, Paris, 1966).

average more than twice the level in Western Europe, the USA and Canada are expected to out-perform most European countries. Canada would have the highest annual rate of change of GNP at 5.2 per cent (except for Portugal which, starting from a low base, shows up a 6.6 per cent rate). France, at 5 per cent, would have the highest 1965-77 growth rate among the EEC countries. For West Germany a comparatively low growth rate of 3.6 per cent, reflecting her low growth of working population, is calculated. The continental EFTA countries emerge slightly better from the calculations than the EEC; not so well, though, when the UK is included. The UK, after the relatively low rate of growth from 1960-65 returns, in the table, to a 3.1 per cent rate for the years 1965-77, the lowest of all those countries listed. But NAFTA, with the UK included, would be expected to have a 4.5 per cent rate of growth, about a quarter of 1 per cent greater than the EEC. If the UK was included in the EEC, then the Common Market's overall rate would be lower at 3.9 per cent. More interesting, perhaps, is the massive size of the NAFTA market. The total GNP of NAFTA countries, on this basis, could be $1,375,000m. by 1977, with the USA alone having a GNP of $1,065,000m. compared with a GNP for the EEC of $453,000m.

What effect could the NAFTA proposal have on Britain's rate of growth? While the dynamic aspects of a larger market are probably of most consequence to the UK in the long run, they are also the most difficult to assess. Various attempts have been made by American economists to quantify the effect of the US market size on the American rate of growth. One has estimated that in the first half of this century a doubling of labour and capital inputs in the US non-agricultural sector was accompanied by a 130 per cent increase in output due to economies of scale.[36] In other words, unit costs fell by 23 per cent as output doubled. Another has suggested that economies of scale accounted for 20 per cent of the growth in output per employed worker in the period 1929-57 when the US market expanded by $842,000m.[37] At 1965 levels of GNP the extra output representing the scale effects of a NAFTA arrangement would be $742,000m. That is, the market would expand by almost as much as the growth in the US market in the years 1929-57.

[36]A. A. Walters, "A Note on Economies of Scale", *Review of Economics and Statistics*. November, 1963.
[37]E. F. Denison, "The Sources of Economic Growth in the United States", (Committee for Economic Development, New York, 1962).

Assuming this expansion would produce the same growth in productivity in the UK as in the US in these years, we arrive at a figure of 0.49 per cent per annum as the added growth of UK *per capita* income as a result of the economies of scale that could be attributed to NAFTA (2.6 × 0.20 × 0.94) where 2.6 per cent is the growth of *per capita* income in the UK in the years 1960-65.

American Investment in the UK

Increased US direct investment in British industry is another factor that could raise Britain's rate of economic growth under a NAFTA scheme. Insofar as American exports are able to expand their share of the UK market, which could be expected in industries enjoying a comparative advantage, perhaps where know-how and capital are important, it seems likely that there would follow a tendency towards increased investment in Britain. There is indeed a historical pattern whereby American firms are induced to invest abroad as they become familiar with foreign markets through exports. The UK as a base for American industry in Western Europe would presumably become more attractive if Britain were in NAFTA. The country could be a convenient place for servicing and exporting across the Channel to countries within both NAFTA and the Common Market (where the tariffs will be substantially reduced by the Kennedy Round). As the British market would be the largest West European one inside NAFTA, and as American firms would no longer be hindered from exporting back to the USA by the tariff, the UK would be likely to continue to be a key area for American overseas investment.

In the recent past the Community has been taking a large share of the flow of US direct investment capital abroad (excluding "ploughing back" by subsidiaries). For example, in 1965 $814m. of new direct investment capital went to the EEC compared with $324m. to Britain and $896m. to Canada. Total US direct investment, though, in the UK in 1965 was $5,119m. against $6,254m. in the Common Market and $15,172m. in Canada.

Professor M. F. Kreinin, of Michigan State University, in his study on the effect of trade liberalisation on the USA, asked 2,000 American firms operating in foreign countries how a NAFTA arrangement, including the EEC, would affect their foreign investment decisions. Half those which replied said such an arrangment would not affect the situation. About a quarter expected either to contract their foreign manufacturing operations or avoid an otherwise expected expansion; slightly less than a quarter anticipated an expansion of foreign production facilities.[38]

Canada, it appears, would be the main loser from a change in investment decisions. Several firms indicated they would contract or liquidate Canadian operations while expanding elsewhere because the Canadian market would (under the NAFTA plan) be better supplied from the USA. Only one company indicated the reverse—a pharmaceutical company, where the US duties on protected imports from Canada are significant. Professor Kreinin concluded that the new Atlantic design might result in a small contraction of total foreign investment, primarily in Canada. But more significant than the overall effect would be the rationalisation of production, involving consolidation of facilities and all product lines, changes in the composition of investments and a shift in location. The principal loser of American capital would be Canada; the shift from Canada, moreover, would be towards Western Europe. Of the fixed geographical areas, the EEC was mentioned most frequently as the site of possible expansion followed closely by the EFTA countries (the study having been made on the basis of the EEC being a member of NAFTA). It appears probable that if the Community is not a member, and tariffs are not important on the products concerned, the UK would be a strong contender for American investment. There is, therefore, little reason to fear that the flow of American capital would dry up; rather, the opposite worry, that it might be too big has to be taken seriously because of actual or supposed political repercussions.

Many fear the large domestic American market would afford US industry an unequal position from the outset in any freer trade scheme. The advantage from the existing, extensive economies of scale would be so overwhelming that freer trade and the removal of restrictions on labour and capital mobility would result in an outward flow from the UK to the USA. History records some examples of regions or countries that have suffered relatively from free trade groupings or economic unions. The classic one is provided by the Kingdom of Naples in the unification of Italy when the free trade policy introduced in 1861 probably ruined southern industry and

[38]M. F. Kreinin, "Trade Arrangements among Industrial Countries: Effects on USA" (Studies in Trade Liberalisation, Johns Hopkins University Press, Baltimore 1967).

led to a capital flight to Milan and the north. Both Scotland and Northern Ireland have experienced lower rates of development than England, brought about by an emigration of labour and capital. But this argument is based on a mistaken analogy. The southern Italy and Northern Ireland situations were largely due to deficiencies in social and economic infrastructure not found in Britain. As Professor Balassa has pointed out:

"The United Kingdom possesses a highly developed industrial structure; hence the relevant question is whether business firms would have sufficient incentive to carry out the transformation necessary to meet the challenge of foreign competition."

5   BRITISH INDUSTRY AND NAFTA

To discover how British industry would react to the NAFTA proposal, Maxwell Stamp Associates sent a questionnaire to a sample of commercial and industrial companies employing members of the Business Economists' Group, a professional body whose membership is representative of a wide range of firms. We considered there was a greater likelihood of economists seriously examining the possible consequences of the proposal – which few UK firms have studied in any depth – than other executives. Of the companies circulated, 54 per cent agreed to take part in the survey. Although a small sample cannot form the basis for a definitive assessment of the attitudes of British industry to the plan, we regard the views expressed as significant, especially since 30 out of the 41 participants in the survey appear in *The Times* list of the 300 leading UK companies (including 15 in the top 100).

The majority did not consider that adaptation to a NAFTA arrangement would create for them major problems. In answer to the question, "To what extent would your company be faced with a problem of adapting itself to a NAFTA scheme", 65 per cent replied, "To a minor degree"; 20 per cent replied, "Not at all"; and 15 per cent replied, "To a major degree".

Only one industry foresaw a major problem of adaptation. That was the computer industry. But three out of the four companies in the industry considered that, changes notwithstanding, when all factors are taken into account, there would be a clear and progressive balance of advantage to their firm from UK membership of NAFTA. The fourth replied that more detailed information and study was required. Only two other companies in the survey considered NAFTA would involve a major adaptation problem. One was a chemical concern which candidly admitted that "the EEC would be a blow, particularly if monopoly and cartel legislation is enforced" and that "membership of NAFTA would spell the end of the road for the company as it is at present". The other was an American-owned company in the food industry. Their position, they pointed out, "may be atypical" because they have subsidiary companies in other potential NAFTA countries as well as a parent company in the USA.

In general, therefore, the companies questioned did not subscribe to the view that British industry would be "flattened" as a result of NAFTA. On the contrary, the abolition of tariff and other trade barriers, they seemed to believe, would be unlikely to erode substantially British markets either at home or abroad. We asked: "UK membership of NAFTA would eliminate tariff protection against imports from, first, the USA and, secondly, (possibly) Japan. To what extent would you expect your company's home market trade to be adversely affected?" With US imports, "Not at all" was the reply of 22 per cent; with Japanese imports, that was the answer of 27 per cent. Just over half expected that their UK trade would suffer a little from the tariff-free entry of American goods, but only 17 per cent expected theirs would suffer very much. As for Japanese goods entering freely, only 12 per cent would expect to suffer severely, 44 per cent taking the view their home business would suffer only a little. The remainder either did not know or did not have sufficient information to form an opinion.

While most British firms did not anticipate big inroads into their home markets to flow from UK participation in NAFTA, the majority did not expect either that the removal of tariffs and other commercial barriers would make a great difference to sales in the USA. Only 17 per cent thought they would expect to gain much in the US markets. Perhaps they were considering only the trade creating effects, neglecting trade that might be captured from other European countries and Japan. Over 60 per cent believed a little would be gained from the removal of American tariffs; and 17 per cent, the same proportion as expected to gain very much, thought they would not gain at all. Various special factors were cited by those that would gain little or not at all. These are probably better analysed industry by industry.

Mechanical Engineering

The majority of the mechanical engineering firms in the survey considered that on balance the net effect of the removal of tariffs under a NAFTA scheme would assist a little, but not much, their sales at home and in the other member countries. Only one out of four thought they would gain very much from the removal of US tariff and non-tariff barriers. None were concerned, on the other hand, about American companies penetrating their home market to any marked degree with the removal of UK trade barriers. One did consider though that the free entry of Japanese engineering products could have an adverse affect.

These views doubtless reflect the fact that tariffs are no longer regarded by the industry as a very important factor. In the USA the average tariffs in 1972, following the Kennedy Round, for SITC groups in division 71, will range from 3 per cent on agricultural machinery to just over 7 per cent for metal-working machinery. Average tariffs in the UK will only be slightly higher, ranging from 8.2 per cent for office machinery to 10 per cent for power generating machinery. In fact, Britain's industry has been able to increase exports to the USA very substantially, despite the existing tariff there, which at present averages on machine tools, for instance, about 15 per cent. The industry's most striking individual increase in 1966, compared with 1965, was a rise of 123 per cent in value of UK metal-working tools. This increase reflected the high level of capacity at which the US economy was running in 1966, but it can also be attributed to the reasonable export performance of the metal-working machine tool makers. An even better export performance has been registered by the British agricultural machinery group. The largest companies in the UK are American or Canadian owned. Since they are already established in most of the NAFTA countries it would seem doubtful whether the removal of the remaining barriers would make an appreciable difference. As one large North American firm commented: "For most purposes this company can be considered to be already part of such a free trade area. Removal of a few tariffs would allow the scrapping of certain uneconomic production facilities."

In general it appears that the dynamic effects of NAFTA would be considerably more important than the actual removal of the tariffs. One expert remarked, with regard to machine tools:

"According to the manufacturers themselves, prices are not of prime importance in determining the pattern of trade in these goods, and it is not altogether certain that the removal of tariffs would have a marked direct effect upon trade. Perhaps the greatest gain to the UK machine tools industry would be the increased dynamism of the whole British economy which might be a hoped for consequence of freer trade."

232

AVERAGE MACHINERY TARIFFS BY 1972
(Per cent *ad valorem*)

SITC		USA	UK (MFN)	UK (Pref.)	Japan	EEC
711	Power generating machinery	7.0	10.0	1.6	12.3	6.3
712	Agricultural machinery	3.0	9.4	1.9	8.2	5.4
714	Office machinery	5.2	8.2	0	14.8	6.3
715	Metal-working machinery	7.1	9.1	0	9.4	4.9
717	Textile machinery	6.9	8.8	0	7.8	5.6
718	Machines for special industries	5.2	7.3	0	8.2	5.0
719	Machinery, appliances and parts	6.0	8.7	0.25	8.8	6.1
71	Non-Electric machinery	5.8	8.8	0.4	9.4	5.7
722	Electric power machinery	13.3	9.4	2.0	10.6	6.4
723	Equipment for distributing electricity	8.3	8.3	1.0	10.0	9.7
724	Telecommunications equipment	7.5	10.8	1.7	9.5	8.9
725	Domestic electrical equipment	7.5	8.0	0	8.8	6.6
726	Medical electrical equipment	10.8	13.3	0	8.8	7.3
729	Other electrical equipment	7.5	11.2	0.5	9.6	7.8
72	Electrical machinery	8.1	10.4	0.7	9.5	7.9

Electrical Engineering

The electrical engineering companies that took part in the survey fell into two groups. There were those, first, involved in computers, as well as other aspects of heavy electrical engineering. In general they considered there was much to be gained in the US market, although business in the home market would suffer considerably. The remainder of the companies believed the removal of trade barriers in NAFTA would only lead to small gains and small losses. Again, the Kennedy Round has reduced tariffs to a level of little significance. On electrical machinery the UK average tariff will be 10.4 per cent by 1972, against 8.1 per cent in the US, 9.5 per cent in Japan and 7.9 per cent in the EEC. One of the British computer companies commented:

"Tariffs are not an important barrier to international trade in the products of this company, so that further reductions of tariffs through NAFTA beyond the agreed 50 per cent cuts in the Kennedy Round would not be of major significance. The

233

most important consideration would be the removal of non-tariff barriers to trade, in particular, improved access to the American market that would result from the abolition of the Buy American Act."

Non-computer companies had mixed reasons for not attaching much importance to the tariff barriers (apart from the question of their height). Two were American-owned and had already a very high export ratio which they doubted could be improved upon. One of these pointed out that the American parent company decided their global operations, which at present did not include the USA or Canada and "therefore we would not as a company benefit to any extent on present policies from British participation in NAFTA. In fact, we may suffer to some degree from the elimination of customs duties against US and Japanese goods."

The abolition of non-tariff barriers, especially public procurement policies, could have a considerable effect on the pattern of trade in heavy electrical equipment. This is an area where one expert considers that the lower labour cost of British and German manufacturers outweighs the technological advantages of the American companies. For example, it was reported that in tenders on power transformers and power circuit breakers submitted to the Tennessee Valley Authority, foreign producers undercut American companies by a wide margin. The Central Electricity Generating Board's monopolistic buying powers allow the British industry to retain the UK market but perhaps at the expense of higher generating costs and an over-capitalised structure. Removing non-tariff barriers would therefore work both ways. But as the American market is so much larger, and the increased competition would work to the long run competitive advantage of the British companies, the removal of these barriers could result in a much healthier, if smaller, UK industry.

Non-tariff barriers are not as important to the domestic electrical appliance industry. Here the level of tariff protection is geared up by the calculation of purchase tax on the price of the imported item plus the customs duty. The real competitors for British manufacturers are in Common Market countries, not the USA. Access to the American market could nonetheless be important to certain British firms at present unable to take advantage of the full economies of scale.

Chemicals

The effect of removing tariffs and non-tariff barriers in the chemical sector will remain uncertain until the US Congress decides whether or not to abolish the American Selling Price (ASP) system of fixing the chemical customs duties on the basis of the wholesale price of a comparable American-made product. ASP was applied to benzenoid chemicals after World War I to afford added protection to the coal tar sector of the US chemical industry. It is applied to imports of benzenoid intermediates and to certain finished products such as dyes and pigments, medicinals and pharmaceuticals, flavouring and perfume materials, synthetic rubbers, pesticides and plastics and resin materials. ASP applies only if the imported item is considered competitive with US domestic production. The application of ASP can have a prohibitive effect on the tariff incidence. A report by the US Tariff Commission has pointed out that a 40 per cent tariff rate applying to the ASP of a particular group of dyes results in an equivalent 172 per cent *ad valorem* tariff. Sometimes ASP can have the effect of arriving at a lower duty when foreign prices are higher than US prices. But on average ASP has the effect of doubling the level of the tariff. As a result 43 of the 108 categories covered by ASP carry effective duties exceeding 50 per cent.

ASP was a *cause célèbre* in the Kennedy Round. It was generally agreed that an automatic and unconditional 50 per cent cut would be made by the USA (except for duties already below 8 per cent), but until ASP is abolished the tariffs of other countries will only come down by 20 per cent. To placate the Swiss the cut on dyestuffs will be by an unconditional 35 per cent. A further 30 per cent reduction will be made by the UK, the EEC and other GATT countries if and when the US Congress removes the ASP system for chemicals. The US chemical industry has been fighting the abolition of ASP very hard and, at the time of writing, the situation is uncertain.

For the purpose of this study we assumed that ASP would be eliminated and that the industrial countries will lower their chemical tariffs by half by 1972. By that date the average level of tariffs in the industrial countries of the world will not present, as the table shows, an unsurmountable barrier to trade. Probably for this reason the chemical companies that took part in the survey indicated that, on the whole, they would only expect a small gain in the American market and correspondingly a small loss in their domestic market from either American or Japanese imports. One exception, already mentioned, said that a NAFTA arrangement would adversely affect its domestic market to a considerable degree. But it seems this particular company is anyway uncompetitive. The majority of the chemical companies believed they would enjoy an overall advantage in the NAFTA plan for sales at home and abroad, although the advantage would be small. Here again, there can be little doubt that the relative level of tariffs, if the full Kennedy Round reductions are implemented, will be quite low, but not low enough to accord British producers the benefits of a large-scale market enjoyed by their competitors in the USA and the Common Market.

AVERAGE CHEMICAL TARIFFS BY 1972
(Per cent *ad valorem*)

SITC		USA	UK (MFN)	UK (Pref.)	Japan	EEC
512	Organic chemicals	19.0	10.6	0.6	11.9	8.5
513	Inorganic chemical elements*	6.3	7.7	0	6.9	5.9
514	Other inorganic chemicals	8.3	7.1	0	7.8	5.8
515	Radio active materials	4.6	10.4	0	3.3	3.2
521	Mineral tar and Crude chemicals	3.9	6.0	0	3.3	2.2
531	Synthetic organic chemicals	19.2	8.8	0	8.1	10.8
532	Dying and Colouring materials	8.0	4.4	0	4.1	5.2
533	Pigments and Paints	11.9	7.9	0	8.7	6.7
541	Medicinal & Pharmaceuticals	10.3	7.8	0.4	9.0	6.7
551	Essential Oils and Perfumes	6.6	11.0	0	9.0	5.2
553	Perfumery and Cosmetics	16.5	13.8	0	16.3	7.5
554	Soaps	6.9	8.8	0	11.3	7.1
561	Manufactured fertilisers	4.6	4.6	0	2.5	3.0
571	Explosives	4.7	8.3	0	11.3	7.3
581	Plastics	10.5	6.4	0	9.5	7.5
599	Other chemical materials	8.8	6.4	0.4	9.6	6.0

*Assumes abolition of ASP (see Page 235)

Vehicles

In 1966 the North American market for UK motor exports was slightly smaller at £116m. than the EEC at £116.9m. EFTA was larger than both, taking £149m. of British motor products. The tariffs on motor cars (at present 7 per cent) in the USA are low and, following the Kennedy Round, will be even lower—only 3 per cent. With motor cycles and bicycles the tariff will be lowered from 10 to 6 per cent. The Japanese tariffs on cars, at present 40 per cent, will come down to between 20 and 30 per cent by 1972. The UK and EEC tariffs on cars will be reduced by then from 22 to 11 per cent.

The vehicle manufacturers did not therefore consider that the abolition of these tariffs would make very much difference to either their home markets or their sales in the US market. One large American-owned UK motor company stated that British membership of NAFTA would not make any difference to their sales in the USA and similarly they did not expect that the abolition of tariffs would affect their home sales, at least as far as US exports were concerned. They considered, though, that Japanese competition could have a small effect.

A large British aircraft producer, however, considered that the NAFTA proposal would create considerable advantages in the US market. The tariff there on aircraft is currently 10 per cent and will come down to 5 per cent. The British tariff of 14 per cent is waived whenever an airline can demonstrate that the equivalent aircraft is not produced in the UK. British planemakers would benefit even more from the removal of the non-tariff barriers, especially the Buy American Act, which requires that goods of domestic origin be purchased by federal agencies for use in the USA except when the domestic cost exceeds by 6-12 per cent the foreign bid price, including duty. The US Defence Department, however, has increased to 50 per cent the price preference given to domestic producers in order to diminish expenditure affecting the country's balance of payments. As Britain's aircraft exports to the USA were

AVERAGE TRANSPORT TARIFFS BY 1972
(Per cent *ad valorem*)

SITC		USA	UK	UK	Japan	EEC
731	Railway vehicles	8.1	9.4	0	7.5	5.8
732	Road motor vehicles	3.5	14.3	5.5	12.5	13.7
733	Cycles and Trailers	12.4	16.1	1.9	9.1	11.0
734	Aircraft	8.0	9.2	0	14.2	7.1
735	Ships and Boats	6.5	2.3	0	6.9	2.5
		7.2	10.5	2.5	9.7	8.5

40.2 per cent of her total aircraft exports in 1966, a waiving of the Buy American Act could substantially increase the size of the UK's largest export market for aircraft.

Metal Manufactures

The largest metal manufacturers in the UK, the steel industry, were unable to take part in the survey because the National Steel Corporation had only just been formed. In general the British average tariff or iron and steel products is 9.0 per cent, compared with 8.7 per cent in the USA, 7.2 per cent in the EEC and 8.9 per cent in Japan. It remains to be seen what difference the formation of the larger units under the National Steel Corporation will make to Britain's relative competitive position. Certainly the US steel industry does achieve a higher return on assets than the British industry, although comparisons of this kind, based as they are on different depreciation rates and asset valuations, are limited in value.

Return on Total Assets %	1961	1962	1963	1964	1965	Average 1961–65
UK	6.5	2.8	2.1	3.5	3.2	3.6
USA	7.8	6.4	8.5	10.2	10.2	8.6
Return on Fixed Assets %						
UK	9.5	4.0	3.0	5.2	4.9	5.3
USA	14.4	11.7	16.3	19.5	19.3	16.2

Other metal manufacturers that took part in the survey had varying attitudes towards the NAFTA proposal. One large mining and smelting concern could see a considerable advantage coming from such an arrangement, especially in the US market. Another large company, a metal user, did not consider that there would be any overall balance of advantage to its sales, either at home or abroad. A third company, a medium-sized one which is a subsidiary of a US company, was "already prevented from selling more to the North American continent by our parent company: NAFTA would not affect this situation".

Textiles, Clothing and Footwear

The Kennedy Round did not have as much impact on textile and clothing tariffs as it did on other sectors. The cuts, on average, work out at about 20 per cent. This could be important for the UK

should, on the whole, benefit from a NAFTA arrangement with the US, Canada and EFTA in textiles, clothing and footwear, where Britain has a strong relative advantage because of relatively low labour costs and a high degree of specialization. This relative advantage is particularly strong in woollen textiles.

Unfortunately not many textile manufacturers have members of the Business Economists' Group in their employment. The only woollen concern that took part believed that they would gain substantially from free entry to the American market. With the luxury woollen industry this should indeed be so. For the tariff on cashmere sweaters will still be 17 per cent at the end of the Kennedy Round adjustments. North America at present takes £37m. of Britain's total £170m. exports of wool fabrics.

With cotton textiles and footwear Britain has a relative advantage over the USA and Canada and should gain from free trade with these countries, although not as much as in the case of woollen textiles. It is unlikely that this relative advantage would continue if Japan was a member of NAFTA, and the relative advantage would quickly disappear if the less developed countries were given a preferential tariff position in NAFTA. An agreement to extend preferences to developing countries, if made by all NAFTA countries (including later the EEC), would take a considerable amount of the pressure off the UK market which, alone among the developed countries, allows tariff free entry for textiles, clothing and footwear from developing countries, members of the Commonwealth.

The reaction of the textile companies in the survey was therefore mixed. One large textile and fibre company conceded that there would be a small overall balance of advantage for their sales effort in both home and export markets, but did not believe it would make more than small gains in the USA. A large clothing retailer also considered that the NAFTA plan would probably result in a small overall gain. Another textile company, which supplies intermediate products direct to clothing manufacturers, was inclined to think that Japanese membership of NAFTA would be advantageous as a supplier of textile raw materials, but disadvantageous as a direct competitor. This company accordingly considered that the balance would turn on whether textiles were treated as a special case.

Other Industries

Among the other industries that took part in the survey, the British paper industry, already confronted with EFTA competition, stands out as the one most likely to lose. A large paper company took the view that NAFTA would provide no overall balance of advantage to them and furthermore, their domestic business would be considerably affected by American paper and board entering tariff free.

The building materials industry, on the whole, thought there was little or nothing to gain or lose from NAFTA. A large building construction firm did not expect that it would be affected as the industry is scarcely affected by changes in tariffs.

A large group in the food, drink and tobacco field considered that although the overall advantage to its sales from the lowering of tariffs in NAFTA would be small, nevertheless there would be a clear and progressive balance of advantage in terms of the general growth that would, in its opinion, be generated by the arrangement. As has already been mentioned, however, an American-owned foodstuffs company held the view that there would be no advantage for it in NAFTA since considerable competition could be expected from American and Japanese sources.

Economies of Scale

The firms that took part in the survey placed more importance on the dynamic aspects of a free trade area. They were asked: "Does your company see advantages concerning economies of scale stemming from NAFTA?" More than three times as many considered that there would be advantages from such economies as the number which believed that the tariff reduction would lead to considerable expansion of sales. Three-quarters of the engineering companies, both mechanical and electrical, considered that they would gain from economies of scale. The chemical companies did not foresee the same advantage in NAFTA, although a recent report by the National Economic Development Council on manpower in the chemical industry came to the conclusion that "the scale of operations is a major factor in the achievement of increased output per man in America". This apparent contradiction could stem from the fact that some major chemical companies have already set their sights on achieving economies of scale in a European market and have not yet considered in any depth the NAFTA proposal. The other major industry which envisaged advantages of scale was the vehicle industry.

We also asked the companies if they considered that British

membership of NAFTA would bring easier access to American know-how. The reasoning behind this question was that American companies might be more likely to arrange contracts to share know-how if there was no fear that tariffs or other barriers might prevent full advantages being taken of specialisation. Here again there were about twice as many companies which considered that NAFTA would facilitate easier access to American know-how as there were who foresaw a considerable expansion of trade stemming from the reduction of tariffs.

The companies were also asked: "How would you expect your company's expenditure on research and development to be affected by British membership of NAFTA?" One third visualised their level of expenditure increasing. Only one believed that its spending on research and development would be cut. The remainder either considered that the level of expenditure would remain the same or else they were unwilling to commit themselves. About a quarter of the companies questioned replied that joint research and development with US companies would expand as a result of NAFTA. A few companies, less than 10 per cent, considered that such joint activities with EEC countries would contract in the event of NAFTA being formed.

Although, as was pointed out at the beginning of this section, companies did not on the whole believe that NAFTA would necessitate major adaptations, between a quarter and a third of them considered that the adaptation that was necessary would involve rationalisation to form bigger units. Even more took the view that NAFTA would involve changing production techniques or switching to new products. Almost all the electrical engineering companies, including the computer firms, held this opinion. Not so many companies, however, considered that adaptation would involve a reorientation of their trading and commercial policies, although the computer companies did believe this would be the case.

The Overall Advantage

Finally companies were asked how they assessed the balance of advantage to their company in a NAFTA arrangement. "Firstly, how would you expect your company's costs on balance to be affected by British membership of NAFTA?" One company, largely engaged in merchanting, thought its costs would rise. About one fifth visualised their costs being decreased; these companies were spread fairly evenly between the various industries. The majority of companies believed that costs would largely remain unchanged. On the question of profitability—how the companies expected their profits would be affected by British membership of NAFTA—the breakdown was more interesting. Of the participants in the survey, 33 per cent believed that their profitability would rise as a result of NAFTA, 40 per cent considered theirs would remain the same and only 10 per cent believed that their profitability would fall.

The final question was posed as follows: "In the light of all the above, do you think there would be a clear and progressive balance of advantage to your company from membership of NAFTA?" Fifty per cent answered in the affirmative. There were 7 per cent who did not consider there was a clear advantage, and 10 per cent were unwilling to commit themselves at this stage. As pointed out at the beginning, the survey conducted as part of this study was too small to be conclusive. But it did include some of the largest British industrial enterprises. Very few believed that taking on the Americans in a free trade area would lead to British industry being overrun; quite the opposite: half the companies in the survey believed that there would be a clear advantage to their company under a NAFTA scheme and about a third saw this working out in terms of improved profitability.

6 CONCLUSIONS

This study has been written largely from a British point of view. We have been mainly concerned with trying to assess the effects on Britain of joining a broad free trade area as an alternative, or supplement, to joining the EEC. So far as can be seen, and provided export prices can be kept competitive, an Atlantic-based free trade area would have beneficial effects both on the volume of British trade and on the country's balance of payments. If there is no deterioration in the UK's relative position, Britain should be able to compete with other participants, even in the face of superior American technology, in a large enough proportion of trade to enable her, in all probability, to improve her position. Having the big, rich and homogeneous American market to "shoot at" would provide the stimulus and opportunity to enable British manufacturers to exploit to the full the economies of scale made possible in a large assured market. American competition in the UK market would, even more than European competition, administer the "salutary jolt" which would encourage or force British industry to improve productivity. But, as must follow if our trade balance with the US improves, as we would expect, this "jolt" would be no more than Britain could healthily absorb.

Our examination of the figures and views expressed by the business economists who answered our questionnaire lead us to the conclusion that fears of American domination, either through takeovers or by beating British firms in competition, are much exaggerated. Indeed, it may be that American fear of British competition may be one obstacle to be overcome in persuading the USA that a NAFTA arrangement would be in American interests.

Almost all the purely economic advantages put forward as reasons for British entry into the EEC apply with equal or greater force to participating in NAFTA. And Britain would not have to suffer the disadvantages of the EEC's agricultural arrangements, with the higher food costs involved and the promise of an inevitable rise in the British cost of living. Instead, the UK could continue to purchase food from traditional cheap suppliers. New "special arrangements" would not have to be negotiated to prevent damage to New Zealand and others.

These advantages are offset in many people's minds by the fear, already mentioned, that US firms would buy up British industry, or, put another way, that Britain "would become the 51st State of the Union". When this last fear was heard after Bretton Woods, Lord Keynes replied: "No such luck!" One of the virtues of the free trade area system is that it is not necessary to surrender sovereignty. Neither Sweden nor Switzerland have become dependencies of Britain as a result of EFTA, despite discrepancies of size and population. If the UK, the USA and Canada want to draw closer together politically, then clearly free trade between them will make the approach easier. But free trade does not make political domination inevitable.

There appears to be equally little reason to believe that the formation of NAFTA, or a wider arrangement, would produce a vast increase in the inflow of US capital into the UK, with British industry becoming mainly American-owned. Of course if NAFTA increases the UK growth rate, as we think it may, then Britain will be a much better place to invest in and more attractive to foreign capital. Britain normally welcomes foreign capital. For her own savings are inadequate to finance all the investment required. American investment up till now has certainly been beneficial to the nation's balance of payments and to its overall efficiency. One of the factors holding back British growth would appear to be a low rate of investment. There accordingly seems to be no reason why this welcome for foreign capital should be reversed. In fact, the need for capital to take advantage of new opportunities would be greater if Britain was to enter NAFTA and therefore the welcome should be warmer. But if, in the event, the inflow of US capital reaches "dangerous" proportions it should not be impossible, or incompatible with a free trade area (which in essence provides only for tariff free entry of goods and need not cover capital movements or the movement of labour), to control this flow. Britain would still have the choice, if she remains an attractive place to invest in, between more American capital, on the one hand, with more American ownership, and less investment, on the other, with slower growth and more "independence".

A major problem likely to be the subject of increasing attention concerns assistance to less developed countries. Of itself NAFTA would do nothing to help African, Asian and Latin American nations to expand their exports. Unless special arrangements are made it may even worsen their position. But it would be possible, within the NAFTA framework, to accord them temporary advantages over the next few years. Thus if the NAFTA agreement provides, as it probably would, for a long period, say 15 years, during which tariffs between members were to be gradually reduced, it would be possible to remove tariffs against the manufactured products of developing countries in a much shorter time, say 5 years. Developing countries would then enjoy a preferential rate for several years, during which time they could develop industrial production. NAFTA would, therefore, be a useful instrument for helping all developing countries, free from the complications of entrenched preferences for a few (the former French colonies) in the EEC.

NAFTA would hold advantages for Britain if it were confined to Canada, the USA, the UK and other EFTA countries. It would hold even bigger advantages if it proves to be not the end of the road, but the first steps on a road towards a much wider free trade area to include Japan, Australia, New Zealand and eventually the EEC. The British interest lies in freeing trade on a permanent basis so that British industry obtains the benefits of the largest possible potential markets and in order that competition can work its usual beneficial miracles at home. To be excluded from a NAFTA-type arrangement, if one were formed, would certainly hurt Britain. The damage she would suffer could possibly be greater than any economic advantages obtained from joining the EEC. Hence even if the UK is successful in renewed negotiations with the Common Market it will be to Britain's economic advantage if the enlarged EEC becomes a member of an Atlantic-based free trade area to avoid being excluded from or discriminated against in the USA and Canada. It must be a matter of judgement whether the chances of the Community ultimately joining NAFTA would be greater if Britain was to join the EEC first or join NAFTA first.

This study has not been concerned with the economic advantages and disadvantages of NAFTA to the other prospective partners. Others are working on this. But because the share of foreign trade in the American GNP is so much less than in the case of Britain—because indeed the USA already has a very large home market—it would seem probable that the USA would gain less than Britain and Canada. That she would still gain is very likely. The USA, moreover, does have an interest in, and a genuine concern for, the prosperity of others. She has a concern for helping developing countries, and NAFTA, as we have seen, could be adapted to those ends; she has, we hope, a concern also for the future of Britain; and she is concerned that Europe should not degenerate into a selfish, inward-looking trade block.

Free trade associations can be effective economic instruments, as EFTA has shown. By comparison with the EEC they do lack glamour. "Building Europe" has a fine ring to stir the imagination. "Building a free trade area" would mean little to the man in the street. A vision though of an economic community of the free world, with hope of sweeping away the trade barriers which do so much to prevent the world reaching its full economic potential, could all the same stir imaginations in Britain and in the USA. And so to the final question: "Would the Americans accept the free trade area concept of a new Grand Design?"

As the world political scene changes, so shifts in policy can be expected, particularly from the USA. With Congressional hearings often a guide to how American opinion is shaping, it is very interesting to note the relevant, early conclusion of the subcommittee of the Joint Economic Committee, referred to earlier, which has been reviewing US trade policy:[39]

"While the USA should pursue the multilateral approach to reducing trade barriers, we recognise that conditions may arise in the future that would favour US participation in a regional trading block. . . . The possibility that Britain will not be accepted as a new member of the EEC raises questions that are not going to be answered satisfactorily by economic measures alone. Should she not be accepted, it is possible that Britain would consider joining an Atlantic free trade area in which the USA would be the leading member."

[39]"The Future of US Foreign Trade Policy" (*Report*, Subcommittee on Foreign Economic Policy, Joint Economic Committee, US Congress, US Government Printing Office, Washington D.C., October, 1967).

TABLE 1
ACTUAL GNP AND PROJECTIONS
(Based on 1965 figures in US $'000 million)

| | Actual | | Projected | | Average Annual % Change 1965–77 |
	1960	1965	1972	1977	
W. Germany	83.4	112.2	140.5	160.7	3.6
France	69.3	94.0	126.9	150.4	5.0
Italy	40.8	56.8	74.3	86.7	4.4
Belgium	13.8	16.9	21.6	25.0	4.0
Netherlands	14.4	19.0	24.9	29.3	4.5
Luxembourg	0.4	0.6	0.8	0.8	3.2
EEC (Total)	222.2	299.5	389.0	452.9	4.3
UK	82.2	98.9	120.4	135.7	3.1
Denmark	7.6	10.0	13.1	15.3	4.4
Austria	7.4	9.3	11.8	13.5	3.8
Norway	5.1	6.9	9.3	10.0	4.8
Sweden	14.7	19.3	25.1	29.3	4.3
Portugal	2.6	3.9	5.8	7.0	6.6
Switzerland	10.6	13.9	117.5	20.1	3.7
EFTA (Total)	130.2	162.2	203.0	231.8	3.6
EFTA (Continental)	48.0	63.3	82.6	96.1	4.3
USA	541.0	681.0	904.8	1065.1	4.7
Canada	39.6	48.3	65.9	78.4	5.2
NAFTA	710.8	891.5	1173.7	1375.3	4.5

	All Manu-	Foodstuffs	Beverages	Textiles	Boot & Shoe	Clothing	Timber & Sawmill
USA	3.20	2.97	3.42	2.23	2.18	2.19	2.20
Canada	2.15	1.79	2.57	1.63	1.45	1.41	1.91
Sweden	1.95	1.76	1.81	1.61	1.62	1.45	1.85
Norway	1.54	1.32	1.47	1.23	1.32	1.18	1.46
Denmark	1.53	1.25	1.65	1.21	—	1.22	1.52
W. Germany	1.52	1.22	1.53	1.19	1.20	1.08	1.35
Netherlands	1.32	1.24	1.22	1.17	1.10	0.97	1.31
Belgium	1.31	1.15	1.25	1.01	1.04	0.86	1.23
France	1.29	1.15	—	1.05	—	1.01	1.11
Italy	1.29	1.20	—	1.00	0.87	0.92	0.88
Finland	1.28	1.16	1.19	0.99	1.00	0.90	1.16
UK	1.20	1.01	1.10	0.98	1.05	0.88	1.18
Austria	1.14	1.12	—	0.90	0.82	0.90	0.97
Japan	0.45	0.39	—	0.31	—	0.26	0.35
Switzerland	—	1.21	—	1.06	—	1.03	1.33

E COSTS (US $)

Rubber	Chemicals	Building Material	Iron & Steel	Engineering	Shipyard	Road Vehicle	Mining & Quarrying	Construction
3.20	3.74	3.20	4.05	3.56	3.70	4.13	3.65	4.38
2.19	2.34	2.15	2.47	2.44	2.54	2.94	2.48	2.50
1.85	1.85	1.96	2.16	2.02	—	—	2.54	2.70
1.48	1.55	1.56	—	1.64	—	—	—	—
1.37	1.37	1.42	—	1.54	—	—	—	—
1.58	1.75	1.63	1.73	1.55	1.64	1.87	—	—
1.37	1.47	1.32	—	1.33	—	—	—	—
1.38	1.52	1.42	1.52	1.46	1.96	1.81	—	—
1.40	1.51	1.54	1.40	1.38	—	—	—	1.15
1.60	1.50	1.25	1.40	1.51	1.48	1.85	1.83	—
1.15	1.32	1.36	1.40	1.35	1.39	1.56	—	—
1.25	1.24	1.17	1.39	1.26	1.24	1.58	1.15	1.21
—	1.35	1.21	1.26	1.11	—	—	—	—
0.39	0.58	0.48	0.66	—	—	—	0.56	0.43
—	1.52	1.43	—	1.46	—	—	—	—

SITC		Increase in Imports from :—					Inc
		USA I & II	Canada I	II	Total I	II	USA I
51	Chemical elements and compounds	5.26	0.05	0.04	5.31	5.30	2.23
52	Crude chemicals	0.13	0	0	0.13	0.13	0.17
53	Dyestuffs and colouring materials	0.66	0	0	0.66	0.66	2.47
54	Medicinal and Pharmaceutical products	0.62	0	0	0.62	0.62	0.99
55	Essential Oils and Perfumes	2.40	0	0	2.40	2.40	0.51
56	Fertilizers	0.01	0	0	0.01	0.01	0
59	Other chemicals	1.79	0.01	0.01	1.80	1.80	0.53
61	Leather manufactures	0.35	0	0	0.35	0.35	1.55
62	Rubber manufactures	1.11	0.01	0.01	1.12	1.12	0.80
63	Wood and Cork manufactures	0.99	0	0	0.99	0.99	0.08
64	Paper and Board manufactures	11.57	0	0	11.57	11.57	1.06
65	Textile Yarn and Fabrics	4.08	0.81	0.61	4.89	4.69	13.89
66	Non-metallic mineral manufactures	0.91	0	0	0.91	0.91	21.25
67	Iron and Steel	2.20	0	0	2.20	2.20	9.76
69	Other manufactures of metal	6.52	0.01	0.01	6.53	6.53	11.56
71	Machinery-non-electric	64.54	0.19	0.14	64.73	64.68	32.76
72	Electric Machinery	26.78	0.20	0.15	26.98	26.93	9.17
73	Transport equipment	18.18	0.43	0.32	18.61	18.50	62.16
81	Sanitary, plumbing, heating, Lighting equipment	0.36	0	0	0.36	0.36	0.18
82	Furniture	0.18	0.03	0.02	0.21	0.20	0.67
83	Travel goods, handbags etc	0.12	0	0	0.12	0.12	0.52
84	Clothing	1.42	0.63	0.47	2.05	1.89	17.08
85	Footwear	0.09	0.02	0.01	0.11	0.10	3.65
86	Professional and scientific instruments	19.10	0.05	0.04	19.15	19.14	9.85
89	Miscellaneous manufactures	16.75	0.15	0.11	16.90	16.86	40.21
	TOTALS	186.12	2.59	1.94	188.71	188.06	243.1

Footnote:—I = No rise in export prices   II = Rising export prices

(Trade Creation) to:—			Increase in Exports (Trade Diversion) to:—			Total Exports		Net Change	
nada II	Total I	II	USA	Canada	Total	I	II	I	II
0.39	2.75	2.06	9.77	0.76	10.53	13.28	12.59	+ 7.97	+ 7.29
0	0.17	0.13	0.12	0.02	0.14	0.31	0.27	+ 0.18	+ 0.14
0.44	3.06	2.29	1.33	0.34	1.67	4.73	3.96	+ 4.07	+ 3.30
0.20	1.26	0.94	1.54	0.20	1.74	3.00	2.68	+ 2.38	+ 2.06
0.09	0.63	0.47	2.45	0.20	2.65	3.28	3.12	+ 0.88	+ 0.72
0	0	0	0.64	0.01	0.65	0.65	0.65	+ 0.64	+ 0.64
0.19	0.79	0.59	1.51	0.26	1.77	2.56	2.36	+ 0.76	+ 0.56
0.33	1.99	1.49	2.64	0.30	2.94	4.93	4.43	+ 4.58	+ 4.08
0.36	1.28	0.96	2.63	0.61	3.24	4.52	4.20	+ 3.40	+ 3.08
0.02	0.11	0.08	6.24	0.71	6.95	7.06	7.03	+ 6.07	+ 6.04
0.38	1.57	1.17	1.32	0.20	1.52	3.09	2.69	− 8.48	− 8.88
3.16	18.10	13.58	59.69	8.77	68.46	86.56	82.04	+ 81.67	+ 77.35
1.04	22.63	16.98	29.61	3.11	32.72	55.35	49.70	+ 54.44	+ 48.79
1.31	11.51	8.63	76.78	10.44	87.22	98.73	95.85	+ 96.53	+ 93.65
3.01	15.58	11.68	29.03	3.20	32.23	47.81	43.91	+ 41.28	+ 32.38
9.80	45.83	34.37	24.13	4.65	28.78	74.61	63.15	+ 9.88	− 1.53
4.15	14.71	11.03	33.01	5.50	38.51	53.22	49.54	+ 26.24	+ 22.61
5.65	69.69	52.27	56.12	8.95	65.07	134.76	117.34	+ 116.15	+ 98.84
0.09	0.31	0.22	2.61	0.25	2.86	3.17	3.08	+ 2.81	+ 2.72
0.13	0.84	0.63	1.59	0.19	1.78	2.62	2.41	+ 2.41	+ 2.21
0.10	0.66	0.49	2.82	0.40	3.22	3.88	3.71	+ 3.76	+ 3.59
1.68	19.32	14.49	54.50	4.84	59.34	78.66	73.83	+ 76.61	+ 71.94
0.46	4.26	3.20	12.78	1.71	14.49	18.75	17.69	+ 18.64	+ 17.59
1.03	11.23	8.42	28.55	3.95	32.50	43.73	40.92	+ 24.58	+ 21.78
2.81	43.96	3 2.97	45.30	5.95	51.25	95.21	84.22	+ 78.31	+ 67.36
36.82	292.24	219	486.71	65.52	552.23	844.47	771.37	655.76	583.31

:ent of tariff cuts + = net exports − = net imports

TABLE 4
INTRA-NAFTA TRADE IN MANUFACTURES*
(Based on 1965 f.o.b. figures in US $ million)

Importing Country Exporting Country	UK	USA	Canada	Total Exports to NAFTA Countries
UK	—	1,059.6	499.82	1,509.42
USA	872.1	—	4,099.6	4,971.7
Canada	179.01	2,063.6	—	2,242.8
Total imports from NAFTA Countries	1,051.1	3,123.4	4,549.4	Total Trade 8,723.9

*SITC Groups 5, 6, 7 and 8, less Divisions 57, 58 and 68. Division 68 was excluded on the grounds that non-ferrous metals under the SITC classification contains largely basic materials. Divisions 57 and 58, on the other hand, were excluded because data for 1960 was not available, and thus projections to 1972 were impossible. Their exclusion from the 1965 figures makes the impact on trade for 1965 and 1972 directly comparable.

TABLE 5
ESTIMATE OF EFFECT OF UK ENTRY TO EEC ON BALANCE OF TRADE IN MANUFACTURES*
(Based on 1965 f.o.b. figures in US $ million)

SITC†	Increase in Imports	Increase in Exports			Net Effect
		Trade Creation	Trade Diversion	Exports Total	
51	8.94	6.73	22.09	28.82	19.88
52	0.07	0.05	0.19	0.24	0.17
53	2.89	5.92	0.87	6.79	3.90
54	0.73	2.36	1.56	3.92	3.19
55	5.02	2.89	1.13	4.02	—1.00
56	1.98	0	0.15	0.15	—1.83
59	2.48	3.58	3.54	7.12	4.64
61	0.66	2.04	1.17	3.21	2.55
62	2.51	3.38	1.25	4.63	2.12
63	1.59	0.29	0.73	1.02	—0.57
64	6.43	7.68	7.30	14.98	8.55
65	19.14	16.11	10.79	26.90	7.76
66	6.66	18.14	4.64	22.78	16.12
67	5.28	6.85	5.23	12.08	6.80
69	10.67	13.52	4.69	18.21	7.54
71	84.25	80.19	42.12	122.31	38.06
72	26.05	32.84	25.81	58.65	32.60
73	41.09	64.65	28.11	92.76	51.67
81	1.19	1.10	0.63	1.73	0.54
82	1.40	1.17	0.19	1.36	—0.04
83	1.32	0.34	0.29	0.63	—0.69
84	14.28	10.17	4.33	14.50	0.22
85	7.34	1.04	0.65	1.69	—5.65
86	15.82	19.43	13.68	33.11	17.29
89	18.35	15.24	10.52	25.76	7.41
Totals	286.14	315.71	191.66	507.37	221.23

*For definitions of divisions see Table 3.
†SITC Groups 5, 6, 7 and 8, less Divisions 57, 58 and 68.
— = net imports.

Part V

SCOPE FOR NEW TRADE STRATEGY

by

David Robertson

1 NEW APPROACH TO TRADE LIBERALISATION

Ever since it was established in 1947, the General Agreement on Tariffs and Trade (GATT) has been supported as the main instrument for expanding world trade. In recent years, though, there have been growing doubts about the traditional GATT approach to trade problems and tariff bargaining. New proposals for dealing with trade restrictions have accordingly been mooted. The most promising involves using Article 24 of the GATT to negotiate a free trade area arrangement to include as many as possible of the agreement's signatory countries, usually referred to as "contracting parties". What is envisaged can be described as an open-ended, Atlantic-based free trade area. Because of the likely initial membership, and for domestic political reasons to do with the debate over relations with continental Europe, the idea is often posed in Britain as a North Atlantic Free Trade Area (NAFTA). But it is as a fresh approach towards liberalising world trade that the case is essentially argued.

In introducing some measure of order into international trading relations after the chaos of the 1930s and 1940s, the GATT has fulfilled a very valuable role. Its two outstanding features are the principle of non-discrimination and the principle of reciprocity; encouraging, that is, the pursuit of freer trade through negotiated reciprocal tariff reductions between contracting parties on a most-favoured-nation (MFN) basis.[1] From the outset there have been theoretical reservations about GATT's principles.[2] Other doubts have since been raised because the application of GATT rules has hardly been uniform. Anomalies abound. Disappointments in

[1] For a history of the development of the GATT and its work see Gerard Curzon, "Multilateral Commercial Diplomacy" (Michael Joseph, London, 1965).

[2] See Harry G. Johnson, "World Economy at the Crossroads" (Clarendon Press, Oxford, 1965). Also see Robert Baldwin, "Toward the Seventh Round of GATT Trade Negotiations", in "Issues and Objectives of US Foreign Trade Policy" (*Compendium of Statements*, Subcommittee on Foreign Economic Policy, Joint Economic Committee, US Congress, US Government Printing Office, Washington D.C., September, 1967).

advance over the probable results of the Kennedy Round[3] put new emphasis on these reservations. Even after this sixth round of multilateral tariff negotiations was satisfactorily concluded in May, 1967, doubts have persisted, and have indeed been burgeoning, over whether the GATT approach can any longer provide a suitable way of attacking the trade barriers that remain.

The GATT was set up to tackle excessive protection in international trade and payments, resulting from pre-war "beggar-thy-neighbour" policies and war-induced shortages and disruption. The many changes since then suggest a need for reappraisal. After six rounds of GATT negotiations, tariffs have been radically reduced in many sectors. Some difficult commodity groups, however, still possess high tariffs or quotas. These have proved impregnable to past assaults. Agricultural protection, moreover, has increased as industrial tariffs have been reduced. Non-tariff barriers have loomed larger in importance. Here, though, the GATT has no mandate. And finally, the development of regional trade blocks under the GATT has greatly altered the nature of tariff bargaining.

In spite of the growing feeling in many countries that a new approach is needed if the movement towards free trade is to continue, the value of GATT is fully recognised. Few countries would be willing to revoke its articles. There would be great reluctance, for instance, to contravene the MFN clause because of the possibility of other countries then resorting to preferential agreements. Revision of the present approach of multilateral tariff bargaining must therefore remain within existing GATT powers.

Article 24 of the GATT

Article 24 could provide a more forceful approach to free trade. It sets out the conditions on which it is possible to deviate from the normal rules of non-discrimination and reflects the belief that any movement towards preferential arrangements should be consistent with the goal of free trade. It states that a new regional free trade scheme must be either a free trade area or a customs union and must:

    i. require complete, not partial, removal of trade restrictions among members;

[3]These tariff-cutting negotiations were made possible by President John Kennedy's Trade Expansion Act of 1962. See later.

ii. cover "substantially all the trade between the constituent territories";

iii. not increase the restrictiveness of trade barriers against non-members; and

iv. be completed "within a reasonable period of time".

From this article it is plain that a customs union, involving harmonisation of policies on at least external commercial relations and domestic economic policies, would go far beyond simple reduction of trade restrictions that most countries could accept.[4] The type of arrangement under discussion, therefore, would be a free trade area; that is, a preferential arrangement in which participating countries eliminate tariff and quota restrictions among themselves in specified commodities, but remain free to retain their national trade barriers and trade policies *vis-à-vis* the rest of the world.

Most of the discussion on the need for a fresh approach to international trade problems has taken place in the United States and Canada. There the realisation that changes have taken place on the international trade scene has led to a reappraisal of commercial policies. The clearest exposition of the NAFTA proposed has come from the Canadian-American Committee. This body is sponsored jointly by the National Planning Association in Washington and the Private Planning Association of Canada. It was established in 1957 to study problems arising from the growing interdependence of the two countries and is composed of leading, influential representatives from industry, labour, agriculture and the professions. In a statement[5] published in May, 1966, the committee made a forthright recommendation which has greatly enlivened the debate in both countries on future commercial policy.[6]

From the discussion in North America it is clear that any new

[4]For a discussion of differences between a customs union and a free trade area see Sperry Lea, "A Canada-US Free Trade Arrangement: Survey of Possible Characteristics" (Canadian-American Committee, Washington D.C. and Montreal, October, 1963). Also see Harry G. Johnson, Paul Wonnacott and Hirofumi Shibata, "Harmonisation of National Economic Policies under Free Trade" (Private Planning Association, University of Toronto Press, Toronto, 1968; Oxford University Press, London, 1968).

[5]"A New Trade Strategy for Canada and the United States" (*Statement*, Canadian-American Committee, Washington D.C. and Montreal, May, 1966). The text of the recommendation is given below on Page 278.

[6]The Canadian-American Committee's proposal, together with the hearings before the Joint Economic Committee of the US Congress on the issues involved, are discussed in Chapter 3 below.

free trade area would have to be open-ended to allow all countries to participate. In Western Europe it has become common, as indicated earlier, to refer to such proposals by the more parochial-sounding title of a North Atlantic Free Trade Area. In this paper NAFTA will be used as shorthand for a wide free trade arrangement open to any country to join if it is prepared to accept the free trade provisions. This is justified because the North Atlantic countries have shown such a degree of co-operation in economic and defence matters in the last twenty years that some group of them would be a natural foundation for a successful free trade area.

There has been little public discussion of the NAFTA proposal in Britain. Yet there are very special reasons why the United Kingdom should examine carefully the proposals for a free trade area of developed countries. The economic problems that have plagued Britain since the end of World War II have become more critical in recent years. As a consequence, Britain's ability to fulfil a political role overseas has diminished. It now seems that the only way in which the British economy can be brought into equilibrium is through the action of external forces in a market larger than the British Isles alone. On a basis of this assessment, the Macmillan and Wilson governments have tried to achieve membership of the European Communities (EEC)[7] as the obvious regional grouping that could provide a treaty-guaranteed reduction of tariffs and an irreversible extension of the market for British industry. President Charles de Gaulle's latest veto, his third, leaves Britain with two alternatives:

i. Wait for some kind of new flexibility to appear in the political balance within the Community, through an internal change or an alteration in the international situation which might revitalise the idea of wider European unity; or,

ii. Find an outside alternative, and here the only viable organisation that would bring the same forces for economic change and political rejuvenation is a wider free trade arrangement with other major industrial countries.

[7] In mid-1967 the European Economic Community, the European Coal and Steel Community and Euratom merged. The new entity is entitled the European Communities. But throughout this study use will be made of the more familiar abbreviation EEC, the term Common Market or simply Community when referring to the Six countries adhering to the Treaty of Rome (and the associated Paris treaties).

The first involves no action. It merely means waiting for a change of heart, or leadership, in France. The second thus needs to be studied. It is unfashionable at present to discuss the political and economic realities of Britain's relationships with other Commonwealth countries and the United States with any constructive purpose, but they may contain important opportunities within a free trade arrangement. If the UK succeeds in joining the EEC in the next few years the effort spent examining NAFTA will not have been wasted because a free trade arrangement to include all members of the Organisation for Economic Co-operation and Development (OECD) and other developed countries might still be desirable in the long run. (It is as well, in any case, to clarify the issues facing Britain in the search for a new place in the world.)

Britain could play a key role in establishing a NAFTA scheme embracing a new universal approach to free trade. In this study, therefore, an attempt is made to assess what kind of agreement might be reached to create an open-ended free trade area. The various proposals that have been made for free trade arrangements in the Atlantic region are examined and an outline of the possible form for an agreement is suggested. An attempt is then made to discover, in a most general way, what might be the principal economic and political forces affecting the reactions of the governments of certain countries to the proposal. In conclusion, some of the problems involved in implementing a free trade arrangement are indicated.

2 REVIVAL OF ATLANTIC IDEA

Atlantic economic co-operation, as a concept, has strong roots in the plans for post-war recovery developed within the alliance between the USA and Britain during World War II. The Atlantic Charter, signed by Roosevelt and Churchill in August, 1941, before America became an active participant in the conflict, contained two articles concerned with trade and economic aims for the restoration of world order after the war. Throughout the war years specialists in international trade and monetary relations in both countries worked on proposals for a post-war system. The institutional framework through which the aims of the Atlantic Charter were to be achieved was agreed at Bretton Woods. The compromise agreement reached on the structure of the International Monetary Fund (IMF) and the International Bank for Reconstruction and Development (The World Bank) is well known. Equally, the failure of the International Trade Organisation (ITO) Charter, owing to the complexity of its articles, has been documented.[8] In the context of Atlantic free trade, however, it is worth mentioning briefly the different proposals put forward by the USA and Britain on commercial policy in the years immediately prior to the Bretton Woods conference.

At an early stage the British authorities proposed "an across-the-board reduction in tariffs according to a pre-arranged formula". Its basis was a paper, "Commercial Union", written by Professor James Meade which first appeared in Whitehall in 1943.[9] This type of agreement would have enabled Britain, and other European countries, to obtain effective cuts in the American tariff, which was prohibitive in many sectors. The intention was that this system of automatic tariff reductions according to an agreed schedule would eventually lead to duty-free access to the American market for

---

[8]See, for instance, Richard N. Gardner, "Sterling-Dollar Diplomacy: Anglo-American Collaboration in the Reconstruction of Multilateral Trade" (Clarendon Press, Oxford, 1956).

[9]This proposal was never published outside Whitehall. It is referred to in Curzon, *op. cit.*; and, also, in Gardner, *op. cit.*

British goods. Generally applied by all countries adhering to the agreement, it would in fact have been very close to the free trade area concept as defined in Article 24 of the GATT. At first it appeared that the Americans would accept this approach. But the rigid adherence of the US Congress to its control of the tariff could not be overcome and the Administration had to reject an automatic, across-the-board approach. Instead, it was accepted that progress towards liberalisation of trade was to proceed by means of bilateral negotiations on the basis of the Reciprocal Trade Agreement Act of 1934. Washington formulated a plan whereby separate trade treaties between countries might be embodied in a multilateral treaty which applied the same rules for each participating country; whereby, moreover, the individual treaties could be agreed simultaneously at one conference. The GATT incorporated the provisional commercial policy rules that had been agreed for the ITO.

The failure of the wartime plan for a pre-arranged schedule for tariff reductions is an interesting historical event in the context of Atlantic free trade. The item-by-item approach to tariff bargaining adopted at the first meeting of the GATT in 1947 provided the negotiating technique for all subsequent rounds of tariff reductions until the Kennedy Round when an attempt was made to streamline the negotiating procedures.

Little more was heard of Atlantic free trade following the creation of the GATT. Two attempts to obtain wider economic policy co-operation on an Atlantic basis in the early 1950s were shunned by the US authorities. In 1951, the Atlantic Council set up a committee of "Three Wise Men"—Mr. Averell Harriman, of the USA; M. Jean Monnet, of France; and Lord Plowden, of Britain—to examine the problems of financing rearmament to strengthen the North Atlantic Treaty Organisation (NATO). Reporting in December, 1951, it advocated the need for closer economic co-operation among the NATO states to facilitate the reallocation of economic resources required for military rearmament.[10] Although the need for co-operation was

[10]A second set of "Three Wise Men" (the Committee on Non-Military Co-operation: Mr. Lester Pearson, of Canada; Dr. Halvard Lange, of Norway; and Gaetano Martino, of Italy) recommended, in 1956, guidelines for the future development of political co-operation in NATO.

A theoretical argument for closer economic co-operation among Atlantic countries was given by Professor James Meade in "Problems of Economic Union" (Oxford University Press, London, 1953). This approach is discussed below on Page 270.

recognised, the recommendation was not implemented in any way. That year Britain tried to have transferred to NATO some of the functions of the Organisation for European Economic Co-operation (OEEC). But the initial aims of Marshall Aid were largely fulfilled and most American financial aid was by this time being directed to defence purposes. This notion was thus firmly rejected by the Americans. They considered that the OEEC still had a useful function in promoting closer integration between the European economies. European members of the OEEC who were not members of NATO also objected to any abbreviation of the powers of the former.

After the early 1950s the political scene in Western Europe was dominated by the idea of unification. The official US version of Atlantic co-operation saw European unity as a pre-condition for any closer association between North America and Western Europe. As for economic integration embracing all North Atlantic nations, that was a very unfashionable idea. The Atlantic Community was instead envisaged by governments, both sides of the ocean, as a defence alliance with some functional co-operation on economic questions, the first objective being a unified Western Europe.

President Kennedy's Grand Design

Towards the end of the 1950s Europe was launched on the division that has prevailed during the 1960s. The EEC was inaugurated on January 1, 1958.[11] Negotiations for a wider OEEC free trade area in industrial goods broke down at the end of that year. The European Free Trade Association (EFTA) of the "outer Seven" was agreed in Stockholm in 1959 and it began to function the next year. In 1961, however, it became known that the British Government was considering an approach to the EEC to discover the terms on which Britain might accede to the Treaty of Rome. After the British move several other EFTA countries announced their intention to make similar approaches to the EEC. In the light of this development, and the beginning of the Brussels negotiations in October, 1961, there was a revival in North America of interest in Atlantic free trade.

The clarion call was made by President John Kennedy in his Declaration of Interdependence in Philadelphia on July 4, 1962:

[11]The first tariff cut of 10 per cent took place on January 1, 1959.

"We do not regard a strong and united Europe as a rival but as a partner. To aid its progress has been the basic object of our foreign policy for seventeen years. We believe that a united Europe will be capable of playing a greater role in the common defence, of responding more generously to the needs of poorer nations, of joining with the United States and others in lowering trade barriers, resolving policies in all other economic, diplomatic and political areas. We see in such a Europe a partner with whom we can deal on a basis of full equality in all the great and burdensome tasks of building and defending a community of free nations."

The practical demonstration was the Trade Expansion Act, given Congressional approval in October, 1962. The powers this legislation gave the Administration were far wider than any previously given.[12] This was probably in response to misgivings about world developments.

The continuance of the US balance of payments deficit was causing concern. The prospect, too, of increasing discrimination from an EEC enlarged by the accession of Britain and other EFTA countries was not being welcomed. For the Common Market, which for many years the Americans had supported and promoted, was beginning at this time to appear like a highly protective system, entailing strong elements of discrimination against third countries. In addition, this rapidly expanding and protected market was proving attractive for American investment, thereby increasing the outflow of private capital to Europe. These were strong motives for trying to reduce the degree of discrimination exercised by the EEC.

Pressure for British Entry

On the other hand, the US authorities were anxious that the Brussels negotiations, over Britain's application to join the EEC, should reach a successful conclusion. For Britain's accession would serve several ends. First, it would, so it was thought, project the British economy into a dynamic market, thus helping the UK to overcome persistent economic ailments.

Secondly, Britain was the most Atlantic-minded, or outward-looking, of the European countries and showed more sympathy towards American foreign policies than many other NATO allies. A Trojan Horse, as it were, the UK could play an important role

[12]For a detailed discussion of the provisions of the Trade Expansion Act of 1962 see Johnson, *op. cit.*

in strengthening ties between the USA and Western Europe, and so build a genuine Atlantic Community. The "dominant supplier authority" provisions of the Trade Expansion Act of 1962 were therefore made contingent upon Britain joining the EEC; this, obviously, was an attempt to put pressure on both parties to reach agreement. The prospect of full free trade in goods where the USA and the EEC accounted for 80 per cent of free world trade would encourage, it was hoped, a successful outcome to the negotiations. Because of the French veto, though, the dominant supplier authority was never used in the subsequent Kennedy Round discussions.[13]

Thirdly, the growing pre-occupation of West European countries with internal affairs was also weakening the Atlantic alliance. Integration in the EEC, and the accompanying rapid rate of economic expansion, had made these countries less dependent economically on the USA and a similar trend was developing in political relationships. World problems were receiving less consideration in European capitals, leaving the USA to bear a relatively greater burden. This applied particularly to peace-keeping operations in the more remote parts of the world and, too, to problems of economic development in poorer countries. Pressures were building up in the Third World for greater assistance and new policies from the industrial nations to help promote trade. The Trade Expansion Act contained special provisions for removing tariffs on products of special interest to developing countries provided other industrial powers co-operated.

As the Kennedy Round progressed during 1964-67, negotiating difficulties caused spreading disillusionment. Issues that had seemed important when the Trade Expansion Act was formulated became even more important. The EEC's attitude to lowering tariffs, the development of the EEC's highly protectionist common agricultural policy and the EEC's refusal to admit new members all illustrated, rightly or wrongly, an unwillingness to co-operate in the furtherance of trade liberalisation. Economic weaknesses in the British economy were dramatically revealed in yet another balance of payments crisis. The US payments deficit also worsened. Meanwhile, growing

[13]It now seems doubtful whether the EEC, or Britain for that matter, would have been prepared to eliminate tariffs against American goods in such technically advanced sectors as electrical machinery, office machinery, insecticides, agricultural machinery and aircraft.

economic strength allowed the French, in particular, to use this as a bargaining device to frustrate progress on such major issues as world monetary reform and multilateral aid to developing countries. These disturbing developments caused a further weakening in the structure of the Atlantic alliance, which was aggravated, in addition, by new uncertainties about the future of NATO.

Despite the many difficulties, the Kennedy Round achieved partial success, although the results fell short of the original hopes contained in the Trade Expansion Act. Tariffs on industrial goods were reduced, on average, by about 35 per cent, to be spread over the five years up to 1972. For agricultural goods the results covered only maximum and minimum prices for wheat, an agreement on the volume of food aid to be provided for less-developed countries, an accord on what kind of agreement should be made for grains and some minor agreements on other products. Some progress was made on the removal of non-tariff barriers, the main agreement concerning the American selling price (ASP) valuation for chemicals which still has to be approved by the US Congress. But the developing countries won very little. Concessions on their exports of tropical products were largely blocked by existing preference arrangements. What concessions they received on their exports of manufactured goods are difficult to isolate. This brief description of a preliminary assessment of the Kennedy Round's outcome does not compare very favourably, it can be seen, with the possibilities deployed to win Congressional support for the enabling Trade Expansion Act.

Alternatives to Another Kennedy Round

All the same, one important conclusion is that, notwithstanding the many frustrations felt at different stages in the negotiations, most participants agree that everything that had been negotiable was in fact wrested from the great confrontation. The general opinion of GATT officials and representatives of governments is that there are very few areas where any countries would be prepared to offer further acceptable tariff cuts. There consequently appears to be little scope for further multilateral bargaining sessions in the GATT for some years to come. The task of persuading domestic industries to accept lower protection and the organisational problems of another major GATT conference are so formidable that such a step can only be undertaken if it is warranted by prospective gains.

This does not imply no further progress can be made through

the GATT towards trade liberalisation. Specific areas remain where some advance is possible without mounting large negotiating exercises. Efforts could be launched to remove, or harmonise, low tariffs—the small residuals left after six rounds of multilateral tariff negotiations that now possess only a certain nuisance value. But, by definition, the benefits to be gained would be very small. Another possibility would be an industry-by-industry approach to tariff reductions. Sir Eric Wyndham White, when he was Director-General of the GATT, suggested three areas where this technique could achieve results; namely, in technologically advanced industries; in products internationally made and traded; and in semi-manufactures. This approach would permit, as well, a full discussion of all trade barriers—not merely tariffs—affecting an industry. A major difficulty would be finding sufficiently wide industrial sectors where countries would be prepared to exchange tariff cuts in order to provide an acceptable bargain to all participants within the MFN clause. The technique was adopted in certain difficult sectors during the Kennedy Round with some success.

Although their results would be limited, these two possibilities would maintain some momentum towards trade liberalisation. The alternative might be a return, by default, to protectionism. But if any major step towards wider free trade is to be achieved in the next few years, the experience of the Kennedy Round suggests that a new technique for tariff reductions must be developed to replace the laborious item-by-item approach of GATT tradition.

One of the initial objectives of the 1964-67 negotiations by Lake Geneva was to speed the bargaining by introducing a technique of cutting tariffs on a linear across-the-board basis[14] instead of the item-by-item approach of earlier GATT rounds. If such a new technique could have been agreed the negotiations would have been simplified. Disagreements over the results of such a system (which focused on the issue of "tariff disparities") and the extensive lists of exceptions claimed by participating countries meant, in effect, that the Kennedy Round was very similar to previous negotiations. Unless a simpler and more flexible technique for reciprocal tariff reductions can be agreed by the major trading countries the prospect for another multilateral exercise will in itself be extremely daunting.

[14]The new approach outlined in the Trade Expansion Act implied that about equal percentage cuts (weighted by the volume of trade) would give reciprocity.

Disappointment over delays in the Kennedy Round gave rise to a suggestion that the MFN clause in the GATT should be modified to allow conditional MFN treatment. By this means the governments least willing to accord tariff concessions would not be able to prevent other countries from making mutual reductions. Article 24 of the GATT, however, permits trade barriers to be removed on a basis of strict reciprocity without the need to offer MFN treatment to non-participating countries, provided only that tariffs should be removed completely "within a reasonable length of time". It seems possible, therefore, that a formula could be devised under this article which would permit countries prepared to remove tariffs to do so on a reciprocal basis without being forced to give unilateral tariff concessions to other countries reluctant to give reciprocal treatment.[15] Many proposals for free trade among the North Atlantic countries have been made in the last fifteen years. These are examined in the next chapter.

[15]For a discussion of the various courses open to governments in efforts to further liberalise trade see Gerard Curzon and Victoria Curzon, "Options After the Kennedy Round", Part II above in this volume. Another Kennedy Round type of negoiation is ruled out. The options are narrowed down to the industry-by-industry technique and the free trade area approach.

3 THEORETICAL PROPOSALS EXAMINED

Most proposals for free trade among Atlantic countries have been made in the 1960s. Before turning to the more recent plans, however, it is worth recalling one of Professor Meade's early contributions on this subject. In 1952, when the problem of sharing the financial burden of NATO rearmament was a major issue, he proposed closer economic integration between the Atlantic countries as a way to a solution.[16] He considered that, working through a council of ministers, agreement could be reached on the allocation of production and on economic measures to be introduced in member countries in order to achieve agreed military expenditure. Professor Meade realised, though, that the tendency towards greater consultation and co-operation on related military and economic issues would be a slow and gradual process. He concluded:

> "Much progress remains to be made even in this the least ambitious type of scheme for joint consultation on economic plans and programmes. But the North Atlantic Treaty Organisation is the one promising organisation through which this could be done and it is greatly to be hoped that it will develop along these lines."

This suggestion resembled the recommendations in the report of NATO's "Three Wise Men" in December, 1951. The theme was also taken up by *The Economist* in 1952 when it published a set of articles on the prospects for an Atlantic Payments Union as a solution to the problems of international liquidity and trade restrictions. None of these proposals received much attention.

During 1955 it became clear that the six countries of the ECSC were determined to establish a Common Market. The UK authorities therefore needed to find an economic solution in Europe which would prevent Britain from being excluded from EEC markets while allowing her to maintain her Commonwealth preferential trading arrangements. The US Administration was enthusiastic

---

[16]Appendix to Meade, *op. cit.*

about the complete integration proposed under the Treaty of Rome. It looked less favourably on the British plan for a wider European free trade area covering all, or most, of the OEEC countries. This proposal did not involve any commitment to political integration and it was seen across the Atlantic simply as a means of discriminating against the USA—albeit legally under the GATT. When the discussions for a free trade area to cover all the OEEC countries began, with Mr. Reginald Maudling heading the British side, the US observer did not disguise his country's dislike for the scheme.

The only Atlantic move at this time was the Thorneycroft proposal for a free trade area between Britain and Canada. Britain's intention to propose a free trade area in Europe was disclosed to other Commonwealth countries in the autumn of 1956. It caused particular disquiet in Canada. At the Commonwealth Prime Ministers' Conference in London in June, 1957, Mr. John Diefenbaker, the Canadian leader, suggested that a new Commonwealth trade summit should be convened to examine means of expanding trade between member countries. The Canadian aim was a genuine, easily understood, desire to increase trade with Britain as a counterweight to American economic domination. Since 1945 Britain's share of Canadian trade had declined sharply. Mr. Peter (now Lord) Thorneycroft, then Britain's Chancellor of the Exchequer, put forward the offer in October, 1957, in Montreal, having been accompanied there by Sir David (now Lord) Eccles, President of the Board of Trade. The manner of its presentation (it was announced at a press conference before being put to the Canadian Government) and the casual nature of the British Ministers' approach (the communique stated that they "did not ask the Canadian Ministers for an expression of their views on the proposal") rather suggests that the Anglo-Canadian free trade area proposal was, in fact, a defensive move by the UK Government intended to discourage further discussion of free trade proposals outside Europe. The details of the British proposal—if there were any—were never disclosed. The Canadian Government could not at that time enter into such a far-reaching commitment. Mr. Thorneycroft's plan, therefore, had a brief and undistinguished life.

The Meade Paper

The first clear proposal for free trade in an Atlantic setting, rather than in a purely European framework, was in Professor

Meade's *Hobart Paper*, published in April, 1962.[17] After a careful analysis of the effects on the pattern of Britain's trade of accepting the EEC's common external tariff and common agricultural policy, Professor Meade concluded that Britain should accede to the EEC only if, simultaneously, all the industrial countries of the North Atlantic reduced restrictions on trade among themselves and with third countries. He recognised that when examining the pros and cons of Britain joining the Common Market "the political issues are ultimately more important than the economic". Nevertheless, he maintained "its political implications can be understood only in terms of its economic effects". The political aims of the EEC, he suggested, should be judged in terms of the way its six members chose to treat special British problems with regard to the Commonwealth and sterling.

The main purpose of Professor Meade's discussion was to ascertain whether the economic effects of Britain joining the EEC would be compatible with the long-run objectives of British commercial policy. These long-term aims were defined as:

> "the formation of a huge free trade community by the highly developed, industrialised countries of the free enterprise world. Basically this would imply that the North Atlantic countries of North America and Western Europe (including, of course, the UK) would progressively remove their restrictions on imports of products from each other and from other outside sources until they had all adopted a policy of virtually free importation from all sources."

This must be the objective if it is assumed Britain seeks to maximise efficiency in production and to raise the living standards and welfare of all people, including those living in underdeveloped regions. The former would be achieved through the increased specialisation and economies of scale permitted in a large market. The latter would be facilitated by free access to rich and rapidly expanding markets without hindrance from trade restrictions. Accession to the EEC would offer British industry the advantages of a larger market. But if the EEC proved to be "inward-looking and protectionist" then joining would not be consistent with the above long-run objective of commercial policy.

[17]Meade, "UK, Commonwealth and Common Market: A Reappraisal" (*Hobart Paper*, Institute of Economic Affairs, London, 1962).

272

Acceptance of the Treaty of Rome's terms by Britain would involve not just a loss of tariff preferences for Commonwealth countries but a complete reversal of this preferred position in the British market into discrimination against them in favour of Common Market producers. Apart from the undesirability of treating friendly nations in this fashion, such a policy would also involve raising new tariff barriers which would be inconsistent with the long-run objective. (The same reversal of discrimination would occur in the case of any EFTA country that could not obtain access to the EEC.) After a considered analysis of adjustments and concessions that might be made by the EEC to certain Commonwealth interests, Professor Meade concluded that a more general solution would be necessary if the Commonwealth countries were not to lose on balance.

One possibility would be a general reduction in the EEC's common external tariff and other protective measures. But to comply with the GATT such a reduction would have to be non-discriminatory. To compensate Commonwealth countries, the EEC would thus be giving unrequited market opportunities to the rest of the world, including some advanced industrial countries. This difficulty would be eased if all industrial nations participated in an agreement to reduce tariffs and other trade barriers on a MFN basis. The agreement, Professor Meade proposed, should include all North Atlantic countries, plus any others who wished to join, such as Australia, New Zealand and Japan. A major step would accordingly be taken towards the long-run objective, as already defined. The agreement, however, would need to go beyond tariffs. Imports of labour-intensive manufactures from developing countries are restricted by quotas as well as by tariffs. Agreement to limit this protection, or to enlarge quotas for Commonwealth producers, would therefore have to be discussed. A wide variety of protective measures are also used by most industrial nations to restrict imports of temperate-zone agricultural produce. But the problem of agricultural protection is deep-rooted in all industrial countries and this would be a tough settlement to achieve. As an incentive to the other countries to agree to undertake discussions Britain might offer to give up existing Commonwealth preferences.

Professor Meade suggested that the agreement should be planned through the OECD and negotiated finally in the GATT. He concluded that Britain should join the EEC only "if as a result of such a general settlement the Commonwealth countries agree that they stand to gain as much by this easier access to the whole North Atlantic area as they lose in the UK market".

Britain's position with regard to the EEC and the Commonwealth has changed since Professor Meade wrote his *Hobart Paper*. France has twice vetoed British attempts to join the Common Market. The Kennedy Round has achieved a considerable lowering of tariff levels by all major industrial countries. And if the proposal for generalised preference on imports from developing countries accepted at the second United Nations Conference on Trade and Development is implemented the importance of Commonwealth preferences will be substantially eroded. Despite these developments, however, Professor Meade's arguments remain very relevant in the context of Britain's uncertain policy and the wider objectives of trade liberalisation.

Reaction to EEC Political Aims

Another international economist who has advocated a similar scheme to Professor Meade, but on a rather narrower base, is Professor Bertil Ohlin, former leader of the Swedish Liberal Party. He believes that in Europe the economic aspects of integration have been subordinated for too long to the political aims of the EEC.[18] In the early stages the EEC needed the common external tariff to facilitate the introduction of common institutions and to establish a community of political interests. But now that the entity of the EEC is beyond dispute, Professor Ohlin argues, the sanctity of the common external tariff should be abandoned in favour of wider free trade in Europe. If the EEC remains inflexible, however, he considers that the EFTA countries should look elsewhere for the wider markets their industries need. In Professor Ohlin's opinion the MFN clause of the GATT should be modified to permit further progress towards free trade. This would enable a preference area composed of the USA, Canada and EFTA to be set up, with initially, perhaps, a one-third preference among member states. The end object would be complete free trade; at the outset, though, this would probably be too much for governments to accept.

[18]Speech to Liberal International (World Liberal Union), Saltsjobaden, Sweden, September, 1965. Also speech to Benelux Union, Amsterdam, October, 1966. In addition, see Bertil Ohlin, "Some Aspects of Policies for Free Trade", in R. E. Baldwin *et al.*, "Trade, Growth and the Balance of Payments: Essays in Honour of Gottfried Harberler" (North Holland Publishing Company, Amsterdam, 1965).

Professor Ohlin's sentiments have been echoed in many proposals mooted in North America in recent years, largely as a response to the EEC's obstructive tactics during certain stages of the Kennedy Round. Professor Randall Hinshaw, of Claremont University, has argued[19] that for American trade policy reciprocity is a more important principle than non-discrimination. Reciprocity is important, he argues, in order to provide new markets for extra outputs made possible by improved efficiency produced, in turn, by domestic tariff reductions. Non-discrimination has the advantage, or disadvantage, depending on the point of view, of restraining tariff-cutting negotiations to the pace of the most reluctant bargaining country.[20] This could be achieved legally by forming a free trade area under Article 24 of the GATT, he points out; or alternatively, by a preferential arrangement for lower tariffs on trade between a group of countries, which would require a change in GATT rules. A free trade area would not only preserve reciprocity. It would also afford businessmen a sense of certainty about future tariff reductions.

Reluctance to Hinder Europe

American opinion on NAFTA in the early 1960s was overshadowed by a reluctance to consider any proposal that might hinder West European integration. Outstanding examples of this view are to be found in two other studies sponsored by the Council on Foreign Relations in New York. In a general examination of the problems of the Atlantic Community, Mr. Harold van B. Cleveland, of the First National City Bank, and formerly in the US Department of State, adjudged that a NAFTA proposal was only realistic if it was recognised as a weapon to threaten the EEC with trade diversion in an attempt to bring down the Community's common external tariff.[21] In a statistical analysis of the consequences for trade of alternative commercial policies Professor Bela Balassa, of Johns

---

[19]Randall Hinshaw, "The European Community and American Trade" (Council on Foreign Relations, Praeger, New York, 1964).

[20]An analogy can be drawn with the slowest ship in a convoy. See Theodore Geiger and Sperry Lea, "The Free Trade Area Concept as Applied to the United States", in "Issues and Objectives of US Foreign Trade Policy, *Compendium of Statements, op. cit.*; reprinted in *Looking Ahead*, National Planning Association, Washington D.C., October, 1967.

[21]Harold van B. Cleveland, "The Atlantic Idea and its European Rivals" (Council on Foreign Relations, McGraw-Hill, New York, 1967).

Hopkins University, reached similar conclusions.[22] And further support for this view was provided in a complementary study by Professor Sidney Wells, now of Salford University.[23]

These last two were part of an Atlantic trade project under the auspices of the Council on Foreign Relations. Both preferred further progress towards liberalisation through multilateral negotiations in the GATT and hoped for an accommodation between the EEC and EFTA that would extend West European integration. They rejected the NAFTA option on the basis of a static analysis of the effects of tariff dismantling on trade flows based on data for 1960. It was recognised, however, that trade between North America and Western Europe would be greatly increased if tariffs were removed.[24] Moreover, Professor Balassa himself pointed out that the dynamic effects are the most important influence derived from trade liberalisation.

Studies of this type, rejecting action on NAFTA while hoping for new developments in Europe, have been undermined by events. The Kennedy Round has been satisfactorily concluded and another major tariff bargaining exercise of this type is widely accepted as unlikely. The latest *Non* from President de Gaulle to Britain's second application for membership of EEC also prevents any progress in West European integration, although various temporising measures have been proposed. Under these circumstances there can be little point left in reasoning that nothing should be undertaken that might impede European unity. The cost of waiting for a change of heart in the EEC would appear too high for all concerned when the NAFTA alternative is available.

Professor Harry Johnson, of the London School of Economics and the University of Chicago, has come down firmly in favour of the free trade area proposal for a number of reasons which he put forcibly in March, 1967, to the European-Atlantic Group in London.[25] He urged that an industrial free trade area should be formed initially between the USA, Canada and the EFTA coun-

[22]Bela Balassa, "Trade Liberalisation among Industrial Countries" (Council on Foreign Relations, McGraw-Hill, New York, 1967).

[23]Sidney Wells, "Trade Policies for Britain" (*Chatham House Essay*, Royal Institute of International Affairs, Oxford University Press, London, 1966).

[24]See Balassa, *op. cit.*, Chapter 4 and Appendix.

[25]See Johnson, "The Atlantic Case", *New Society*, London, May 18, 1967; reprinted in *The Atlantic Community Quarterly*, Atlantic Council of the United States, Washington D.C., Fall, 1967.

tries. It should, however, be open-ended and he envisaged the eventual participation of Japan, Australia and New Zealand "and, if they so choose, the Common Market countries". His preference for a free trade arrangement was based on its consistency with GATT rules and the fact that it would be a purely commercial arrangement, carrying no longer-run political obligations and allowing participating countries complete freedom in their commercial policies towards third countries. Moreover, Professor Johnson asserted, "complete free trade within a reasonably large international market has the advantage over partial free trade in the world market of guaranteeing maximum freedom of access to the large market".

Professor Johnson also suggested that the formation of NAFTA would assist with two very important international trade problems: the demands of the less-developed countries for wider markets for their exports,[26] which were clearly expressed at the first UNCTAD in 1964, and the problem of devising suitable rules for trade with the East European countries, which are becoming important sources of new outlets for industries in Western Europe and which themselves wish to expand trading links to the West.

Professor Johnson is associated with a major research programme on Canada's economic relations with Atlantic countries that is being sponsored by the Private Planning Association in Montreal. The project is under the direction of Professor Edward English, of Carleton University, who was one of the first to put the NAFTA idea in Britain,[27] and is based on earlier work by the Canadian-American Committee. The three-year programme represents the culmination of years of research into problems of freer trade between Canada and the USA. In 1963, the Canadian American Committee published a report[28] on the possible types of free trade arrangement permitted under Article 24 of GATT. This was followed in 1965 by a second report,[29] which gave a more detailed outline of the form a

[26]See Johnson, "Economic Policies Toward Less Developed Countries" (Brookings Institution, Washington, D.C., 1967; Allen and Unwin, London, 1967).
[27]H. Edward English, "Atlantic Trade Policy: The Need for a New Initiative", *Moorgate and Wall Street Review*, London, Autumn, 1965. See also English, "Transatlantic Economic Community" (Private Planning Association, University of Toronto Press, Toronto, 1968; Oxford University Press, London, 1968).
[28]Lea, *op. cit.* Mr. Lea is American Director of Research, Canadian-American Committee.
[29]"A Possible Plan for a Canada-US Free Trade Area" (Canadian-American Committee, Washington D.C. and Montreal, February, 1965).

North American free trade area might take. In May, 1966, as mentioned earlier, the committee broadened its approach to take account of the latest developments in the GATT. In "A New Trade Strategy for Canada and the United States" the committee recommended:

1. That as a first step the governments of the United States and Canada initiate discussions with the United Kingdom and its partners in EFTA to explore their interest in establishing under GATT rules, a broad free trade association of developed nations, recognising that special consideration must be given to less developed countries.

2. That the two governments and interested private groups in Canada and the United States encourage the study and discussion of the economic and political implications of such an arrangement for our two countries.

The type of organisation proposed by the committee was a free trade area to cover all industrial products and raw materials. Agriculture would probably be excluded at the outset as it was in EFTA.

Congressional Hearings

Hearings in the US Congress in the summer of 1967 before the Joint Economic Committee's Subcommittee on Foreign Economic Policy on the future of US trade policy produced some valuable papers and opinions[30] that revealed the growing support among professional economists for American participation in a new regional free trade agreement. In its conclusions the subcommittee, headed by Mr. Hale Boggs, stated:[31]

"While the United States should pursue the multilateral approach towards reducing trade barriers, we recognise that conditions may arise that would favour American participation in a regional trading bloc".

Support for regional free trade is based on a feeling that US economic policy, as an instrument in overall foreign policy, should pay attention to changing realities of power.

Some witnesses before the subcommittee advocated an American

[30]"Issues and Objectives of US Foreign Trade Policy", *op. cit.*
[31]"The Future of US Foreign Trade Policy", *Report, op. cit.*

initiative to create a wide free trade area to include all advanced economies that are interested and to incorporate a special system of tariff preferences for less-developed countries. Such a proposal was made by Mr. David Rockefeller, President of the Chase Manhattan Bank. Consideration of the proposal was also urged by Dr. N. R. Danellian, President of the International Economic Policy Association.[32]

In a paper called for by the subcommittee,[33] Mr. Theodore Geiger and Mr. Sperry Lea, both of the National Planning Association, argued that American participation in a free trade area was virtually inevitable in the long run. Even if for the present the US authorities continued to prefer multilateral tariff negotiations through the GATT, there would come a time when, in order to make further progress towards free trade, a formal commitment to zero tariffs would be necessary. This would occur either because multilateral bargaining broke down without hope of a compromise or because a major trading country, or group of countries, refused to offer reciprocal tariff cuts to the satisfaction of other participants in the negotiations. In either case the only way forward would be through a free trade agreement under Article 24 of GATT. If tariff negotiations through the GATT continued to give satisfactory results in the years to come a point would be reached eventually when the contracting parties would be very close to free trade. They could then be expected to arrange to remove all remaining trade barriers and set up institutions to implement such a step through a formal free trade agreement. Under these circumstances, the creation of a free trade arrangement would be inevitable in the long run so there would be a strong case for proceeding in this direction sooner rather than later.

Further evidence of the growing support for free trade in the USA was given at the congress of the International Chamber of Commerce held in Montreal in May, 1967. The leader of the US delegation proposed that the international chamber should investigate a scheme for a world free trade area. The congress approved a study programme for the next two years that included work on this plan.

The basis for the US Chamber of Commerce proposition had

[32]"The Future of US Foreign Trade Policy", *Hearings*, Vol. I, *op. cit.*
[33]Geiger and Lea, *op. cit.*

been outlined earlier by Mr. Ralph Straus,[34] one of the founders of the Committee for a National Trade Policy, spearhead of the liberal trade lobby. The proposal was for a world free trade agreement to cover all the developed countries, based on EFTA arrangements, but with the notable exception that agriculture would be included. It would be an "open-ended" organisation; any country could join as long as it accepted the basic conditions. In the first instance, the agreement would include the USA, Canada and EFTA. While the EEC should be entreated to join, Mr. Straus argued, the organisation should be established regardless of the Six's attitude. It would also be desirable to include Australia, New Zealand and Japan as founding members. The developing countries would be accorded special treatment by granting them on a non-reciprocal basis all tariff reductions under the agreements.

Some of the free trade area proposals discussed so far are more detailed, like Mr. Straus's for instance, than others. But there is emerging a clear consensus on the basic outline of any new trade initiative that might be taken along these lines.

There has been support for the NAFTA concept from certain like-minded US senators. Senator Jacob Javits, of New York, urged the idea on Capitol Hill on August 12, 1965. In London shortly after, on November 8, he suggested that if Britain could not join the EEC she should:

"consider phasing into a trade partnership with the US, Canada and other industrialised countries. To be practical, such an alternative must be prepared in advance, or it will not be available when it is needed . . . the USA must now indicate the degree of support it is prepared to give. . . ."

On the constitution of a treaty for free trade the senator was vague on this occasion. But he returned to the theme two years later[35] and indicated the need to develop "a free trade area of the broadest possible grouping of the industrialised nations of the free world who have the capacity to compete with each other on relatively equal terms". He went on to suggest that an Atlantic free trade area "will be a reality in ten to fifteen years".

[34]Ralph I. Strauss, "A Proposal for New Initiatives in US Foreign Trade Policy", *Orbis*, Foreign Policy Research Institute, University of Pennsylvania, Philadelphia, Spring, 1967.
[35]Jacob Javits, "Britain and the Future of Europe", speech to The Pilgrims, London, June 27, 1967.

Another exposition was presented by former Senator Paul Douglas of Illinois, in a book[36] published in the autumn of 1966. This work received scant attention in Europe and it was obviously written in anger over the EEC's growing independence of American designs, particularly in view of the difficulties raised in the intermediate stages of the Kennedy Round. In the Senate, Mr. Douglas had sponsored in 1962 the Douglas-Reuss amendment to the Trade Expansion Bill, seeking to include EFTA in the "dominant supplier authority" clause, which would thus have avoided the problems created when Britain and other applicants were barred from the EEC in 1963. The amendment was rejected by the Administration, for political reasons. One recommendation of Mr. Douglas was that this amendment should be adopted in new tariff legislation. A second suggestion was:

"If the other five members of the Common Market choose to stay with France . . . we should then seek a trade alliance with Great Britain and the other EFTA nations, together with Canada, Australia, New Zealand and, in qualified fashion, Japan. This would create a trading area of over 400m. people which would be stronger than the Common Market."

This implied the use of some kind of modified MFN clause. Mr. Douglas did not consider a free trade area under Article 24 of GATT.

Sir Robert Menzies, Commonwealth elder statesman and former Australian Prime Minister, has also alluded to the need for wider free trade arrangements. In a speech at Ditchley Park, Oxford, in July, 1967,[37] he suggested a closer association of the English-speaking nations as an alternative to Britain joining the Common Market. If special economic arrangements could be established between Britain, the rest of the Commonwealth and the USA, it would not only strengthen the existing links between these countries but would enable them "to do great things for the under-developed nations". It was plain, however, that Sir Robert was thinking of an informal arrangement covering co-operation in a number of economic and political spheres, and not a commitment to a complete freeing of trade.

[36]Paul H. Douglas, "America in the Market Place" (Holt Rinehart and Winston, New York, 1966).
[37]Reported in *The Times*, London, August 1, 1967.

4 PRINCIPLES OF FREE TRADE TREATY

What might be the outline form of an open-ended free trade area treaty? The most detailed plan so far produced is that of the Canadian-American Committee. It provides a basic framework on which to hang additional ideas drawn from other proposals and facilitate discussion.

Agreement on a NAFTA arrangement would probably follow the plan outlined in the Canadian-American Committee publications cited in the last chapter. These have been greatly influenced by the EFTA precedent. A NAFTA agreement would be necessarily more complex because of the possible dimensions and wider aims for achieving free trade between all industrial nations. An important consideration would be flexibility. Differing industrial structures would have to be accommodated. The agreement would need to be designed so that new members can be admitted with minimum fuss. There is a strong case for making the treaty as simple as possible, assuming that specific problems can be dealt with as they arise within a set of broad guidelines. Yet members would be understood to have accepted an irreversible movement towards full free trade. The technicalities of drafting a treaty are not, however, the subject of this study.

Commodity Coverage

The treaty would be open to any country, or group of countries, prepared to accept its provisions. It would offer the maximum benefits from free trade with minimum interference with national policies and commercial relations with outside countries. This form of trade agreement is the most likely one to be acceptable to the US Congress. It is also likely to be the form most acceptable to other prospective members. EFTA countries have revealed their preference. Australia and New Zealand chose to embark on a free trade area in 1964-5. Canada has examined the possibility of a free trade area, not a customs union, with the USA. To maintain a minimum of interference in the domestic affairs of member countries, the institutional arrangements should be functional. Common institutions would be set up solely to implement the agreement and assist its application.

There seems to be general accord over the commodities that should be covered by a NAFTA agreement. All raw materials and industrial products should be included. But the Canadian-American Committee has declared that "unless the participants were prepared to form a common agricultural policy, they would exclude this sector, at least at the outset, as did the EFTA".[38] This blithe dismissal of agricultural trade from the free trade agreement appears to be in conflict with the stated desire to embrace as many countries as possible in the agreement. Neither Australia nor New Zealand could give serious consideration to the proposal if they were not offered freer access for efficiently produced agricultural products in the markets of industrial countries. Moreover, the US Administration would probably require provisions for expanding agricultural trade in order to persuade Congress to accept a free trade arrangement.[39]

Agricultural Trade

The GATT draws no distinction between trade in agricultural and industrial products. But while trade in industrial goods has been considerably liberalised in the last twenty years, the reverse has occurred with trade in agricultural goods where a vast array of protective measures has developed. In addition, quantitative restrictions, almost eliminated on trade in industrial goods, have become increasingly important in agricultural protection where tariffs have little effect. The difficulties of achieving a NAFTA agreement for lessening agricultural protection would concern only temperature-zone produce. The removal of restrictions by the industrial countries on imports of tropical produce should provide few difficulties since they are of export interest principally to developing countries.

Agricultural trade has been described as a national rather than an

[38]"A New Trade Strategy for Canada and the United States", op. cit.
[39]The Trade Expansion Act of 1962 contained very specific measures on agriculture. If they had not been included it is doubtful whether the legislation would have been passed. Since nothing was achieved in the Kennedy Round in the way of obtaining an expansion of commercial trade in temperate-zone agricultural produce it is likely that the farm lobby on Washington's Capitol Hill will be even more active when new trade legislation is next placed before Congress.

international problem.[40] At the root of the present disorganised system of trade in agricultural products are to be found short-term policy expedients adopted by national governments to safeguard domestic farmers. Professor John Coppock, of the University of Stanford, California, has remarked: "Agricultural policies in the industrial countries are essentially isolationist, and international relations—trade—are little more than a patchwork of import restrictions and export subsidies, both essentially opportunistic in origin".[41] The reasons for these protectionist policies are legion—self-sufficiency for defence purposes or to safeguard the balance of payments, price controls to guarantee incomes to farmers, subsidies to enable farmers to sell their surplus, import quotas or levy systems to enable farmers to sell their surpluses, import quotas or levy systems to stabilise the market and so on. The basic reason in all industrial countries, however, is that the agricultural sector has a powerful political lobby. Many of the protectionist policies introduced in the inter-war period, or since 1945, were intended to meet special short-term problems. The difficulties have arisen because in spite of expansion in agricultural output resulting from improved farming techniques (mechanisation, fertilisers, crop programming) and changes in the structure of markets these policies have been retained. In consequence, new measures have had to be developed by the main exporting countries in order to sell their expanding output in the face of growing self-sufficiency in high cost industrial countries. The EEC's common agricultural policy is the ultimate, so far, in protectionism. Its "politically determined" prices for commodities are likely to produce enormous surpluses in the years to come.

The problem of international trade in agricultural goods has thus become one of guarantees for "market access". Production costs and prices are considered irrelevant. A more rational attitude by governments would be to reduce agricultural protectionism, which is probably a better way forward than seeking an international agreement in the GATT. Some consensus was reached during the Kennedy Round on the need for negotiations on agricultural trade liberalisation to be related to all aspects of domestic support and protection policies affecting output and trade in both importing and exporting countries. Negotiations centred on grain.

[40]See John O. Coppock, "Atlantic Agricultural Unity" (Council on Foreign Relations, McGraw-Hill, New York, 1966).
[41]*Ibid.*, Ch. 2.

The fact that very limited progress was made on a Kennedy Round grains agreement suggests some agreement on agricultural trade should be possible in a NAFTA scheme. The same comprehensive approach to all aspects of national agricultural policies would be necessary. Negotiating positions in NAFTA would be fairly clear. Britain and Japan are two of the world's largest importers. Canada, Australia, New Zealand and the USA are major exporters. Denmark would also have an important say on dairy produce. (If the EEC countries also decided to join a multilateral free trade area the situation would be wide open and the comprehensive Kennedy Round approach might be tried again.) A glance at the agricultural trade of prospective NAFTA members indicates that the group would be a net exporter even with Japan participating. NAFTA could not, therefore, provide a complete solution to the problems of the major exporting countries. Some further help with export surpluses might be agreed by means of a scheme to finance programmes of food aid for developing countries.

In the remainder of this paper it will be assumed that the NAFTA agreement will cover industrial goods and raw materials. Agriculture will only be mentioned where it will play a crucial role in the discussion; for example, where the inclusion or exclusion of agriculture may be vital to the participation of a particular country. The difficulties of reaching an agreement to include temperate-zone produce in NAFTA make it impossible to judge what effects it might have on members. It should be made clear, however, that it is difficult to see how a wide-ranging free trade area to include such countries as Australia and New Zealand could be envisaged without at least a limited agreement on agricultural trade. In this study it will be assumed that any agreement on agricultural trade between NAFTA countries can be treated as outside the basic NAFTA plan.

Trade Regulations

All the member countries would be required to progressively remove tariffs and quota restrictions applicable to imports of products covered by the agreement. The timetable of this liberalising programme would need to extend over as short a period as possible. The wide range of income levels and the great disparities in the sizes of the economies might make it advisable to provide differing timetables for some countries where too rapid a lowering of protection might pose serious adjustment problems. Special timetables might also be considered necessary for some difficult commodities. If the NAFTA scheme is open-ended as proposed, then as new countries acceded to the agreement new timetables would have to be devised for them.

In a free trade area each member country maintains its own external tariff against imports from third countries, while the free trade arrangements apply only to goods produced in member countries. Some measures are thus necessary to prevent trade deflection, which occurs when goods imported into the free trade area via a country with a low tariff are shipped with free trade area treatment to higher tariff countries in the area. The "origin rules" adopted by EFTA have proved very successful and similar arrangements could be made for NAFTA.[42] Goods passing in trade between member countries would be treated as originating in the area on either of two counts:

i. A content criterion: A minimum stipulated percentage of the export value must be added within the area (in EFTA the figure fixed was 50 per cent) ; certain specified basic materials may be specified as originating in the area regardless of actual sources.

ii. A process criterion: Certain stipulated manufacturing processes must be performed within the area.

These rules might be simplified by a harmonisation of external tariffs on certain inputs, particularly where the tariff differentials are small, performing only a nuisance function. The simpler the rules the easier they will be to operate.

In accordance with the objectives of a free trade area, the agreement would be defined to minimise interference with the fiscal arrangements of member countries. Special consideration would have to be given to revenue duties possessing a protectionist element. Revenue duties form a particular type of non-tariff barrier to trade where the protective element is readily measured by the differential in tax rates charged on foreign goods compared with domestically produced substitutes. There are many other non-tariff barriers, however, that must also be taken into account; for example, quotas, methods of assessment for duties, border tax adjustments, health regulations, special border charges for imports, marking and labelling regulations and differences in standards and patent laws.

[42]See S. A. Green and K. W. B. Gabriel, "The Rules of Origin" (European Free Trade Association, Geneva, 1965).

Non-tariff barriers become more significant as tariffs are reduced. In creating a free trade area some non-tariff barriers will disappear in the natural course of events. For instance, methods of assessing duties will no longer affect intra-trade when duties no longer exist. To avoid delay in setting up a free trade agreement, it should be possible to provide machinery for dealing with non-tariff barriers. An expert committee could be established to prepare a comprehensive list of them and to investigate how they should be eliminated. The complexities of these restrictions will require separate studies of each.

Rules of Competition

The removal of tariffs and quotas would not by itself give free trade its full meaning. Member countries must also modify policies and practices that distort competition among producers in the free trade area and interfere with the free movement of goods within the area. One important infringement of free trade has already been mentioned above—non-tariff barriers against imports.

It is difficult to give an exhaustive list of policies and practices that could distort competition and prevent the full benefits of free trade. Provisions must be made in the articles of the agreement to cover the following:

i. Discriminatory government aids, such as export subsidies, production subsidies, discriminatory freight rates on internal transport networks and preferential treatment for domestic suppliers in government procurement policies.

ii. Restrictive business practices, which as an objective or result prevent, restrict or distort competition within the free trade area. These might include specially prescribed standards for goods which discriminate against non-domestic suppliers.

iii. Rights of establishment for firms and individuals from all member countries in all other countries. If agents and dealers cannot be freely established in partner countries the free flow of goods between member countries might be distorted.

Agreement on rules to prevent distortions of competition would involve some degree of harmonisation of policies, but not more than is necessary to achieve the aims of free trade. It is clear that it would not be possible at the start to draw up a full system of rules to cover all practices or policies that might affect free trade. It is not possible to foresee which existing policies or practices will constitute a frustration of free trade benefits. This would only be possible after careful study of each case as it is revealed. But it should be relatively straightforward to trace any new practices introduced to replace trade restrictions dismantled under the free trade agreement. A system to control unfair trade practices could evolve over time as a result of continuing vigilance by all member governments.

Provisions would need to be made, too, for trade in invisibles and capital movements. Very little progress has been made in freeing these items from control. The Code for Invisible Transactions of the Organisation for Economic Co-operation and Development (OECD) has been agreed, but agreement over regulations under the code has not yet been achieved. Capital movements would be even more important in an Atlantic free trade area. Restrictions on such movements have lately been increased. Britain has successfully tightened exchange control since 1963 as the balance of payments position has deteriorated. The USA adopted a policy of voluntary controls on overseas investments until January 1, 1968. Both Britain and the USA now have restrictions on capital movements that are discriminatory in their impact as between different countries.

Since capital flows and trade flows are to a large extent substitutes for each other, and since capital flows are so important for growth in many economies, there is good reason for reaching an understanding on what controls can be allowed within a NAFTA scheme. Moreover, the discriminatory element in capital controls would need to be adjusted in line with NAFTA membership.

Economic Development and Adjustment Policies

The questions of economic development and adjustment assistance are closely related and at times they are difficult to separate. Economic development, which should include regional development, is a continuing process which will take place regardless of whether a free trade area is formed. Nevertheless, a major aim of the free trade arrangement should be:

"to promote in the area of the association and in each member state a sustained expansion of economic activity, full employment, increased productivity and the rational use of resources, financial stability and continuous improvement in living standards".[43]

Some co-operation to foster economic development in member countries would follow, although its form might take time to agree.

[43]See Article 2, Stockholm Convention.

Any undertaking of this type would hardly conflict with national policies.

The problems of economic development would be difficult to keep apart from the adjustment assistance that would be required by certain industries and workers faced by unbearable competition from foreign suppliers as a result of free trade. This assistance could take the form of financial aid, tax reliefs, retraining grants and financial compensation. Assistance could only be provided for a limited period. The aim would be to facilitate adaptation and specialisation. The organisation dealing with adjustment programmes (the Adjustment Assistance Board[44]) could also serve to appraise the regional economic development policies of member countries to ensure that they are consistent with other treaty provisions.

Provisions for adjustment programmes and economic development would be determined in the agreement, as would the method of financing and administering the schemes. Their function would be limited to full signatories of the free trade treaty and would not cover associated countries or countries on slower time-tables for tariff elimination. These countries could be covered separately in the agreements of association.

Trade with Third Countries

All countries would be free, under the agreement, to pursue their own commercial policies with third countries, but there are two groups of countries where special arrangements might be made. First, it has been suggested that all tariff reductions and quota dismantling between NAFTA members should be granted unilaterally to under-developed countries or that some form of preference arrangements should be granted by participants in the free trade association. This would meet the call from the United Nations Conference on Trade and Development (UNCTAD) for greater trading opportunities for developing nations in the markets of industrial countries. Second, trade with East European countries might be subject to special "rules of competition" preventing unfair practices in this rapidly expanding area of trade.

Special articles would deal with the problems of less developed

[44]This is the title suggested in "A Possible Plan for a Canada-US Free Trade Area" (Canadian-American Committee, Washington D.C. and Montreal, February, 1965).

countries. Indeed, an important objective of the free trade area approach would be to widen multilateral trading opportunities for less developed countries. Care must be taken, most proposals agree, that NAFTA does not discriminate against developing countries. The new Part IV of the GATT, dealing with trade and development, incorporates a clause to the effect that complete reciprocity is not required from the less developed countries when trade barriers are reduced by other GATT members under MFN agreements. This clause should be written into the NAFTA treaty. If it is thought necessary to provide preferences in NAFTA markets for the exports of less developed countries this could be achieved by an agreement accelerating the liberalisation of trade for these goods. The functioning of a system of qualified membership for less developed countries could be controlled by a Trade Review Board. This could supervise the operation of concessions by industrial members and determine to what extent, and at what rate, the associated less developed countries would be required to reduce their restrictions on imports from the industrial countries. For example, preferences granted to less developed countries in such fields as textiles might be pre-empted by some of the more advanced developing countries, like Hongkong and India, without bringing any benefit to less developed countries as a whole.

Trade between West European and East European countries has been growing rapidly in recent years. Canada and the USA have also been developing such East-West trade. In 1950, free world exports to Eastern Europe (including the Soviet Union) were estimated at $1,100m. This figure rose to $4,800m. in 1963 and to $6,200m. in 1965. Because of the bilateral nature of most of this trade, the volume in the other direction was of the same value. There are many problems created when market economies trade with ones centrally planned. As this trade has expanded the need to determine what amount to "fair practices" has grown. Within a NAFTA arrangement it should be possible to reach agreement on guidelines for this trade which would reduce uncertainties on this score. For instance, trade credit provides special problems in connection with trade with Eastern Europe. Systems of export guarantees differ widely between Western countries and may be unreliable at certain periods. Financial backing and other forms of technical and marketing assistance may be difficult to get in some Western countries when seeking to sell in Eastern Europe. If a regulated system could be established with special arrangements to facilitate trade from the West, the trade might be substantially increased, particularly in view of the relaxation of political tensions.

Institutional Arrangements

It was earlier pointed out that most prospective member governments of NAFTA would prefer to avoid policy harmonisation as far as possible and to keep institutions to minimum requirements. The range of countries contemplated in an open-ended arrangement, however, would necessitate a considerable technical staff in a central secretariat to maintain a smooth-running organisation. If an initial agreement is supplemented by subsequent agreements on the accession of new members, the intricacies of the system are likely to increase. Moreover, if developing countries become associate members and are required to make tariff concessions as their industrial development progresses, there will be a need for a review body to investigate each case. The minimal institutions therefore would seem to be as follows:

i. A Ministerial Council to resolve problems and reach decisions to achieve the aims of the agreement;

ii. An Adjustment Assistance Board to smooth the processes of structural change brought about by the implementing of the agreement, to alleviate social hardship and to promote industrial development in backward regions;

iii. A Trade Review Board to assess the tariff and trading positions of developing countries as they accede to the agreement, and to adjust their positions as development progresses;[45]

iv. An Appeals Committee to investigate problems arising from the NAFTA agreement and its operation.

These bodies would need to be serviced by a secretariat, but it would not have to be very large. As mentioned earlier, it may also be decided to set up expert investigating committees to examine non-tariff barriers, which frustrate the full benefits of tariff-free trade, and another special problem, that of trade in temperate-zone agricultural products.

[45]See Straus, op. cit.

Escape Clauses

A key element in any free trade agreement is the procedure for general consultation and complaints. There has to be a mechanism for resolving differences between the member governments and an apparatus by which individual infringements of the articles of the agreement can be investigated. The normal place for such complaints to be examined could be the council, probably meeting below ministerial level. In more difficult cases special committees could be established by the council, as has been done in EFTA. Since there are likely to be few issues that cannot be resolved by discussions between representatives of interested governments this simple framework would probably be sufficient.

It has become practice in free trade agreements to allow countries with severe balance of payments difficulties to reimpose import restrictions consistent with existing international obligations under the GATT and the IMF. Such measures are permitted only after consultations with partner countries and the restrictions must be temporary and for a specified period.

The reimposition of restrictions of any kind on imports from partner countries plainly frustrates the expectations of partners in the agreement. In special situations where the dominant member of a free trade area is forced to impose new protection against imports owing to balance of payments difficulties, a serious disruption of the agreement may ensue. EFTA experienced as much with the import surcharge that Britain imposed in 1964. The position, economically, of the USA in NAFTA would be even more dominant than Britain's position in EFTA. The possibility of unilateral action would undoubtedly be in the minds of the EFTA countries and probably Canada as well. These fears would be considered in any official discussions on the content of a multilateral free trade area treaty.

It is difficult to see how a balance of payments crisis in one member country could be overcome without some of the burden of adjustment falling on partners. Some kind of permanent consultative machinery, which could create effective economic co-operation and give warning of incipient balance of payments difficulties, could offer some help in such cases. The presence of the USA in NAFTA should mean that temporary financing of a deficit by any other member country could probably be readily arranged. Economic consultative machinery would hardly deal with any threats of unilateral abrogation of the free trade agreement by the USA. On the other hand, such a step would only be taken as a last desperate measure and the US economy is not confronted with the structural problems that have plagued Britain in recent years. A more realistic fear, however, might develop through periodic protectionist demands in the US Congress. But here history has shown that the checks and controls of the American political system usually thwart extravagant Congressional proposals. A treaty commitment to free trade should be sufficient to overcome domestic pressures among NAFTA countries for protection and, in any case, these pressures usually represent the interests of only a small section of a country.

The problem of balance of payments adjustment cannot be solved within the free trade agreement alone. Existing international agreements on international trade and payments and the main-tenance of fixed exchange rates between national currencies already restricts the choice of policy measures available to governments faced with external disequilibrium. Any measures introduced to regulate the domestic economy must affect other countries. A system of consultation on economic developments and adjustment policies in member countries would help to maintain harmony within the free trade association. The final solution to this problem of the international economy, however, rests with a new and more flexible approach to balance of payments adjustment and the international monetary system by governments and central banks in all the advanced countries.

5 GEOGRAPHICAL SCOPE OF ARRANGEMENT

The initiative for a free trade area approach towards further trade liberalisation would have to come from North American and EFTA countries; that is, from those that are being obliged to grapple with the problems of being discriminated against in the Common Market. But the treaty is envisaged as being open to all industrial nations prepared to accept its provisions. In this connection Japan, Australia and New Zealand are possibilities. It would be hoped, in particular, that the EEC countries would join, if not at the outset then not long after. First of all, though, what are the attractions of an Atlantic grouping for the USA and Canada?

Inducing a New Cohesiveness

For a wide-based free trade arrangement to be successfully established it must include either the EEC or the USA. Common Market refusal to extend free trade, in its most meaningful sense, to a wider area in Western Europe,[46] indicates that, initially at least, the EEC would decline to join a NAFTA scheme. The question of American participation is therefore crucial.

In Chapter 2 some attention was given to the reasons why Atlantic free trade became a topic of interest to the Kennedy Administration in 1962. The Trade Expansion Act gave the President extensive powers to negotiate a liberalising of trade restrictions that would dilute the discriminatory effects of the EEC's common external tariff. The final results of the Kennedy Round fell considerably short of the anticipated outcome, but a substantial cut was achieved in industrial tariffs. It remains in some doubt whether Washington is interested in further trade liberalisation in the next few years. There may be a wish to have the Kennedy Round cuts digested before new moves are made.

International political objectives, however, are the primary considerations which shape US trade policy. This was emphasised in the testimonies before the Congressional hearings on trade policy conducted in the summer of 1967 by the Joint Economic Committee's

[46]See Curzon and Curzon above, p. 32. Also see "The European Free Trade Association and the Crisis of European Integration" (Michael Joseph, London, 1968), a study by a group at the Graduate Institute of International Studies, University of Geneva.

294

Subcommittee on Foreign Economic Policy. It was earlier reaffirmed
—as, indeed, it has been many times before and since—in the new
trade strategy proposed by the Canadian-American Committee.
Foreign trade, after all, accounts for only 4 or 5 per cent of the US
national income. But the USA does not appear to have revised her
international objectives to better suit the new world situation that
has arisen so rapidly in the mid-1960s. The threat from Russia in
Europe has greatly diminished, although it has far from disappeared,
while the threat to world stability from China has manifested itself
more clearly in Asia.

The difficulties of adjusting international economic policies to
meet new situations have been underlined by the opposition to
President Johnson's measures to relax restrictions on trade with
Eastern Europe. The preoccupation of Washington with complex
Asian-Pacific issues contrasts with trade policies orientated towards
European-Atlantic issues. Relations with European countries have
suffered somewhat and the Third World has been mounting a
protest against an international trading system which favours the
industrial nations. Important political questions are thus raised.
It would be very much in order if a new initiative for further trade
liberalisation could revivify not only the North Atlantic Alliance
in particular but the Western alliance generally, meaning the
Pacific wing as well as the Atlantic, and in addition achieve a
multilateral approach to the trading needs of developing countries.

The North Atlantic Treaty will be subject to annual notice of
withdrawal by any member after 1969. As relations between East
and West have improved in Europe some West European countries
have begun to question whether a defence pact that includes the
USA is the best way to safeguard European interests. At one extreme
there are those who favour a central European 'defence pact as a
way to German reunification. At the other end some would prefer
a less formal military arrangement than the North Atlantic Treaty
Organisation (NATO) based not on combined defence but on the
North Atlantic Treaty itself. In this way the American nuclear
umbrella could be retained as an ultimate defence while a commitment to the USA could be avoided. This is what France has achieved
by withdrawing from the NATO defence forces. The Fifth Republic
now has independence of action while still being informed on
NATO policy decisions and remaining under American nuclear
protection. But it is doubtful whether the USA would be prepared

to accept such a one-sided proposition, providing the "free rides" to which some Europeans feel entitled.

Despite doubts about NATO in some West European circles, the value of the Atlantic community for promoting international co-operation is widely accepted. If the defence bond is under reconsideration, or anyway subject to political strain, there may be added point in examining the possibility of strengthening economic links in order to provide a new cohesiveness. The political interest in employing a free trade area arrangement to hold together the Atlantic community would require EEC participation. But, as mentioned earlier, the Six probably would not be willing to undertake any new reductions in their common external tariff until the internal aims of political and economic unity have been carried further. Yet the reaction of some Common Market countries to what promised to be a large and flourishing trade arrangement from which they, as a matter of EEC policy, were abstaining might provoke the pressure necessary to achieve free trade between Western Europe and North America.[47] The EEC countries would thus be forced to become "outward-looking" and to seek their cohesion in ways other than mutual discrimination against the rest of the world. In this way the division of Western Europe into two trading blocks could be healed.

The problem of expanding trade opportunities for developing countries is incentive enough for the US Administration to examine seriously a broad-based free trade area, providing as it could the co-operative basis on which a system of tariff preferences for less developed economies might be launched so that the burden of low-cost imports would be shared by most developed countries. Washington is committed to promoting economic development in poor countries and is demanding through UNCTAD a freer access to industrial markets. If, following the second UNCTAD in New Delhi, world-wide agreement is not reached on the details of a generalised scheme of tariff preferences, there will be a danger of separate preference areas being established. Particular regional groups of developing countries could become the special interest regional groups of industrial countries along the lines of the EEC's associated overseas territories. Latin America might be given

---

[47]See Curzon and Curzon above, p. 51. Also see Maxwell Stamp, "The Free Trade Area Option", Speech to the European-Atlantic Group, London, February 26, 1968, reported in *The Times*, February 27, 1968.

preference treatment by the USA (and perhaps Canada). The world could thus be divided into North-South preference zones, resulting in political and economic repercussions of great disadvantage to all. The NAFTA proposal would provide an excellent co-operative basis for the USA to grant preferences to developing countries in conjunction with other advanced countries.

While economic considerations are generally less important than political ones in determining US trade policy, their significance should not be under-estimated. There were very significant economic factors involved in the preparation of the Trade Expansion Act of 1962 and of course the Administration remains very sensitive on the balance of payments deficit. As regional trade blocks have multiplied and become fully operative, the competitiveness of American exports has been affected by tariff discrimination in favour of member countries. A multilateral free trade area would lower these foreign trade barriers and at the same time open the US economy to greater foreign competition. Another effect might be that when faced by lower foreign tariff-barriers American firms would be satisfied to export from existing domestic plants rather than investing in new plant within the tariff walls. This would help reduce the outflow of private capital.

An attempt to assess the impact of various trade policy alternatives on the US trade balance has been made by Professor Mordechai Kreinin, of Michigan State University[48]. He examined four options on a static analysis based on 1960 trade figures. The most favourable result for the US trade balance, it was found, would be in a free trade area with Canada, Britain, the rest of EFTA, Japan, Australia and New Zealand. Agriculture, though, was excluded from the assessment. (These results are set out on the following page.)

Professor Kreinin recognised the limitations of this kind of measurement. All the same, the figures did indicate that American trade policy was important from an economic standpoint. They indicated, too, that a free trade arrangement could substantially benefit the US trade balance. If the pre-Kennedy Round position continued with discrimination by EFTA and EEC against American exports, the costs probably would have been of the order of $450m. a year compared with the 1960 position. The successful outcome of

[48]Mordechai Kreinin, "Alternative Commercial Policies: Their Effect on the American Economy" (Institute for International Business and Economic Development Studies, Michigan State University, 1967).

the Kennedy Round is likely to ameliorate this effect by around $100m. a year. Professor Kreinin concluded that, although political considerations would be important in any decision about trade policy, the effects of the present discrimination against American exports could not be ignored.

KREININ RESULTS
(US$m.)

Options	Net effect on US trade balance
NAFTA (including EEC)	+300
NAFTA (excluding EEC)	+400
GATT 50% Tariff Cut	+150
Continuation of European Integration	−450

If the US Administration accepted the value of a wide-based free trade area arrangement doubts would remain whether it could get sufficient support from Congress and industry. In late 1967, widespread demands were launched for new quota restrictions on a wide range of imported goods. Several special reasons can be given for this disturbing development. The comparative success of the Kennedy Round would naturally have affected the timing of an attack on trade liberalisation. The strength of the attack has been assisted by the slight decline recently in US economic activity and the very rapid rise in imports that has occurred in recent years. There has in any case been a very long history of protectionism in the USA and periodically since 1945 there have been bursts of political pressure for more import restrictions. But the post-war record of the USA freeing trade suggests that most new bills seeking to impose import controls are normally intended to satisfy domestic political pressure groups and, in fact, have little effect on national trade policy. The Administration's opposition to the latest batch of bills for import quotas has been expressed in no uncertain manner.

The USA is unlikely to reach a decision to accept a free trade commitment through an internal debate on trade policy. It must be remembered that only about 4 per cent of American output is exported. The economic effects of any change in trade policy, however drastic it may appear, can only be small. On the other hand, the Administration might well respond favourably to a free trade area proposal from another country, provided it made political as well as economic sense. American interest could only be aroused, it is argued, if the free trade area were open-ended, permitting the widest possible membership.[49]

Canada: Danger of being Isolated

Canadian interests in a new free trade arrangement differ from those of the USA. Although fully involved in all international institutions, Canada is probably more interested than the USA in international economic relations; this is more because of their importance to the country's economy and standard of living than because of their contribution to international stability. The dismantling of formal trade barriers within the two West European trade groupings leaves Canada as the most important industrial country that is not integrated into a market of at least 80m. people and enjoying the advantages of specialisation and competitiveness that such integration implies. For this reason proposals for a multilateral free trade area arrangement have received much attention in Canadian circles.

Britain's continual flirtation with the EEC has caused increasing concern in Canadian trading circles: Commonwealth preferences being placed in jeopardy and other serious uncertainties provoked. Loss of preferences in the British market, and the subsequent removal of preferences for British goods in Canada, which would almost certainly follow if Britain joined the EEC, would leave Canada in even greater isolation than at present. This would be incompatible with the present policy interest in developing Canadian manufacturing industries through wider markets and increased competition. On the infant-industry argument, Canadian manufacturers have traditionally been sheltered by high tariffs and, in consequence, they are now hampered by high costs and short production runs. The Canadian authorities, many industrialists and a strong body of professional economists[50] therefore argue that, in

[49]President Johnson's Special Representative for Trade Negotiations, Mr. William Roth, disclosed on February 19, 1968, that his staff is studying four possible future negotiating techniques for further liberalising world trade, of which one is the multilateral free trade area approach. "We are trying to measure the economic impact of such arrangements", he said, "as well as their advantages and disadvantages to United States trade." See Mr. Roth's testimony to the Joint Economic Committee hearings on the future of US trade policy, reprinted as William Roth, "The President's Trade Policy Study", *The Atlantic Community Quarterly*, Spring, 1968.

[50]See the Atlantic Economic Studies Programme organised by the Private Planning Association of Canada. In particular, see English, "Transatlantic Economic Community", *op. cit.*

299

Canada's present stage of development, schemes which provide for the complete removal of trade barriers, on a reciprocal basis with her main trading partners, would be more advantageous than more limited reductions in such barriers. Trade policy is thus of vital interest to the Canadian Government and industry. Exports account for around 20 per cent of gross national product (GNP), although only just over half of this total consists of manufactures and semi-manufactures.

The Canadian authorities have favoured another multilateral approach to reduce trade barriers through the GATT. Such an approach should, however, be selective and not an "across-the-board" approach like that intended in the Kennedy Round. As Minister of Finance, Mr. Mitchell Sharp said that "for Canadians it will make sense to proceed, as I've said before, not according to formulae (under which I include schemes for percentage tariff cuts or for complete free trade between groups of countries) but selectively, seeking deep tariff cuts in sectors of production where tariff changes mean new business".[51] This "industry-by-industry" approach was also urged by Sir Eric Wyndham White when he was Director-General of the GATT.[52] It depends, however, on the willingness of negotiating countries to bargain for tariff cuts over sufficiently wide industrial classifications to permit reciprocity. In other words, it requires "giving" concessions in one area while "receiving" concessions in another. The greater the number of countries involved in the bargaining the wider will need to be the industrial sector covered. One advantage is that all restrictions on trade, and not merely tariffs, can be included in the bargaining. This approach nevertheless involves a confrontation and, in the end, an agreement among all the negotiating parties. Moreover, it will produce only a partial removal of trade barriers over a lengthy period of years.

But the free trade area approach to trade liberalisation has also been widely discussed in Canada, and indeed largely developed

[51]Mitchell Sharp, "The Outlook for Trade Policy", Address to the Canadian Manufacturers' Association, Toronto, May 29, 1967.

[52]Eric Wyndham White, "International Trade Policy: the Kennedy Round and Beyond", Address to the Deutsche Gesellschaft für Auswärtige Politik, Bad Godesberg, October 27, 1966.

Since then Sir Eric has come out in favour of "a broadly based free trade association" as a "desirable development in the wake of the Kennedy Round". See Eric Wyndham White and Others, "Strengthening the World's Economy", Letter to *The Times*, July 5, 1968, further quoted on Page 337 below.

there, as has been indicated in the previous chapter. The first possibility explored in this direction was a free trade arrangement with the USA. Many industrialists think that access to the large and rich American market would bring a necessary improvement in industrial efficiency and lower costs to Canadian manufacturing industry, provided adequate transitional assistance and a suitable period for adjustment are allowed. A forceful economic case for free trade with the USA has been made by Professor Paul Wonnacott, of the University of Maryland, and his brother, Professor Ronald Wonnacott, of the University of Western Ontario.[53] Their study shows that the benefits for Canada from free trade would primarily take the form of increased industrial efficiency. This would be revealed in lower consumer prices—directly from the lower cost domestic production and indirectly by enabling cheaper Canadian exports to pay for additional low-cost imports—and higher wage rates deriving from higher productivity of labour in Canadian manufacturing industry. It is estimated that the aggregate effect of these changes would eventually be to increase GNP by 10 per cent more than it otherwise would have been. The Wonnacotts' analysis also shows that a free trade arrangement with the USA would not reduce Canadians to "hewers of wood". On the basis of certain assumptions, some areas of Canada would provide satisfactory locations for manufacturing industry to supply the integrated North American market. The study concludes:

> "Because the Canadian economy is much smaller than the American, Canadians would not have to compete all along the line but rather could select specific products in which they enjoyed a special advantage."[54]

It is also pointed out that the results of the examination of the bilateral free trade possibility would broadly apply to Canada in any larger grouping.

There is very little appeal for the USA in a bilateral free trade arrangement with Canada, which represents only the most recent of a series of proposals of this type which began in the middle of last

[53]Paul Wonnacott and Ronald J. Wonnacott, "Free Trade Between the United States and Canada: The Potential Economic Effects" (Harvard University Press, Cambridge, Massachusetts, 1967). The results of this study are set out more briefly in Wonnacott and Wonnacott, "US-Canadian Free Trade: The Potential Impact on the Canadian Economy" (Canadian-American Committee, Washington D.C. and Montreal, February, 1968).
[54]*Ibid.*

century. Differences in the size and the breadth of economic structure in the two countries indicate that the USA could expect to derive little economic benefit from forming a trade arrangement with Canada alone. The US population is ten times larger than Canada's; the GNP is thirteen times greater. Both countries have large extractive industries for fuel and raw materials, which play a large part in Canadian exports. Furthermore, a large proportion of Canadian industry is American-owned.[55]

Politically, a bilateral free trade area would lead to serious problems in both countries. There are fears in Canada that closer association with the USA might undermine economic and political independence. The bonds holding Canadian federation together are not strong. It is feared in some political circles that it might disintegrate under the forces of change generated by a bilateral free trade agreement. It is also thought that Canada's independent voice in world councils might be weakened by so obviously a close relationship with her powerful neighbour.

For the USA, a free trade arrangement with Canada would lead to political difficulties in other directions. Mexico would almost certainly wish for similar treatment for her exports to the American market and for this there would be much support in Congress. Trade arrangements with Latin-American countries generally, because of traditional links, would also be urged both from within and without. The development of a Western Hemispheric economic block would not be desirable from the US point of view since it would restrict freedom of political manoeuvre in other parts of the world. It might also antagonise the developing countries excluded from such arrangements. Two problems that would still remain for the USA would be exports of agricultural products and accommodating Japanese interests in the American market. The latter would involve difficult access problems if competitors in other industrial countries were not to be upset.

By contrast to a bilateral arrangement, a more extensive free trade area, such as the NAFTA proposal, has greater appeal for many Canadians. Mr. Lester Pearson said, when he was still Prime Minister, that "discriminatory inward looking regional groupings

[55]According to Roy A. Matthews, "Canadians for Free Trade", *The Round Table*, London, April, 1967, "some 45 per cent of Canadian manufacturing industry, 50 per cent of mining and smelting activities and over 50 per cent of oil and gas production are owned by American interests".

are no answer to the problems of the world today. Unless such groups are so organised as to look outward, as to lead to wider arrangements, or are linked with such wider arrangements, they can be a step backward rather than forward."[56] And in an important speech on January 30, 1968, Mr. Robert Stanfield declared, shortly after becoming the new Leader of the Opposition, that a Conservative Government would "consider the necessity of Canadian participation in a larger trading unit".[57] Statements such as these, and there have been many similar ones, show that leading Canadians consider that any proposal for free trade should be as extensive as possible. They emphasise, too, that the various NAFTA proposals are receiving very considerable political attention in Canada.

A multilateral free trade area, one started by North Atlantic countries, but open to all countries prepared to accept its principles, offers greater opportunities for Canada, and is far more acceptable politically, than a special trading relationship with the USA alone. A full commitment to free trade on a reciprocal basis within a given period and on a broad regional basis would be preferred to partial tariff reductions on a non-discriminatory basis under the GATT. The basis of the Canadian problem is a high-cost manufacturing industry operating in a limited and protected market. Foreign tariffs impede Canadian producers from achieving larger markets through foreign sales and Canadian tariffs reduce the efficiency of domestic industry by permitting several small producers to exist in a small market. Under these circumstances partial tariff cuts through the GATT bring only small benefits of increased exports of high-cost Canadian manufactures while increasing penetration of the home market by already lower cost foreign goods. There is insufficient incentive from partial tariff cuts for the basic restructuring of Canadian industry that is needed. But full commitment to the removal of all trade restrictions over a given period could have the desired effect. Uncertainty about future trade restrictions would be removed and businessmen could plan investment and marketing programmes accordingly.

The economic appeal of a free trade arrangement to many Canadians as a means of bringing about the necessary structural

[56]Speech at an international conference on "Canada and the Atlantic Economic Community" organised by the Private Planning Association of Canada at Montebello, Quebec, November, 1966.
[57]Speech to the Macdonald-Cartier Club, Windsor, Ontario, January 31, 1968.

changes in the economy is also supported by the political characteristics of a free trade area. In a wide-based free trade arrangement the political disadvantages of association with the USA could be largely offset by the balance of other members such as Britain, Japan and the EFTA countries. Moreover, the US Administration would be more likely to react favourably to a free trade proposal which would include most of the present GATT members than it would to a simply bilateral arrangement with Canada.

EEC: Danger of Trade Diversion

On the evidence of the external trade policy of the EEC there is unlikely to be interest there in a proposal for a multilateral free trade arrangement among industrial countries, at least in the initial stages anyway. Within the EEC, the common external tariff and the common agricultural policy are regarded as essential to cohesion and identity of the Community. Until these are augmented by more far-reaching elements of integration among the Six, through the harmonisation of taxes, a common transport policy, common legislation on competition and so on, there can be expected to be a great reluctance to any move to weaken in the existing outward signs of unity. The sanctity of these external barriers has been illustrated many times. Policies adopted in the Kennedy Round, together with the rejection of the various attempts by the EFTA countries to create a wider European market, are specific examples.

Concern about preserving the external tariff is tied up with the importance of achieving the full benefits of the Treaty of Rome before any dilution is allowed. But this means different things to different people. To the European "purists" it involves the achievement of full political integration as well as economic unity. To the Gaullists, on the other hand, it means squeezing the maximum assistance from a treaty that can, with careful manipulation, be a vehicle to serve nationalistic aims. Industrialists and farmers may be satisfied with the economic benefits available from a full implementation of a Common Market in manufactures and agricultural produce. There is a feeling, however, that only when specialisation has brought maximum advantages from the large EEC market, behind its protective tariff wall, will European industries be able to face the full force of US competition. Further trade liberalisation should, therefore, wait until this has been achieved.

The long-run aim of political unity in Europe, which was so

important in determining US support for European integration throughout the 1950s, has receded with changes in the international situation. The relaxation of tension between East and West in Europe removed one of the principal motives behind the integration movement. Subsequent French attacks on the supranational aspects of the Community—such as the 1965 crisis manufactured out of the problems of the common agricultural agreement and the subsequent Luxembourg agreements to prevent majority voting[58]—have weakened further the forces for political integration among the Six. Nevertheless, the political aims of the Treaty of Rome still exist. Until full integration is achieved the "classical Europeans" will present this as a reason for rejecting any wider free trade arrangement that might further weaken European resolve in this direction.

The present political atmosphere in the EEC countries would make unacceptable any proposal involving closer association with the USA in any field. President Charles de Gaulle has on many occasions expressed his complete antipathy towards the USA and anything American. In his present role he is intent on leading the rest of Europe away from the American sphere of influence. Whatever the views on France's President's inadequate means and policies for achieving his aim of a Third Force in Europe under French leadership, the reaction to any proposal for closer economic ties would be unequivocal. Since the late 1940s the main cohesive force in the Atlantic community has been NATO. President de Gaulle's efforts are hence directed to reducing NATO's role. He is not likely to accept a new form of agreement to give renewed life to the Atlantic link he scorns. The only likelihood of a change in President de Gaulle's policy that would allow consideration of an Atlantic free trade proposal would be a drastic change in the present international situation, which would be undesirable for everyone, or a change in the political balance in the EEC. In his efforts to promote French nationalism, President de Gaulle has destroyed the institutional chains that were to bind West Germany so close to the rest of Europe that "she could never again get to her gun". This was one of the main motives for European integration in the early 1950s. The stability, prosperity and restrained policies of the Bonn

[58]The Luxembourg agreements were negotiated at meetings of the EEC Council of Ministers on January 17-18 and 28-29, 1966. The text may be found in "The European Free Trade Association and the Crisis of European Integration", *op. cit.*, Appendix II.

Republic since 1948 have reassured her neighbours. But Germany is still divided and reunification is still a live issue. For the present West Germany is happy to allow President de Gaulle to lead the EEC and to accept his vague and often contradictory statements about German reunification as the most practical way to its achievement. If the French political system reverted to the chaos of the Fourth Republic, however, the leadership of EEC would fall by default into the hands of West Germany. The great economic strength of West Germany has not been used, so far, to support political objectives, but this does not mean it never will be used in this way.

Most writers on the Atlantic free trade area idea are inclined to recognise that at the present time the EEC countries would probably reject membership of such an arrangement for political reasons. Many hope, though, that the economic advantages of free trade in one large market for all industrial countries might attract some members of EEC sufficiently for them to overcome the political opposition. In particular, West Germany, with its highly competitive and efficient industry, might yield to the glowing opportunities that such a rich market might offer and this country would least welcome the trade diversion effects of an Atlantic free trade area from which the EEC was abstaining. West Germany has always been the member of EEC most willing to examine free trade arrangements outside the Treaty of Rome.

There would be very considerable gains to be had in an Atlantic free trade area for the EEC countries.[59] At the same time there would be very considerable losses to the EEC countries, as a whole, if NAFTA were established without their participation. Mr. Maxwell Stamp and Mr. Harry Cowie have estimated that, even on fairly conservative assumptions, around 10 per cent of EEC exports to the USA and Canada would be displaced by British exports if NAFTA should be created without the EEC joining. On the basis of 1965 trade figures this would represent a loss of around $300m. to EEC exports.[60] This trade deflection would be even greater when the effects of other EFTA countries' and Japan's participation were added. If a NAFTA proposal became a reality, therefore, the attitudes of some EEC countries to membership might change when

[59]See Balassa, *op. cit.*
[60]Maxwell Stamp and Harry Cowie, "Britain and the Free Trade Area Option", Part IV of this volume, pp. 167-253.

faced by the prospect of trade losses of this magnitude. Moreover, a free trade arrangement on an Atlantic, or an even wider basis, could offer many rich and attractive markets to EEC producers. It is possible that in future these opportunities will prove more attractive than in the past. The "dominant supplier authority" clause in the US Trade Expansion Act of 1962 was not greeted with much enthusiasm in the EEC where it was regarded as a means of increasing American penetration of European markets in advanced manufactures before the EEC's external tariff protection could permit competitive products to be developed. The latest OECD forecasts, however, suggest that the very rapid economic expansion that EEC has enjoyed in the past twenty years may be slowing down. In future, EEC growth rates for GNP may be lower than those in the USA. If this is the case, progressive industrialists in the EEC countries may see great attractions in a wider free trade area arrangement.

The Kennedy Round showed that the EEC were prepared to bargain for multilateral tariff reductions. The Six's preoccupation with their own affairs in the last few years, and the present political atmosphere in the EEC, leave few doubts that a proposal for an open-ended, Atlantic-based free trade area would be rejected in the first instance. The NAFTA proposal would therefore present two possibilities where the EEC is concerned. First, the size and the value of the NAFTA market would increase the bargaining power of the other industrial countries with respect to the EEC's common external tariff if they co-operated in forming a suitable strategy in any further tariff negotiations.[61] But secondly, and more likely, the prospect of losses to the EEC countries because of trade deflection brought about by NAFTA would, in the longer term, encourage the Six to seek accommodation in the multilateral free trade area.

EFTA: Economics Out-weighing Politics

If Britain chose to join an Atlantic free trade area it seems probable that most of the other EFTA countries would follow. This is not to say though that there would not be uncertainties or hesitations. These doubts would be mostly of a political nature, reflecting

---

[61]Individual countries within NAFTA would retain autonomy over their tariffs *vis-à-vis* third countries. NAFTA could not bargain with non-members, such perhaps as the EEC, because of the differences in the tariff structures of members. The bargaining power of the NAFTA arrangement would need to be harnessed by a co-ordinated strategy.

a concern that an Atlantic free trade arrangement from which the EEC abstains would aggravate the divisions in Europe and a suspicion, emotional if nothing else, that closer association with the USA might reduce their influence in world councils and possibly undermine the increasing relaxation in relationships with Eastern Europe. But the economic advantages of wider free trade would be attractive, especially if hopes for a single European market were postponed by the EEC's reaction to the most recent approach by EFTA countries.[62] The small industrialised countries have most to gain from widespread tariff cuts. While they have relatively low duties, which allow competition in their domestic markets, their export possibilities are often restricted by the higher tariffs of other industrial countries, which can limit the extent that economies of scale can be exploited by their industries. This is an important reason why, for the past twenty years, the small EFTA countries have been among the strongest advocates of trade liberalisation.

Any discussion of an Atlantic free trade arrangement would cause some disturbing policy reappraisals in the four Scandinavian countries.[63] One area of difficulty would be defence. Norway and Denmark are members of NATO; Sweden is a militarily strong neutral from choice; and Finland is a neutral at the insistence of Russia. A rethinking of defence policy is under way in the two NATO countries as 1969 approaches. Norway, in particular, has a pivotal role at its northern border with Russia. The essential problem created by a closer association with the USA would be Russia's attitude towards Finland becoming more attached to Western Europe and the USA. The Fin-EFTA association agreement has been very successful in drawing Finland into the main flow of industrial development in Western Europe. But it is very doubtful whether Russia would permit the Finns to associate with a wider free trade area that included the Americans. An important strategic reason for Sweden's continued neutrality is the desire not to isolate Finland. Sweden's decision to remain neutral in the early post-war years contained other elements, too, and this feeling had much sympathy in Norway. However, if the *détente* between East and West

[62]For a discussion of the attitudes of EFTA countries to European integration see "The European Free Trade Association and the Crisis of European Integration", *op. cit.*

[63]Finland is an associate member of EFTA and has a slightly slower timetable for dismantling tariffs, but despite the separate association agreement the country participates fully in EFTA.

continues it might be possible to obtain special treatment for Finland in a free trade arrangement. Scandinavian solidarity has a high priority in all four countries and if Finland were prevented from joining NAFTA the other three countries would be placed in a difficult position.

The US authorities could also face some controversial questions on defence policy in connection with NAFTA; namely, whether non-NATO members should be included in a free trade arrangement. To raise such questions might cause the Scandinavian countries to dismiss any NAFTA proposals. The political content of a free trade area agreement would be closely scrutinised. Any suggestion of infringements of other countries' independence would immediately kill the idea. For some time political disenchantment with the USA has been growing in Scandinavia, chiefly over American policy in Vietnam. There is strong resentment against the USA over this issue, particularly among young people, which may be one reason why joining the EEC is looked upon more favourably than formerly. Nevertheless, the cultural, ethnic and economic links with the USA are strong and if the Vietnam conflict could be terminated the present antipathy would probably disappear in a few years.

It is probable that in most Scandinavian countries the anticipated economic advantages of free access to the US market would outweight political hesitations about closer ties with USA. But any hint of political pressures, real or imaginary, from the USA in the proposed multilateral free trade area could tip the balance in the opposite direction. At best the NAFTA scheme would be interpreted in all Scandinavian countries as a second-best alternative to an integrated European market. This is understandable from an economic point of view. The four Scandinavian countries sell almost 28 per cent of their exports in EEC and obtain around 33 per cent of their imports from this source. In 1966 they had a combined trade deficit of $1,100m. with the EEC. By comparison, just over 8 per cent of their exports go to the USA and Canada and less than 10 per cent of their imports are from these countries.

The economic advantages of being inside an enlarged EEC have been known to the Scandinavians for many years. Only recently though has there been talk of the political reasons for joining the Community. One reason is probably the movement away from the US line of foreign policy in South-East Asia, which leads to a compensatory movement towards the EEC's agnostic attitude. But there has also been an increase in self-confidence in Scandinavian political circles. Formerly there was a strong predisposition against associating too closely with the conservative-led Catholic countries to the south with their record of political instability. The present view, however, is that the Nordic democracies could give stability to the Community's system. For the time being, however, the Scandinavian countries would not join the Community without Britain. The most likely reaction of the Scandinavian countries to the latest British failure in Brussels will be to reopen discussions on a Nordic economic union. To a large extent this union has already been achieved through EFTA and Nordic co-operation in transport, customs control, the labour market and so forth. A Nordic block could form a viable counterweight to Britain in EFTA.

If a wider European market cannot be achieved by an expansion of the EEC and Britain became genuinely interested in a NAFTA proposal, Scandinavian industrialists would probably look favourably on the export opportunities offered by tariff reductions in the North American markets. EFTA has shown all the Scandinavian countries that there is much to be gained through wider free trade when larger markets are available and the efficient industries are now anxious to exploit new opportunities. Professor Balassa has shown that, in static terms, the gains to the four Scandinavian countries from joining a free trade area that did not include the EEC, would only be about half that from joining an enlarged EEC. All the same, the gains would be very substantial. Moreover, Scandinavian industries have strong links with the USA. Access to American technology and finance is very important for industries in small countries where resources are limited. A closer commercial association with the USA in a wider group could offer opportunities for economic expansion and greater industrial efficiency.

The Scandinavian countries would obviously prefer a free trade arrangement that included the EEC, but if that is not possible a smaller grouping could still bring many benefits. As small countries, they all appreciate the importance of international laws and treaties to safeguard their interests and any agreement must embody such characteristics. The chance to achieve at least a partial multilateral solution to some of the problems of the developing countries would also appeal to Scandinavian Governments. The small industrial countries face special problems if the less developed countries are given preferences by the larger rich countries. There is always a danger that unconscious and informal preferences would develop in the reverse direction, which would be, in effect, discrimination by the less developed countries against the smaller industrial countries. For this reason, the Scandinavian countries are strong advocates of multilateral solutions to the trade and aid needs of the Third World through existing international bodies.

Thus, the Scandinavian countries would examine any NAFTA proposal with interest, if the prospect of joining the EEC seems to be postponed indefinitely. Or, they would welcome such a proposal if it included the EEC, and as long as suitable arrangements could be made for Finland.

On the other hand, the Scandinavian countries are pleased with the results of the Kennedy Round, where, for the first time, a single negotiating team was used in the GATT to bargain for the Nordic block. They are also pleased with the Nordic integration that has occurred through EFTA and the chances offered in the large UK market, although these have not proved as great in the last three years as had been hoped owing to restrictive domestic policies in Britain. Furthermore, the EEC's common external tariff has not proved insurmountable in many commodity groups. In consequence, the Scandinavians are not looking for a new initiative in trade liberalisation. Any proposal would be fully considered, but these countries are not likely to strive for new plans in present economic circumstances.

The position of Switzerland if a NAFTA proposal were made is more difficult to assess. On the one hand, Swiss neutrality is very rigidly observed and any association with the USA might seem to infringe the constitutional neutrality, even in a free trade area agreement. On the other hand, Swiss industry, which is on the whole very efficient in its export sectors, would be eager to gain access to wider markets.

Switzerland's international position is difficult to unravel. For example, she is a member of OECD and the Group of Ten, but is not a member of the IMF[64] or the United Nations. Switzerland is anxious to maintain a careful balance in relations with East and

---

[64]Switzerland has been an observer at the IMF for several years. In *The Times*, January 28, 1968, it was reported from Berne that the Swiss Finance Ministry is considering making a request for full membership of the IMF and the World Bank. Switzerland has become a full member of the Asian Development Bank.

West which has led at times to political convulsions. Although there are occasions when *de facto* Switzerland seems to deviate slightly from this virtuous path it is rigidly adhered to *de jure*. In recent years Switzerland has shown a cautious willingness to participate more fully in international responsibilities. Whether it would be possible for Switzerland to join NAFTA would depend upon the pressures of domestic politics and the fear of being discriminated against in trade if she failed to join.

The economic benefits of joining NAFTA would probably be smaller than for the Scandinavian countries. As another manifestation of its neutrality, Swiss industry has concentrated on achieving a world-wide market for most of its goods. This has been assisted by the high quality and technically advanced character of most of its exports. In consequence, tariffs are less important for Swiss exports than for those of many other countries, although there are undoubtedly some sectors where tariffs are restrictive (for example, chemicals). This is not to imply, however, that freer access to any market, and particularly the rich American market, would not be welcomed by Swiss industry.

For the present, Switzerland is not anxious to open new initiatives into trade liberalisation. The Kennedy Round was considered successful from a Swiss standpoint and in EFTA Switzerland has been revealed as the least willing to seek any change in the existing European position. Switzerland does more than half of her trade with her EEC neighbours. This trade has continued to expand rapidly even though tariff discrimination between EFTA and EEC has increased. Moreover, Switzerland's statutory neutrality would create special problems if she considered joining the EEC. The country, therefore, would probably regard any NAFTA initiative without great enthusiasm. But again if the proposal seemed likely to become a political reality, Switzerland, too, would probably want to participate.

The remaining two EFTA countries are apparently easier to assess with regard to a NAFTA proposal. Austria has shown herself to be prepared to join EEC on almost any terms, but has been held back by the Russian ban on any association of Austria with Germany as contained in the Austrian Peace Treaty of 1955. It is clear that a NAFTA scheme without EEC would not attract Austria. If the Russians remain intransigent about Austria's membership of the EEC, however, the NAFTA alternative would still be available. Austria has gained far more from membership of EFTA than the

Austrian authorities ever admit[65] and further economic gains could be earned from NAFTA.

The attitude of the Portuguese authorities to a NAFTA proposal is clear. Portugal would welcome a wider free trade arrangement with or without the EEC. But as in the EFTA convention she would seek special treatment under a NAFTA agreement because of the country's relative lack of competitive industry and low income levels. It is probable, therefore, that Portugal and any other less developed Mediterranean country would receive special arrangements under the agreement. This could be administered and adjusted by the proposed Trade Review Board.

A general conclusion on the reactions of the continental EFTA countries to a NAFTA proposal is not too difficult to reach. Two countries, Austria and the associate member, Finland, would face peculiar difficulties because of special agreements with Russia. The Soviet authorities could be expected to bring pressures to bear to stop these countries concluding any formal association with the USA. If the détente between East and West continues, however, there may be some hope of a relaxation in the Russian attitude. Portugal would probably be afforded special treatment under the agreement, owing to her lower standard of living. In principle all these countries could be expected to welcome a proposal for free trade under article 24 of the GATT.

The four remaining countries—Denmark, Norway, Sweden and Switzerland—would all be sceptical of American motives in such an arrangement. The political implications would need careful handling by all concerned and would probably require special treatment in a free trade agreement. Industrial sectors in all these countries would probably give support to membership of NAFTA, though with varying degrees of enthusiasm, if an agreement for an enlarged EEC was indefinitely postponed. Industrialists and governments in these countries still see many untapped market opportunities to exploit from the Kennedy Round and EFTA. In consequence, they would be unlikely to promote actively a proposal of this type which would give rise to many complicated issues.

It would obviously be desirable to include Japan in a free trade arrangement among the advanced economies since it is now one of the largest industrial countries and certainly the fastest growing.

[65]"The European Free Trade Association and the Crisis of European Integration", *op. cit.*, Ch. III.

The US Administration, in particular, would be anxious to include Japan. Since 1945, trade relations and industrial co-operation between these two countries have grown rapidly. Nevertheless, there would be apprehension about the impact on industry and labour if increased Japanese imports were allowed.

Japan: Query Over Non-tariff Barriers

Freeing trade with Japan would cause uneasiness in many industrial countries which already feel the effects of strong competition from Japanese industry. None the less, since Japan joined the OECD in 1964, she has gone some way to meet the trade liberalisation procedures that membership demands. Even so, there remains an array of trade restrictions to be dismantled before free trade can be fully realised. The other prospective members of a free trade arrangement would not be willing to offer any tariff concessions to Japan without full reciprocity. The Canadian-American Committee's proposal, in discussing membership of a free trade area, noted that "the unique character of some of the Japanese trade controls could introduce a special problem for Japan".

Although the Japanese have been slow to liberalise their economy, in recent years significant steps have been taken, especially in the area of foreign investment. The subject of regional free trade agreements is also in the minds of Japan's administrators and economists. This is understandable given Japan's position as the dominant industrial country in East Asia. Interest has been shown in two types of regional trading arrangement. First, a free trade arrangement among the advanced economies of the Pacific area—the USA, Japan, Canada, Australia and New Zealand—which would also make efforts to assist economic development in South-East Asia.[66] Second, an economic community among the countries of South-East Asia with Japan as the hub, but with financial and technical backing from the adjacent advanced countries like the USA and Russia.[67] The aim of both these proposals is to secure for Japanese

[66]Kiyoshi Kojima, "A Pacific Economic Community and Asian Developing Countries", *Hitotsubashi Journal of Economics*, Hitotsubashi University, Tokyo, June, 1966. Also see Kojima (ed.), "Pacific Trade and Development" (The Japan Economic Research Centre, Tokyo, February, 1968) and English, "Japan's Developing Trade Strategy", *The Round Table*, April, 1968.
[67]Interview with Mr. Sohei Nakayama, President of the Industrial Bank of Japan, from Ralph Hewins, "Japanese Miracle Men" (Secker and Warburg, London, 1967), in *The Times*, September 25, 1967.

industry the vacuum left by the colonial powers in the Far East. Meanwhile, the Japanese realise that they must rely on increasing their exports to the rich industrial markets of North America and Europe if their rapid economic expansion is to be maintained. While they have been developing the markets in neighbouring countries through financial aid (two-thirds of Japanese aid, which represents around 0.66 of GNP, goes to Asia) their marketing efforts in the West have been increasing during the 1960s.

But the Japanese ambitions in South-East Asia need not be in conflict with membership of a wider free trade area of industrial countries because help could be offered to these countries through such an organisation. Any plan for a free trade arrangement supported by the USA would hope to include all the major countries of the proposed Pacific free trade area as well as European countries. Membership of such a group would open many new markets for Japanese industry. Japan is a country that has been discriminated against by other major industrial countries for many years because of its highly competitive exports based on cheap domestic labour. Many of the quotas operated against Japanese goods are now on a "voluntary" basis, but the effects are the same. Any chance to gain easier access to the markets of the industrial countries must appeal to Japanese industry. The question would remain, however, whether the Japanese would be prepared to give reciprocal treatment to imports from other participants to the agreement. Some industrial countries would also be reluctant to grant free access to cheap Japanese manufactures, and some transitional arrangements might need to be introduced. If Japan did not participate in NAFTA she would stand to lose substantial exports to the USA and Canada through trade deflection. Mr. Maxwell Stamp and Mr. Harry Cowie have estimated that Britain would capture almost as much trade from Japan as from the EEC countries—around $225m.[68] This alone would provide a strong motive for Japan to join the free trade area. In addition, Japan would stand to gain very substantially from trade creation as a result of the removal of high tariffs and specific quotas levied on some of her exports by other industrial countries. On balance, therefore, Japan would show a very substantial benefit on her visible trade balance from membership of such a free trade arrangement.

The Japanese attitude towards the granting of trade preferences

[68]See Stamp and Cowie, *op. cit.*, p. 211 above.

315

to developing countries is unequivocal. The Ministry of International Trade and Industry has estimated[69] that if tariffs were lowered on a preferential basis the loss to Japanese exports would be $135m. to $180m. a year. Around 18.4 per cent of Japanese exports are light industrial products and textiles of interest to developing countries. The Japanese could only accept such a procedure if the "burden" of the preference could be shared equally among all developed countries, if all existing preference systems were abolished and if products where developing countries are competitive were excluded. While Japan would probably accept any scheme that was approved by UNCTAD, she might find more acceptable a preference arrangement through a multilateral free trade area arrangement. Adjustment assistance would be available through such an organisation and the timing and incidence of concessions could be controlled to some extent. Nevertheless, the Japanese could be expected to be sticky negotiators on this issue in any agreement because of their own intermediate position in development and their dependence on exports directly competitive with those of developing countries.

Japan's position is therefore difficult to assess. On the one hand, Japan is anxious to expand her overseas markets for new sophisticated manufactured goods. On the other, there must be doubts whether Japan is prepared to dismantle altogether her remaining trade restrictions and whether some industrial countries would be prepared to face competition in their home markets from Japanese exports of cheap manufactures. Japan would also be very worried about the granting of general trading preferences to developing countries on goods which compete with Japanese exports. The conclusion must be that Japan would not be ready to participate fully in a free trade arrangement among industrial countries. After a period of adaptation and further rapid economic expansion, however, she could find herself more prepared to examine the economic advantages and disadvantages.

Australia and New Zealand: Problem of Agriculture

Australia and New Zealand figure among the richest countries in the world and for this reason it seems desirable that they should be included in any extensive free trade arrangements. Moreover, they have strong ethnic, cultural and political ties with Britain and

[69] *The Times*, September 22, 1967.

North America. It must be remembered, however, that the national wealth of Australia and New Zealand is based upon their natural endowment and derived from agriculture and minerals. New Zealand is a small country with a population less than 3m. and it has very little industry. Australia is as large as the USA in land area, but it has a population of only 12m. Both these countries consider that, on balance, they need their existing tariff and quota restrictions: New Zealand, because of the need to restrict imports of manufactures to avoid a worsening of balance of payments problems, and Australia because of the need to protect developing industries from foreign competition until they are established. Neither country exports manufactured goods to any great extent. Nor would either expect to gain very much from reductions in tariffs on industrial goods by other participants in the free trade area agreement.

Agricultural exports account for around 80 per cent of total Australian merchandise exports, and mineral ores and metals account for a further 15 per cent. The predominance of agricultural exports is even greater for New Zealand where more than 95 per cent of exports are from this sector. For both these countries Britain is an important trading partner and is indeed by far the most important commercial outlet for agricultural exports. These figures indicate that in order to attract Australia and New Zealand into a NAFTA scheme, there would have to be a very substantial liberalisation of commercial trade in agricultural products within the agreement.

There is much concern in Australia and New Zealand over the development of regional free trade agreements which have tended to leave these two countries in isolation. The future of Commonwealth preference, which has been so important for the development of commercial markets for their agricultural produce in Britain, is very uncertain after Britain's various attempts to join the EEC.

If Britain ever joins the EEC the effect of the common agricultural policy would be to reduce severely the markets for Australian and New Zealand meat, dairy produce and cereals. Even if some transitional arrangements could be made for those goods they would probably be of short duration. Thus in a period of three to five years the marketing policies for agricultural produce for the two countries would have to be completely revised. The uncertainty now attached to the security of the British market is viewed very seriously in Australia and New Zealand. If Britain participated in

NAFTA, however, free access to the British market for Australian and New Zealand agricultural produce would continue, even if Australia and New Zealand were not members of the free trade arrangement. Apart from guaranteeing a very important share of these countries' export earnings this would also serve to keep down food prices in Britain, with its consequent impact on production costs. In addition, a close and unequivocal trading relationship—unaccompanied by such fundamental uncertainties as have been provoked by Britain's refusal to renew the Anglo-Australian trade agreement—might help to restore the UK's rapidly declining share in the exports and imports of these two Antipodean nations.

In recent years Australia and New Zealand have made strong efforts to develop markets for their agricultural produce in Asia. Japan, in particular, offers a very attractive market, but that country has a highly protective agricultural policy. The Australian and New Zealand Governments have shown some interest in Japanese proposals for Pacific economic integration. An arrangement with Japan alone, without Canada and the USA, would not be acceptable.[70] The prospect of gaining freer access to the Japanese market for agricultural produce is enticing, but both countries are reluctant to allow freer entry for Japanese manufactures. Australian-Japanese trade has nonetheless been expanding rapidly and in 1967 Japan purchased around 20 per cent of total Australian exports and supplied around 10 per cent of total Australian imports. This meant Japan displaced Britain as Australia's largest export market; in the same year, the USA displaced Britain as the major supplier of Australian imports.

In an effort to promote mutual trade and economic expansion, Australia and New Zealand formed a free trade area between themselves which began to function on January 1, 1966. The agreement followed the general form of such arrangements under the GATT with proposals to remove all trade barriers and tariffs over eight years. There are liberal powers for temporary suspensions

[70]For two Australian views on a Pacific free trade area see H. W. Arndt, "PAFTA: An Australian Assessment", *Inter Economics*, Hamburg Institute for International Economics and the German Overseas Institute, Hamburg, October, 1967, and also see Peter Drysdale, "Pacific Economic Integration: An Australian View" in Kojima (ed.), *op. cit.*

For two New Zealand views see L. V. Castle, "New Zealand Trade and Aid Policies in Relation to the Pacific and Asian Region", and I. A. McDougall, "The Prospects of the Economic Integration of Japan, Australia and New Zealand", in Kojima (ed.), *op. cit.*

of obligations if the agreement leads to hardship in a particular industry or if a protected market is needed for the development of a domestic industry. The agreement was reached after two years of difficult negotiations and many people in both countries are apprehensive of its effects on their own economies. The agreement so far covers only 60 per cent of commodity trade between the two countries. Australia and New Zealand are anxious not to be left outside the main flow of trade expansion through liberalisation and their governments would doubtless wish to negotiate for terms to join a wide-based free trade area.

The two Antipodean countries face many problems similar to those of the developing countries. They have narrow-based economies which rely mainly on agriculture for foreign exchange earnings. They are nevertheless high income countries. If all the major developed countries in the West were either in a NAFTA scheme or the EEC there would undoubtedly be strong pressures operating in political and economic circles directed to achieving a satisfactory agreement to permit Australia and New Zealand to particpate. On the other hand, both countries also need to establish manufacturing industries to maintain their prosperity in the future. Their interest in joining NAFTA would depend on what could be offered on agricultural trade. If substantial market opportunities were provided in the NAFTA agreement, Australia and New Zealand, especially the latter, would probably be prepared to forsake their protective policies on manufactured imports. Leading politicians from both countries have indicated as much. The difficulties of reaching an agreement that would include agricultural trade in NAFTA have been discussed earlier. Full membership of NAFTA might therefore be difficult for Australia and New Zealand to accept initially. The flexible type of agreement advocated in this paper, however, could be adapted to allow associate status for Australia and New Zealand.

Developing Countries: Preference Scheme

Economic development for the world's poor countries is probably the most urgent international economic problem. Any prospective free trade arrangement among the advanced industrial countries must take account of this. Among the less developed countries there has been a mounting conviction that the principles governing international trading relations, as set out in the GATT, are against their trading interests. The most important demands of the developing countries were strongly expressed at the first UNCTAD in 1964 and these grievances have been formalised by the establishment of the Trade and Development Board as a permanent agency of the United Nations. This body enables the developing countries to bring organised pressure to bear on the trade and aid policies of the more advanced countries.

The UNCTAD meeting in 1964 revealed wide differences between the attitudes of the developed countries to the principal demands of the developing countries for trade preferences for their industrial goods and for more world commodity agreements to stabilise and raise commodity prices. If the advanced industrial countries of the North Atlantic were to establish a free trade area for industrial goods this would be an extension of the type of discrimination embodied in the GATT that has led the developing countries to attack it. The form of tariff bargaining carried on in the GATT is controlled by the major trading nations—those with the largest trade volumes and the highest tariffs. They choose the products to be liberalised on the basis of their own interests. The tariff cuts are extended to developing countries under the MFN clause and normally no reciprocal tariff cuts are demanded. Nevertheless, the goods in which trade is liberalised are not usually produced by the poor countries. The goods that are of interest to them—for example, tropical agricultural produce, processed materials and cheap, labour intensive manufactures—are either not included in the tariff bargaining negotiations or are protected by quotas and other non-tariff barriers.

The main hope at present for assistance with new trading opportunities for the developing countries rests with the recommendation of the Trade Committee of the OECD in October, 1967. This proposes that a system of generalised, non-reciprocal preferences should be introduced for imports of manufactures and semi-manufactures, and possibly some basic commodities, from developing countries. This offer was put forward at the second UNCTAD in New Delhi in February, 1968, and accepted in principle. So far this scheme has not received approval from the US Congress and the OECD report[71] on which the proposal is based leaves wide

[71]Report of Special Group on Trade with Developing Countries" (Organisation for Economic Co-operation and Development, Report TC[67] 16, Paris, October, 1967).

scope for disagreements on the details of the plan. There were many differences between the four members of the study group—France, West Germany, Britain and the USA—and the report contains only very general recommendations.

There is a grave danger that if the developing countries do not soon get some satisfaction of their demands in UNCTAD, the GATT will be undermined by a series of separate preference arrangements between individual, or groups of, developed countries and groups of developing countries. The evolution of such preference arrangements would be an attack on the GATT's principle of non-discrimination. An agreement could be reached within NAFTA to meet the trade demands of the developing countries.[72] The industrial countries of NAFTA could grant all tariff reductions among themselves to developing countries unilaterally. Alternatively, they could accelerate the tariff dismantling of goods of special interest to the developing countries, even to the extent of abolishing duties on certain categories of goods as soon as NAFTA began to operate. Another approach could be to arrange some kind of associate membership on developing countries which would allow some control over their rights to raise infant industry protection against countries granting them tariff concessions. A differential system might be necessary to get maximum effect for all developing countries. One danger of a unilateral concession to all developing countries would be that the most advanced among them would pre-empt the market and possibly cause wide disruption in certain industries of the developed countries. In this event some sliding scale for preferences granted might be organised.

The need for special treatment for the trade of the developing countries can be clearly illustrated. Exports of manufactures by these countries increased rapidly during the 1950s and to raise their income levels further expansion of exports of cheap manufactures is essential. But the industrial countries tend to protect their own industries that compete with the cheap manufactured exports of the less developed countries through their tariff structure. Professor Harry Johnson, of the London School of Economics and the University of Chicago, has referred to this problem as "the effect of the escalation of tariff rates by stage of production".[73] This is

[72]For a full discussion of possible NAFTA preference scheme see David Wall, "The Third World Challenge: Preferences for Development (The Atlantic Trade Study, London, January, 1967).
[73]See Johnson, "Economic Policies Towards Less Developed Economies", *op. cit.*

not necessarily shown in their tariff schedulus, but it is clear when "effective tariff rates" on production processes are examined; that is, when the nominal tariff rate is compared with the value added in a particular industrial process. Professor Balassa has estimated that the effective tariff rates on imports of commodities of interest to developing countries "often exceed 30 or 40 per cent in industrial countries",[74] and are substantially higher than nominal rates of duty. Under these circumstances, reductions in apparently low nominal tariffs could provide increased export opportunities in these goods by lowering the effective protection to domestic industries in advanced industrial countries. But even more secure protection against low-cost producers is provided by quotas imposed on certain categories of imports from developing countries—particularly cotton textiles and certain agricultural goods.

The intention of extending unilateral concessions on trade to the developing countries under a NAFTA agreement is not to argue that this would in itself give the permanent answer to this problem. On the other hand, it would give some satisfaction to the demands for trade preferences from the developing countries. NAFTA would also provide a framework for a multilateral approach within the GATT to the trading problems of the developing countries.

[74]Balassa, *op. cit.*, Ch. 7. Also see Balassa, "Tariff Protection in Industrial Countries", *Journal of Political Economy*, University of Chicago Press, Chicago, December, 1965.

6   BRITAIN IN A BROAD FREE TRADE ASSOCIATION

The revival of interest in North America in the proposals for an extensive open-ended free trade area arrangement for industrial goods centred on the Atlantic countries would be expected to lead to an immediate interest in Britain. After all, the NAFTA proposals accord with many of Britain's policy proposals made in the last twenty-five years. In the immediate post-war years Britain showed over-riding concern for the North Atlantic Alliance. When it became clear that the Treaty of Rome would establish the EEC in the mid-1950s, Britain proposed an industrial free trade area to cover all the OEEC countries. And when dealing with European affairs in the period up to the early 1960s British governments went to great lengths to explain the need for them to safeguard their many political and economic links with areas outside Europe. Yet in the seven years since Mr. Harold Macmillan decided that Britain's role was with Europe, efforts have been directed to cultivating a European aspect and playing down traditional relationships.

The official policy of the Labour Party in the early 1960s opposed the Macmillan Government's attempt to join the EEC. Yet, eighteen months after taking office, the Wilson Government decided to make another approach to the EEC. After some face-saving exploratory talks with leaders in the EEC countries, the British authorities embarked on a determined effort to join the Community, in spite of the many doubts that still existed about French attitudes. The British Government was prepared to go to almost any lengths to achieve this end. Any suggestion of an alternative policy, such as the NAFTA proposal, was rejected for fear of seeming "un-European" or of weakening the resolve to achieve entry to the Community.[75] Yet French opposition to the application was rapidly made clear. In May, 1967, immediately after the formal letter of application for entry had been delivered in Brussels, President de Gaulle explained at a press conference that he did not consider Britain was prepared

[75]See the speech by Mr. George Brown, the Foreign Secretary at the time, on Britain's application to join the EEC at the 1967 Labour Party Conference; reported in *The Times*, October 6, 1967.

for EEC membership. He explained, pointedly, how it would be difficult to admit Britain and other EFTA countries into "the framework of the Common Market without bringing about drastic upheavals".[76] The statement by M. Maurice Couve de Murville, France's Foreign Minister, in Luxembourg on October 23, 1967, seems to have been a more specific exposition of French objections to Britain joining the EEC, but it reached the same conclusion. The EEC Commission's report on the application for admission of Britain and other countries, published at the beginning of October, 1967, spelt out in detail the many constitutional and economic problems that would arise. The prospect, therefore, was for a long period of pre-negotiation and negotiation on the many economic and organisational issues. Fortunately, the French Government brought an early death to the British application and did not repeat the wasteful process of the 1961-63 Brussels' negotiations. President de Gaulle spelt out his objections to Britain's application for membership of EEC at his press-conference on November 27, 1967.[77] M. Couve de Murville gave a final *Non* at the meeting of the EEC Council of Ministers on December 19, 1967.

Folly of "Wait and See" Policy

The British Government maintains that the application for membership remains in effect and ministers repeatedly reiterate that there is no alternative available. This attitude contains all that is worst for Britain and this is becoming more generally recognised in industry and commerce.[78] The British economy still faces tremendous problems of structural adjustment if the external balance is to be restored, even with the aid of the devaluation of sterling in November, 1967, and the severe cuts in overseas defence expenditure announced in January, 1968. If all policy decisions are directed to persuading the French that Britain is truly European and worthy of membership of the EEC this will greatly restrict freedom

[76]President de Gaulle's press conference on May 16, 1967.
[77]Reported in *The Times*, November 28, 1967.
[78]See, for example, Kenneth Keith, "After the Veto—What Should Britain Do?" *British Industry Week*, London, January 5, 1968. Mr. Keith, Chief Executive of Hill Samuel and Co. Ltd., merchant bankers, and a spokesman for the City of London, being a member of the National Economic Development Council, argued: "We shall not help our long-term chances by adopting a wait-and-see attitude which will be interpreted abroad as just another excuse for doing nothing. We must show we mean business. A British initiative for NAFTA could make a great deal of sense."

of action to introduce the necessary policies. It would also be fruitless since President de Gaulle has plainly inferred that his real reason for not wanting Britain to join EEC is that she would contest with France for the political leadership of the Community. Moreover, rather than wanting Britain to correct her economic difficulties, French industry fears the effects of competition from British industry, especially following the sterling devaluation.[79] A policy of waiting for permission to join the EEC can only weaken further Britain's bargaining position. In the event of Britain joining the EEC the terms of entry are likely to be even more severe. The British economy and the morale of the British people, who are already faced by difficult adjustments in Britain's position in the world, will be adversely affected by a policy of waiting for a change of heart in France. And it is not only France that prevents British membership of EEC. Other EEC countries also doubt whether the Community could be enlarged without destroying its fabric.[80]

Britain's problems of the last twenty years are primarily attributable to economic weakness. There is good reason, therefore, for examining any proposal that might offer a way to rectify the weakness. A formal agreement to dismantle tariffs with a wide-ranging group of other countries offers Britain a number of advantages that are not available through multilateral tariff negotiations under the GATT. In a formal agreement Britain would be committed to a schedule to remove trade restrictions against partner countries and, likewise, restrictions against British exports would be reduced. Under these circumstances British industry would have to face a controlled introduction of competition from abroad, while at the same time new export opportunities would be opened up. Because of the commitment to a treaty, British industry would be fully aware of both these phenomena; it would know the schedule for changes and would be able to plan accordingly. In other words, apart from bringing new export opportunities, the benefits of selling in a large market and the salutary jolt of foreign competition, a formal commitment to a free trade agreement would reduce boardroom uncertainty and permit businessmen to plan investment, production and market-

[79]Statements by the French Patronat and representatives of French industry in Paris in December, 1967, indicated opposition to British membership of the EEC. See, for instance, *The Times*, December 2, 1967.

[80]See, for example, testimony of Signor Aurelio Peccei, "The Future of US Foreign Trade Policy", *Hearings*, Vol. I, *op. cit.* Signor Peccei is Vice-Chairman of Olivetti, a member of the steering committee of Fiat, and President of Italconsult, Rome.

ing to meet the scheduled changes. With multilateral tariff negotiations the final bargains achieved cannot be foreseen and the effects of partial tariff cuts are also difficult to assess so that uncertainty is not reduced. The British Government continues to hope the Treaty of Rome will provide these new forces for change in British industry. But NAFTA could provide similar forces.

Comparing NAFTA and the EEC

The economic case for joining the EEC is that British industry will prosper and thrive in the more competitive and dynamic environment provided by the larger market. NAFTA would offer a wider-based free trade area than the EEC. NAFTA would be bigger, richer and technologically more advanced than EEC. The volume of Britain's trade with the members of the proposed NAFTA is already larger than that with the prospective members of an enlarged EEC. If an enlarged EEC included all the EFTA states, which is giving it the optimum size, these countries accounted for around 33 per cent of Britain's total imports and exports in 1967: the prospective initial membership of NAFTA (assuming EEC abstenance) accounted for around 40 per cent of Britain's trade and, in addition, existing preferences in trade with the Commonwealth countries would be retained. It is also worth noticing that exports to the North American market have been growing very rapidly in the past few years. In the period 1964-68, UK exports to the USA have increased at a rate approaching 25 per cent per annum. The rate of growth of exports to EEC, on the other hand, has decreased since 1963. In actual value, exports to Canada and the USA combined earned $2,350m. (f.o.b.) in 1967 compared with $2,700m. (f.o.b.) earned in EEC and $2,120m. (f.o.b.) in EFTA.

It is very difficult to measure the effects dismantling of tariffs under a free trade agreement might have on trade and income. The dynamic forces are at least as strong and as important as simple measurements of tariff effects on static assumptions. Mr. Maxwell Stamp and Mr. Harry Cowie have attempted to analyse, on a basis of post-Kennedy Round tariffs, the effects the setting up of NAFTA could have on British trade.[81] This is primarily a question of the effects on Britain's trade balance of entering into free trade with Canada and the USA, and with Japan if she became a full member of NAFTA. British manufactured exports already have

[81]See Stamp and Cowie, *op. cit.*, pp. 203-16 above *et seq.*

almost free access to Australia and New Zealand through Commonwealth preference, and tariffs have been eliminated on trade with EFTA countries. The study shows that joining the EEC would not be as advantageous as joining NAFTA.

INCREASE IN TRADE RESULTING FROM BRITISH MEMBERSHIP OF NAFTA AND EEC
(US $m.)

UK	NAFTA	EEC
Export Increase (Trade Creation)	292	316
Export Increase (Trade Diversion)	552	191
Import Increase	189	286
	655	221

The estimates are based on 1965 trade figures. They were made on the assumption that the prices of British exports would not rise relatively to domestic prices in other NAFTA countries. The study used fairly conservative co-efficients of demand elasticity for imports with respect to price changes. These estimates do not take account of the effects of the devaluation of the pound on November 18, 1967. The effect of devaluation must be to increase the net benefits to Britain from trade diversion and trade creation. The extent of the gains will depend on the effects of devaluation on British export prices and foreign demand elasticities.

The figures in the table assume that Japan would not be a member of NAFTA. If Japan participated fully in NAFTA the rise in exports due to trade diversion would be reduced by $248m. The Stamp study shows that direct trade flows between Britain and Japan would rise about equally in response to the removal of tariffs, so the net effect on the trade balance would be unchanged. Even if Japan became a full member of NAFTA, the net benefit to Britain's trade balance would be almost double that from joining the EEC or the basis of those calculations—$407m. compared with $221m. On balance, it seems probable that this difference would be reduced by the impact of greater competition in markets where Britain has preferences. If a European solution should be found, Britain's exports to some EFTA countries might be adversely affected by competition from present EEC countries. On the other hand, increased competition from Japan and the USA, as a result of loss of preferences in Canada, Australia and New Zealand, would be greater. Nevertheless, even if allowance is made for these diversionary trade effects, the favourable effects on Britain's trade balance would still be greater from NAFTA than from EEC membership. Another study, the one carried out by Professor Balassa,[82] gives some support to this conclusion, although this analysis was for a rather different purpose and was based on a different approach.

Retaining Commonwealth Trade Links

Membership of a multilateral free trade area permits freedom of commercial policy with respect to third countries. In NAFTA, therefore, Britain would retain her present access to Commonwealth markets, although the value of this preference would be eroded over time if Australia, New Zealand and other Commonwealth countries joined NAFTA. It is difficult to assess the importance of Commonwealth preferences for British exports. The effects of preferences cannot be measured simply by knowing preference margins. These tell nothing about the responsiveness of suppliers to the preference. It would be used as a competitive weapon to lower prices or to allow greater selling efforts; or all the preference could be taken as profit; or there could be a division between these two. In the case under discussion it would nonetheless be interesting to know what price (or profit) advantage British sellers would lose if preferences ceased. A recent Board of Trade survey[83] shows that in 1961 around one-

[82]Balassa, "Trade Liberalisation Among Industrial Countries", *op. cit.*, Ch. IV and Appendix.

Professor Balassa's estimates were based on 1960 trade figures. He was investigating the impact of removing tariffs on trade between all industrial countries. including the EEC. He did not estimate the amount of trade that might be diverted to British exports if EEC and/or Japan did not participate in NAFTA. If the discriminatory effects are taken into account, the figures given in Professor Balassa's study would give a clear balance of advantage to Britain in joining NAFTA (excluding EEC).

EFFECT ON UK TRADE OF REMOVING TARIFFS AMONG INDUSTRIAL COUNTRIES

UK	EEC	USA	Japan
Exports	233	199	20
Imports	322	249	15
Net Effect	− 89	− 50	+5

[83]R. W. Green, "Commonwealth Preference: Tariff Duties and Preferences on United Kingdom Exports to the Preference Area", *Board of Trade Journal*, Board of Trade, London, June 11, 1965; and also Green, "Commonwealth Preference: United Kingdom Customs Duties and Tariff Preferences on Imports from the Preference Area", *Board of Trade Journal*, December 31, 1965.

half of British exports to other Commonwealth countries, which are around 30 per cent of total British exports, enjoyed an average preference of 6.5 to 7.5 per cent. These preferences have been eroded slightly since 1961 by tariff reductions in the GATT and further erosion will take place as a result of the Kennedy Round. But probably more significant is the distribution of countries that afford preferences to British goods. Australia and New Zealand offer preferences on more than 80 per cent of imports from Britain and Canada gives preferences on around two-thirds of imports from Britain. Other high income Commonwealth countries offer preferences on fewer goods. The developing countries of the Commonwealth offer much smaller preference margins on much smaller ranges of goods.

The preferences Britain affords to other Commonwealth countries are generally smaller. Most agricultural goods and raw materials enter Britain either duty free or with very low levels of duty. In consequence, opportunities for Commonwealth countries to expand sales through price competition are small. If Britain joined EEC, however, some Commonwealth exports, particularly agricultural goods, would face a disadvantage in the British market compared with EEC producers. The outstanding case, of course, is New Zealand, which is heavily dependent on the British market for exports of some agricultural products. Around 90 per cent of butter, lamb and cheese exports go to Britain, representing 40 per cent of the country's total export earnings. The reverse preference that would be created if Britain joined the EEC would cause much hardship in certain Commonwealth countries, if—as would seem highly likely—there is little assistance or compensation from the Community.

If Britain joins the EEC, the preferences in Commonwealth markets will be bargained away, which could cause a sharp fall in the value of exports to these markets. The Australian Government has estimated that trade with Britain might fall by one-third[84] (£160m. fall in Australian imports from Britain; £80m. fall in Australian exports to Britain). As noted earlier it is difficult to determine exactly how much effect loss of preferences might have because nothing is known about elasticities of supply. The Australian study suggests though that the figures in the various official

[84] *The Times*, August 22, 1967.

and semi-official British estimates that have been published of the effects on Commonwealth trade of Britain joining EEC may be optimistic. On the other hand, if Britain joins a multilateral free trade area arrangement she could retain the preferences in Commonwealth markets indefinitely, or until such time as countries like Australia and New Zealand decided to join the arrangement. In the latter case, rather than the sudden loss of preference that would occur on joining the EEC, which would tend to cause prices to rise sharply (or profits to fall similarly) the existing preference would be retained. They would merely be extended gradually to other participants under the agreement. Moreover, the advantages of cheap imports into Britain of food and material from Commonwealth sources would continue. Thus there would be clear advantages for Britain in NAFTA with regard to Commonwealth preferences.

Dynamic Effects

The economic advantages for Britain of the dynamic forces that would result from membership of the EEC would be at least equalled by the NAFTA proposal. Opportunities for greater efficiency in industry through competition and economies of scale in a large, dynamic market would be readily available in a NAFTA scheme, which would include the richest countries in the world in terms of income per head. The opportunity to exploit the markets would also be made easier by access to American capital, technology and managerial expertise. These would be advantages that are not so evident in membership of the EEC where the present members have fragmented capital markets much encumbered with legal formalities and restrictive practices. Expenditure, moreover, on research and development in all the EEC countries is lower than in Britain.

The growth potential of the EEC market does not appear to be so great now as in former years. The slow-down in economic activity in West Germany and France has led to a sharp fall in Community imports and the OECD forecasts indicate that economic growth in the EEC countries will be lower than in the past ten years. On the other hand, the growth prospects in North America and Japan appear greater. Latest estimates indicate that the growth rate for GNP in EEC is marginally below the average rate that could be expected in a NAFTA.[85]

[85]Stamp and Cowie, *op. cit.*, Table 1, p. 247 above.

Some British industrialists fear that American capital and technical superiority would enable Americans to dominate British industries. This reflects an insular and parochial attitude and should not be accepted too readily by the consumer. American industrialists and financiers will only invest capital in British industry if they feel it is possible to raise profits through greater efficiency. Ownership of firms may pass to Americans, but the labour force should benefit through higher wages from being more productive and consumers in general would gain from cheaper products. In any case, one of Britain's greatest needs at present is more capital investment. [86] An inflow of American capital would help to raise productivity. The capital used to acquire ownership of any British companies would be available for investment elsewhere in the economy. An inflow of American capital and managerial expertise, however, does not mean a take-over of Britain; if necessary, the Government can legislate to safeguard British interests. An influx of US capital and management enterprise could do much to improve the competitive position of British industry. In recent years there has been a stream of first-class inventions by British scientists that have never been fully developed for the market; particularly in highly technical fields like aircraft and transport, where the cost of developing a marketable product from a prototype is often very high. Access to American technology could increase possibilities for product development in Britain.

Dollar-Sterling Co-operation

It has also been suggested that if Britain removed tariffs on imports of American manufactures there would be less reason for US firms to invest in Britain since they could supply the British market from their home plants. This could well be so, other things being unchanged. But if the rate of economic growth is raised in Britain, owing to more competitive conditions in NAFTA as well as increased exports, then the returns on investment in Britain should become greater. The future of US private overseas investment is difficult to forecast in view of the balance of payments measures announced by President Johnson at the beginning of 1968. Nevertheless, Britain is in a privileged category under them. If NAFTA should be established, special attention would have to be given to restrictions on capital movements.

[86]See Angus Maddison, "Economic Growth in the West" (Allen and Unwin, London, 1964), and G. R. Denton and S. Trench, "Growth in the British Economy" (Allen and Unwin, London, 1960).

A further advantage afforded by NAFTA, if launched, is that it would include both the international reserve currencies. All prospective members of NAFTA have an interest in finding a satisfactory solution to the problems of the international monetary system. If a universal solution does not appear feasible, NAFTA members, including the two reserve currencies, could possibly make a substantial contribution towards improving the system: a wide multilateral payments system could be established to economise on reserves and relieve pressures on the two reserve currencies. This kind of action could encourage other countries to co-operate in seeking a universal solution through the IMF. This must be welcomed by the British authorities. Sterling, as the weaker of the two reserve currencies, has, until the latest devaluation, received most of the pressure in the world's money markets. But the Americans have treated sterling as the first line of defence for the gold exchange system and have provided liberal support for the pound whenever it has been in difficulties. In the early stages of discussions to strengthen the world monetary system, Britain and the USA often presented a common front. As the British Government has become more committed to a further attempt to join the EEC, however, they have tended to take a less positive line in the discussions, in spite of their vital interests in the outcome. Presumably this withdrawal of support for the American policy was for fear of giving the French cause to class Britain as "Atlantic" rather than "European". There can be little further value in this policy after the French attitude towards the Special Drawing Rights agreed at the IMF meeting in Rio de Janeiro in September, 1967, and in view of the latest failure to achieve entry to the EEC.

Yet another reason why Britain should welcome the NAFTA proposal is the intention to introduce special measures to assist the developing countries to expand their exports. Britain, like most other advanced countries, is committed to help the developing countries. In addition, she has a particular responsibility towards the poor countries in the Commonwealth. Owing to Britain's economic difficulties she has not been able to increase financial aid. But the UK remains a substantial donor and has a more liberal policy on imports of cheap manufactures from these countries than many other advanced nations. The British Government played a significant role in the 1964 UNCTAD conference and has always expressed support for multilateral solutions to the aid and trade problems of developing countries. All these aims could be assisted by the NAFTA proposals and if the poorer Commonwealth countries could be persuaded to associate with NAFTA they could reap substantial benefits.

EFTA and Commonwealth Disenchantment

British foreign trade policy in the last decade has alienated the affections of many of her closest trading partners and there is a growing feeling among them that Britain is an unreliable associate. This applies particularly to EFTA countries and the old Commonwealth. The British Government has twice now turned away from EFTA towards the EEC without much thought for the interests of her partners. In 1961, the other EFTA countries forced from Britain the London Agreement whereby accession to the EEC would not be signed until all the EFTA countries had been satisfactorily accommodated. At the EFTA meetings in December, 1966, and February, 1967, it appears that even this assurance was discarded. The furore created by the import surcharge in October, 1964, is well known and the difficulties for the small countries to live in the same organisation with a single large economy like that of Britain was fully brought home by this action. If Britain failed again to join the EEC it has been on the cards that the interests of the smaller EFTA countries could well lead them in the longer term to seek, independently of Britain, an accommodation with EEC. Austria has made her wishes clear already and Denmark is in an equivocal position. If these countries, and maybe others, were tempted away from EFTA by offers of association agreements, for example, Britain would be left isolated in Europe. For the moment such a break up of EFTA is unlikely. But if Britain continues to treat EFTA in a cavalier fashion and declines to offer economic leadership within this area such a state of affairs is possible.

The Commonwealth countries have become similarly disenchanted with British trade policy and for similar reasons. The system of Commonwealth preferences was placed in jeopardy in the 1961-3 Brussels negotiations. Although it has continued to operate since it was again put at hazard by Britain's latest application for membership of the Community, the uncertainty attached to their position in the British market does not breed confidence in Commonwealth countries with regard to their future earnings. Moreover, the slow rate of economic growth in Britain does not give much prospect for expanding markets. In consequence, the Commonwealth countries are looking elsewhere for markets, more actively than they would otherwise, and investigating possibilities for regional trade agreements. Many African and Asian Commonwealth countries have already ceased to offer preferences to Britain. Nigeria has signed an association agreement with the EEC. The richer Commonwealth members are seriously disturbed about the way Commonwealth trade relations are treated in London.

Technological Association with USA

In addition, a British initiative on NAFTA would move Britain closer to the USA in economic matters. This is obviously to the advantage of Britain in the short-run following the latest French veto on membership of EEC, and what this means in terms of leaving Britain in limbo between North America and the EEC. The policy that has been followed by the British Government involves flirting with the EEC—at the expense of Britain's wider interests—in an effort to get some kind of accommodation with the Europe of the Six. This appears to involve a "co-ordination" on technology and research where Britain holds a short-term lead over the EEC countries. If technological co-operation is undertaken, without Britain becoming a full member of EEC, then, the short-term advantage Britain holds in this field is unlikely to be sustained in the longer term. If this bargaining card is given away then British membership of EEC could become even less likely in the longer term. On the other hand, closer association with the USA would probably increase Britain's lead over the rest of Europe in technology— British industry would be operating in a more dynamic atmosphere in NAFTA and, probably, with greater access to American research and technology. The "technological gap", and the possible effects of trade diversion from NAFTA would be likely to bring EEC into NAFTA once it had begun to operate.

A British initiative for NAFTA could also help to seal over some of the gaps that have been opening up between London and Washington as a result of Britain's continuing economic weakness, with subsequent repercussions on the dollar in the international monetary system and the latest reduction in Britain's world role. Both these effects have put increasing burdens on the USA. Much irritation has been caused in Washington by the acceleration of Britain's military withdrawal from the Indo-Pacific theatre. It is not in

Britain's interests to become estranged from the USA when her position in Europe is also weakening. Apart from restoring Britain's position in Washington by initiating a free trade arrangement that could bring solutions to many of the world's trading problems, a NAFTA initiative would bring substantial economic benefits to Britain herself.

Membership of NAFTA also presents Britain with a chance to stabilise trading relations with EFTA and the major Commonwealth countries by removing uncertainty about the future. It is clear that NAFTA could provide Britain with substantial economic opportunities. The benefits that might accrue from NAFTA would be at least equal to those offered by membership of EEC on the basis of the estimates available. Moreover, Britain would not be faced with the consequence of accepting the EEC's agricultural arrangements or the need to conform to other common policies agreed in the future. Finally, membership of NAFTA is not inconsistent with greater European unity in the longer term. If, as it is hoped, the EEC countries could be persuaded to join NAFTA the process of political integration in Europe could proceed without the disruptive influences of discriminatory trading arrangements.

7 THE PROSPECTS FOR NEW STRATEGY

The GATT system of multilateral bargaining for tariff reductions has provided the main approach to trade liberalisation in the last twenty years. There are several reasons for doubting whether this approach will provide the most suitable method to pursue future trade liberalisation. The nature of the GATT bargaining has always meant that the strongest countries—those with the highest tariffs and largest markets—have tended to control the proceedings. In the last decade the development of regional trade blocks under Article 24 of the GATT has caused a major shift in bargaining power. This must cause doubts about any future negotiations for countries outside these groups.

Tariffs on industrial goods have been substantially reduced in the six rounds of GATT negotiations since 1947. This is relevant to future trade relations in two respects. First, most superfluous tariff protection has now been removed. Hence, any further tariff reductions can be expected to have significant effects on the reallocation of resources into more efficient activities. Secondly, with the "hard core" of protection reached, bargaining in any future negotiations is likely to meet greater resistance from industrial sectors that consider their protection has been cut sufficiently. In other words, the sectors where multilateral tariff bargaining is difficult will have increased in number.

Wyndham White favours Free Trade Association

The Kennedy Round has cast severe doubts upon the future of multilateral tariff negotiations. The complicated and detailed preparations for the Kennedy Round and its difficult bargaining procedures took five years and an immense effort by governments. It is the general opinion of participants that such an effort is unlikely to be tried again for many years. At the Kennedy Round's conclusion, the Director General of the GATT, who at the time was still Sir Eric Wyndham White, said that "the Kennedy Round is probably the last of the major pure tariff exercises. The next stage may come in establishing free trade among major international industries."[87] Shortly after he retired from the GATT there was a shift in Sir Eric's position on the form of a new initiative. He headed the signatories of a letter to *The Times* which suggested that "it would be highly desirable for the leading trading nations to undertake a joint effort to bring about a broadly based free trade association in which all like-minded nations should be invited to participate. We feel," they wrote, "that such an initiative would hold out the greatest hope for the continued expansion of the world economy for the benefit of developed and under-developed countries alike."[88] While a new approach to trade liberalisation is necessary to prevent the world from slipping back towards greater protectionism by default, the GATT Secretariat would continue to function as a guardian of the 1947 agreement, to tie up loose ends left after the Kennedy Round negotiations and to pursue unfinished reforms in agricultural trade and non-tariff barriers.

The GATT provides the legal framework for international commercial relations. The most suitable means to pursue trade liberalisation would appear to be to generalise as far as possible the contents of Article 24 of the GATT. All countries that joined a free trade arrangement under this article would be committed to remove trade restrictions against other member countries according to an agreed schedule over a specified period. Such an agreement would provide opportunities to deal with some of the more intractable problems in commercial relations. As tariffs have been reduced the impact of non-tariff barriers on trade has become more important. It is difficult to include non-tariff barriers in multilateral bargaining sessions because of their diversity, but they might be more easily dealt with in discussions under a free trade agreement. Indeed, the institutional mechanisms of a free trade area treaty, it is being argued, probably offer a better means of harmonising policies and practices that are part of the non-tariff barrier problem than the intermittent and *ad hoc* procedures of multilateral experience. Under a treaty commitment, a code of fair competition, such as has been proposed by the Canadian-American Committee,[89] could go a long way towards meeting the criticism in the USA that as tariff barriers

[87]See *The Times*, May 16, 1967.
[88]See *The Times*, July 5, 1968.
[89]"Constructive Alternatives to Proposals for US Import Quotas" (Canadian-American Committee, Washington D.C. and Montreal, February, 1968).

have been lowered some foreign governments have actually been raising non-tariff barriers.

The attitudes of the developing countries to the GATT are already very unfavourable and the announcement of a new free trade proposal between the advanced countries would appear as another form of discrimination against the developing countries. It is essential, therefore, that the proposal should include specific provisions to give preferential treatment to imports from the developing countries. These preferences would be intended to promote trade in simple manufactured goods produced in developing countries and would be granted unilaterally. As a *quid pro quo* the developing countries could be encouraged to examine their trade and development policies to see if they would maximise benefits from such preferential arrangements. If the proposals agreed in principle at the second UNCTAD for generalised preferences to be granted by the developed countries cannot be transformed into a worthwhile scheme, a similar approach through NAFTA could still be successful.

NAFTA would be basically a free trade arrangement for industrial goods and raw materials. Agriculture would introduce specific and difficult issues, but they would have to be faced. Tropical agricultural produce is primarily of interest to developing countries and by granting free access for this produce a step would be made to help these countries. A comprehensive agreement on temperate agricultural produce is unlikely at the outset. Yet prospective members of NAFTA with important agricultural exports would require considerable assurances for increased agricultural exports if they were expected to reduce protection on manufactured goods. There is no reason why agricultural production should not be rationalised on an international basis, perhaps through a harmonisation of domestic support policies.

Attitudes towards NAFTA Initiative

Many special interests will have to be taken into account and considerable heavy bargaining will be necessary before a NAFTA agreement could be signed. The discussion in this paper has shown that initially the signatories to such an agreement would be the USA, Canada, Britain and the other EFTA countries. A slightly modified membership, taking account of special circumstances, might also be accepted by Japan, Australia and New Zealand. It is probable that initially the EEC would not wish to join NAFTA. It was shown in Chapter 5, however, that once a wide-based free trade area for industrial goods began to operate, forces would be created that would almost certainly attract, even oblige, the EEC countries to join.

An obvious prerequisite for an effective free trade arrangement among a larger group of industrial countries is that the US Congress and the Administration should accept such a proposal. The American attitude is vital because traditionally Congress has been a highly protectionist-minded body and very susceptible to the arguments of those industrialists who fear foreign competition. Congressional approval of the Trade Expansion Act of 1962 indicates that this restrictive bias is diminishing. But until the full results of the Kennedy Round negotiations are approved by Congress—including the ASP agreement for chemicals—doubts will remain about the influence of the protectionist lobbies. New cause for concern has arisen with the flood of Senate bills seeking import quotas to cover almost half of total American imports.

There is much evidence, though, that Americans are giving serious consideration to the various multilateral free trade area proposals. The US Chamber of Commerce has come out strongly in favour of a world-wide free trade area. The National Planning Association has clearly expressed strong interest through the Canadian-American Committee. The powerful Joint Economic Committee of Congress commissioned and published in 1967 a wide range of studies on trade prospects and alternative commercial policies for the USA, to which reference has been made already (see Footnote 2, Page 257). The report of the Joint Economic Committee's Subcommittee on Foreign Economic Policy recognised that "conditions may arise that would favour American participation in a regional trading bloc". The enquiry headed by Mr. William Roth has examined the free trade area approach. Whilst no formal proposal has been made by the Administration, the possibility of American interest in an Atlantic-based free trade area is not as unlikely as it would have appeared ten years ago. No trade steps could be expected until after the 1968 Presidential election.[90] But groundwork has been

[90]Even so, one of the late Senator Robert Kennedy's leading advisers, Professor Arthur Schlesinger, a former Special Assistant to both President Kennedy and President Johnson, came out very strongly in favour of the NAFTA idea during the presidential election campaign. See Arthur Schlesinger, Jun., "After the Super-Powers: The Anglo-American Prospects", USAF Memorial Trust Lecture, University of East Anglia, Norwich, May 14, 1968; published under the title "America's Need for Allies", in *The Round Table*, July, 1968.

cleared for a possible new trade initiative to be taken when the new Administration is formed. This will be vital not only as a counter to protectionism. It will also be vital to maintaining the momentum of trade liberalisation. Britain has a big interest in the form this initiative takes.[91]

The relative lack of importance of foreign trade in the American economy indicates that for the USA to be attracted by a free trade scheme it must offer something further. For example, the USA would not be attracted by membership of a restricted regional grouping, such as a free trade area confined to the North Atlantic region. This would inhibit US policies in other parts of the world. In particular, it would create political difficulties in Latin America and with respect to the developing countries. In all the free trade area proposals that have been discussed in the USA, the common characteristic has been that the agreement should be open-ended and and that it should extend to as many countries as possible.[92]

Also important in the American view of the NAFTA idea is the monetary aspect. As long as the USA is obliged by the political realities of the age to bear the chief responsibility for maintaining the security of the free world it is likely to continue being confronted by balance of payments problems. In the light of divided opinions over the acceptability of a continuing US deficit, there has accordingly been some discussion of a dollar-sterling block, on the one hand, and a gold block, on the other, with a system of variable exchange rates between them. This course was proposed as a "second best" solution to the international liquidity problem in a Brookings Institution report published in 1964.[93] It has since been raised again by, among others, Dr. Merlyn Trued, who was at the US Treasury as Assistant Secretary for International Affairs under the Johnson Administration until mid-1966, but acted as an adviser

[91] For a discussion of the multilateral free trade association proposal as a dramatic means of countering protectionism on both sides of the Atlantic see Gerard Curzon, "North Atlantic Free Trade Link Could be a Powerful Magnet", *The Times*, August 26, 1968. Also see Curzon and Curzon, op. cit., p. 21 above.

[92] This was underlined in Henry S. Reuss, "An American Perspective on Proposals for an Atlantic Free Trade Association" (Address to the Trade Policy Research Centre, London, November 21, 1968). Mr. Reuss is chairman of the Subcommittee on International Finance in the US House of Representatives.

Also see David Rockefeller, "Prospect for New World Monetary and Trade Patterns" (Address to an investment forum convened by the Chase Manhattan Bank, of New York, in London, October 18, 1968).

[93] "The United States Balance of Payments in 1968" (Brookings Institution, Washington D.C., 1964).

to Mr. Richard Nixon during the 1968 Presidential campaign.[94] Another modification of the theme has been developed by Dr. Fred Bergsten, of the Council of Foreign Relations, New York.[95] By affording Britain access to a large-scale market, thus facilitating a strengthening of sterling, pressure might be expected to be taken off the US dollar and a restoration of confidence achieved.

The attitudes of other countries to NAFTA proposals can be divided into a political reaction and an economic reaction. The main objections or doubts rest on the possible effects on these countries of closer association with the USA. The Canadians are apprehensive about extending formal economic links with their giant neighbour in case it should interfere with their independence in foreign policy and diminish their influence on world councils. On the other hand, the Canadian Government recognises the economic risks of exclusion from all the regional free trade arrangements. Under these circumstances, therefore, the Canadian authorities prefer a very wide free trade arrangement with sufficient members to counterbalance the forces from the USA and neutralise any apparent American influence on policy as far as outsiders are concerned.

The problem for European countries is rather different. There are strong forces in Western Europe, not only in the EEC, for greater independence from the USA. This is expressed in many different forms. The present American policy in Vietnam gives an opportune outlet for expression of these feelings, but it goes deeper than a simple anti-war emotion, although this is strong enough. Many European countries have just withdrawn from their remaining colonial outposts at great cost and they now wish to avoid entanglements outside Europe. They fear that any form of association with the USA will mean association with American foreign policy and a renewal of unwanted responsibilities. This is undoubtedly one of the reasons why the EEC seems very inward-looking to some non-members.

Moreover, many European countries see no immediate need for new arrangements to reduce trade barriers; the existing schemes provide the opportunities for trade expansion that they need—

[94]Merlyn N. Trued, "Flexible Exchange Rates and a New Free Trade Initiative", *The Times*, London, October 14, 1968.
[95]C. Fred Bergsten, "US-UK Economic Relations: Scope for Policy Co-ordination" (Paper given at a conference jointly sponsored by the Institute of Defence Analyses, Washington D.C., and the Royal Institute of International Studies, London, at Racine, Wisconsin, October, 1968).

that is, the EEC and EFTA and the tariff cuts from the Kennedy Round. However, if a new opportunity to expand markets should be initiated the EFTA countries could be expected to respond favourably, especially if the prospects for forging a link between the EEC and EFTA remain as remote as they are at present. The only European country with a positive incentive to seek a new free trade arrangement is Britain. The door to the EEC remains firmly shut against Britain. Yet, British industry and the Government see the need for guaranteed access to a wider market than is at present provided by EFTA and the Commonwealth. An agreement to eliminate tariffs on trade with a group of industrial countries would remove much uncertainty about the future and provide incentives for planned increases in output and investment. It was shown in Chapter 6 that any advantages that could be provided by the EEC could be provided equally or to a greater extent in NAFTA.

Timing of Initiative

To be successful, the timing of an initiative for a broadly based free trade association is very important. If launched in 1969, early in the term of office of the new US Administration, it would still take several years before an agreement could be concluded under the auspices of the GATT. On the basis of the Kennedy Round negotiations, it would probably be 1972-3 before the first phase of tariff dismantling, under the agreement, could commence. The schedules for removing tariffs would extend over at least ten years and the removal of non-tariff barriers is bound to take longer.

With Britain's position so central to this issue, it is worth noting that the above assessment of the time span before a NAFTA arrangement would become operative compares favourably with the most optimistic assessment of the anticipated delay before Britain could expect to join the EEC. The period of transition before Britain could be a full member of the Community would probably be at least five years and there would appear little chance of any new moves to accommodate the UK for several years yet. Thus the present policy of the British Government does not seem likely to give Britain a full say in the Community's policy before 1978 at the earliest.

The political problems that appear to impede any constructive movement towards an Atlantic free trade area, or wider agreements aimed at world free trade, are often over-emphasised. The cross-fertilisation of ideas, techniques and expertise within Western Europe and between these countries and the USA is far greater than most politicians would be prepared to admit. These exchanges of knowledge are of far greater consequence in practice than short-run political differences. The formal co-operation on economic matters has progressed a long way since 1945, but the invisible network of contacts between individuals and firms in different countries provides a much stronger form of economic integration in the Atlantic area. The movement of knowledge and techniques across national boundaries is less tangible than the movement of merchandise in trade but its importance must not be under-estimated. As long as the Atlantic economies are integrated in this concealed manner, the prospect for formal free trade among them cannot be too lightly dismissed for political reasons.

In many respects the present system of tariffs and other restrictions on trade used to protect national markets are anachronistic in view of the many developments in international economic relations in the last twenty years. The development of regional trade groupings under Article 24 of the GATT has largely invalidated the concept of non-discrimination. Advanced technology has become international and it is transferred across national frontiers without the need to pay duties. It is easier to set up a new plant using new technology in a foreign country than to export the new products with the need to overcome tariffs and other restrictions; or, conversely, it is easier to buy the technology abroad and import it rather than import the goods produced by using that knowledge. The growth of inter-national companies has increased the tendency to shift technology, management and capital across frontiers. The giant international companies have grown in importance in international trade and investment and this invalidates many of the effects of national tariffs and other trade barriers against foreign firms.

The open-ended NAFTA concept provides a solution within GATT which is in keeping with the trend in international com-mercial relations of the last two decades. It would be a regional grouping with special provisions for extension to cover all industrial countries. At the same time it would have sufficient flexibility to permit special arrangements to be made for less developed countries and for regulations to facilitate East-West trade. Britain is in a position to encourage, if not initiate, discussions of the NAFTA proposal. The USA and Canada could not be expected to do so as long as Britain only shows interest in a narrower European solution to her problems. Both these countries, however, could be expected to support a British proposal for NAFTA and the other EFTA countries would probably follow suit. The most recent veto from President de Gaulle gives Britain strong reasons to examine carefully the advantages of such a step.